Praise for European Aesthetics:

"Robert Wicks has an encyclopedic knowledge of the history of continental European aesthetics between 1790 and 1990. His book will be of use to both scholars and advanced students."
Dabney Townsend, Secretary-Treasurer/Executive Director, American Society for Aesthetics

"A highly accessible and richly contextualized guide to the history of continental European aesthetics... A valuable resource for historically-oriented courses in aesthetics and philosophy of art."
Sandra Shapshay, Assistant Professor of Philosophy, Indiana University

European Aesthetics

A Critical Introduction from Kant to Derrida

ROBERT L. WICKS

ONEWORLD

A Oneworld Book

Published by Oneworld Publications 2013

Copyright © Robert L. Wicks 2013

The moral right of Robert L. Wicks to be identified as the Author
of this work has been asserted by him in accordance with
the Copyright, Designs and Patents Act 1988

Hardback ISBN 978-1-85168-818-0
Paperback ISBN 978-1-85168-819-7
eBook ISBN 978-1-78074-077-5

Typeset by Cenveo Publisher Services, Bangalore, India
Printed and bound in Great Britain by TJ International, Padstow, UK

Oneworld Publications
10 Bloomsbury St
London WC1B 3SR
England

Stay up to date with the latest books,
special offers, and exclusive content from
Oneworld with our monthly newsletter

Sign up on our website
www.oneworld-publications.com

For Gladys, Valentina and David

CONTENTS

PLATES

1 Design from the Lindisfarne Gospels manuscript (*c*.700) located in the British Library in London.

2 The image of Tukaroto Matutaera Potatau Te Wherowhero Tawhiao, Second Maori King – d.1894 (provided courtesy of the G.M.Collection, Alexander Turnbull Library, Wellington, New Zealand).

3 *Discobolus* (Discus Thrower), copy of the original statue by Myron, *c*.460-450 BCE located in the Copenhagen Botanical Gardens.

4 Carl Wilhelm Hübner, *The Silesian Weavers* (1846) located in the Kunstmuseum, Düsselsdorf.

5 Taj Mahal, Agra, India.

6 The original photograph of *Nomadic Kyrgyz Family on the Golodnaya Steppe in Uzbekistan* by Sergey Prokudin-Gorsky (1911) located in the Library of Congress, Washington, D.C.

7 The original photograph of *Lewis Thornton Powell* (a.k.a. Lewis Payne) by Alexander Gardner (1865) located in the Library of Congress, Washington, D.C.

8 Diego Velázquez, *Las Meninas* (1656) located in the Prado Museum, Madrid.

9 Vincent van Gogh, *A Pair of Shoes* (1886) located in the Van Gogh Museum, Amsterdam.

10 Honoré Daumier, *Third-Class Carriage* (1862) located in the National Gallery of Canada.

ACKNOWLEDGEMENTS

I would like to extend my gratitude to Oneworld Publications, who initially suggested the idea for this book, and to Mike Harpley at Oneworld, who allowed it to mature slowly.

Thanks are also due to the Heads of the Department of Philosophy at the University of Auckland whose tenures covered the duration of this book's composition, Tim Dare and John Bishop, along with the Dean of Arts, Jan Crosthwaite, who respectively scheduled reduced administrative assignments, granted academic leave and secured special building access that allowed me to complete this book more effectively than would otherwise have been possible.

In connection with the Kant chapter, I would like to thank Donald Crawford; for the chapters on Hegel, Schopenhauer, Freud and Benjamin, Ivan Soll; for the Marx chapter, Paul Warren; for the Heidegger chapter, Julian Young; for the Gadamer chapter, Matheson Russell; for the Foucault chapter, Stephen Davies. These individuals have been among my friends, colleagues and teachers who, through discussions or professional interactions of one kind or another, have shaped my views on the theorists here addressed. I am also indebted to two anonymous reviewers for Oneworld, whose insights and constructive criticisms significantly improved the manuscript. Thanks are also due to Routledge Publishing, for having given permission for me to draw from my Foucault entry in *The Routledge Companion to Aesthetics*.

My gratitude also extends to my research assistant, Daniel Wilson, and to the students in my History of Aesthetics, Kant and Hegel, Schopenhauer and Nietzsche, and Twentieth-Century French Philosophy classes at the University of Auckland, whose presence, maturity and intellectual enthusiasm motivated me to formulate some of the leading ideas contained herein.

The birth of my son, David, during the course of this book's development, almost on the birthday of Immanuel Kant, our initial theorist, and exactly during the scheduled time of my Kant–Hegel class at the University of Auckland (which had to be cancelled that morning for his arrival), rendered the memories of this book's composition that much more exciting and meaningful. My wife, Gladys, and my daughter, Valentina, also deserve great thanks, as they open-mindedly allowed me some peaceful months of time to write in New York that otherwise would have been spent travelling happily with them while they were in South America. I dedicate this book to my beautiful wife and children.

Auckland, April 24, 2012

INTRODUCTION: ART AND THE DISILLUSIONMENT IN REASON

This book surveys sixteen theorists – mostly philosophers, but also representatives from literary criticism, psychiatry, classics, and history – whose work informs European aesthetics during the last two centuries. The arrangement is chronological on the whole, where the sequence of writers is further grouped according to their geographical origination and shared assumptions. For the sake of expository balance, the presentation divides evenly within each century between those who tend to respect reason's capacities for enlightenment versus those who question its power. Reflected in their various conceptions of reason are ethical or political agendas that, as we shall see, usually predominate over their aesthetic views. Two broad strands of thought are consequently exposed, one rationalist and the other anti-rationalist, that extend side by side from 1790 to 1990, where our account ends, but where contemporary history also continues along the same dual tracks, albeit now more confusingly amalgamated. These are "broad" strands, for each thinker embodies a particular proportion of rational and anti-rational aspects which render the comparisons and contrasts between them more subtle and often less oppositional.

This expository design reflects a seminal theme that extends across these 200 years and illuminates this time-segment of aesthetic theorizing, namely, the disagreement over the nature and value of reason. During the Enlightenment and culminating in the French Revolution, reason reaches a point where it is celebrated absolutely as the essence of God himself, or simply as the new God to replace those of traditional religions, and in particular Christianity. Optimistic applications of reason in science, politics, social organizations, and psychology – a trend that continues today – are prescribed here as the most truth-oriented and advisable ways to understand and manage our surroundings. Such ideals inhere in some of the French Revolution's advocates and sadly, eventual victims, such as the Marquis de Condorcet (1743–94).

The French Revolution's descent into a Reign of Terror left subsequent thinkers perplexed about how reason could turn irrationally and violently upon itself. Some philosophers, such as G. W. F. Hegel, reacted by developing a new, conflict-absorbing conception of reason – a reconciliatory and integrative style of rationality based on the structure of self-consciousness – upon which to ground a more comprehensive vision of metaphysical truth and social harmony, as well as a position on beauty and art in human history. Others, such as Friedrich Nietzsche, regarded excessive reason as mainly a source of illusion and illness, despite how it can console weaker souls, often through art, in the face of the world's irrationality. Notwithstanding the contrasting attitudes towards reason that Hegel and Nietzsche represent, most theorists of the time share the idea – one that endures to the present, and which accounts for much contemporary interest in aesthetic theory – that *a resurrection of art and beauty* offers a means to greater insight and social salvation. Some link art and beauty to reason in a continued pursuit of Enlightenment ideals, whereas others establish a sharp antagonism between poetry and science, but both camps regard art as a means of rescue and recovery. Virtually all of the thinkers in this study assign ethical, political, and pedagogical roles to beauty and art, roles which govern their aesthetic theories, sometimes to the point where aesthetic values are rendered dramatically subservient, as in Marxist aesthetics.

Our survey of European aesthetics is further informed by how the last decade of the eighteenth century and the first decade of the nineteenth century marked the emergence of an increasingly historically-oriented style of thinking – one that leads to a more down-to-earth and, in some cases, amoral appreciation of the physical world, including the human body, and eventually to philosophical movements such as twentieth-century phenomenology and existentialism. In conjunction with this, the notion of the "unconscious" begins to gain intellectual currency at the beginning of the nineteenth century, soon precipitating an attention to instinct, feelings, life-forces, inspiration, sexuality, violence and, broadly speaking, some of the more uncomfortable dimensions of human nature, as we see in Freud's view.

Insofar as the Reign of Terror of 1793–94 reveals how reason can support an exclusionary and terrifying system of order, undermining its attractive presentation as a well-motivated, clear-thinking, and praiseworthy source of social ideals, we can use it as a benchmark for the outset of reason's loss of status which structures the history of aesthetics during the cultural period we are considering. Nietzsche and Heidegger notably represent this suspicion of reason, since both look back to the roots of rationalistic thinking, and identify the ancient Greek culture that was contemporary with Socrates, Plato, and Aristotle as the initial point where reason first became tyrannical. Foucault is yet another theorist who identifies a violent side to reason. For him, this aspect presents itself at the outset of the Enlightenment, when those whom society had deemed unreasonable, such as the mentally ill, the infirm, and the unemployed, were indiscriminately incarcerated and treated with degrading cruelty, as at the *Hôpital Général* in Paris which opened in 1656.

Throughout the nineteenth and twentieth centuries, and in light of the French Revolution's failure to preserve a sense of universal human respect, a mistrust of human reason tempers the reception of the tremendous advances in the sciences that were simultaneously taking place. In almost every instance, the theorists who write on art and aesthetics embody a discord inherent in the spirit of these times, expressed in the problem of how to assign a positive value to scientific attitudes as they admittedly reveal the laws of nature and bestow great controlling powers over our environment, while they simultaneously dehumanize people to the status of numerical values in cost–benefit analyses, or as cog-like wage-laborers in an impersonal factory mechanism, or as the faceless members of a social organization, or as bodies of unemployed flesh. Reason, once considered to be God, transforms for many during the nineteenth and twentieth centuries, into a tyrant to be resisted, typically and consistently through non-rational means, among which is the weapon of art. Hence, we witness the efforts to dethrone reason that generate the pronouncement that God is "dead." Just as the French Revolutionaries decapitated their monarchs in 1793, an impressive series of nineteenth- and twentieth-century writers aim to decapitate the ideals that had rationally constructed the Revolutionaries' very guillotine.

These global considerations set the stage for the present narrative, which, through the examination of specific thinkers, traces the roles of beauty and art across two centuries of theorizing. It illustrates within the context of aesthetic theory how, for example, the values accorded to art and beauty in Nazi Germany were not aberrations or exceptions to a supposedly more powerful, civilized, and humane trend that had been brewing in European society, but were the exaggerated and superficially instantiated extensions of respectable and entrenched outlooks that are present at the French Revolution's outset, and in Kant, Schiller, Hegel, and Marx. In the Nazi instance, the more fiendish side of reason bursts forth with oppressive intolerance. An important strand of Nazi art nonetheless remains well situated within the neoclassical tradition, as it celebrates perfectly formed human bodies, and as, in a Reign of Terror of its own, it detests all forms that vary from its mathematical and unrealistically demanding ideals.

Within this context of the various attempts to dethrone reason over the last two centuries, as they stand historically side by side with inspiring scientific advances, we will survey an assortment of attitudes towards art and beauty. Insofar as it can be opposed to art, beauty traditionally bears a close relationship to rationality in light of its formal balances and proportions, and we will see how beauty slowly loses favor as a positive aesthetic ideal, and is replaced by alternative values that center upon creativity, ingenuity, virtuosity, playfulness, and expressiveness.

The constellations and degrees of support versus antagonism towards reason among our theorists vary, as their diversity resembles a museum exhibition of artworks that devote themselves to the same general theme. Each can be appreciated as part of a wider historical trend, while each also stands on its own as expressive of an innovative vision of the world. So, in addition to setting the various aesthetic theories within the historical context of reason's oppressive turn over the last couple of centuries, the rise of historically oriented theorizing and the strong influence of ethical and political agendas, each chapter constitutes a small world of its own, relatively isolated from the others for the sake of a more self-sufficient appreciation and potential academic use. Our study focuses on the contents of the respective philosophical theories and theorists, and although it develops a picture of the overall historical development thereby, it does not provide a detailed history of aesthetics during this period, as might be written by a historian, which would require a different style, contain less philosophy, and extend for a longer length.[1]

Underlying the sequence of individual expositions, the organizing theme is that during the nineteenth and twentieth centuries a profound ambivalence towards reason inheres in most of the aesthetic theories and respective cultural formations, noticeable in a number of ways: (1) the search for universality and fixed truth, often associated with morality, conflicts with a more earthy sense of transient, instinctually driven and contingently occurring history; (2) the traditional definition of human beings as rational animals conflicts with the growing realization that we are biologically and psychologically constituted by accidental and rationally unfathomable feral energies; (3) the efficiency and attractiveness of regarding people as scientific objects, not to mention the awesome successes of theoretical physics, conflicts with our basic sense of human respect; and (4) the pleasures and security afforded by the perception of beauty conflicts with the association of beauty's systematic form with fascism and oppression.

This narrative of European aesthetics from 1790 to 1990 reveals the more distressing question of whether the alternatives to rational inquiry afforded by artistic creativity and poetic consciousness are even more dangerous than the forms of rationalism they intend to replace. Without objective criteria to establish a reliable community of opinion, with appeals merely to insight, intuition, and a prescribed openness to new dimensions of the world alone, the

---

[1] There are over one hundred theorists during this period that could be cited. A classic and comprehensive survey of these figures is Benedetto Croce's *Aesthetic* (1909). Not mentioned even by Croce, an underappreciated theorist of the early period worth noting here is Ludwig Gotthard Kosegarten (1758–1818), who influenced German Romantic painters such as Caspar David Friedrich and Philipp Otto Runge. See Holmes, *Kosegarten's Cultural Legacy*.

opportunities for being ideologically misled are multiplied. The upshot is a double bind, where reason becomes plagued by objectionably oppressive systematicity, and where poetic and artistic awareness become too complacent towards propaganda.

This double bind is the maddening koan of our times, raising contemporary anxiety about humanity's future as globalization begins to touch everyone, and as scientifically grounded means of surveillance slowly saturate our experience. Within the short span of an hour, these means can range from the recordings of one's internet web browsing at home, to the computer chips in one's mobile telephones and automobile GPS mechanisms that emit traceable signals as one drives to the grocery store, to the speed cameras that await at the traffic intersections, to the surveillance cameras attached to the store's ceiling, to the recording in some distant database of one's payment with a credit card, and to the potential satellite photograph of one's return back home. At home, one turns on the television to watch a news program or political presentation that has been constructed by professionals well-seasoned in the psychological techniques of persuasion. This is the contemporary form of social dilemma that motivates many of our writers, each of whom considers how art either contributes to it or helps resolve it.

Given the limited space within which this survey of European aesthetic theory must be presented, sixteen major thinkers have been selected. Inevitably, some philosophers worthy of inclusion are treated in less detail and only in passing. The diversity of views presented here amongst the sixteen, though, should establish a solid foundation upon which any other aesthetics-sensitive thinkers of the time period can be approached usefully, such as Schelling, Wagner, Lukács, Marcuse, Lyotard, Merleau-Ponty, Dufrenne, and Bakhtin. Although there is no specific chapter devoted to Jean-Paul Sartre's view on art, he appears substantially in this book.

In connection with the nineteenth-century philosophers especially, it is difficult to appreciate their aesthetic theories without being familiar with the metaphysical theories within which they are situated. One of the major drawbacks of many studies of nineteenth-century aesthetics and aestheticians is that the expositions commence with the aesthetic theories themselves, in abstraction from the metaphysical theories from which they grew, like flowers clipped from their roots and stems. Atypically for a book on aesthetics, some of our chapters self-consciously spend extra time providing an exposition of the philosopher's metaphysical outlook, before introducing his aesthetic theory. The chapter on Hegel's aesthetics is exemplary, and requires patience. The aesthetics of Marx, Schopenhauer, Nietzsche and Freud are also presented in this contextualized manner, adding some depth to their aesthetic theories by sketching the wider philosophical theories in which they are embedded.

Kant's aesthetic theory – a theory in reference to which subsequent thinkers are either sympathetic or antagonistic – grounds most of the reflection on art and beauty that takes place during the 200 years following its publication, so the opening chapter on Kant is more detailed than the others. The treatments of the twentieth-century thinkers tend to be more focused, and, in most cases, they attend to one or two of the thinker's most influential aesthetic writings, where these stand as the model for the rest of their discussions. Derrida – who published many volumes of work during his lifetime – is the most obvious instance, where we attend closely to his lengthy and controversial treatment of an 1886 painting by Vincent van Gogh, *A Pair of Shoes*.

Within the context of ascertaining the value of reason, the history of European aesthetics from 1790 to 1990 is significantly motivated by the effort to understand the roles of beauty and art in connection with morality and with a variety of conceptions of the good society, wherein the respectively preferred moral values are to be instantiated. In this focus upon art and society, the theories usually have implicit answers to theoretical questions such as "What is art?," "What is good art?," "What is the nature of artistic expression?," "What is an artistic genius?," "How do works of art express emotion?," "Which qualities of artworks are aesthetically relevant and which are not?," "What is the value of popular art versus fine art?," "What is the relationship between art and metaphysical knowledge?" and, "What is the nature of artistic creativity?" The answers to such questions will appear as they arise within the context of each theorist, as opposed to their being separated for singular thematic attention, as one might do in a more topically centered study.

After surveying how over the past 200 years a leading determinant of European aesthetic theories is the question of whether to value reason positively or negatively – and in conjunction with this, the ethical, political, and pedagogical roles assigned to art – we will conclude that this preoccupation has obscured the more fundamental fact that *both* rationalistic and non-rationalistic modes of expression are inherently double-aspected. Either mode can humanize or dehumanize, so neither is *prima facie* preferable to the other, as most theorists have assumed. This requires us to set aside the simple answer to the question of how to develop the powers of judgment, taste, and wisdom for achieving the social goals that motivate most of the theorists we are considering, where the standard choice would be to adhere predominantly to either reason or its opposite. There are no easy prescriptions in aesthetic education, and following the interests of the writers in our study, the limited suggestion will be that headway can be made by considering artistic ways to cultivate trust, interdependency, and sharing among people, in an effort to enlighten our place in the world. If one is interested in using art as a means for social improvement, as were most of the intellectual figures we will discuss, then one can try positively to cultivate trust, or try more modestly to clear the way for trust with art that conveys an intelligent social critique.

Part I

1790–1900

Part 1

1

THE BEAUTY OF UNIVERSAL AGREEMENT

Immanuel Kant

Consider this scenario: intending to strike up some friendly conversation at a dinner gathering, one mentions casually how a vase of brightly colored flowers so pleasantly enhances the table's appearance. Not everyone agrees. Someone mumbles the word "garish," and a mildly devilish voice at the end of the table quotes a poem about the "faint, sickening scent of irises." Steering away from the conflict, one praises the chef's talents to draw attention to the excellent food. Some people report, unfortunately, that the vegetables are soggy and the meat tough. With tensions on the rise, one then, having noted the wine's rarity, extols its virtues, imagining how heads will nod in an easy-going accord. This is met with a remark about the wine's insipid taste. Only a short step from submitting that, indeed, there is no disputing about tastes, one mentions the intriguing spiral designs on the nearby wallpaper, almost in jest. The group turns, and a strange silence settles as each person quietly reflects upon the geometrical patterns … It is exactly here, in the playfully aimless formal designs, so suggestively intelligent, that Kant's aesthetics offers some hope for agreement.

1. SPACE, TIME AND LOGIC

Immanuel Kant (1724–1804) expresses an interest in beauty and sublimity in his *Observations on the Feeling of the Beautiful and*

Sublime as early as the 1760s, but his reputation as the father of modern aesthetics resides in his *Critique of the Power of Judgment* (1790) – a work composed and published almost three decades later. This is the third of his highly influential *Critiques*, all of which reflect and develop Kant's intellectual breakthrough in the early 1780s that defines the philosophical tenor of his mature writings. These three *Critiques*, namely, the *Critique of Pure Reason* (1781/1787), the *Critique of Practical Reason* (1788) and the *Critique of the Power of Judgment* (1790) are shaped by an assumption that runs contrary to the British empiricist views of the late 1600s and early 1700s. Kant maintains that when our minds passively receive sensations, those sensations do not simply and immediately reflect the world's physical objects, as if the mind were a mirror or blank sheet of paper.

Our knowledge may begin with sensory experience, Kant acknowledges, but our mind does not compare well to a blank sheet of paper upon which sensory experience writes its messages or impresses its information. We have additionally, so he observes, a set of fixed intellectual capacities through which we actively transform those raw sensations, such as tiny bits of color, texture, sound, odor, and taste, into comprehensible objects of awareness, such as tables and chairs. Sensations may vary in quality from person to person and from circumstance to circumstance, but they are processed and organized according to mechanisms that he believes operate identically in everyone. Kant's theory of beauty draws our attention to those shared mechanisms and, importantly, to the universal feelings they emit during their operations.

This conception of the human mind may seem obvious, for it is difficult to deny that a cat must think like a cat, a dog like a dog, a bird like a bird, and a human like a human. The originality and radicality of Kant's theory of knowledge resides not exactly here, but in his inventory of the mechanisms that supposedly define our human nature and according to which we organize our sensations. His view is innovative, although he remains in perfect line with the history of Western philosophy that defines human beings as rational animals.

For instance, humans apprehend natural events in logical, causal terms: when experiencing two events in close sequence, we imagine that one causes the other, and until proven otherwise, we suppose that the events are causally related, even if the exact pathways are unclear. Indeed, it is difficult to imagine how any event could *lack* a cause, although as an abstract possibility it is not impossible to hypothesize that some event could happen spontaneously, out of nowhere. It is not inconsistent to think so, but the possibility remains intellectually bewildering. Kant believes that with respect to our logical nature, we have no choice but to interpret our experience in terms of the principle that every event has a cause, which implies that we cannot but expect our experience to be scientifically understandable and predictable. This is a point about how we are constituted to think about things, rather than how those things are in themselves.

More radical than the proposition that for us, every event must have a cause, is Kant's innovative and hallmark position that *space* and *time* are among the forms we use to organize our sensations, and, most extremely, that space and time are nothing more. This is not to deny that there is a mind-independent reality. There is a reality beyond our ken, but Kant insists that our experience of it as being spatio-temporal tells us nothing about its true nature. We can only know how this mind-independent reality appears to us humans, not how it is in itself.

Strange-sounding at first, Kant's idea is not as alien to our common conceptions as it might seem. Supposing that God is a being that in itself is beyond space and time, then if God were to communicate with humans, this communication would need to occur within the parameters of our finite human world. It must at least occur at some time. To relate to us, God's presence would have to assume a temporal aspect, and perhaps a spatial one as well, even though neither aspect would characterize what God is like in itself. Kant accordingly maintains that we have a public, spatio-temporal experience of a mind-independent reality that is beyond time and space.

Kant's philosophical position that space and time are merely subjective forms of sensory awareness, common to all humans, is attractive for a reason that bears on his aesthetic theory: when experiencing any given object, these spatio-temporal features are identical for everyone. For a crowd of people watching the final seconds of a sports event, the dramatic movement and location of the time-clock is objectively the same for everyone in the crowd. The universally shared quality of time and space establishes an agreement among our experiences, unlike the situation where the group of people at our dinner party all taste the same wine and food, and yet disagree about whether the food or drink is pleasurable to their palate.

We have spoken about Kant's views on space and time, because the public quality and invariant structure of space and time are at the heart of his aesthetics. By focusing our attention on an object's spatial and temporal configuration, he establishes *a ground for universal agreement* in some important kinds of aesthetic judgments, namely, those concerning pure, or truth-oriented, beauty. Establishing the theoretical grounds for this universal agreement is one of his leading philosophical interests. Having argued in his *Critique of Pure Reason* that geometrical relationships express the qualities of space, and that mathematical relationships express the qualities of time, he invokes these relationships to ground the universal agreement that is attainable in judgments of pure beauty.

These objective considerations inform Kant's aesthetic theory, since he regards geometry and mathematics as formal specifications of space and time, and since he argues that space and time are invariant forms of human experience. The result is this: if someone attends purely and exclusively to the geometrical relationships and/or mathematical relationships in an object – whether the object happens to be a snowflake, tulip, painting, sculpture, or wallpaper design – that person can be sure that in principle, other people can apprehend the *same formal relationships* and, as Kant argues, *feel exactly the same way* about the object's design. By referring to this special kind of universal feeling, Kant's aesthetics concerns itself primarily with establishing the basis for universal agreement in judgments of beauty, along with a conception of beauty that corresponds to empirical truth.

2. JUDGMENTS OF PURE BEAUTY AND UNIVERSAL AGREEMENT

Writing in the late 1700s, Kant is captivated by a rigorous conception of knowledge that he inherited from René Descartes (1596–1650). Descartes had been frustrated by the tensions between his Roman Catholicism and the newly emerging sciences of his day, and he aimed to settle their differences through a valiant attempt to set aside all of his prior beliefs, hoping to discover a fresh and unprejudiced foundation for his philosophizing. To this end, he prescribed a "method of doubt" in his *Meditations on First Philosophy* (1641) through which he presumed to be false, any belief that could be subject to the slightest uncertainty, even if he had to introduce wild conjectures to discern this doubt. At one extreme point, he wondered what, if anything, would remain indubitable if a powerful evil demon were trying to confound his reasoning at every possible turn.

Descartes sought a belief that could resist this relentlessly skeptical attitude, and, realizing that sometimes his senses deceived him, he set aside all beliefs based on sensation. This led him to imagine the entire physical world as possibly illusory, and himself as perhaps nothing more than a disembodied spirit. Realizing further that he sometimes made errors in reasoning, he set aside all beliefs based on methodical, step-by-step thought-sequences as well, which include elementary mathematical truths such as $2 + 2 = 4$. After having thus eliminated – so he believed – all of his sensation-based and logic-based beliefs, it dawned on him that although he now found himself with almost nothing left in which to believe, he could not doubt that he was then actively engaged in the process of doubting, as he observed himself setting aside all of these common beliefs, type by type. That very awareness confirmed his presence to himself. Descartes concluded that whenever he stated it, the proposition "I think, I exist" is certain, and he proceeded to rest his positive philosophy upon this foundational act of self-awareness, as if it were unshakeable bedrock.

By the time we reach Kant's philosophy almost 150 years later, this unyielding Cartesian quest for certainty had been transformed into a search for propositions that are universal and necessary. Here, mere probability will not suffice: if the subject under consideration lacks a necessary foundation, then we must conclude that there is no genuine knowledge of that subject. Different types of necessity nonetheless can be distinguished. There is the conceptual or logical necessity that if someone is a bachelor, then the person is male and unmarried. There is the psychological necessity of feeling pain, if boiling water splashes onto one's normally functioning hand. There is the mathematical necessity that *2 + 2 = 4*, not to mention the geometrical necessity that the angles in a Euclidean triangle add up to 180 degrees. Yet another type of necessity – and the one central to our discussion of Kant's aesthetics – is the necessity of having to be consistent with the kind of being one is. An apple tree necessarily produces apples, and not oranges.

If we assume with Kant and most of the Western philosophical tradition that human beings are essentially rational animals, then our rational quality cannot be set aside. Given his historical position, Kant characterizes our rationality in reference to the elements of Aristotelian logic, and maintains that as rational animals, we are logical beings who organize our sensations according to basic logical patterns (for example, "If A, then B" or "This individual S has some general quality P"). As finite beings, as noted above, we also organize our sensations in accord with spatial and temporal patterns. That our knowledge must adhere to these forms of space, time, and logic is an epistemological necessity, that is, a necessity relative to how we are constituted to know things. Our condition compares to the apple tree that, if it produces fruit, it must necessarily produce apples.

It took Kant some time to discern how the epistemological necessity of space, time, and Aristotelian logic could be reflected in aesthetic judgments, which he defined as judgments based entirely on feeling. Having been influenced by the eighteenth-century British empiricist tradition in aesthetics, as we find in the writings of the Earl of Shaftesbury (Anthony Ashley Cooper) (1671–1713), Joseph Addison (1672–1719), Francis Hutcheson (1694–1746), Alexander Gerard (1728–95), Edmund Burke (1729–97), Archibald Alison (1757–1839), and David Hume (1711–76), aesthetic judgments had always appeared to Kant to have a contingent foundation in sensory feeling that varies inevitably from individual to individual, not to mention very little connection to scientific truth. Depending upon how a person's eyes, ears, nose, tongue, or basic skin sensitivity happens to be structured, a person's feelings and aesthetic judgments will differ. Some people will enjoy the smell of roses, some will not; some people will delight in the taste of wine, others will not; some will take pleasure in the sound of a flute, while others will love trumpets, and so on. In light of such examples, and at first believing that sensory feelings encompassed all aesthetic judgments, Kant assumed for decades that it is pointless to dispute about tastes – and also not much point in philosophizing about them – since it is absurd to expect someone whose tongue, nose, eye, or ear is structured differently from one's own to feel and enjoy exactly the same foods, drinks, aromas, paintings and music as oneself. On this conception, judgments of beauty are not referring to what is objectively "out there" for everyone to appreciate.

Kant's original view that judgments of taste have an exclusively sensory basis is evident in his critical assessment of his German rationalist predecessor, Alexander Baumgarten (1714–62), the theorist who first used the term "aesthetics" to refer to the study of beauty in relation to a "science of perception":

> The Germans are the only ones who presently use the word "aesthetics" to refer to what others call the critique of taste. This stems from a failed hope, held by Baumgarten, that excellent analytical thinker, of bringing the critical treatment of beauty under rational principles, and raising its rules to a science. But this effort is fruitless. The rules or criteria in mind here are, as far as their main sources are concerned, merely empirical, and therefore can never serve as determinate *a priori* laws, according to which our judgment of taste must be directed. To the contrary, our judgment is the true test of the correctness of the rules.[2]

Assuming that aesthetic judgments are about how something makes us feel, and acknowledging that feelings about roses, beer, flute sounds, and the like depend upon the structure of a person's sense organs, and hence vary from person to person, Kant believed that *if* all aesthetic judgments are based on sensory feelings, then disputing about tastes is pointless, since the judgments lack universality, necessity, or any kind of scientific basis. He never departed from this position, from this "if." Qualifying his view, however, was a crucial realization in 1787 that a special group of aesthetic judgments are *not* based on sensory feelings.[3]

---

[2] Kant, *Critique of Pure Reason* (A21n/B35–36n). Unless otherwise noted, all translations are by the author.

[3] See Kant's letter to Karl Leonhard Reinhold in December 1787, in Kant, *Correspondence*, pp. 271–2.

Prior to attaining this realization relatively late in life – he was sixty-three at the time – he focused his philosophizing on more productive subject matters such as science and morality that do, in fact, yield judgments that are universal and necessary, and he set aesthetics into the background. The results were his *Critique of Pure Reason* (1781/1787) and his *Critique of Practical Reason* (1788), mentioned above. When he published the *Critique of the Power of Judgment* in 1790, he was sixty-six years old.

Before Kant developed his more innovative views about how *some* aesthetic judgments are based on a kind of non-sensory feeling, he had succeeded in characterizing a different kind of non-sensory feeling at the basis of *moral* judgments, namely, the feeling of self-respect that we have for ourselves as rational beings. This is not a sensory feeling, for it is grounded solely in our intellect. It thus carries a necessity that sensory feelings lack, and it is a superior feeling for this reason. For instance, if there are conflicting demands between moral feelings and sensory feelings, the moral feelings always have the power to prevail, since (for Kant) they derive from our unconditional, rational qualities, whereas the sensory feelings derive from our variable physical conditions.

Sensory feelings do not entail any activities that we ought to engage in unconditionally, and, to illustrate this weakness, Kant offers the following example in his second *Critique*: although an intimidating death threat might easily persuade someone to stop engaging in extraneous sensory pleasures, the threat might be powerless to coerce someone into telling a lie that would deliver an innocent neighbor fatally to corrupt authorities. A person subject to such bullying might choose rationally to sacrifice himself, rather than send an innocent neighbor to his death.[4]

Since moral feelings require us to know what sort of object or situation we are judging, they are not feelings of beauty. When Kant reflects upon the nature of beauty, he discerns that to find something purely beautiful, we need not know what kind of thing it is, for the judgment requires merely registering how the thing's abstract design – whatever sort of thing it happens to be – makes us feel. This leads him to appreciate that whatever the nature of

---

[4] See Kant, *Critique of Practical Reason*, Chapter I, §6, Problem II, Remark.

the feelings that ground judgments of beauty happen to be, they differ from the non-sensory feelings that ground moral judgments. Only two possibilities follow: either judgments of beauty are based on a kind of non-sensory feeling that is distinct from moral feeling, or they are based on sensory feelings such as pleasant scents, textures, and tastes.

Kant's theories of science and morality define the intellectual mood of his philosophy, given how they rest upon universal and necessary principles. We can appreciate this atmosphere in the conclusion of his second *Critique*, the *Critique of Practical Reason*, where he mentions how two things constantly fill his mind with admiration and awe, the more and more he thinks of them: the starry heavens above (that is, the laws of nature) and the moral law within. Kant is awed by the existence of two distinct realms of law, one outer and one inner. Science follows the mechanical laws of cause and effect; morality respects the more generally rational, but nonetheless unconditional (or categorical) imperative to act such that the rule under which one's action falls can be a universal law for everyone. The Kantian philosophy's supreme task is to reveal the possibility of perfect cooperation between these two realms of law, and his aesthetic theory serves this purpose of integrating what is, with what ought to be.

Having identified a non-sensory, universal and necessary feeling at the basis of morality, we would expect Kant to search for a corresponding non-sensory, universal, and necessary feeling at the basis of scientific inquiry. This is the feeling of pure, or truth-oriented, beauty that he discerns in 1787, which is based on the apprehension of spatio-temporal configurations that are, in principle, publicly accessible to everyone. The feeling of pure beauty arises at a higher level of generality than is required for the formulation of any specific scientific laws, however, for it expresses simply the basic mental disposition that scientific knowledge requires for its realization.

Specifically, the feeling of pure beauty occurs at the level of elementary cognitive functioning where two complementary aspects of the mind pleasurably resonate as they operate together, poised to produce knowledge of the physical world in reference to spatio-temporal configurations. These are (1) "the imagination" (*die Einbildungskraft*), which is the faculty through which our sensations coalesce to produce an object's rudimentary sensory image, and (2) "the understanding" (*der Verstand*), the faculty that applies concepts to that sensory image for the sake of comprehending it as a thing of a certain kind.

The feeling of pure beauty functions consequently as a mental gauge that, through the pleasurable intensity of the felt harmony between the imagination and understanding, indicates the potential knowability of a given object. It reflects how cognitively at home we are in relation to some given object's formal design. The beauty-related aspect of this attunement between the imagination and the understanding does not involve specifying what kind of thing the object happens to be; it is a general feeling that issues from a detached, impartial and completely open-minded response to the object's spatio-temporal form. The feeling reveals in relation to that object, that our cognitive faculties are working in harmony well enough to know the object effectively in a scientific sense. The judgment is always a matter of degree. Within Kant's aesthetics, the baseline position on judgments of beauty depends, in sum, upon these cognitive considerations. Judgments of pure beauty rest upon the feeling of harmony between the cognitive faculties (the imagination and the understanding) as these faculties are jointly geared towards some given object in the appreciation of its abstract design.

One of Kant's leading aesthetic distinctions, then, is between feelings of pure beauty as opposed to sensory feelings, since unlike sensory feelings, we can assume *everyone* can feel those related to pure beauty to the same degree in relation to an object's design. These feelings depend only on how the common structures of our minds are directed towards knowing some thing, where what we attend to in the thing is its configuration of objective, scientifically relevant, spatio-temporal qualities, that is, what some British empiricists (John Locke, for example) refer to as primary qualities such as extension, figure, and motion. Kant's main discovery in aesthetics emphasizes how, in reference to an object's appearance, the way it makes us feel has not only a sensory dimension that can vary from person to person, but, more importantly, a non-sensory, formal dimension that is *invariant* between people and is the basis for universal agreement. The object's pure beauty is a reflection of this invariance.

Three types of feelings are thus distinguishable, and they can occur together in various mixtures, as we will see below: (1) sensory feelings; (2) intellectually based feelings that involve knowing what sort of thing we are judging; (3) intellectually based feelings that do not involve knowing what sort of thing we are judging, namely, feelings of pure beauty. We can also refer to the latter as feelings of truth-oriented beauty in that the qualities of the object to which we are attending (namely spatial and/or temporal qualities related to the object's design) are objectively valid for everyone. As Kant defines it, pure beauty is truth-oriented insofar as the feeling of pure beauty in relation to a given object gauges our capacity to acquire scientific knowledge, or empirical truth.

We are now getting a glimpse of how Kant is chiefly concerned with identifying a universal and necessary dimension within the sphere of aesthetic judgments for the sake of advancing our understanding of the interrelationships between science and morality. A manifestation of this interest is his emphasis, as we have been discussing, upon *establishing the possibility of universal agreement* in judgments of pure beauty. Since Kant has identified a non-sensory feeling that is associated with some aesthetic judgments, he distinguishes between aesthetic judgments that are based on feelings that vary from person to person, from those that are not. The former are "aesthetic judgments of sensation"; the latter, aesthetic judgments of beauty, or as he often describes them, "judgments of taste," which admit of universal agreement. For the sake of terminological clarity, we will refer to judgments of taste as judgments of pure beauty, or as judgments of truth-oriented beauty in the sense mentioned above.

To appreciate the non-sensory feelings that ground our judgments of pure beauty, it helps to recall that according to Kant, the universal and necessary qualities of the human mind are only formal qualities, like the contours of a cookie-cutter in relation to the dough it cuts. These lack sensory content and can be described as innate structures, forms, functions, or ways of organizing our given sensations. In judgments of pure beauty, we accordingly attend only to an object's formal qualities, to ensure that our judgment will resonate only with those of the object's qualities that we know *everyone* can identically experience, like a stopwatch's hand that moves objectively at a sports event. These qualities center upon the object's spatio-temporal design, and involve the object's sensory content only to the extent that it illuminates that formally defined design.

3. PURE BEAUTY, VULGAR BEAUTY, ADHERENT BEAUTY AND BEAUTIFUL PEOPLE

Kant's account of judgments of beauty rests significantly upon his leading observation that to judge a thing's pure beauty we need not know what kind of thing it is. It is necessary only to consider how the object's design makes us feel, and however we describe that feeling, concepts of the object's kind should not enter substantially into the account. Moreover, since judgments of pure beauty limit themselves to an object's mere appearance, this appearance could be that of an actual object, a dream image, or a self-conscious construction of fantasy. From wherever the images derive, if two images appear exactly the same, then their degree of pure beauty is exactly the same. Judgments of pure beauty, in other words, are *disinterested* in the sense that whether or not the judgment's object actually exists, it has nothing to do with the image's pure beauty. Judgments of pure beauty are consequently not identical to judgments of natural beauty. Dream images can be purely beautiful, and equally so, although they are only creatures of the imagination.

We can now summarize Kant's account of judgments of pure beauty, upon which the remainder of his aesthetic theory rests. When making a judgment of pure beauty, we must disregard: (1) the kind of object that we have before us; (2) whether or not the object actually exists; and (3) the object's sensory content (for example, its color, its odor, its taste, and its felt texture). The object's formal design remains to reflect upon, and, when reflecting on that design, we judge by the very feeling of how well it resonates with our cognitive, scientifically oriented faculties. The object is subsequently said to be beautiful, or not beautiful, or more precisely, beautiful to this or that intensity, depending upon the intensity of the felt resonance.

Kant's association of judgments of pure beauty with the forms of space and time stems from his discussion of space and time in the *Critique of Pure Reason*, where he highlights the forms of space and time by performing a series of abstractions from conceptual and sensory content. These abstractions perfectly match what is required to make judgments of pure beauty. He writes:

> In the transcendental aesthetic we shall, therefore, first *isolate* sensibility, by removing from it everything that the understanding

thinks through its concepts, so that nothing but empirical intuition is left. Secondly, we shall also remove from this, everything that belongs to sensation, so that nothing remains except pure intuition and the mere form of appearances, which is all that sensibility can supply *a priori*. Through this investigation it will be found that there are two pure forms of sensible intuition, namely space and time, as principles of *a priori* knowledge, the evaluation of which we will now be concerned.[5]

If we restrict our aesthetic judgment to an object's spatio-temporal design, setting aside the conceptual and sensory constituents that vary from individual to individual, then other people can identify that same design, and should feel about the object exactly the same as we do, if they perform the same abstractions. Only by attending exclusively to the formal design can we expect others to have the same feeling about the object. Insofar as we are confident about having performed the requisite abstractions from concepts, existence, and sensory content, we may even demand that other people agree with our judgment and feel the same way. Such a demand is the result of having taken ourselves beyond differences in sensory organ structures to a more fundamental level of spatio-temporal apprehension that everyone shares, for this commonality grounds the expectation that others should agree with our judgments. In the experience of pure beauty, then, attention is given to the qualities of the object that, if they were features of an actual physical object, would be qualities relevant to scientific knowledge. The formal design is composed of objectively valid configurations, and this is the source of the universal agreement it supplies. Pure beauty, in sum, is about an object's primary qualities, either real or apparent.

Owing to this focus upon an object's pure design, the attitude appropriate to making judgments of pure beauty is of the same kind that we would adopt – were we to attend more specifically to the kinds of objects that we were judging – if we were interested in formulating scientific laws that would apply to those objects. In this sense, the disinterested attitude required for making judgments of pure beauty serves as an aesthetic educator for scientific thinking, since through that disinterested attitude

---

[5] Kant, *Critique of Pure Reason* (A21/B36).

we become more mentally disposed to perform the types of abstractions that are useful to formulate scientific laws, both individually and as a system. The disinterested attitude required for making judgments of pure beauty also serves as an aesthetic educator for moral thinking, as we will see below. In Friedrich Schiller's aesthetics, written only several years after the publication of the *Critique of the Power of Judgment* and inspired by Kant, the notion of aesthetic education along such moral lines is developed, as the next chapter will describe.

Let us now consider the feeling of pure beauty in more detail. If this feeling is of the harmony of our cognitive faculties in view of an object's spatio-temporal design, then insofar as the design makes us feel that we can obtain scientific knowledge of that object, we can ask what specific quality of that design is resonating so pleasurably with our cognitive faculties. Since the ultimate aim in acquiring scientific knowledge is to achieve a systematic comprehension of the world for the sake of predicting the future, formal designs whose configurations strongly suggest that they are the products of intentional activity, that is, that, through their form alone, express the presence of intelligent, systematic thinking as their source, will be the ones that produce the feeling of beauty most effectively. The pleasure in pure beauty, in other words, resides in the disinterested and immediate apprehension of systematic, spatio-temporal design.

In Kant's terminology, such beautiful designs exhibit a purposiveness (*Zweckmäßigkeit*) or designedness through their systematic form. Since we set aside considerations of the kind of object we are judging within the context of estimating pure beauty, this purposiveness cannot be specified, as would alternatively be the case if we were to consider the object's purpose and relate the design to that purpose. The purposiveness at hand is a more generalized purposiveness "without a purpose" (*Zweckmäßigkeit ohne Zweck*) that arises at a higher level of abstraction. It is a merely formal systematicity that we apprehend, for example, in geometrically well-organized and creative patterns such as floral designs and arabesques that have no particular purpose. When the designs are complicated and yet systematic, they become examples of impressively beautiful arrangements, as in the structure of snowflakes or in the calligraphy typical of medieval illuminated manuscripts (Plate 1).

To sum up: Kant's inheritance of a rigorous Cartesian approach to knowledge generates a philosophical quest for judgments that are universal and necessary, and discovering such commonly shared judgments is one of his philosophy's central concerns. Within the field of aesthetics, Kant considers how we would need to understand judgments of pure beauty, if they are to exhibit such a universality and necessity. To arrive at this, he realizes that we must disregard the object's sensory appeal and its conceptual contents, restrict our judgment to the object's formal design, and attend especially to the design's inherent systematicity. The result is a formalistic aesthetics that coheres with scientific interests and with systematic interests of all kinds. It also coheres with Kant's moral theory, which is also formalistic.

A reasonable reaction to such a theory of pure beauty is to criticize it on several counts, the weightiest of which is its apparent inability to account satisfactorily for the artistic value of works that are rich in meaning, since the artworks' meanings and values go far beyond their pure, scientifically grounded beauty that is related simply to an object's spatio-temporal design. Hans-Georg Gadamer advances such an objection, as we will see in Chapter 12. Another drawback resides in how Kant's restriction of judgments of pure beauty to considerations of formal, systematically organized design does not match some ordinary uses of the term "beauty." Roses are paradigms of beauty, but Kant's theory implies that a rose, if beautiful, can be genuinely or truly beautiful on account of neither its delicate colors, nor its petals' soft texture, nor its seductively sweet aroma. Sunsets are also paradigms of beauty, but on Kant's theory, if a sunset is genuinely or truly beautiful, it cannot be so on account of its bright colors, for he regards the colors as nothing more than charming sensory stimuli, whose appeal varies from person to person.[6] Many of the objects that we typically pronounce to be beautiful prove themselves to be merely charming or pleasant within Kant's theory of beauty, and this raises the question of how remote Kant's theory of pure beauty is from ordinary conceptions of beauty.

---

[6] Kant admits that colors can be beautiful, but only on account of their purity. So the beauty of pure green and pure blue would be the same; the sensory differences between the colors would not figure into the judgment.

Kant denies that charming sensory qualities are beautiful, and upon those occasions when the beauty of formal design significantly mixes in with sensory charm, the object's overall beauty can become crass or vulgar. One way to interpret this is to say that our ordinary language mentality – one that has entrenched the images of roses and sunsets into our standard vocabulary of beauty – is itself deficient in taste, despite the presence of what seems to be common agreement. Kant would remind us that some people find the smell of roses to be sickening, or the colors of some dramatic sunsets to be too loud. These cases cannot reflect universal agreement or any kind of true beauty, so the frame of mind that regards them as paradigmatic cases of beauty does not express a common taste in any strict sense. Such would be Kant's estimation of situations where the pure beauty of formal design mixes with sensory charm beyond the point of merely highlighting the design, but extends to the point where the sensory charm predominates. This can be called "vulgar beauty." It does not demand universal assent, and it includes some paradigmatic cases of beauty.

In the complementary case where the pure beauty of formal design combines with conceptual factors, Kant offers an account that, owing to its connection with art and morality, resonates positively throughout the rest of his aesthetic theory. Within this kind of combination, the judgment of an object's beauty rests initially upon the consideration of what sort of object we are judging, for example, whether it is a work of art, or whether it is a human being, or a horse, or a church. Here, the beauty *adheres to*, or depends upon, the concept of the object's purpose, and Kant accordingly refers to this kind of beauty as adherent, or dependent, beauty. The term "adherent" is apt, since within these contexts the object's beauty must respect the concept of the object's kind. The beauty adheres to – in the double sense of "respecting" and "attaching itself to" – the kind of object under consideration. A few examples will illustrate what Kant has in mind.

We can judge a thing's beauty insofar as it is an object of a certain type and say that *as a rose*, the object (which is a rose) is beautiful, or that *as a snowflake*, the object (which is a snowflake) is beautiful. There might be a rose that has lost most of its petals, or a snowflake that has had some of its points broken, and yet as formal designs, they could still be very beautiful. They would not be very beautiful as roses or as snowflakes, though, since their forms would not measure up well to how roses or snowflakes ought to look. In the latter instances, the object's limited beauty would adhere to the concept of a rose or snowflake, respectively.

We can usually choose unproblematically to judge a thing's beauty in a pure way, or in a way that adheres to the kind of thing it happens to be, as in the case of a rose or a snowflake. Sometimes, however, there is no reasonable choice to make, for some objects *oblige* us to recognize them as the kinds of objects that they are, on pain of violating a moral imperative. This, rather importantly, is the case for the aesthetic judgment of human beings according to Kant. We are morally required to show respect to other human beings, and if we were to judge their bodily configurations merely as formal designs while ignoring that we are judging the configuration of a human being, we would be displaying a lack of moral sensitivity. It would be tantamount to regarding the visually satisfying contours of a person's body as being no different in kind from those of a visually satisfying rock formation. Since, for Kant, moral imperatives are unconditional, the demand to respect other people overrides any concern about their pure beauty. His consequent position is that we ought to judge a person's beauty always in a specific and respectful manner, namely, as *human* beauty, so that our aesthetic judgment will adhere to the idea that humans are rational, moral beings, and, in conjunction with this, acknowledge nature's plan for the ideal human bodily configuration.

This requirement to recognize that human beauty must adhere to a moral concept explains why Kant objects to some forms of tattooing. Many tattoos are purely beautiful as abstract designs, but they can conflict with or obscure the body's natural contours and lines of emotional display that Kant believes are consistent with moral expression and behavior. For this reason, he objects to the facial tattooing of the New Zealand Maoris, where the same kinds of beautifully circular figures that we see in the Lindisfarne Gospels design (Plate 1) are inscribed upon the human face (Plate 2).[7]

---

[7] For a defense of Maori tattooing, however, see Wicks, "Kant on Beautifying the Human Body."

Within the sphere of adherent beauty, Kant describes how a beautiful human being ought to be, stating that this ideal has two components, a physical one and a conceptual one. One component is the physical pattern that nature has in mind when producing human beings – a pattern, according to Kant, discernible in the rationalized bodily proportions typical of an ancient Greek sculpture (Plate 3). The other component is the idea of the human being as a rational and moral being. In the fusion of these two components, the ideal figure would be morally expressive while embodying nature's pattern for the human form. Clean, physically well-contoured, virtuous-looking characters are good examples.

The result is that for Kant, the most beautiful human beings will be attractive in both inner character and outer physical appearance – each will have a morally sound mind in a physically sound body – and their moral awareness will shine through in their bodily movements and overall shapes. Such people would be rational within and without.

Implicit here is a vision of a beautiful society, populated by people with strong, attractively proportioned bodies who, owing to their good wills, express themselves in a rational manner. The rationality of natural physical proportions (the laws of nature without) and the rationality of non-natural, moral rationality (the moral law within) are fused together in this ideal of beauty – an ideal that more generally represents the harmony of science (or nature) and morality. In later chapters, and especially in the next chapter on Schiller, when we imagine an entire society of such people more concretely, we will see various developments and transformations of this idealization of the human being that is here represented initially and positively in Kant's account of human beauty.

With respect to Kant's estimation of the aesthetic value of Maori tattoos and other such designs that allegedly conflict with how human beings ought to look, there is an open question regarding the extent to which the beautiful forms and associated satisfactions should be valued. It is implausible to assert that these should not be valued at all, as if we were speaking of pleasures that issue from thoroughly immoral behavior. Neither, however, is it plausible that they should be equally valued with those forms of satisfactions that do not violate moral dictates.

As the situation stands, Kant's position is that insofar as tattoos and other bodily modifications do not cohere with the natural ideal, the beautiful forms and satisfactions related to them are tainted. Since he regards moral dictates as unconditional, bodily modifications that conflict with moral expression would be objectionable, just as someone who maintained a severely naturalistic aesthetic would find unacceptable the depiction of dogs or human faces as bright green, blue, or purple.

4. JUDGMENTS OF THE SUBLIME

Kant's theory of the sublime complements his theory of beauty, and together they strengthen the connections between aesthetics and morality. Unlike the experience of pure beauty, sublimity includes a dimension of pain, fear, or frustration. To regard as sublime a crashing thunderstorm, or an imposing mountain range, or an earthquake, it is necessary to overcome the fear of being hurt or killed. Only then can one appreciate the aesthetic qualities of the physically threatening phenomena. Starting from this observation about the sublime, Kant articulates a theory that reflects his philosophical interests and his account of how the mind operates. In particular, he describes the experience of the sublime in reference to the operations of the imagination and *reason* – which contrasts with the activity of the imagination and understanding that we encounter in the theory of beauty – and he ascribes value to the sublime experience in view of its capacity to accentuate moral awareness via the connection to reason.

Kant identifies two general types of sublime experience – the "mathematically" sublime that involves the perception of intractably large objects or phenomena, and the "dynamically" sublime that involves the perception of overwhelmingly powerful objects or phenomena. Both types subject us to some sort of pain, fear, or frustration. When we aesthetically appreciate objects or phenomena of extremely large size, natural or artifactual – we can imagine here the infinite extent of time or space, the wide expanse of the ocean, extremely spacious buildings such as St. Peter's Basilica, lengthy fortifications such as the Great Wall of China, or enormously weighty constructions such as the Pyramids – most perceivers will try to encompass the size with a single perceptual sweep. The inevitable failure and feeling of frustration reveals our imagination's limited power. Concretely imagining the infinity of space is impossible, since it would take forever to picture ourselves literally passing through it all.

To comprehend the object successfully, we must abandon our imagination and employ another mental function, namely, our "reason" as Kant conceives of it, whose purpose is to construct abstract ideas for the sake of comprehending totalities. As we more effectively comprehend the totality with a rational idea, the frustrations associated with the perceptual or imagination-related effort, transform into a satisfaction that arises through a shift of attention from sensory, to non-sensory, mental functions. Since, for Kant, our moral awareness resides within this sphere of non-sensory rational functions, he believes that the experience of the mathematically sublime ultimately reinforces moral awareness by stimulating a transition from the sensation-entrenched imagination to a more elevated, rational mode of awareness that stands at the threshold of morality.

A comparable process occurs in the experience of the dynamically sublime, except that the concern is initially with our physical perishability rather than with our limited ability to comprehend excessively extensive expanses. As alluded to above in the initial examples of thunderstorms, mountains, and earthquakes, to experience the dynamical sublime it is necessary to overcome the fear of being seriously hurt or killed. Kant importantly believes that when we feel the threat of death, we can be awakened to a dimension within ourselves that is *immune* to physical threats. This, once again, is our reason, which is non-sensory and is the legislator of moral laws that prevail amidst all physical changes and threats.

In the above two ways, the experience of the sublime serves as an aesthetic educator that directs our attention to our unconditional, more elevated, non-sensory moral selves. Kant believes that the experience of beauty significantly does the same, and with respect to beauty, there are yet further ways in which it reinforces our moral awareness, to which we will now turn. The first concerns how beauty is the expression of aesthetic ideas; the second, how it is the symbol of morality. From the discussion so far, though, we can already appreciate that Kant's aesthetic theory fundamentally reinforces his moral theory.

5. BEAUTY AS THE EXPRESSION OF AESTHETIC IDEAS

After Kant describes pure beauty, human beauty, and the sublime, he attends to artistic creation and artistic beauty, both of which he characterizes further as the expression of "aesthetic ideas" (*ästhetische Ideen*) – a notion that is easy to misconstrue. Kant defines an aesthetic idea as an individual image, or creature of the imagination, that is highly resonant in meaning. It is not an abstract concept, as one might expect from the term "idea." It is a metaphor-filled, multi-interpretable image, either artifactual or natural. For clarity's sake, we will refer to aesthetic ideas as "rich aesthetic images." According to Kant, such a presentation is a perceivable individual whose form and/or meaning stimulates more thought than can be determinately specified, like a literary text filled with suggestive metaphors. A rich aesthetic image is a visionary product and any individual artwork, if resonant in meaning, would embody the artist's aesthetic idea, or artistic vision.

One of Kant's underlying intentions is to formulate a definition of beauty that corresponds to his original account of pure beauty (that is, that coincides with his main notions of purposiveness without a purpose, the harmony of the cognitive faculties, disinterestedness, and formal relationships), but which applies more effectively and obviously to works of fine art. He consequently asserts expansively that *all* beauty – whether it is pure beauty, natural beauty, or artistic beauty – is the expression of aesthetic ideas.

Problems immediately arise, owing to the rich semantic content that rich aesthetic images contain. Insofar as they are semantically rich, it is difficult to see how Kant's centrally motivating quest for universal agreement in aesthetic judgment can be preserved. Works of art are subject to many different interpretations, and the meanings of metaphors can vary from person to person, or from population to population, almost as much as can the effects of wines and foods. This leads to the following dilemma: either we remain focused exclusively upon the qualities of objects that are constant for everyone, and set aside images with rich metaphorical (and hence variable, multi-interpretable) content, or we more broadly allow semantically resonant images into the account of pure beauty and sacrifice the universal agreement that was initially so carefully sought and which originally motivated this aesthetic theory.[8]

Insofar as a rich aesthetic image is a veritable fountain of suggestive associations relative to some given subject, it has two functions within Kant's aesthetics. The first is to cohere with his account of how judgments of pure beauty admit of universal agreement, which, as we have noted, is unlikely. The second, more plausible, function is as an aesthetic educator that indicates a realm beyond determinate conceptual formulation and our finite understanding. It is questionable whether rich aesthetic images necessarily generate the feeling of beauty, but their semantic density can lead us to experience the feeling associated with moral awareness in a manner more akin to the sublime. They are consequently supposed to serve a double function that integrates science via the connection to truth-oriented beauty, and morality via the manner in which they resonantly display ideas that defy definition and whose content can never be exhausted, such as those of God, the kingdom of the blessed, eternity, creation, death, hell, love, envy, fame, and the like.

Kant's theory of artistic genius supports the above connections, for he states that as a matter of natural ability and as a natural creature, the artistic genius produces rich aesthetic images. Nature works through the genius to produce works of

---

[8] One might wonder, as do some Kant interpreters, whether Kant's theory of pure beauty and his theory of aesthetic ideas can be rendered compatible by speaking generally of formal relationships of *any* kind (as opposed to only spatio-temporal relationships) as can obtain between colors or thematic elements. This strategy fails because it cannot preserve universal validity. Some people are color blind, and some people prefer some colors over others, given their retinal structure, so formalistic relationships among colors cannot preserve universal validity. Neither can formalistic relationships among thematic elements, since, for instance, one cannot expect a person who has no conception of a thematic element(s) that arises in the artwork of another culture, to be able to appreciate the formal relationships it bears to other elements in the work. See the chapter on Gadamer below for a reiteration and expansion of this point.

fine art, and, in this respect, works of fine art are like natural products such as snowflakes, tulips, or seashells. Insofar as rich aesthetic images indicate the moral realm through their display of rational ideas, the artistic genius – a figure whose theoretical function parallels that of the ideally beautiful human being – is a natural being who expresses, as well as embodies, the compatibility of nature and morality. This compares to how rich aesthetic images themselves produce the feeling of beauty as they indicate the moral realm, and by implication, the feeling of moral self-respect.

6. BEAUTY AS THE SYMBOL OF MORALITY

Kant concludes his aesthetic theory with the revealing claim that the faculty of taste is fundamentally a capacity to judge the presentations of moral ideas in a sensory form, as when a poet or painter tries to render God's presence public in words or in paint. In connection with the rational ideas involved (for example, heaven, hell, eternity, life, and death), it would be crucial to judge the artwork's degree of resonance of meaning in both consistency and depth. In connection with judgments of natural beauty, and, again, in reference to the idea of rendering God's presence public, the faculty of taste would lead us to regard the object as if it were the product of supernatural design. Here, taste becomes the capacity to appreciate the possibility that there is a supernatural designer.

When Kant speaks specifically of beauty as the symbol of the morally good, he thinks in more general terms than occur in the above two examples, for he is concerned with the abstract structure of judgments of pure beauty and the comparable structure of judgments of moral goodness. This interrelationship recognizes how both kinds of judgment rest on a non-sensory feeling, albeit of different kinds. As the basis of the "symbolism," or more precisely, their parallelism in structure, Kant observes that both kinds of judgment have the same core features, namely, that the feelings that ground the two kinds of judgment are immediately felt, and that the judgments involve relationships to freedom, disinterestedness and universality.

Owing to the isomorphic structure that judgments of pure beauty and judgments of the morally good share, Kant states that beauty *symbolizes* the morally good, suggesting that purely beautiful objects compare well with artworks produced by genius. Just as a beautiful artwork expresses – mainly through the presence of metaphor – a rich aesthetic image that cannot quite capture the rational idea it aims to express, a purely beautiful object symbolizes the morally good in a way that also involves a gap between sensible objects and rational ideas. The kinds of distance between the sensible objects and the rational ideas differ in each case, but Kant is keen to show that in each kind of beauty, whether it involves pure configurations, natural objects, or artworks, the beauty indicates morality. He concludes that an exercise of our capacity to make judgments of beauty can educate us towards the attitude of mind that is proper to moral judgments, and alternatively, if we could more effectively realize that our essential nature is moral, then the beauty in the world – especially the natural beauty – would shine before us as never before. With respect to the latter, Kant is convinced that someone whose interest in natural beauty exceeds any concern with artistic beauty, shows the mark of a good person and deserves to be called a beautiful soul.

7. BEAUTY AS A RHETORICAL DEVICE

Kant's association of beauty with morality and science has a general implication for instances where we add beauty to arbitrary subject matters: the addition of some beauty attaches both a moral dimension and an appearance of scientific validity to the subject at hand, whatever the subject might be. Consider a person's idealized portrait: when the facial contours are reshaped to achieve a more balanced set of proportions, when the blemishes are removed, when the facial expression is rendered pleasing and consistent with a moral expression, the process of rationally guided idealization adds an authority and attractiveness to the figure.

These formal modifications can be applied to any subject or subject matter, and, as such, the process of rationally guided idealization can be used rhetorically to persuade people to accept the subject matter. Within Kant's aesthetics, pure beauty expresses an object's suitability for scientific knowledge, but owing to the merely formal character of this purified beauty, it has no connection to any specific kind of thing. It can, therefore, be added artistically to any given thing. If we fail to maintain the distinction between pure and adherent beauty, it will be easy to associate the beautiful form with the object's content, and fallaciously ascribe a scientific validity and moral attractiveness to that content.

This fallacious association between an object's formal beauty and its content explains why some people – call the group, "*A*" – would find the aesthetic idealization of their heroes to be attractive, but the aesthetic idealization of their enemies to be offensive, and why a strictly opposing group "*B*", in social conflict with *A*, would find the aesthetic idealization of *A*'s heroes to be offensive, and the aesthetic idealization of their own heroes to be attractive. Independently of *A*'s and *B*'s content, the aesthetic idealization is achieved in each case by adding a rationality-grounded legitimation, which within Kantian aesthetics carries a specifically scientific or documentary quality, along with a moral quality. Within the field of rhetorical analysis, adding such pure beauty as Kant conceives of it, would be to employ *logos* – as when one portrays a fictional construction using an image that looks like a news photograph – to achieve the persuasive effect. Given the association between beauty and morality, it would also employ *ethos* to achieve the persuasive effect, since ethos is the appeal to respectable character, as when an actor dons a dentist's professional attire to sell toothpaste.

If we remain within the parameters of Kant's aesthetics, the rhetorical use of the sublime operates in a more complicated manner. Suppose we portray a person, say, a king or an emperor, as overwhelmingly powerful, like a fearsome god, or as overwhelmingly perceptive, like someone of all-seeing wisdom whose stretch of insight touches every corner of the world. The image would stimulate respect, and we could interpret such a representation as portraying in connection with the person, either the world's infinite power or expanse, or the infinity of soul within ourselves towards which the experience of that physical expanse ultimately directs us.

Similarly, the characterization of a person using rich aesthetic images, as when one writes poems, makes movies, or paints portraits of the person, renders the person larger-than-life and adds a documentary and ethical quality to the person's image. If beautiful, the rich aesthetic images add a documentary quality; they also portray the person in relation to lofty rational and morally related ideas such as heaven, hell, eternity, life, and death.

In none of these examples need the portrayed person be morally good, worthy of artistic portrayal, especially powerful, insightful, or respectable. The aesthetic effect is only rhetorically and formalistically achieved. In relation to Kant's aesthetics and his theory of genius in particular, this formalistic quality is at the source of a problem that shows itself more saliently in later writers, namely, that of beautifying immoral content. Tempering this situation's inherent danger is Kant's view that the artistic genius is "nature's favorite," which conveys the thought that nature speaks through artistic geniuses, and that the imaginative, beauty-producing power of the artistic genius is a natural power.

Since from a moral standpoint, Kant is convinced that nature is rationally grounded in a divine, benevolent intelligence, his conception of artistic genius implicitly follows suit: he believes that the artistic genius has the special capacity to produce rich aesthetic images, and that these images help us become aware of the rational and moral side of things. The disturbing fact, however, is that an artist can apply rich aesthetic images rhetorically to any subject matter, as when a first-rate painter or novelist portrays a mass murderer angelically, predictably generating moral outrage.

Kant typically describes selfish interests as indicative of bodily inclination or sensory feeling, so we can ask whether in the case of the naturally inspired artistic genius who uses his or her genius rhetorically to substantiate and authenticate subjects unworthy of moral respect, we have an instance of nature in contradiction with itself, and evidence that nature is not as coherently constructed as Kant imagines it to be. Consider those who self-consciously present known villains as unconditionally good and respectable in their paintings, sculptures, photographs, films, plays, television, or video productions.

The question of whether it is appropriate to beautify immoral themes or people arises more explicitly in the theorists who follow Kant, and the larger issue concerns the depth of the connection between morality and beauty. In Kant's aesthetics, as we have seen, the connection is deep. In the bud, we have here the project of rendering people more morally aware through some type of exposure to beauty or fine art – a project that seems to require controversially that we suppose that the world is inherently rational. Once it becomes more questionable that rationality resides in the basic fabric of things, beauty and morality will begin to disengage from one another, with the result that theorists will understand the value of beauty in connection with other, non-moral ends.

2

THE BEAUTY OF MORAL CULTIVATION

Friedrich Schiller

1. FINE ART AND MORAL CULTIVATION

The historical reputation of Friedrich Schiller (1759–1805) rests mainly upon his achievements as one of Germany's finest dramatists and poets. His "Ode to Joy" (1785), whose words feature in the last movement of Beethoven's *Ninth Symphony* (1824), is widely recognizable even to those who have had only a brief exposure to Western classical music. Within a variety of scholarly circles that include philosophers, aestheticians, political theorists, Germanists, and literary critics, Schiller's philosophical writings – especially his *Letters on the Aesthetic Education of Man* (1795) – have also become influential. His philosophical writings further include a less familiar set of essays and letters composed between 1792 and 1796 such as the *Kallias-Briefe*, "On the Sublime," "On Grace and Dignity," "On the Tragic Art," "On Tragic Pity," and "On Naive and Sentimental Poetry" that illuminate his views on beauty and art.

To appreciate Schiller's interest in the educative power of beauty, it will help to mention some details of his life prior to composing the above essays. Schiller's father, an army captain in the service of Duke Karl Eugen of Württemberg, sent his young son to the Duke's private military academy – the *Karlsschule Stuttgart* – that instituted a strong disciplinary ethic. The school's authoritarian administration grated harshly against Schiller's freedom-loving temperament, and remembering his miserable experiences in later years, he argued against soul-destroying tyranny in an effort to uphold liberty, freedom, play, and a return to a more beautiful, pastoral, and idyllic world. To conclude his formal education, Schiller trained in medicine and became a regiment doctor, albeit briefly, at the age of twenty. The censorship of his play, *The Robbers* (*Die Räuber*, 1781), performed only a year later, forced him into exile from his former province, and this led him to shift his residence from city to city for the next several years, during which time his health often suffered.

Although it had been brewing for years, the French Revolution began officially when Schiller was thirty, and for many who observed its course from neighboring counties, a roller-coaster of sentiments marked the event, as the lofty idea of a rationally driven society governed by universal justice and a sensitivity to human rights raised everyone's hopes in 1789, and, as the Reign of Terror dealt swiftly and murderously with all perceived opposition, those aspirations were soon dashed beyond repair. At the midway point, the King, Louis XVI, and then in later months, Marie Antoinette, his wife and Queen, were executed in 1793. The time coincided with Schiller's revisiting of Kant's writings, which he had first encountered five years earlier. In 1794, the Reign of Terror's bloodbath marked the depths to which the Revolution's original mission had sunk: during the most vicious months of May to July, an average of twenty-two people per day were guillotined in Paris. For the six months from January to July of the same year, ten people per day were guillotined on average. By almost any reasonable standard, the number of people being executed was frightening and intellectually troubling.

These events generated the riddle of how such a politically beautiful and inspiring movement could gravitate into a state of brutality. Schiller's answer was both direct and global: before a group of revolutionaries can effectively promote a socially improving idea, they must first cultivate their moral character. No matter how excellent a political idea might be, if the people who advocate the idea are not of sufficiently high integrity, then the sensuous dimension – and for Schiller this is our more animalistic quality – can easily take over. He consequently sought ways to educate people to become more refined, noble, and free with methods that were *independent* of existing governmental and general political situations. Inspired by Kant, he discerned these civilizing powers in beauty and in fine art. Most of Schiller's aesthetic writings accordingly reflect his medical training and philosophical interest in restoring spiritual health. Complicating his formulation for a cure is the sensuous nature of beauty and fine art, which seems to conflict with the moral awareness he believes beauty and art have the power to reinforce and uphold.

To conceptualize the therapeutic problem of how to produce an aesthetically informed civilization of a higher personal integrity, Schiller relies upon a Kantian framework, where at the foundation is the divide between the sensuous natural realm and the non-sensuous moral realm. In what seems to be a small departure from Kant, Schiller entrenches beauty more deeply within in the sensuous realm, and by thus widening the gap between beauty and morality, he creates for himself the problem of how beauty can foster moral awareness at all. Compounding his difficulties is the observation that although fine art can have a powerful aesthetic presentation, the main subjects of its narratives can be of immoral character, for example, robbers and murderers. When immoral subjects aesthetically predominate, it will not easily follow that if a work is excellent as fine art, moral awareness will be cultivated.

Notwithstanding his recognition of beauty's sensuous dimension, Schiller is moved by Kant's claim in the *Critique of the Power of Judgment* (§42) that if someone automatically, naively, and naturally takes an interest in nature's beauty, then this is evidence that the person is of good character and is a "beautiful soul" (*schöne Seele*). Kant's estimation of the evidentiary quality of fine art was less enthusiastic, as he noticed around him the number of selfish connoisseurs of fine art. If these individuals are any example, he reasoned, then if a person spends his or her life exposed to fine art, it will do little to develop moral character.

Schiller is of a different mind in the *Letters*, and, anticipating the prevailing opinion of theorists who will be writing during the nineteenth century, he judges fine art to be superior to natural beauty. This issues from locating the human being at the crown of creation and regarding creative, freely expressive human works as the embodiments of what is best in us. Schiller writes accordingly that fine art can be an outstanding cultivator of moral character.

He thus faces a difficult task in the hope of securing, for fine art, a noble place within the moral realm, given his more sensuous understanding of beauty, his recognition of immoral characters in great drama, and his departure from Kant's negative estimation of artistic connoisseurs.

On a broader scale, and further motivating Schiller's interest in beauty, is the variety of ways in which Kant describes beauty as the intermediary between nature and morality, claiming that (1) beauty is the symbol of morality, (2) aesthetic ideas (that is, what we referred to earlier as rich aesthetic images) direct us towards both nature and morality, (3) artistic geniuses naturally express rich aesthetic images with a moral content, and (4) the ideal of beauty locates a moral character in a physical body that reveals nature's rationally idealized design for the human species. Finally and fundamentally, Kant maintains that the feeling of pure beauty is the free play and harmonious interrelationship between the sensation-oriented imagination and the concept-oriented understanding. Following this latter definition, Schiller assigns a central place to the notions of "freedom" and "play" in his own conception of beauty and aesthetic education.

2. THE *LETTERS ON THE AESTHETIC EDUCATION OF MAN*

Historically overlapping with the French Revolution, the Industrial Revolution was also making its mark in Europe at the end of the 1700s and into the 1800s. Although the development of manufacturing and the increased availability of material goods had its obvious benefits, a repugnant price was being paid in adverse labor conditions and human suffering. Of particular concern to Schiller was the dramatic increase in the division of labor that factory production entailed, as it constricted human imagination and the possibilities of spiritual development. Many workers spent the bulk of their waking lives confined to repetitive, mind-numbing jobs, and, in Schiller's judgment, not only did this condition offend human dignity, it prevented the spiritual integration of the human psyche as it drove a wedge between its sensuous and rational aspects. Perceiving that industrial development was blocking the road to moral development, Schiller was among the first to characterize the demeaning nature of capitalism. In the Sixth Letter of his *Letters on the Aesthetic Education of Man*, for instance, he wrote the following:

> As soon as, on the one hand, broadened experience and more exact speculation made necessary a sharper division of the sciences, and on the other, the more complicated mechanism of States made necessary a more rigorous division of ranks and occupations, the inner bond of human nature was torn apart, and a disastrous conflict set its harmonious powers at variance. The intuitive and the speculative understanding withdrew in hostility to their respective fields, whose boundaries they now began to guard with mistrust and jealousy, and by confining our activity to a single sphere we have handed ourselves over to a master within, who frequently ends up suppressing the rest of our capacities. While in one place a luxurious imagination ravages the hard-earned fruits of the intellect, in another the spirit of abstraction stifles the fire at which the heart could have warmed itself and the imagination been kindled.

Aggravating the situation were the political divisions among the many German principalities, not to mention the prevailing philosophical attitude of the time: the scientific breakthroughs of the 1600s and 1700s had reinforced a mechanistic view of the world as a large clockwork, and although this attitude led eventually to dramatic advances in the human sciences, it also encroached upon the idea of human freedom. When the human body is regarded as a mechanism governed by causal relationships throughout, the slightest behavior becomes predictable and human freedom – a necessary condition of morality – either proves to be an illusion or becomes redundant. Already at the end of the 1700s, we can see reason beginning to square off against itself: mathematical, mechanical, instrumentally geared reason characteristic of scientific thinking was invading the territory of the reflective, legislative, rule-forming reason definitive of our higher intellect and moral capacities.

Schiller maintains that nature's physical laws can cohere perfectly with the moral law, and, following Kant, he also appreciates the difficulty of coordinating them, for he likewise characterizes nature and morality as being fields apart. Like the colors red and yellow, so different in visual quality, but admitting of a smooth connection through shades of orange, Schiller sees that although no direct jump can easily be made from nature to morality, or from raw instinct to purely rational moral awareness, a passage can be forged effectively through beauty and fine art.

Taking the lead from Kant's aesthetics, he understands the experience of beauty to involve a free play of the imagination that resonates symbolically with moral awareness. He consequently regards beauty as a transitional phase on the civilizing path to morality, without which a person would remain entangled within an instinctually driven life, with attendant tendencies to violence. Convinced that only through beauty can we arrive at moral freedom, he is captivated by the project of rendering people more virtuous through an intensification of their aesthetic experiences, and considers this civilizing aim to be one of the most important educational undertakings of cultural life.

Schiller's first task in the *Letters* thus aspires to lift people from a more instinctual condition, servile to the senses, to a point where moral awareness can shine through and eventually dominate. This path from the perceptual to the intelligible world is a well-trodden one, notably outlined in Plato's belief that to arrive at the unchanging truth, we must transcend the daily world of changing things. To remain in the world of otherworldly forms, however, is nonetheless unrealistic: our communal nature and sense of obligation soon call upon us to carry our hard-won knowledge back to practical activity for everyone's benefit. With this objective in mind, Schiller supplements his ascending notion of aesthetic education with a descending aspect – one that re-integrates us into the world of sensory experience with a higher level of awareness, and that regards beauty and fine art as more than simply a means to a moral end. At the completion of our aesthetic education, beauty and fine art become ends in themselves as the constituents of the sophisticated awareness required to render moral awareness a concrete, civilized reality.

It is difficult to develop oneself into a solid moral character, and it is also difficult to appreciate beauty and fine art to the extent where their moral effects can be felt in a life-changing way. Supposing that we can attain the moral heights that require our disengagement from the sensory world, then Schiller offers a guide for managing the result of having become so absorbed in abstractions, conceptions, forms, and intellectual matters. Since such a condition, so detached from competitive and survival-related concerns, does not last for long, there is the inevitable need to act, and with it, a need to address the question of how to transform one's abstract moral awareness into a concretely lived reality. Once again, beauty and fine art define the returning path, the culmination point of which invokes the notion of the beautiful soul and Kant's ideal of human beauty.

Schiller perceptively describes the condition of a morally aware person who has succeeded in absorbing and incorporating beauty into his or her practical life, as a complex one where beauty simultaneously cancels the distinction between sensuousness and morality, preserves the presence of sensuousness and morality, and enhances them both. The infusion of moral content enhances sensuousness, and, in turn, sensuousness enhances moral content by rendering it concrete within the daily world. Beauty serves to synthesize the two to establish a genuine organic unity of opposites. With a great anticipatory insight, he describes this amalgamated condition with the verb "*aufheben*" (to lift up, cancel, and preserve, all at once) and introduces an image pregnant with the dialectical reasoning that predominates in German idealistic thought during the first several decades of the nineteenth century. As we shall see in the next chapter, among German Idealists such as Hegel, words such as "*aufheben*," "*Aufhebung*" and "*aufgehoben*" describe a non-mechanical, dialectical synthesis of opposites, characteristic of a living, organic unity.

Reacting strongly to the unresolved theoretical divisions that remain in the Kantian philosophy, to the political divisions in his homeland, and to the social divisions of labor in the growing industrial atmosphere, Schiller, like many other German intellectuals of the time whose ideals were shaped by the art historian Johann Winckelmann (1717–68), finds his redemptive image in the ancient Greeks, who were perceived as having a deep fondness for healthier times past. Winckelmann had steeped himself in Greek and Roman sculpture, the result of which was an influential image of the ancient Greeks as expressing "noble simplicity and tranquil grandeur." Indeed, this phrase became a slogan during the end of the 1700s and early 1800s, as did the attendant conception of the Greeks as having embodied the epitome of rationality in balance with concrete life.

"Organic unity" also became a leading idea in its suggestion of a different, more dignified kind of rationality grounded in the image of living things, and which stands in sharp contrast with the dehumanizing rationality of mechanical causality. Schiller himself imagines the Greeks to have been well-balanced, beautifully thinking people, who, as they embodied the ideal of a sound mind in a sound body, represented the ideal attitude required to integrate the sensuous and moral dimensions of the human psyche. To him, they combined a fullness of form and content, as he conceives of them as philosophic and creative, tender and energetic, youthfully imaginative, and rationally mature. Surpassing the Greeks' spiritual achievement is difficult for Schiller to imagine, and he wonders how far we can emulate the ancient Greeks, to become ancients once again.[9]

When Kant described the ideal of human beauty, he injected a moral component into the image of the perfectly patterned human body – an image that reflects what nature ideally and supposedly has in mind for our physical presence. The social result of this fusion between the abstractly rational and the concretely physical is a set of attractively proportioned people with good moral characters. A certain rigidity and lifelessness, however, accompanies this Kantian ideal: formally proportioned objects can convey a feeling of emptiness or spiritual vacancy, and as such they can disappoint. Recognizing the vacant quality of such abstract, purified beauty, Schiller modifies Kant's ideal of human beauty and characterizes the beautiful soul in a more animated, noble and inspired way.

To do this, he introduces the expressive quality of *gracefulness*, which he believes more effectively embodies a harmony between reason and sensation, duty and feeling. Schiller conceives of the beautiful person's movements as easy, sweet, serene, gentle, and melodious as music. The ideal person walks lightly, like a dancer, with animation and confidence, carrying a facial expression

---

[9] Even Hegel, who preferred Christianity over Greek religion, could not help but celebrate the Greeks. In *The Positivity of the Christian Religion* (1796), he wrote the following:

> But anyone who has made the simple observation that the heathen too had intellects, and that in everything great, beautiful, noble, and free they are so far our superiors that we can hardly make them our examples but must rather look up to them as a different species at whose achievements we can only marvel … (in Hegel, *Early Theological Writings*, p. 153).

inspiring love, expressive of freedom and goodwill. We have here in Schiller's ideal of the perfect, beautiful person and the result of aesthetic instruction, a strong, saintly type, filled with life and exuding grace and dignity, more attractive than Kant's more frozen ideal of human beauty. The extrapolated result is a society filled with people of elevated character, as Schiller envisions a community of physically healthy, well-proportioned, attractive-looking souls.

This vision is more ambitious and demanding than Kant's conception of the highest good, where everyone does their duty and is happy on their private terms. Within Schiller's ideal, not merely does each member of the population act according to his or her duty, but character-wise, each member embodies the highest caliber of acculturation and refinement, and not merely a rationally motivated behavioral consistency. Schiller envisions a noble society in a rich and evolved sense, and, of course, whether anyone can embody such an ideal is questionable. More importantly, we should ask whether such an ideal is even desirable.

To appreciate the inspiration behind Schiller's ideal of human beauty, we can refer to some of the social innovations that were being put forth simultaneously in France. Side by side with the mass executions, there was a revolutionary effort to reconfigure the French society along rationalistic and philosophic lines. The calendar was recalibrated to begin anew and festivals were proposed to celebrate reason itself, with holy days designated for universalistic concepts such as "truth," "justice," "infancy," "old age," "agriculture," "the human race", and "our ancestors." These are not nationalistically defined festivities, but are holy days worthy of a world government, that could be respected by any human being at any time.

The abstractions designating these holy days are so lofty, that it would require an enlightened general population to institute them and identify with them wholeheartedly. As such, the French Revolutionary ideals were innovative and valuably advanced, and so much so that one can understand how their leaders became desperately defensive and murderous when failure approached. In line with this universalistic spirit, and as unrealistic or still too far ahead of its time as it might presently seem, we can appreciate the impact of the French Revolutionary ideals as they entered into Schiller's advocacy of a society of culturally noble characters, and its embodiment of a different, more spiritual kind of human being.

Schiller's vision for humanity's future is perhaps unattainable, but he is not insensitive to practical realities. Having been interested in physiology from his early years, he frames his notion of aesthetic education in reference to quasi-physiological "impulses" – the formal impulse, play impulse, and sensuous impulse – that can work either in harmony or in conflict within the human psyche. With this concrete characterization, he tries to outline a genuinely experienceable mentality associated with his ideal of human beauty and social perfection. Contributing to his attempt to be practical-minded, Schiller uses the notion of dialectical synthesis or *Aufhebung*, mentioned above, as a way to express the reconciliation of opposing forces, themes, or aspects within the human situation. This advent of dialectical thought introduces some notable philosophical distance between him and the traditionally logical Kant, and it allows us to step forward into the nineteenth-century German philosophical and aesthetic spirit proper.

We can appreciate Schiller's dialectically minded approach in his theory of beauty, where the "play" impulse related to beauty serves as the intermediary and synthesis of two initially opposing impulses, namely, the "sensuous" impulse and the "formal" impulse. This yields a physiologically grounded interpretation of truth, beauty, and goodness that integrates through the experience of beauty, the main subjects of Kant's *Critique of Pure Reason* (scientific truth), *Critique of the Power of Judgment* (beauty) and *Critique of Practical Reason* (goodness).

For Schiller, the question of harmonizing the sensuous and formal impulses is none other than the question of reconciling scientific determinism with morality. In this regard, his physiological interpretation of beauty has a sweeping metaphysical function. Taking his inspiration from Kant, who conceives of beauty as an intermediary between nature and freedom, Schiller describes the play impulse as the synthesis of natural "life" and moral "shape." The upshot is a new idea of beauty as "living shape," which, in its synthetic quality, fosters the harmonious presence of opposing qualities in a work of art. The best and most beautiful works of art will be, for instance, powerful, but also clear; or energizing, but also relaxing; or lively, but also tranquillizing; or awakening, but also peaceful. This amalgamating disposition, with its leading interest in integrating, strengthening, ennobling, and inspiring the human personality, is the hallmark of Schiller's aesthetics.

3. "ON NAIVE AND SENTIMENTAL POETRY"

Consistent with the utopian vision and amalgamating style are Schiller's reflections on the ancient Greek spirit in his essay, "On Naive and Sentimental Poetry" (1796), where he considers how that ancient spirit stands opposed to our more modern awareness. Written a year after the *Letters*, the essay is an extended meditation on his optimistic suggestion that we should rejuvenate Greek attitudes, composed within a growing awareness that the present, modern mentality within which we are immersed, is more reflective, less natural, and less satisfied with itself than what we encounter in the Greek world. Our modern problem is how to become more attuned to our natural dispositions as we stand within a more highly civilized context, so we can unite the best of both worlds. It is the problem of how to acquire and preserve the Greeks' noble simplicity and tranquil grandeur within a world of advanced culture riddled with artificialities.

The Greek ideal leads Schiller to consider the value of naturalness more carefully, and to regard more positively Kant's view that beautiful souls gravitate to the contemplation of nature's beauty. Schiller writes that the pleasure taken in natural beauty is a moral pleasure related to feelings of love, much like our affection for children and their innocence. It is also enhanced by the awareness of great potentials, inspiring power, and effortless calm. Natural beauty, especially in its idyllic landscapes, represents what we once were, and what, he maintains, we must become again someday. He imagines an ideal future world – a Garden of Eden, Mount Olympus, and Shangri-La combined – laced with the full and sophisticated recollection of advanced civilization.

Having assimilated Kant's claim that the artistic genius is nature's favorite, and that the creative powers of genius are natural, rather than reflectively rational or deliberation-oriented, Schiller associates genius with the natural itself, or what he calls "the simple" or "naive." We can imagine here innocent country folk or trusting tribal peoples, as they stand uncorrupted by exploitation and deceit, who would regard providing hospitality to perfect strangers as a sacred and welcome activity. Schiller speaks of honesty, unpretentiousness, childlike naivety, simplicity of expression, natural wisdom, and, most importantly, a gracefulness that modern times seem to have lost. In contrast to the *Letters*, where he associates the sensuous world more negatively with raw instinct and violence, the idea of the natural is now clothed in terms that more closely reflect the synthesis of sensuousness and morality that was the goal of aesthetic education.

Schiller considers essentially whether the ideal of beauty, and of the beautiful soul he describes in the *Letters*, is possible to achieve within modern times. As modern characters, he observes that we are more reflective, more inward, more "sentimental," and that we define ourselves as longing for a reinstatement of more natural times – times that we recognize as lost, now that we have become more socially attuned to abstracted, rationalized, and subjectively oriented ways of being in the world. Whereas the ancients lived more closely to nature, with a purview centered locally and practically on finite objects, we moderns focus more expansively and inwardly on the infinite and conceptual. At one point, Schiller wonders seriously whether genuinely natural poets are even possible in our modern, artificial age and, in effect, whether the simple, natural spirit of profound innocence will remain nothing more than a memory.

This reflection upon the very possibility of natural poetry and poets in contemporary times shows nonetheless that Schiller does not abandon his concern for fine art that he expresses in the *Letters*, but tempers it with the factor of naturalness as a criterion of creative genius. His essay on naive and sentimental poetry begins with a reference to the Kantian appreciation of natural beauty as a way to ennoble people, and soon turns to fine art and a discussion of the kinds of poetry that can serve the same morally cultivating end. Through a long survey of contemporary poets, Schiller searches for a modern writer, almost in vain, that he can present as the perfect synthesis of ancient simplicity and modern subjective inwardness. He finds his hero in his respected friend, Johann Wolfgang von Goethe (1749–1832), referring to him as the ideal poet who effectively combines these two spirits.

An unthematized dilemma of the neoclassical disposition – a problem related to all nostalgia – underlies Schiller's discussion, as he urges us to return to the Greeks while realizing that the ancient Greek culture is historically long gone. Resurrecting the Greeks entails resurrecting them within a contemporary form, and this requires revising their attitudes compatibly to suit our own, perhaps to a point where through the infusion of modern concerns, their inherent naturalness will mostly dissolve. As one of the first theorists to become aware of this hermeneutical problem, Schiller remains optimistic and calls for a synthesis of the naive and sentimental, ancient and modern attitudes in an ideal of beautiful humanity that can arise only through an intimate union of both. In this respect, his intellectual temperament is consistently reconciliatory and optimistic. Insofar as he always writes with a vision of what is best in humanity, he is also remarkably inspirational.

4. THE TYRANNY OF REASON

When Schiller describes our moral nature, and as much as he believes that morality must harmonize with our passionate side, he adheres to Kant's view by characterizing morality as being seated exclusively in our intellectual, rational faculty. This assumption introduces Kant's claim that moral demands in their abstract purity are unconditional, unlike the pushes and pulls that sensation-grounded feelings and desires make upon us. If reason – supposedly our most unshakeable, divine, aspect – demands that we *ought to* act rationally, then in principle we *can* act rationally; if reason demands that we ought to perfect our humanity accordingly, then in principle we can do so. If the perfection of humanity, as both Schiller and Kant understand it, consists in the unity of our sensuous and intellectual aspects, or, more informally stated, the rational integration of body and mind, then we should dedicate ourselves to making that combination a reality.

Schiller emphasizes that the unity of our sensuous and intellectual aspects is genuine human beauty, understood as a graceful, physical expression of a good moral character. Given the nature of morality in Kant's and Schiller's understanding, and given that we ought to perfect our humanity, then there arises an unconditional rational demand to produce beautiful characters or "beautiful souls," in both ourselves and in others. Our essential rational nature imposes the obligation to produce an aesthetic state and its attendant society of beautiful people. Lest we betray ourselves, it obliges us to be graceful, to walk like dancers, and to be poised, composed, and dignified.

One can challenge this rational demand by considering the assumptions upon which it rests. A main assumption is that morality has exclusively rational grounds, where rationality is itself construed timelessly and unconditionally. Another assumption, closely related, defines human nature as rational, in agreement with the bulk of the Western philosophical tradition. A third involves accepting a fairly rigid conception of rationality in the form of Aristotelian logic, as was the prevailing position before the emergence of nineteenth-century dialectical conceptions of reason. In the chapters that follow, we will see how different thinkers question these assumptions and develop views to the contrary. As a prelude, and as a next step after Kant, we can begin by considering the depth and attractiveness of this rational obligation to create a society of beautiful people that we find in Schiller.

Consider one of the most elementary structures of traditional logic, "*S is P*." This formally says that some thing or subject *S* has some quality or property *P*. As a factor in human experience, it represents a foundational structure of human awareness, for our first bits of knowledge involve realizations that, for instance, that thing is pleasurable, this thing is warm, that thing is uncomfortable, this other thing hurts, and so on, all of which can be described as apprehensions that have the basic form, "*S is P*."

Another way to express "*S is P*" is to state, as we find in some early logic books, "the individual is the universal." This is a peculiar phrasing, but it transforms quickly into the revealing notion of "the universal individual." We can see this through the following. Suppose as an instance of "*S is P*" we say more objectively, "the sky is blue." The latter expression represents our basic awareness of the blue sky. So "the sky is blue" expresses the idea that we find in the phrase "the blue sky," and vice versa. In this manner, "*S is P*," "the individual is the universal" and "the universal individual" become interchangeable phrases.

This notion of a universal individual that hides within the most basic logical form is filled with implications, for it invokes an individual that stands for everything. If the universal individual is taken to be a person, then that person would be someone who stands for everyone, or who would be a model for everyone. Such a person would be generically and facelessly conceived – and we can think of classical Greek sculpture here – but the person would also thereby express the essence of humanity as its content, and would be the image of humanity itself. It would be the ideal person, in other words. One of the most elemental forms of our rational essence, considered logically, provides an image for us to live up to.

Such a highly abstracted conception of a person is what Kant directs us to employ imaginatively, and to try to identify with, when engaged in moral reasoning. When thinking morally along such Kantian lines, we should not imagine ourselves as our unique personal character defines us, or as a member of a local social or larger cultural group with which we identify, but should think more impersonally, regarding ourselves as a human being in general. A judgment made from this standpoint will apply to anyone in the same, or in the same type of, situation, unprejudicially, universalistically and unconditionally. The force of one's judgment attained through this method is attractive in its power, for one does not make a pronouncement merely for the particular time, place, and context, but puts forth an assertion from a timeless standpoint.

In Schiller's notion of the beautiful person, we face the universal force of Kant's conception of moral judgment, combined with a specific way of understanding the best materialization of moral awareness in general. Schiller is not thinking of this or that moral judgment, but has in mind the psychological *atmosphere* that a moral attitude produces in a person, and is considering how this atmosphere would show itself in overall behavior, as an atmosphere or mood is expressed by an artwork. For Schiller, the rationality akin to morality shows itself physically in well-proportioned bodily forms, but it also shows through in the poise of one's movements, which he considers to be related to organic unity, life, and a kind of inner harmony.

Ugly physical configurations, inelegant movements, and disorganized manners all aesthetically contradict the rational essence of morality, and, as such, they do not represent ideal human behavior. Schiller's ideal calls for rationality within and rationality without, but more alarmingly, it admits to a moral obligation to realize that outwardly rationalized, morally expressive physical form. Just as we ought to become a universal individual within the field of abstract moral deliberation, we ought to become a universal individual in how we aesthetically appear and behave, for this aesthetic expression is nothing more than the physical embodiment of one's subjective, moral quality. Here, beauty is morality's physical appearance; it is morality's body. If we link morality with divinity, as many (such as Kant) do, beauty would be defined as *the sensuous appearance of the divine*, which is the definition we see explicitly in Hegel's aesthetics.

The image of an aesthetically sophisticated culture composed of sane, reasonable, poised, gracefully moving, physically attractive, well-proportioned people is idyllic, and it resonates with traditional images of heaven. When we situate this image within the context of a theory such as Kant's, namely, one that assigns an unconditional status to reason in its association with morality, and set that heavenly image upon that unconditional moral ground, we create a demand from within ourselves to become beautiful people. This becomes the rational thing to do, and if we are essentially rational beings, as the philosophical tradition that stems from ancient Greece would have it, then a heaven on earth will follow if we become who we are.

The inherent tyranny of reason and of this heavenly vision should now be obvious, for it makes it easy to justify imposing aesthetic demands on others, many of whom might not agree with the validity of the assumptions that underwrite it. To soften this vision, as suggested earlier, one can dissolve the link between morality and beauty, or dispute the idea that humans are essentially rational beings. It is also possible to subordinate beauty to sublimity, or expand the number of legitimate aesthetic categories to include, in addition to beauty, categories such as sublimity, the picturesque, the grotesque, or the generally "expressive." One can also assert that everything is beautiful within a tempered context that worships imperfection, or one can reject the very importance of behaving morally in connection with human advancement. Finally, one can accept the validity of morality, but deny that it can or should be expressed in a physical form, beautiful or otherwise.[10]

Much of the consequent history of European aesthetics revolves around theories that maintain rational demands at their center, and that respect beauty's deep value, as these stand opposed to theories that sacrifice the supreme value of either beauty or rationality, or reject unconditional values altogether, often in the interests of preserving creative freedom. In the course of this history, we will, in effect, be observing the dissolution of reason's power to dictate unconditionally, and with it, the dissolution of beauty's aesthetic hegemony.

---

[10] Walter Benjamin's interpretation of the Judaic prohibition against images of God is revealing in this regard. He states that the ban is not only against idolatry, but "obviates any suggestion that the sphere in which the moral essence of man is perceptible can be reproduced" (*The Origin of German Tragic Drama*, p. 105).

3

THE BEAUTY OF METAPHYSICAL TRUTH

G. W. F. Hegel

It is itself a beautiful thought that if we were to perceive God's face, its appearance would be breathtakingly beautiful, serene, and satisfying. This is the underlying idea of Hegel's aesthetics, despite the complexity of his philosophical vision and his unorthodox conception of God. Hegel defines beauty as the sensuous appearance of the divine, as if when we perceive beauty, we were apprehending God's spatio-temporal incarnation. More technically, he defines beauty as the sensuous appearance of the "absolute Idea," introducing his conception of the highest development of abstract thought, independently of any worldly or sensory contents. To appreciate Hegel's aesthetic theory, it is consequently important to outline his philosophical system's structure, so his conception of the absolute idea – for this is what he believes appears to us in the experience of the beautiful – can be grasped with a greater determinacy than is usually the case. As we shall see, the apprehension of "God's face," as described above, is tantamount to a supreme idealization and glorification of the human being as an essentially rational being.

1. HEGEL'S PHILOSOPHICAL SYSTEM

When, at the height of his career, G. W. F. Hegel (1770–1831) delivered his lectures on fine art at the University of Berlin between the years 1820 and 1829, he characterized the nature of beauty and fine art from the standpoint of his comprehensive systematic philosophy. His interest in philosophical systematicity was unshakeable, but this did not prevent him from treating aesthetic matters more extensively and in more detail than any philosopher before him: at over 1,200 pages in length, his lecture manuscripts on the philosophy of fine art address all of the topics central to the aesthetic theorizing of the time.

Hegel formulates his aesthetics as part of a broad-ranging philosophical enterprise, and understanding his views on art and beauty requires a grasp of his conceptual system. We will begin with this background, focusing upon two of its main ideas: (1) ultimate reality is knowable, and (2) its essence is the structure of self-consciousness. These ideas reveal Hegel to be an optimist in the theory of knowledge and a philosophical idealist in the field of metaphysics.

Prior to Hegel, Kant had concluded skeptically that human beings lack the capacity to know how things are in themselves. Metaphysical knowledge of the universe's origins, constituents, purposes, and general nature is, according to Kant, forever barred from us. No matter wherever, whenever, or however a person lives, that person will die without ever knowing what the purpose of existence, if any, happens to be. To live surrounded by mystery in a state of perpetual questioning, only to receive silence as the answer to our deepest queries, is the human condition, on Kant's view.

This skepticism issues from Kant's theory of the human mind, which characterizes us as information-processing mechanisms that synthesize incoming sensory data into perceptible products, as when a coin-sorting machine organizes a large bag of assorted-shaped coins into rows of neat stacks, or as when a baker's intelligent actions combine eggs, flour, water, and spices into a cake. In such instances, the appearances of the end products differ from those of the initial ingredients. With respect to our own information-processing, Kant maintains that we experience only the endpoint of the knowledge process, like the coin stacks or cake, and that we are never in a position to know how the initial ingredients are independently. Our experiential products are all humanly informed, and as we are bound to our way of experiencing things, we cannot know how things are in themselves.

Everything tangible of which we are aware thus depends upon the raw sensory information that is given to us from without, since the original condition of our minds is empty, like a coin-counter without coins, or a water-wheel without water, or a cookie-cutter without dough, or a computer without electricity. As we initially lack content to fill the abstract forms of our minds, we depend upon given sensory inputs to function cognitively, just as a coin-counter needs coins, a water-wheel, water, a cookie-cutter, dough, and a computer, electricity, for without the raw sensory inputs, there would be no experience at all.

Kant defines "intuitions" (*Anschauungen*) as individual objects of which any conscious being – even a god – would or could be aware, adding that for humans, our intuitions are always and restrictedly of a sensory nature. Since our intuitions arise from synthesizing raw sensory information into objects of awareness according to the innate forms of space, time, and logical categories, none of those intuitions represents how things are in themselves. Time and space may be infinite magnitudes in their measurable extent, but they remain among the features of human finitude. Now one can surmise that a person who has a taste for metaphysical knowledge – a person like Hegel – would feel imprisoned, even suffocated, by space, time, and logic as Kant understands them, for within the Kantian philosophy they form an impenetrable wall that stands between us and the absolute truth for which human beings cognitively aspire.

To characterize our finitude, Kant contrasts how God's mind supposedly operates, with how our mind more feebly works. Since the objects that we know all presuppose some raw sensory information that has been given from without, we do not entirely create what we apprehend. This is an essential difference between God and us. The objects we apprehend are the appearances of a reality independent of us, and insofar as the objects are mind-independently grounded, we say that they exist.

In contrast, Kant describes God as having the power to make objects exist through the mere thought of those objects. For us, it would be like imagining a glass of water on a table, and spontaneously and magically having a real glass of water materialize thereby.[11] Only God can perform such a miracle – and presumably,

---

[11] The theme of physical creativity by mere thought figures dramatically in the 1956 science fiction classic, *Forbidden Planet* – a movie that ingeniously

this is how God created the physical universe – and it is a mark of our finitude that we lack such a creative power. Our awareness of objects depends upon our being receptive to sensations, whereas God's intuitions issue from God's own thinking substance, and can be referred to accordingly and importantly as purely *intellectual*, that is, purely mind-created, intuitions. This provides another way to express the idea that human beings, as finite, cannot know the nature of things in themselves: we lack the capacity for intellectual intuition.

If the capacity for intellectual intuition is fundamentally godlike, then if it could be established that humans actually have this power, it would connect us with the absolute nature of things in a single step, would reinforce Hegel's quest for metaphysical knowledge, and would undermine Kant's position that humans cannot know the nature of things in themselves. An important question for philosophers immediately following Kant, accordingly, is whether any human capacity corresponds to Kant's conception of intellectual intuition. Although Kant never discerned any such capacity, if we do have it, then we would be able to create the existence of something through the mere thinking of it. As we discover in the writings of Johann Gottlieb Fichte (1762–1814) and Friedrich Wilhelm Joseph Schelling (1775–1854), this search for intellectual intuition within the human being initiates German Idealist philosophy, and it draws a metaphysical line between Kantian and Hegelian aesthetic theories.

To appreciate the result of this search for intellectual intuition, we can recall the Cartesian style of philosophizing at the point where Descartes introduces his method of doubt. As we know, Descartes' quest for certainty sets aside all doubtful beliefs as if they were false. A peculiarity of his method is that it leads a person briefly to regard himself or herself as a disembodied spirit, for in that process one inevitably suspends the belief that there is an actual physical world. Since the senses are sometimes deceiving, all sensory-based beliefs could be false, among

---

combined Freudian psychology with futuristic fantasy and later inspired the television series, *Star Trek*.

which is the belief in the physical world, which includes one's body.

Relevant to our discussion of Hegel's aesthetics is the uncommon conception of existence that operates when Descartes concludingly asserts within the method of doubt as an act of self-consciousness, "I think, I exist." As if it were self-evident, he pronounces, "I exist," but the kind of existence to which he refers can be neither existence in the physical world, nor some kind of mind-independent existence, since he considers himself to have, at this solipsistic point, nothing more than a disembodied presence. This is a significant kind of existence nonetheless, and one that he takes to be so strong and legitimate that he grounds his entire philosophy upon it.

Now Kant's definition of intellectual intuition refers to the ability to create the existence of something through the mere thinking of it, as God – here conceived of importantly also as a being without a physical body – thinks things into existence. Fichte and Schelling insightfully discerned that the act of self-consciousness, as contained in Descartes' pronouncement "I am, I exist," magnificently fits Kant's definition of intellectual intuition. This was their key to reality. Insofar as I (that is, anyone) am self-consciously aware of myself, there is a sense in which I create myself as an object of awareness. When I bring myself into self-conscious existence – and this compares to the process of waking up from a deep sleep, for although not consciously realizing it, I had, earlier on, nonetheless been there when immersed in my dreams – I say to myself that "that," namely, the object that comes into being when I reflect, is "me."

This act of self-consciousness was prized as an intellectual intuition, for one comes into existence for, and to, oneself merely through an act of sheer thought. Self-consciousness, along with the freedom it introduces, thus becomes the godlike spark in us, and the essential principle of reality. Through this rationale, self-consciousness assumes a supreme role within Hegel's philosophy, and its development structures his aesthetic theory. Hegel regards self-consciousness as the universal metaphysical principle, operative from the universe's very beginning, that, like the star-filled skies that physically surround us, has grown to present itself as a set of bright, illuminated spiritual points that constitute the assembly of individual human self-consciousnesses, and, when working in concert, as humanity as a whole.[12]

Hegel accordingly rests his philosophy upon the underlying principle of self-consciousness, understood to reach absolutely into the metaphysical heart of things. Since self-consciousness is a kind of thought, and if, as Hegel believes, the universe *is* this thought in its self-development, then everything that exists is an aspect of an absolute thinking process, including the history of art and the phenomenon of beauty. His philosophical project thus aims to display in detail how the world is conceptual or thought-like in its metaphysical substance and how this thinking substance has the structure of self-consciousness.

One of the most remarkable features of Hegel's philosophy is its encyclopedic attention to almost every subject matter, aesthetics included, in progressive, growth-oriented terms. Hegel is able to achieve this grand organization by arranging all subjects in reference to the growth of self-consciousness. Most recognizably, he regards human history as a continual, pain-filled, struggling and eventually blossoming and justifying movement towards freedom, increased awareness, and social harmony. This eye towards developmental patterns – a distinguishing feature of Hegel's aesthetic theory as well as the rest of his philosophy – issues from his analysis of self-consciousness's dialectical structure. He observes specifically that self-consciousness's oppositional and reconciliatory structure is inherently self-reiterating, expansive, and increasingly comprehensive – once it starts, there is no avoiding its field of comprehension – and insofar as any subject matter incorporates the structure of self-consciousness, it will exhibit an expanding quality of its own.

When a person reflects, much like looking into a mirror, a subject S thinks of an object O, and then recognizes himself or herself as that object. The reflecting person notes in reference to the initially opposing object, that "that is me," where the "is" designates that S is the same as O. The puzzling aspect of this process is that from a traditional philosophical standpoint, "subjects" and "objects" are apparently irreconcilable kinds of being, as we can

---

[12] This Hegelian image of humanity as a set of brilliant stars bears an informative contrast to the Nietzschean image of humanity as a set of mutually expanding and conflicting suns (see the beginning of Chapter 6).

easily appreciate when considering the difference between a brain that weighs a few pounds, and the weightless consciousness that mysteriously inhabits it. If we acknowledge this difference, then *S* cannot be the same as *O*.

The oppositional and reconciliatory structure of self-consciousness thus leads us to admit, with some bewilderment, that *S* is not identical to *O and* that *S* is identical to *O*, that is, *([S ≠ O] & [S=O])*, or more simply, *(-A & A)*. When facing this contradictory quality of our self-awareness, there are two options. First, one can reassert traditional logic and deny that we can genuinely become aware of ourselves. This resolves the contradiction by negating one of its elements, namely, the identity between *S* and *O*. Through a more radical route, we can alternatively restrict the jurisdiction of traditional logic to introduce a new logic that allows for the reconciliation of oppositions. Hegel adopts this latter path, absorbing traditional logic into the more comprehensive field of dialectical logic, which we will now describe, since it forms the basis of his aesthetic theory.

Certain that self-awareness is not an illusion, Hegel renders more coherent, what appears to be an immediately contradictory structure of self-consciousness, by unfolding its conflicting elements into a developmental sequence that brings the "*S*" and the "*O*" together into a reconciled blend, or organic unity of opposites. These initially conflicting aspects, or "moments," as Hegel sometimes calls them, are then amalgamated and rendered *aufgehoben*, that is, preserved, cancelled, and uplifted, all at once. This logic of self-consciousness begins similarly to traditional Aristotelian logic, namely, with an opposition between *S* and *O*, but it does not rest with that opposition, since it allows further for a dynamic blend and reconciliation of the conflicting elements. The process is reminiscent of chemical compounding, as well as human reproduction, where offspring present a visual blend of the parents' characteristics.

We can now describe this dialectical logic – one that Hegel understands to be the elementary form of reason – in less personal terms to appreciate its universal applicability. First, corresponding structurally to the condition of the "I" before the act of reflection, the logical process begins with some initial position (or "thesis," as we find in Fichte's statement of the process). Second, matching the point where consciousness projects or imagines an object (this is the object we later recognize to be an image of ourselves), we have an opposing object, juxtaposed to the original position. The projection negates the initial position, and is the initial position's antithesis. In the third step, corresponding to the point in self-consciousness's activity where one realizes that the object projected is oneself, albeit in an objectified form, the position and negation, or thesis and antithesis, are reconciled into a more complex blend, or synthesis. The process compares to noticing some object moving near one's side while walking in a darkened room. At first taking the object to be another person, one comes to appreciate entertainingly that one had only been looking at a mirror on the wall and that the foreign object had been an image of oneself all along.

The reconciliation immediately assumes the role of a new position or thesis whereby the three-step thought process automatically reiterates itself at a more comprehensive level, positing yet another opposition that reconciles into yet another new position. This inherently expanding quality of dialectical logic is unlimited, ending only when it embraces the entire universe in a fabulous reconciliation of everything that is. Hegel's philosophical system describes this course of increasing comprehension, and it culminates in a rationally integrated, all-inclusive, absolute, self-recognizing totality. The goal is the realization of the universe's inner potential, like a plant that grows into maturity and realizes the ideal plant thereby. His account of beauty as the "sensuous appearance of the Idea" is a key aspect of this development.

As Hegel describes it, this all-permeating dialectical process, although lengthy and involved, begins with an abstraction, namely, the thought of empty being. This abstraction soon transforms itself into a complicated network of abstractions, and thereafter, into the physical world of raw matter and living things. The emergence of human beings follows – human beings who, through a turbulent, but steadily progressing world history, develop towards a rationalized society permeated by spiritual balance and mutual respect. Within this framework, *fine art* – which along with the rest of the universe Hegel believes has the same logical basis – plays a pivotal role in human history and in the progress of the universe's self-realization.

Hegel maintains that the three main divisions of his philosophical system describe the universe's unfolding: (1) logic, (2) nature, and (3) the human spirit. Exemplifying the dialectical structure of self-consciousness, these stand in a relationship of initial position (logic), ensuing opposition (nature), and reconciliatory synthesis (the human spirit). Through this three-aspected sequence, the universe's development reveals itself to be a supreme act of self-awareness on the part of the universe itself. As it describes everything as an aspect of a grand explosion of self-consciousness, Hegel's philosophy is like a Big Bang theory that begins with a simple logical thought and ends with a thoroughgoing rational enlightenment. The difference is that as time goes on, Hegel's universe becomes intellectually brighter and more integrated, rather than more played out and chaotic.

Within this cosmic process, fine art has an essential and culminating role in the development of social consciousness, or spirit (*Geist*), for according to Hegel's definition of fine art, its fundamental purpose is to express, in a sensuous form, the rationally grounded issues that are of supreme concern to any given culture. Fine art shares this leading position with religion and philosophy, and Hegel groups them together as the highest manifestations of any cultural spirit, as the dimensions of "absolute spirit." His lectures on aesthetics consequently characterize fine art in connection with its contemporaneous religious and philosophical expressions. Underlying each of these specific historical characterizations is the principle upon which Hegel comprehends all of world history, namely, the dialectical principle of self-consciousness as manifested in time, described above, along with all that that materialization entails. In Hegel's aesthetics, we witness how fine art participates in the increasing cultural realization of freedom, rationality, and mutual trust that he believes to be the universe's main purpose.

2. HEGEL'S PHILOSOPHY OF FINE ART

For comparison and contrast, we can recall that according to Kant, an object's pure beauty becomes apparent when we contemplate the object exclusively as a systematically organized, spatio-temporal form. Owing to its systematic structure and the associated indication that an intelligence produced the object, the form is rational. One could say that for Kant, beauty is *the sensuous presentation of a rational, systematic form* that appears to have arisen accidentally and serendipitously within the field of human experience. Precisely in light of its contingent appearance, we take pleasure in how the world aesthetically confirms, or at least seems to confirm through beauty, the presence of a rationality over and above our own. The experience is most impressive in the case of natural beauty, where we know that no human had a hand in the rational form's presence. In the case of art, the experience is echoed in view of how good art looks so naturally done, as it issues unreflectively from the natural powers of the artistic genius.

Comparing well with Kant, Hegel's account of beauty is likewise based on the sensuous appearance of rational form. The difference resides in Hegel's understanding of the rational form that appears sensuously in the experience of beauty – a form expressive of the absolute idea that both culminates and retrospectively encapsulates his *Logic*. Let us now consider this absolute idea more specifically, noting its concluding and summary place in Hegel's conception of logic.

For Hegel, self-consciousness and reason are metaphysically one and the same. As such, he derives the new kind of logic characterized above – dialectical logic – from the structure of self-consciousness, regarding instances of dialectical form as manifestations of reason. In Hegel's *Logic*, which begins his philosophical system and outlines the initial presence of the universe's inherent rationality, the leading, and extreme, assumption is that the basis of a thoroughly rational world, as well as any philosophical understanding of it, requires a non-controversial, simple start. Such a supposition-free foundation must be empty, trivial, and tantamount to almost nothing at all. This is different from, if not the very opposite of, the richly developed concept of "God." Little can satisfy this empty condition, and as far as Hegel can see, the only appropriate starting point is an extremely abstract concept – since anything that physically exists would already be too complicated – that serves as a mere placeholder from which a complicated world can subsequently grow. This foundation is the concept of "being" in its most abstracted, contentless, and utterly meaningless form.

The concept of "being" potentially contains everything precisely because it excludes nothing. It is the thinnest thought of all, and it is uninformative. As an abstraction, this concept is so lightweight, that its content *coincides* with the concept of "nothing," when we consider the latter similarly as a bare abstraction. Pure, abstract Being has nothing in it.

When the situation becomes more determinate, the concepts of "being" and "nothing" fall into opposition with one another, but to start, their emptiness is exactly the same. Insofar as "being" is opposed to "nothing" in its general meaning, and yet is the same as "nothing" at the level of its most superficial content, we see here at the beginning of the *Logic*, not to mention at the foundation of the universe according to Hegel, how dialectical logic is already implicit at the beginning. With this reflection upon the neutral relationship between being and nothing, Hegel commences his account of how the universe's inherent rationality expands of its own accord.

The next step in the process is to consider what concept expresses the dialectical reconciliation of being and nothing, since the two concepts are identical in their mutual emptiness, as they remain sharply opposed in principle. No mechanical procedure produces this concept, but when Hegel states that the synthesis of being and nothing is "becoming," the rationale is clear. The concept of becoming refers to a condition that not quite "is," which at the same time is not nothing at all. Every transitional point fits this description, such as the exact moment of death, or of birth. At the exact moment of its death, for example, a living being is neither wholly living nor wholly dead, but is a blend of both; at the exact moment of birth, neither is one completely alive, nor is one non-existent. At any beginning, things are not yet underway, and yet they are also not without a start. The flux of things is paradoxical, but understandable as the synthesis of being and nothing.

Out of this initial triad of "being," "nothing" and "becoming," the developmental sequence of concepts that constitutes Hegel's *Logic* grows – a sequence that, along its complicated length of over a hundred concepts in all, contains the concepts familiar to traditional metaphysical speculation and logic. As we trace this development of abstract thought across and through the whole, each newly emerging concept comprehends those that preceded it, as a fruit presupposes a blossom, and as a blossom presupposes a bud. At the *Logic*'s end, we arrive at the richest development of pure, abstract thought, expressed in a single concept that includes the entirety of the preceding concepts as its aspects and content, and which represents the totality of abstract thought's development. This single, all-inclusive concept is the "absolute Idea," which is crucial for understanding Hegel's aesthetics, for in his *Lectures on Fine Art*, he defines beauty as "the sensuous *appearance* of the Idea" (*das sinnliche* Scheinen *der Idee*).[13] Beauty is the incarnation of the divine logical order as a surface appearance.

It is of vital importance to appreciate the richness of this conceptual factor – the "Idea" or divinity that superficially appears – in Hegel's definition of beauty, which is why we have been considering Hegel's *Logic* and philosophical system at a substantial introductory length. Whereas the concept of "being" contains everything insofar as the concept is completely indeterminate, the concept of the absolute Idea comprehends every pure thought as an aspect of a greater organic unity, like the totality of divine thought before the creation of the universe.[14] With respect to their contents, the two concepts are worlds apart. If we compare the *Logic* to a symphony, the concept of being is like a silent auditorium at the anticipatory moment just before the symphony starts; the concept of the absolute Idea is like the final, crashing moment of the symphony's performance that contains, in its auditory significance, the entirety of the symphony that preceded it.

Hegel defines beauty as the sensuous appearance of the absolute idea, sometimes referring to beauty alternatively as the sensuous appearance of the divine. Underlying these two definitions is the single thought that as time goes on, self-consciousness,

---

[13] T. M. Knox phrases this as "the pure appearance of the Idea to sense" (*Hegel's Aesthetics – Lectures on Fine Art*, Volume I, Part I, Chapter I, Section 3, "The Idea of the Beautiful," p. 111).

[14] In the introduction to his *Science of Logic*, Hegel describes the full logical sequence as the thoughts of God before the creation of the universe, although in Hegel's system, there is no God that exists prior to this sequence. The sequence "is" God as a being that stands as a potential to be realized.

freedom, dialectical structure, reason – all of which describe the same basic metaphysical principle – become more manifest in the world, and as this happens, the world becomes a more beautiful, trusting, friendly, and peaceful place. With respect to beauty, this manifestation of reason first appears as physically centered beauty, and second, as spiritually centered beauty. Hegel's definition of beauty as the sensuous appearance of the absolute Idea, or as the appearance of self-consciousness as taken to be the metaphysical principle of all things, refers primarily to physically oriented beauty, since he understands "sensuousness" in terms that relate immediately to the perception of tangible, physical objects. Upon arriving at the depths of spiritual beauty in later stages of historical development, the realm of beauty proper becomes only a prior phase, as the exciting years of adolescence would appear to a middle-aged person.

Kant and Hegel are usually conceived of as opposing thinkers with respect to their aesthetic theories, but we can now appreciate how they concur by defining beauty in reference to *the sensuous appearance of rational form*. The difference is that Hegel's conception of rationality has a stronger metaphysical import and is infused with the dialectical structure of self-consciousness, whereas Kant's conception of rationality is more one-dimensionally combinatorial and less metaphysically committed. Both philosophers ascribe an integrative function to beauty, where it serves either to unite nature and reason (as morality), as we find in Kant, or to unite nature and reason (as self-consciousness, metaphysically understood), as in Hegel.

The two philosophers appear to philosophize on different registers, mainly because Kant does not combine his theory of beauty with a theory of human history. This additional historical factor arises in Hegel owing to his conception of reason, since it stems from the structure of self-consciousness, is inherently more developmental and dialectical, and requires for its realization, a gradual intensification of reason's presence in the world. It contrasts with Kant's notion of rationality, centered more in traditional logic, which does not attach itself to cultural development and can be instantiated equally and immediately at any time or place.

Due to his more historical and developmental orientation that locates the self-conscious human being at the highest point in the chain of living things, Hegel sidelines natural beauty, viewing it as a rudimentary expression of self-consciousness on a par with natural laws, geometry, and other mechanically definable principles related to the inorganic world. His primary concern is to trace the development of the human spirit in view of its most sophisticated forms, so fine art rises to supreme importance within his theory.

Hegel's philosophy of world history describes history's development from an initially more animalistic condition, where people are tied down to instinctual concerns, authoritarian forms of domination, and undeveloped philosophical conceptions of the world, to an increasingly reflective and civilized condition where freedom, democracy, trust, and mutual respect increasingly prevail, violence is reduced, and society governs itself more rationally. We have developed a long way towards this final endpoint, but there is still much to realize. Hegel avoids predicting the future, but his philosophy implies that if human beings do not realize the thoroughly rational society he envisions, for instance, if some accident were to befall us, then some other species will inevitably develop the self-consciousness that is inherent in the world and carry through the universe's rational aim. This is because he projects the ideal society as a function of the universe's own rational development; the forces that produce the ideal society are already there in the rocks, trees, and everything else that is, and many paths to the same ultimate and necessary end are possible.

When Hegel surveys the cultures that have emerged from earlier times until the present, he observes general patterns of development that confirm his leading idea that self-consciousness is at the core of things, and that it manifests itself more explicitly with time. Along one dimension, for instance, people move gradually from an outwardly focused orientation towards the world to a more inward, subjectively centered one. Along another, people's philosophical conceptions of the world begin with general, more superficial notions, and develop into more specific and complicated ones. Along a third, people move from a more instinctually centered set of interests to a more conceptually and intellectually centered set. Combining these, earlier cultures are seen to have a practical orientation towards the world, generalized philosophical conceptions, and a domination by instinct, whereas more advanced cultures have a higher level of reflection and inward-ness, more refined philosophical conceptions, and an intellectually based relationship to the world. There are surely bumps, set-backs, and individuals who are left out of the mainstream, but Hegel asserts that rationality inevitably intensifies its presence as time goes on, and that the history of fine art plays one of the leading roles in this intensification.

Hegel frames fine art's historical progress in reference to the relationship between how an artwork physically appears (its "form") and what the artwork meaningfully expresses (its "con-tent"). Sometimes the form and content are in balance, sometimes not. He observes that during earlier historical times, an imbal-ance prevailed as people were typically inspired not specifically by human life, but by all living things, as they apprehended a thoroughly animated and overpowering universe. As people lived with fear, respect, and gratitude towards nature and its usually reliable cycles, upon which so much of their survival depended, their conceptual capabilities were limited by lack of experience and reflection, and their ability to express their ultimate concerns in art, and in general, was limited. To portray artistically over-whelming power, there were often long listings of items, such as are found in literary works that seem to provide an inventory of everything in creation. One can also see as an artistic device, numerical reiterations of the same thing, as one finds in many-armed statues, as in Indian art. To portray the mysterious nature of life, sometimes hybrid figures were constructed that were partly animal, and partly human, aiming to signify the general blend of living things through strange and thought-provoking juxtapositions of forms, as in Egyptian art.

In such instances, relatively thin metaphysical concepts are expressed with forms that are either unduly reiterative or notice-ably peculiar. Hegel describes this situation as one where the artwork's perceptual *form* is in excess over its conceptual *content*, calling the works "symbolic," as they indicate meanings more than they embody or exemplify them. This, according to Hegel, is the style that ancient cultures used, to convey their cultural aspirations. The symbolic style, of course, can appear or serve artistically at any time, although it does not cohere well with later cultures in connection with expressing their highest values or interests. Hegel's notion of symbolic art can nevertheless be understood as either a historical or stylistic designation, since the style can be detached from the historical contexts in which it has its proper home.

Hegel states that symbolic art prevailed during the times when Babylonia, Assyria, India, and ancient Egypt stood at the forefront of world culture, and that this artistic style led the way until classical Greek civilization emerged. The Greeks displayed a greater ability and enthusiasm to use reason more exclusively, as opposed to invoking arbitrary and worldly authorities as the final judge and decisive principle in their cultural activities. In conjunction with this amplification of reason's presence, an awareness of a sharp difference between humans and other animals grew to a point where Greek philosophy set forth an explicit definition of the human being as the distinctively rational animal. For Hegel, this is a turning point in human history, since it is the first time that rationality and self-consciousness present themselves within a culture with such a high profile. It also marks a point where *beauty* finds a most appropriate place to manifest the spirit of a culture's main interests, perhaps never to be repeated with such clarity and innocence.

Although the classical Greeks advanced in metaphysical awareness, allowing self-consciousness and rationality to emerge as definitive human characteristics, they remained philosophically immature insofar as their world view retained a substantial proportion of perceptual, earth-centered features. Their gods remained anthropomorphic, with their abodes located on perceptually visible mountaintops and other natural settings. Humans were defined as essentially self-conscious beings, but with a very sensuous orientation towards the world – a sensory entrenchment that, although primitive, provided an optimal atmosphere for fine art and the expression of beauty.

If beauty is the sensuous presentation of rationality, then an ideally beautiful form will balance perfectly its perceptual and conceptual components. The conceptual dimension will not be too introspective, to ensure that the associated depth of feeling does not extend beyond what a perceptual presentation can wholly manage. Neither will excessive details, reiterations, and strange configurations congest the perceptual presentation to the point of distracting us from the object's basic meaning. To achieve this balance between form and content, an economically composed perceptual form and a metaphysical content that is reflective, but not too complicated or dominated by a self-absorbed inwardness of feeling, is required.

In Hegel's view, the Greeks' historical position put them in exactly the right frame of mind to achieve this ideal compositional balance: the general cultural preference to use reason for guidance imparted a simplicity and economy to the artistic designs, while the newly emerging conception of humans as rational beings did not yet admit of extensive elaboration. This defined a cultural atmosphere conducive to the creation of the *most beautiful* objects in Hegel's metaphysical sense of beauty. Overall, the atmosphere conveyed a profound and inspiring tranquillity of character, a solid and enduring strength in the midst of chaos, an elevated and noble composure in the face of tragedy, and a tone of joy, achievedness, and satisfaction, none of which were too convoluted.

Prefiguring the above thoughts, and accepted as canonical when Hegel was writing, Johann Winckelmann's characterization of the ancient Greeks as the epitome of "noble simplicity and tranquil grandeur" thus found a majestic explication in Hegel's philosophical rendition of the brightest days of beautiful art. The Greeks stood at the crossroads of perceptual versus conceptual orientations towards the world, and as they incorporated this balance into their character, fine art attained a supreme level of achievement as the expression of beauty, even though it would become more spiritually profound as people became more reflective with the passing of time.

Hegel observed that when self-consciousness becomes more developed, it becomes more inwardly focused and individualized in the form of contemplative feelings, subjective states, and more personalized attitudes towards the world. The condition soon reaches a point where a more meditative attitude about ultimate things becomes culturally dominant. Rather than referring to mountaintops, trees, rivers, oceans, and other external places and objects as the abodes of the gods, the search for the divine primarily moves towards the contents of the human heart. The Sermon on the Mount embodies this change in attitude, as we hear Jesus say that it is one and the same to sin in one's imagination as it is to sin in actual deed. Such an evaluation of private, merely subjective intentions as if they had the objectivity of actual, physical behaviors indicates the beginning and essence of

Christian thought, and it shows how times had changed since the days of the Greeks, whose glory had been shining only a few hundred years before.

For Hegel, this more pronounced Christian emphasis upon inner subjectivity reveals a pattern that occurs in every line of cultural development, whether we happen to be speaking of European culture, Asian culture, African culture or any other. Hegel observes it most obviously in the Christian culture, with which he is familiar, and he speaks primarily about how the rise of Christianity displays the development of self-consciousness within world culture. His consequent characterization of the kind of fine art that is more at home with this deeper inwardness – he calls it Romantic, as opposed to Classical, art – relies mainly on examples from and references to Christian art. This should not obscure how his general concern is to show that self-consciousness develops in the world as a whole, and that from a metaphysical standpoint, the world is gradually becoming what it ought to be, as it moves towards self-perfection and a more intense self-awareness.

To appreciate Hegel's conception of Romantic art, along with the consequences it carries for the history of fine art in general, it will help to describe how he conceives of the interrelationships between the particular arts. Given the times in which he lived and the traditions he inherited, Hegel focuses on five main arts in the following developmental order: architecture, sculpture, painting, music, and poetry, where the latter includes all of the literary arts, as well as theatrical performance. As the ordering reveals, Hegel begins his discussion with arts centered in three dimensions (architecture and sculpture), advances to those constructed upon a two-dimensional surface (painting; we can now add photography), and finally considers arts whose media are more intangibly single-dimensional, that is, temporal (music and poetry). Hegel organizes his discussion in reference to the five fine arts, but his conceptualization accommodates itself to any conceivable art form, as one might regard dance as moving sculpture, or gourmet cooking as akin either to music (taste-wise) or sculpture (presentation-wise), or the art of bas-relief as an interface between sculpture and painting.[15]

---

[15] In *Beauty and Truth*, Stephen Bungay offers (on p. 92) a more generally applicable, modern reconstruction of Hegel's taxonomy of the arts that can accommodate film, dance, theatre, holography, and so on.

Within this organization of the fine arts, Hegel associates each particular art with a stage of self-consciousness's cultural development, and accordingly coordinates each art with a cultural period in which it is most at home. When the majority of human cultures focused primarily on external objects, were initially discovering mechanical and geometrical laws, and were at a level where the terrain of subjective inner life remained mostly uncharted, architecture – Hegel's paradigm art of the symbolic period – was the most appropriate vehicle for expressing such a cultural spirit. We see this in the ancient construction of large-scale palaces, temples, monuments, and tombs. This is not to say that Egyptian culture, for example, lacked the arts of sculpture, painting, music, and literature. Hegel's claim is that among all of the arts, the interest in architecture predominated, as in how the interiors of the Pyramids were decorated with paintings that served the tomb's religious function.

A genuine architectural interest persists in ancient Greece, mainly in the construction of temples. Large sculptures adorned the temples as well, as did the statue of Athena in the Parthenon. In Greece, however, the art of sculpture attains a higher perfection in its own right as sculptors discovered ways to display less rigid, more poised representations of the human body. The discovery coincides with a method of idealizing the human body according to mathematical proportions – ones that were themselves applied to architectural constructions to lend them a human appearance. Polycleitus' sculpture, the *Doryphoros* (the Spear Bearer, 450–40 BCE) is exemplary of the finest classical Greek sculpture, and the sculpture serves in later years to represent the ideal human body, expressive of the natural plan that underlies that body. Kant, for instance, refers to this sculpture illustratively in his conception of ideal human beauty. The same can be said of Myron's sculpture, the *Discobolus* (the Discus Thrower, *c*.460–50 BCE) (Plate 3), which presents a timeless ideal of athletic energy.

This interest in the sculptural human form represents an advance over earlier times, for with the emergence of the Greek definition of the human being as a rational animal, there is an implicit intensification in the cultural awareness of the proposition that self-consciousness is the key principle of things. In Greek times, this rational self-awareness takes the form of mathematical, geometrical, and logical patterns that manifest themselves in a variety of cultural spheres, ranging from politics, to legal debate, philosophy, religion, and the fine arts. The Greek gods are sculpturally represented as having perfectly contoured, mathematically proportioned bodies, and, as such, the divine in that culture assumes a noticeably rational form. For Hegel, this phenomenon represents the perfect alignment and combination of perceptual forms (as in the well-proportioned human body) with the leading concept in their metaphysical view of things, namely, the notion of the human being as rational and self-conscious.

As art *per se*, considered here to be the sensuous presentation of the divine, where the divine is conceived of as the developed rational principle of self-consciousness, Hegel believes that one cannot aspire to a higher level of artistic perfection. In this sense, he maintains that fine art, conceived of as an art of beauty, reaches its summit in ancient Greece: the perceptual forms it employs are sufficiently rationalized, and the conceptual content that it expresses is sufficiently rational and oriented towards self-consciousness, but is not so complicated that it contains too much for the rationalized form to express. On account of this outstanding balance between perceptual and conceptual content that defines the general atmosphere of Greek art, Greek sculpture carries an aura of satisfaction, achievement, closure, composure, and transcendent cheerfulness, as if one could remain personally intact, untouched, and optimistic, even after the worst tragedy. Now that the ancient Greek culture is gone, and along with it the days when beautiful sculptural forms stood at the peak of cultural expression without any competitors, there is a sense in which, as Hegel says, beautiful art is a thing of the past.

With this excursion into Hegel's system of the arts, where architecture coordinates with Symbolic art, and sculpture with Classical art, it is possible to understand his conception of Romantic art more effectively. As world history passes sequentially through its cultural forms, Hegel observes that the leading ideas of each culture become increasingly expressive of subjectively complicated and reflective feelings, and, eventually, of forms that are almost exclusively conceptual, inward, and complex. The art form most suited for expressing such feelings and concepts is, at first, painting, which compresses the three-dimensional presentations onto a two-dimensional surface, while retaining the sensuous quality of the ordinary perceptual world. Music follows as a more subjectively oriented art that embodies the abstract forms of human feeling. The literary arts are at the spiritual peak of the fine arts, since they are constituted by conceptual forms that can duplicate, in dialogue or exposition, what another person happens to be thinking. Literature brings us into direct contact with another person's subjectivity, as if we were thinking along with the other person upon reading or hearing his or her words.

Painting, music, and literature are all Romantic arts that express a deeper level of subjectivity, and by virtue of their respective media, they implicitly convey a world view where reflective, inwardly seated content dominates over physical form. They are more appropriate for Christian art, insofar as Christianity emphasizes a person's quality of character and personal intentions over a person's bodily appearance. As they are synchronized with the developmental flow of human history, the Romantic arts signify that fine art, now having already realized itself as art *per se* in the ancient Greek world, has assumed a new task of advancing the development of self-consciousness within other key realms, namely, religion and philosophy.

Whereas fine art as beautiful art is the sensuous expression of the divine, religion expresses the same absolute idea in terms of mental imagery. Philosophy expresses the same in the field of pure, non-sensory concepts. The divine is understood here as the structure of self-consciousness considered metaphysically and logically, and within the context of art, religion, and philosophy, we are referring specifically to the structure of self-consciousness as it is instantiated within human culture. This is equivalent to social consciousness, considered rationally. It is the "I" that is "we" and the "we" that is "I," much in the spirit of Kant's and Schiller's rational society, as well as the spirit of Karl Marx's conception of the ideal human community, to which we will next turn, where exploitation has been dissolved and where people live with trust and mutual respect for each other. After its own self-realization in the ancient Greek world, fine art continues to foster the development of the remaining spiritual spheres.

3. AFTER THE "DEATH OF ART": FINE ART'S CONTEMPORARY ROLE

We live presently in an age where fine art is entrenched within the more reflective, conceptually oriented Romantic period that Hegel describes. Some fine art has even become philosophically geared in its references and challenges to the nature of art itself. Consistent with the Romantic spirit, painting, music, and literature have become the predominant art forms, as they fuse together in motion pictures and television. In contrast to the wide publicity given to the latest movies, even the most technically advanced skyscrapers trail behind in popularity. Partially in view of our Romantic condition, Hegel's aesthetics has been described by the Italian aesthetician, Benedetto Croce (1866–1952), as a funeral oration for beauty, raising the question of how significant the experience of artistic beauty can be nowadays, if Hegel's historical account is on the mark.

Any advocate of Hegel's aesthetics, upon encountering someone who hopes to resurrect the days when fine art presided over the culture, would regard the proposition as unrealistic. This is despite how common this project was among neoclassical thinkers at the end of the 1700s and the beginning of the 1800s, just before Hegel composed his lectures on fine art. Hegel, perhaps more than Schiller, realized the problems that attend any resurrection-oriented quest, whether we aim to resurrect the Greeks, Egyptians, Early Christians, Renaissance, or any other time, such as the days of the Beatniks or the psychedelic 1960s. Times change. As we mentioned in our discussion of Schiller, if we are to resurrect the Greek spirit, or any other culture's spirit, this would need to be achieved within a contemporary form, where the infusion of the contemporary form into the older mentalities will always cloud the waters. Hegel's philosophy of world history speaks against any type of authentic resurrection of the Greek (or any other) spirit, and it is fair to say that within Hegel's view, the purity of those past times and glories is out of reach, now that contemporary sensibilities prevail. It suggests that we have grown beyond the days of beauty.

Croce's assessment of Hegel's aesthetics nonetheless overlooks how past traditions continue to reverberate within our own, despite how our modern advancement affects the present appearance of those traditions. Our world remains constituted by past forms of thinking. Many people gaze at the stars, but few apprehend each star as located at a different distance away from the earth, or appreciate the staggeringly lengthy distances involved in a precise way. Many perhaps also do not reflect that, as one stands upon the ground, far below oneself is the other side of the earth, and beyond that, more space filled with stars. We naturally see the stars as points of light set away from us at an equal distance, perhaps upon a dark dome, configured two-dimensionally in constellations that represent hunters, archers, crabs, bears, scorpions, eagles, giraffes, goats, dogs, mythological figures, and the like. This way of seeing predates the 1600s and the age of the great astronomers.

In the same way, many people's religious beliefs still contain human-like figures in elaborate clothes, sometimes imagined with long flowing hair and a multitude of servants, who are thought to watch over us from a distant world, much like the Greek gods looked down from Mount Olympus. Again, this represents an outlook antecedent to the French Revolution and its worship of purified reason. Even more to the point, much of the world's violence and criminality brings us back to times well before the dawn of human civilization, in common with animals that fight one another over the same bit of food or over the same sexual partner. In this respect, the attitudes involved are less rational and civilized. Also, few look at a simple artifact such as a pen and reflect, as would a Hegelian, upon the history of writing, the individuals who designed the pen, the workers who drove the trucks or flew the airplanes to deliver the pen to the store in which it was bought, and the thousands of others who were involved in the pen's production and social meaning. If we were to consider in detail the causal history of the objects that immediately surround us, we would soon be imagining the history of humanity and the universe as a whole. Such is an important aspect of the comprehensive Hegelian mind-set within which he sees everything growing and expanding around him, including the history of art.

This suggests that despite the advantages associated with our contemporary times and the knowledge of how to behave more rationally, there are dimensions of contemporary human existence – in particular the more violent ones – that have not yet reached the level of general civility that, according to Hegel's conception, the ancient Greeks displayed. For those who exemplify these less developed mentalities, fine art in the form of Classical art can remain uplifting, inspirational, and aesthetically educative, much as Schiller imagined it. Since everyone at one time or another faces trials of patience, temptations to engage in violence, and assaults by more brutal world views, the noble and tranquil images of the human being that Greek sculpture and fine art provide can function to uplift everyone's spirit to a more cultured and civilized level at one time or another. In this regard, the most beautiful art, as Hegel conceived of it, is far from being old-fashioned. For those dimensions of our life that are less spiritually developed, classically composed works of beauty can appear like the blessed gods, as they inspire and educate.

4

THE ART OF SOCIAL REVOLUTION

Karl Marx

1. ECONOMICS AND SOCIAL DEVELOPMENT

To understand Marx, let us begin briefly with Hegel. A common misunderstanding of Hegel's philosophy is that as a proponent of metaphysical idealism, he regards our world unrealistically as a vast system of ghostlike, unsubstantial abstractions. In fact, though, Hegel recoils against "abstract thinking," typified by the use of superficial concepts, labels, and generalizations that fail to capture a subject matter's inherent detail. To think abstractly is to label a man a saint, murderer, hero, or racist, and forget that he is also someone's son, brother, uncle, father, grandfather, husband, and cousin, or that he weighs 160 pounds, once visited Venice, and may have had scrambled eggs, toast, and tea for breakfast this morning. To add more features to one's conception is to think more realistically, and not only does Hegel advocate concrete thinking in this sense, he self-consciously formulates his philosophy to include more and more of the world's detail in an ever-increasing sphere of comprehension.

Another distinguishing trait of Hegel's view, and one that separates him from other thinkers whose philosophies also aim to be down-to-earth, is his coupling of concreteness with reflection and rationality. Hegel maintains that the more we reflect, the more detail we bring to light, and the more the world's rationality presents itself to encompass that detail. Only if the real is the rational and the rational is the real, however, can his system achieve complete comprehensiveness.

Hegel's effort to think concretely induces him to think historically, and he often expresses this historical dimension by structuring his discussions with life-centered models that correspond to the natural movement that begins with birth, moves through childhood, adolescence, young and aspiring adulthood, steady middle age, and ends, finally, with old age and eventual disintegration through death. His commitment to discerning rationality and growth at every juncture generates a historically centered style of philosophizing that seeks out developmental patterns – ones that allow him to describe rational movements and tendencies within history and the world as a whole.

A point arises within Hegel's system when it exhausts its capacity to unveil rational patterns, and where its conceptual network lets the world's wealth of sensory detail pass through unassimilated. As comprehensive and as committed to concrete thinking as it is, Hegel's philosophy cannot deduce the pen that moves within one's hand, the number of hairs on one's body, and other such minutiae, as much as it aims to acknowledge the presence of these details. His philosophy is more effective for discerning broad designs and long-term historical patterns, and it weakens when it faces the contingencies of raw sensory detail. The sound of a bird's chirp, the movement of a waving branch, the rattle of the machines in some factory, the sweat glistening upon a prisoner's brow, and the rhythm of one's pulse, are aspects of the world that Hegel's philosophy does not emphasize as such, but whose significance is absorbed by higher-level abstractions and social movements. In a continual advance towards freedom, his realistic philosophy nonetheless includes a place for the immeasurable volume of human suffering – the slaughterbench of world history as he calls it – and he speaks inspiringly against superficial, stereotypical thinking that disregards the widespread misery in the world. Even so, the kind of concreteness that his philosophy achieves remains limited, as it leaves a significant amount of sensory experience untouched by its rationalizations.

Although Hegel's philosophy cannot be justly criticized on the grounds that it ignores historical detail, the metaphysics of self-consciousness that propels his view interferes with the adoption of a yet more practical, down-to-earth outlook. To appreciate this alternative, we can reflect upon how animals survive by building nests and other types of protective enclosures, and how they consume other living things to sustain themselves. Their primary relationship is with the earth and other living things, and within this survival-related context, they typically develop inter-relationships among themselves to render their connection to the earth and other groups more effective, as when animals form social hierarchies, or as when they hunt together in groups.

Human beings are understandable in the same way. People survive by means of their connections to the earth, and social structures form as an upshot of material, practical, survival-related relationships. Within a tribal group, some may devote themselves to hunting or farming, others to tending the dwellings, others to making clothes, tools, weapons, and other necessary items, others to general planning, others to maintaining order and justice, others to raising the children, and still others to maintaining spiritual relationships with nature. The latter religious functions – and these are accompanied by artistic activities, as in the construction of temples, altars, statues, images of the gods, and music for the gods – often involve ensuring the harvest, producing rain, securing relief from disease, or protection against natural disaster, and soliciting power to combat enemies. These roles and relationships are not accidental, but stem from the fundamental working relationships that people have with their environment. They also issue substantially, although not entirely, from the various kinds and divisions of labor within the society. By locating survival needs and labor at the center of our reflections, we arrive at a more materially focused and pragmatic way of comprehending human beings, society, and art, and this is what the outlook of Karl Marx (1818–83) positively offers.

For Marx, how people think of themselves, and of the world at large, depends heavily on the system within which they work – and here we should keep in mind the imaginatively artistic, skill-related dimension of labor – to obtain their food, clothing, and other necessities. The economic context within which people work significantly determines their attitudes towards themselves, other people and the universe as a whole. Specifically, Marx maintains that the economic system's basic structure prescribes the contours of a society's legal and political systems, along with its art, religion, and philosophy. Recall in contrast how Hegel locates art, religion, and philosophy at the crown of a culture's development and self-awareness. These forms of "absolute spirit," as Hegel refers to them, are understood inversely within Marx's view as superstructural social phenomena that issue from the society's economic base, along with the property relationships that this base defines. For Marx, economic interests constitute the primary lens for understanding the nature of art and other cultural phenomena.

There are countless examples where cultural phenomena are interpretable in economic terms. An obvious case is where, on a political level, a war is officially and ideologically justified in reference to humanitarian intervention or the promotion of freedom, when the true motive is to appropriate another country's natural resources. Similarly, within a religious context, the sacredness of certain animals in some cultures is not fundamentally due to any spiritual value that the animals have, but stems from the animals' value as sources of clothing or transportation. Within an artistic context, a particular artistic style might be condemned as degenerate or corrupt, not owing to any deficiencies in the style itself, but rather as a result of economic competition between those who advocate the style and those who find it threatening.

Although Marx adopts an economic style of analysis as opposed to Hegel's more philosophical one, this does not undermine his sympathy with Hegel's developmental understanding of human history. This is evident in how Marx adds a progressive dimension to the materialist approach that we have been outlining. This dimension does not rely upon the advance of self-consciousness *per se*, as we find in Hegel, but follows the pathway of developing economic relationships. Given a certain way of managing the production of food, clothing, shelter, defense, and such, specific cultural attitudes issue from the economic structure. If the economic structure transforms, then new forms of consciousness, along with new sets of values, arise along with that change.

This can be appreciated if we imagine how a family's acquisition of a spinning wheel, in a village where previously all thread was spun by hand, could affect the family's self-conception and status, or how the development of printed media, and later, electronic visual media, have affected how cultures function communicationally. Even more dramatically, if in the present day a type of clean energy were to replace the use of oil worldwide, the international system of social relationships would face an upheaval, since many countries presently oil-rich and strategically important, perhaps beneficially, could fade into relative geopolitical and economic insignificance. We can also recite the impact that technological advances such as interchangeable parts, the airplane, telephone, television, computer, atomic energy, and the Internet have had on the restructuring of social consciousness.

Within the field of art, there is the comparable impact of the pointed arch, oil paint, the steel girder, and probably, with respect to future art, holography and virtual reality. A further example is how the development of photography during the nineteenth century diminished the demand for portrait artists, since photographs portrayed people with greater perceptual precision, while they were also less time-consuming and less expensive to produce. Insofar as photography's success forced many painters to redefine their professional goals, more abstracted and non-representational forms of painting soon became popular.

The capitalist system's exploitative quality infuriated Marx, and his views on art reflect this distress. We speak here of a system where business owners, by virtue of the power that private ownership legally confers, aim to increase their profits as if the sheer accumulation of money were intrinsically valuable. As an economic ideal, capitalist owners employ workers at the lowest possible wages, manufacture products at the lowest possible cost, sell the products at the highest possible price, retain the resulting profits for themselves, and reinvest them for the sake of generating more profits in an upward spiral. The keynotes of this system are self-enrichment through the ownership of private property, money-making for its own sake, competition for markets within the group of self-interested capitalists, and self-preservation through the exploitation of wage laborers.

Within this system of production, the capitalist owns the workers' products – products that often embody significant artistic imagination – and as the capitalist sells those products, the workers work against themselves, for their alienated labor enriches and empowers their capitalist employer, and consequently widens the financial gap between themselves and their employer.

This situation is undesirable from the standpoint of artistic creation, humanly considered, for any artistic expression that the worker puts into the product is immediately and legally disenfranchised from the worker. Since the capitalist owns the artist's or worker's product from the very start, not only does the capitalist appropriate the value of the laborer's time and physical energy, the capitalist appropriates the value of the laborer's creative talent.

Marx does not regard the capitalist mode of production as socially conclusive, since he believes that it contains inherent economic and social tensions that eventually trigger its self-destruction. He envisions an initially competitive situation between numerous businesses playing out to generate monopolies and a decrease in competition, profits gravitating into the hands of fewer and fewer, increasingly wealthy capitalists, ever greater numbers of impoverished workers, and a widening social division between the moneyed bourgeois class and the underprivileged proletarians. Marx predicts mathematically that the division between these social classes will intensify to a point where the exploited workers, eventually realizing their overwhelming numbers and greater power, will overthrow the exploiting capitalists to assume control over the instruments of production themselves.

This idealized situation is dialectically, ironically, and justly structured: as the workers' labor serves initially to increase the capitalists' accumulation of wealth and power, the capitalists' excessive accumulation of wealth and dwindling numbers gradually renders them vulnerable to an overthrow by those whom they have been exploiting, as the capitalists' ability to defend themselves against a mass uprising diminishes. In the perfect outcome, a revolutionary overthrow would dissolve the exploitative opposition between factory-owner and worker, and precipitate a non-exploitative synthesis wherein the factory-owners and workers become the same body of individuals. The result is community ownership of the means of production, permeated with an atmosphere of mutual respect, sharing, and trust amongst everyone involved.

Once this principle of communal, non-exploitative ownership extends across the society as a whole and defines the prevailing economic system, we will have come a long way towards establishing a condition that exemplifies the general spirit of Kant's ideal moral community, Schiller's aesthetically educated society, and Hegel's fully developed social consciousness or *Geist*. The difference between Marx and these earlier theorists is that Marx focuses realistically upon the economic dimension – as Schiller focused concretely and hopefully upon the aesthetic dimension – and foresees that with the development of economic conditions, most of the society's superstructural aspects, namely, the legal, political, artistic, and religious aspects, will follow suit.

Still applicable to our own historical place, as it is presently entrenched within an advanced, psychologically sophisticated and globalizing capitalist mode of production where vast populations in economically disadvantaged countries work for the minimal pay, Marx regards it as our human responsibility to replace this mode of production with a non-exploitative, commune-oriented system. A major aspect of this undertaking, much in the spirit of Schiller's aesthetic education and expressed with the same feeling of obligation and enthusiasm, is to *educate* people about how the capitalist system is inherently exploitative and selfish, since capitalists try to obscure this fact to prevent mass rebellion. The capitalists would prefer to see their workers assume an attitude of localized domestic contentment conjoined with an ignorance of the system's broader economic mechanisms.

As one weapon among many in the effort to raise people's awareness about the objectionability of the capitalist system, Marx regards *art* as a tool for social education. It plays a role similar to television, radio, and internet communications which, in principle, can reach into the most remote corners of the world, ideally to carry a revolutionary message to those who would otherwise remain uninformed.

2. ART'S REACTIONARY AND REVOLUTIONARY ROLES

In Marx's writings, the most salient social conflict is between those who reinforce the capitalist system and those who aim to replace it with a less exploitative system, and, in due time, by a thoroughly commune-oriented system. This defines a battle between those whose actions are sympathetic with the exploited workers, and those whose actions reinforce, either explicitly or tacitly, the exploiting capitalists or bourgeoisie. To reinforce tacitly is to advocate or participate in social institutions that support, either directly or indirectly, the exploitative activities of the capitalists. Within the field of art, we can accordingly identify two basic forms of art, namely, revolutionary art that reinforces the commune-oriented, socially sharing attitude, and bourgeois art that reinforces the selfish system of exploitation, often unsuspectingly.

Since Marx maintains that a culture's economic system significantly determines the culture's collective psyche, we find that within the capitalist system, a large majority of workers have been psychologically absorbed into the world of capitalist values. This absorption is especially pronounced within the capitalist context, as Marx observes how capitalist values have entered the spheres of the family, religion, and personal worth to the point where cash payment has become the sole measure of value.[16] A person's worth as a human being is measured here in reference to what he or she earns, or owns, or can spend.

Such attitudes typify even those who are among the exploited, insofar as many individuals feel humanly worthless merely because they are poor or overwhelmed with debt. To compensate, the victims of exploitation tend to identify with capitalist symbols of wealth by adopting clothes, personal adornments, and behaviors that mimic those who are more wealthy, expressing a desire to become members of the capitalist class themselves. This presents a despairing situation for revolutionaries – a group that would include revolutionary artists – whose goal is to reduce exploitation by changing the attitudes that underlie it, for when the victims of exploitation positively assimilate the value system that enslaves them, it becomes difficult to dislodge the oppressive system and achieve a measure of liberation.

Rendering the situation even more bleak with respect to art's efficacy in raising consciousness, Marx observes that the adoption of capitalist values numbs aesthetic sensitivities. As he states in the *Economic and Philosophic Manuscripts of 1844*, "a dealer in

---

[16] See the first chapter of Marx, *Manifesto*.

minerals sees only the mercantile value but not the beauty and the unique nature of the mineral: he has no mineralogical sense."[17] Moreover, when a person is hungry and desperate, the aesthetic quality of the needed things is lost in view of their practical value. An underpaid worker who has absorbed capitalist values is thus doubly resistant to the project of aesthetic education.

Contributing to the imposition of capitalist values within the society at large is an array of arts that implicitly support or convey those values. This is art produced or supported by the elite, financially privileged classes, and it cuts across the traditional divide between popular and fine art. The activities in this bourgeois artworld sometimes call for massive sums of money for the production of artworks, as is the case for commercial motion pictures and television presentations. In the realm of fine art, it can also require the purchase of expensive tickets for admission into museums, operas, theatres, dance performances, and concerts, appropriately refined clothing, and often an advanced education as a condition for appreciating the artistic presentations. The kinds of artworks involved are often not socially critical, but are entertaining, pleasurable, and politically neutral. Although the works can reach the height of aesthetic perfection, their effect is to distract the exploited population from the unjust nature of their economic position, sometimes operating as the cultural equivalent of an anesthetic or narcotic.

The depth of the problem becomes evident at the level where we consider longer-term cultural trends. Let us assume that Hegel was on the right track when he observed that societies have a tendency to become more reflective, more integrated, more self-conscious, and less vicious in the long term. Let us also observe that his account of art history is consistent with the state of contemporary culture, as we noted earlier. The present culture does not emphasize architecture or sculpture as its main arts, but rather two-dimensional art forms that are grounded in painting, such as photography, television, video, computer-embodied presentations, and motion pictures. We can include music and literature, since the prevailing two-dimensional media often

---

[17] "Economic and Philosophic Manuscripts of 1844," in *The Marx-Engels Reader*, p. 89.

incorporate them as sound and dialogue. The dominant art form is "Romantic" in Hegel's sense, and, according to Hegel, expressive of a cultural condition more communally enlightened than ever before.

Working against this condition, we have powerful capitalist enterprises that control the presentation and distribution of the most visible of the contemporary artworks, possibly to the point of rendering remote the chance that revolutionary art will become dominant. Although by Hegelian lights, artistic culture has developed to an enhanced level of communal spirit in its movement away from architecture and sculpture into the realm of two-dimensional media, one can observe to the contrary as a Marxist, that the corporate control of popular and fine art, not to mention their control of contracted artists, is retarding the emergence of a non-exploitative social consciousness as never before in the history of art and culture. Marx did not write much about art and aesthetics, so we speak here by means of extrapolation, as would an orthodox Marxist.

We can note that within this Marxist perspective, estimations of artistic value do not attend to aesthetic quality for its own sake, but consider aesthetic quality insofar as it reinforces or detracts from the artworks' moral content and/or social meanings. Marxist aesthetics prescribes aesthetically related ways to enhance the expression of those meanings. In Brechtian theatre, for instance, a reality-oriented attitude in the audience is sustained by interrupting the dramatic illusion periodically. Similarly, we encounter hierarchies of the arts where the highly valued arts or genres are those considered to be most effective in conveying Marxist ideals, as György Lukács (1885–1971) maintains is true for the novel in his *The Theory of the Novel* (1920).[18]

Despite how socially objectionable artworks may be worthy of attention as purely aesthetic objects, they remain offensive

---

[18] Writers on art within the Marxist tradition vary in their commitment to orthodox Marxism. Some enhance Marx with Freudian insights, as does Herbert Marcuse (1898–1979); some focus on art as an instrument in social production, but with a more pronounced appreciation for bourgeois art than is usual, such as Christopher Caudwell (1907–37). This chapter aims to identify the qualities of the strict Marxist view, against which such Marxist variants can be understood.

from an orthodox Marxist standpoint insofar as they reinforce groups that engage in economic exploitation. The negative association here is akin to the state of mind represented by a thought such as, "This cup belonged to the people who stripped us of our land and left us destitute, and it thereby represents those people. The cup might be nicely crafted, but it is a bad cup."

Such a condemnation is independent of what the cup looks like, and it is not an aesthetic judgment. Suppose, though, a picture painted on the above cup displayed the capitalists in question, posing in finely tailored suits in front of the appropriated property, proudly displaying their social power. In this case, the artifact's subject matter would only render explicit the original claim that the cup's genealogy represents those who appropriated the land in question. From the standpoint of those who lost their land, one would call the cup "bad art" for the same reason as before.

From a Marxist perspective, capitalist art beautifies or positively aestheticizes injustice, and it compares to elegant portraits of criminals, even if it only tacitly and indirectly refers to the capitalist system it supports. Kant's notion of human beauty illuminates this negative attitude towards capitalist-supportive art, since it states that if an artwork has a human content, then it must respect human dignity. Capitalist-supportive art does not respect human dignity, because at bottom, it reinforces a system of exploitation. Objections to this kind of art are akin to the reasons for boycotting conflict diamonds, or refraining from vacationing in countries with oppressive regimes. Marxist aesthetics is a moralistic aesthetics, for its judgments of good art and bad art situate moral values above aesthetic values. This is no different from how Kant criticizes Maori facial tattooing because the tattoos' purely beautiful forms do not respect his moral conception of how a human being ought to look.

Not everyone who lives within a capitalist system strongly identifies with capitalist values, if only because Marx himself – who had many followers during his time – wrote his anti-capitalist theory in the midst of a capitalist culture. Some people within the culture always discern the exploitative situation and stand in resistance. In this respect, Marx hopes that the truth in his writings will set people free, despite the surrounding cultural impediments. In a parallel manner, certain liberating instances of art arise within capitalist culture, and serve to educate people aesthetically about the exploitative social system and prepare people's minds for socialist ideas. A work that Friedrich Engels refers to enthusiastically is Carl Wilhelm Hübner's painting, *The Silesian Weavers* (1846) (Plate 4), which depicts a woman trying to sell her linen cloth to a wealthy, hard-hearted capitalist, who scorns the material and leaves the woman and her family in despairing poverty. The work functions educatively as would a documentary photograph of illegal activities being enacted by some supposedly socially legitimate group.

Hübner was a talented painter, but one rarely finds him included in company with Raphael, Michelangelo, Rubens, Velázquez, Manet, or Picasso, and this reveals what orthodox Marxist aesthetics considers to be artistically important. Expressing this thought positively, we can say that Marxism advocates arts that are honest, truth-oriented, and focused especially and realistically on portraying social conditions that reveal capitalist exploitation. As a challenge to capitalist values, such works serve educationally for those among the exploited (and also those among the exploiters) who have assimilated those values. Art's complementary purpose is to present visions of a non-exploitative, communal society, where mutual respect, sharing, and trust prevail, where people work in harmony, where they can be freely creative, and where they can appreciate the fruits of their labor, without feelings of alienation between themselves and what they produce. The best artists are ones who have a social activist consciousness.

As an ideal for artistic creation, Marx imagines a situation where artistic labor is non-alienated, remembering past times when artisans in trade guilds made their entire product, and where the product was free to bear their personal style. The future social conditions of artistic creation would correspondingly allow someone to create an object that would be personally exemplary, as if it were the person's accurate mirror reflection. An artist could look at his or her product, appreciate a personal reflection in the work and achieve a measure of self-realization in a context where labor has not been sold to profit an economic oppressor.

The Hegelian theme of self-recognition is evident here, except that within the Marxist context, the development of reason is not mainly responsible for generating the conditions for adequate self-recognition. The development of the economic system along a non-exploitative path creates these conditions, and it advances the interests of reason only as a side-effect. Consistent, however, with Hegel's notion of social consciousness that overflows with a sense of oneness and mutual respect, the artist who creates in the non-alienated social context that Marx envisions for the future does not aim primarily to see him or herself embodied in the work as a particular individual. Having already developed a communal consciousness of his or her own, the artist creates with our human community in mind, having dissolved attitudes of selfish individuality within a spiritual consciousness where the "I" is "we" and the "we" is "I," as Hegel would describe this commune-oriented situation. Artistic production in some tribal contexts has this quality, where members of the tribe express the tribe's spirit in the artworks, rather than their own individual spirit.

3. CONCLUSION

We have seen how Kant, Schiller, and Hegel subordinate art and beauty to wider interests, mainly due to their concern with morality and social harmony. The same is true with Marx, who employs an economically driven theory with moral and social-political ends in view. Within Marx's practical outlook, there is a stronger tendency to sacrifice the attention to aesthetic quality for its own sake, as compared to the other three theorists.[19] For Kant, human beauty adheres strictly to moral expression, and although Kant does not accentuate aesthetic quality in this adherence, he does note that classical Greek sculpture generically establishes the paradigm of human beauty. Schiller – perhaps owing to his position as an accomplished

---

[19] This is not to say that Marx is insensitive to autonomous aesthetic values. In the "Economic and Philosophic Manuscripts of 1844" he speaks enthusiastically of a non-capitalist condition where, in contrast to the mineral dealer mentioned above, people do not regard objects simply as items to buy and sell for a profit, but are liberated to the point of being easily and naturally able to appreciate an object's aesthetic qualities for their own sake.

dramatist himself – more insightfully characterizes the nature of beauty by underscoring the importance of being graceful in one's rational appearance. Hegel's conception of classical art, which for him is the highest form of art as measured by beauty, also attends substantially to aesthetic quality, as he refers us to the balance of form and content, and notes that during the classical phase of its development, fine art attains the highest level of beauty as the sensuous expression of the divine. This supposedly occurred, as we have seen, within ancient Greek society, where the sense of high aesthetic quality matched the Greek cultural development in its advanced condition from the days of ancient Babylonia and Egypt.

In orthodox Marxism, we find a theory less concerned with aesthetic quality for its own sake, and more interested in the values that artworks socially reinforce. If an artwork serves well to convey or otherwise assist a communist message, then it is basically a good artwork in Marxist terms; if it works intensely against that message, it is already deeply flawed, even if it is a masterpiece. Of the four thinkers so far, Marx – who is the most realistic of the group – is also the least concerned with understanding, on their own terms, the nature of beauty, artistic genius, depth of inspiration, semantic resonance, and aesthetic factors of this sort. It is thus unproblematic for a Marxist to regard some of the greatest artists as producers of inferior or defective art, once it becomes clear that their art expresses capitalist interests and is complicit with a system of exploitation.

This sharper detachment of an artwork's pure aesthetic quality from the moral purpose that it may or may not serve, is akin to how Schiller's outlook uncomfortably requires us to beautify ourselves as a moral duty. Marx describes capitalist economics as offensive to human dignity and he comes close to demanding, as a matter of common responsibility, that we transform the present system into a non-exploitative one. This compares in force to how Kant describes the unconditional moral demand that our reason sets upon us. In light of the moral motivation in Marx's aesthetics, and given how pure aesthetic quality – *l'art pour l'art* – is not the central concern, and is in fact an object of criticism, we face the problem of evaluating the products of an artistic genius' free creativity, insofar as they either conflict with or constitute a distraction from the importance of working towards establishing a non-exploitative society.

The results of some of the actual choices that have been made to promote communal works of art in a single-minded manner (for instance, in the early Soviet Union) generate concern about the losses to be sustained when the task of social improvement is adopted monolithically. They raise the question of whether reason, or some moral vision associated with it, should ever fully dominate, if it entails the exclusion of innovative visions of the world that do not cohere well with the prescribed social and rationalistic goal. This question of tolerance for forms of artistic expression that do *not* positively support the liberating aims of the exploited working class, is perhaps the most pressing one within orthodox Marxist aesthetics, for it requires a sacrifice in the kinds of subject matters for which an artist can expect social support or address legitimately.

With respect to this sacrifice, the Hegelian emphasis upon concrete thinking shows itself within Marxist aesthetics as a demand for social realism. Artworks that remain immersed in personal fantasy or subjectivity to the point of disregarding objective social realities are subordinated to more balanced works that may describe a person's inner states in detail, but which complement these with a strong characterization of the person's historical, social, and economic being. Highly abstract and apparently socially unconcerned works, as we find in much modernist art, are consequently condemned as being one-sided, independently of whatever aesthetic quality they might otherwise have. In a similar light, the notion of "art for art's sake" is criticized as being in logical company with the capitalist's unnatural idea of accumulating "wealth for wealth's sake," that Marx described in *Capital*, Volume I.[20]

One can defend Marxist aesthetics by arguing that for the time being, given how capitalist values continue to infuse

---

[20] This reference to art for art's sake in association with wealth for wealth's sake is mentioned at the beginning of G. V. Plekhanov's 1912 essay "Art and Social Life." For Marx's discussion of the accumulation of wealth for wealth's sake (the M-C-M process), see *Capital*, Volume 1, "Part 2: The Transformation of Money into Capital," and "Chapter 4: The General Formula for Capital."

themselves dangerously into most of the mass media and public awareness, it is imperative to focus artistic activity and evaluation concertedly upon social revolution and the project of consciousness-raising. Artistic production should contribute to this important task before engaging in other, less important purposes. There are many kinds of art, and since most are politically neutral, their acquiescence to the status quo implicitly supports whatever social system happens to be in place. In a commune-oriented society, the same arts are likely to remain politically neutral, and they might flourish within a non-exploitative society, if that social organization were strong and secure. Their present objection-ability resides in their political complacency during highly unfair times. In a commune-oriented society, such arts could remain free, since censorship would apply mainly to arts whose content explicitly expresses and reinforces exploitative values, much as one might place restrictions on art that supports gratuitous violence within almost any civilized social system.

The narrowness of the field of preferred art within the Marxist aesthetic is thus arguably provisional, and relative to the sur-rounding, oppressive capitalist context. The narrowness need not obtain within an established, commune-oriented society that has largely eradicated exploitation. Just as the nutritious value of citrus fruits sold by outlaw regimes might be of the same high quality as that sold by the more respectable members of the international community, a large segment of present artistic activity is not objectionable on purely aesthetic grounds, but is objectionable owing to the social connection it bears to its capi-talist sponsors. One can alternatively envision the widespread presence of public television, theatre, museums, and concerts, refined artistic achievements, where the corporate influence over the artistic content for the sake of accumulating profits has been for the most part removed, and where a diversity in the modes of artistic expression remains encouraged and sought.

The perennial problem with the strict Marxist view, and others like it that regard art as an instrument for realizing a singly-defined social goal, where everyone is called upon to participate in its realization, is that before such liberation can happen, the pri-mary task is always to address the social situation that is perceived to be crying out for change. Judging from past attempts, this usually leads to the imposition of oppressive social measures that damage the roots of masterpiece-producing artistic creativity.

In the opposite direction, we should observe that the well-intended Marxist prescription that art remains straightforwardly realistic and socially practical is significantly eroded by the majority of the theorists who write during the later nineteenth century and the twentieth century. Our next four thinkers emphasize how artistic expression involves, to the contrary, either the expression of otherworldly realities (Schopenhauer), the general forces of life (Nietzsche), or the deepest reaches of personal subjectivity (Kierkegaard and Freud). They together trace a non-rationalist route for artistic expression that precipitates into a surrealist orientation that carries on throughout the twentieth century. Of the next four theorists, only Nietzsche is explicitly interested in understanding artistic expression as a means to develop a better, healthier society.

To appreciate this modern trend towards increased subjectivity, an observation from our conclusion of Hegel's aesthetics is informative. As discussed earlier, Hegel's developmental sequence of the five fine arts ranges from three-dimensional (architecture and sculpture), to two-dimensional (painting), to one-dimensional arts (music and poetry). When we combine this movement with his complementary interest in theorizing in the direction of increased concreteness, tensions emerge in the culminating structure of poetry, with which he concludes his aesthetic theory. As Hegel describes it historically, the art of poetry begins with the objective epic form, develops oppositionally into the subjective lyric form, and then in the drama, amalgamates the two forms. Poetry is the highest of the five fine arts, and drama is the highest form of poetry.

When experiencing drama in actual performance, though, we witness not a purely conceptual presentation (as would be the case when reading a novel), but what one might refer to as living sculpture infused with poetry, as actual players recite their theatrical lines during the performance. Drama is sculptural as well as poetic, and despite the tension it causes with the rest of his aesthetics, one of Hegel's reasons for locating drama at the conclusion of his aesthetic theory is the attractiveness of its concrete, living, three-dimensional quality.

The Marxist prescription to be realistic and socially aware coheres well with this Hegelian regard for drama-in-performance as the highest form of social consciousness, or spirit, within the field of art. Given how technological developments in artistic creativity are presently moving towards holography and virtual reality, it is tempting to think that the present-day prevalence of visual culture in printed photographs, television, motion pictures, and computer imagery indicates a historical movement towards the ideal that Hegel and Marx were identifying. Most movie presentations, televisions, and computers will soon be equipped with three-dimensional viewing options, almost as if the art of painting were to transform into the art of sculpture, if we were to speak in Hegel's traditional terms. A three-dimensional movie closely approximates the experience of living theatre, and in this respect, one might think that we are experiencing a confirmation of Hegel's aesthetic theory.

There is one troubling qualification in the inevitable development of three-dimensional media. The peculiar aspect of these seemingly more realistic visual presentations is their inherent *surrealism*, rather than realism: digital photography – the principles of which one can transfer to the cinema – has already negated the difference between traditional documentary photography and imaginative painting, for it has become close to impossible to determine whether a digital image represents an actual condition or event, simply by inspecting the image. The result is a kind of "electronic painting" or "electronic cinema" that presents itself as a mix of the realistic style of art that Hegel and Marx envision, at least with respect to its formal qualities, and the imaginative, socially unconcerned or distortive style of art that Marxists condemn when speaking about the political detachment of modernism. In light of this tendency towards a more surrealistic style of artistic experience, we can frame our next theorists as prefiguring the contemporary immersion into the artistic world where virtual reality predominates.

5

THE ART OF TRANSCENDENT PEACE

Arthur Schopenhauer

1. SCHOPENHAUER'S METAPHYSICS OF THE WILL

Arthur Schopenhauer (1788–1860) proudly refers to himself as a pessimist, for he is convinced that no form of optimism sufficiently takes peoples' and animals' suffering to heart. Having an uncommon sensitivity and compassion for those in distress, he curiously couples this humane thoughtfulness with a streak of misanthropy: when he lived in Frankfurt, he recoiled when he watched visitors to the zoo laughingly taunt the caged animals, and he could hardly endure restaurants and social gatherings where the group's enthusiasm centered only around sports, local gossip, money, and sex. As Schopenhauer suffered when he saw people suffer, the centuries-long parade of individuals who have squandered their time bickering, struggling, and betraying each other for trivialities also stood depressingly in the back of his mind.

For Schopenhauer, such discouraging scenes and activities represent the bulk of humanity's social engagements, past, present, and foreseeable future, and they contribute to his philosophical decision to look elsewhere for a more satisfying level of awareness, a higher quality of being, and a measure of relief from daily chatter. His aesthetic theory enters into play at this point, initiating his quest for salvation. In accord with how Roger Fry

describes van Gogh, Schopenhauer was convinced that "some-
where one might lay hold of spiritual values compared with
which all other values were of no account."[21]

As is true for most nineteenth-century philosophers,
Schopenhauer's aesthetics is difficult to appreciate without some
knowledge of the metaphysics that motivates it. Unlike his
socially well-regarded philosophical contemporaries and immediate predecessors, the bulk of whom either believed in God or
assumed that the universe is essentially rational in its operations
and aims, Schopenhauer maintains that the universe is goalless
and meaningless.[22] He also believes, like Hegel, that the universe's substance is more thought-like than material, despite his
anti-Hegelian position that its inner reality is not rational, conceptual, or self-conscious, but is a blind, insensate, unconscious
force that is best characterized as unrefined, driving Will. For
him – and Schopenhauer discovers this through an introspective
acquaintance with his own inner being – the universe is an
immense, pointless impulse, going nowhere and attaining nothing
everlasting.

Since human beings are woven into the cosmos as much as
any other creatures, Schopenhauer believes that if we examine
ourselves carefully and apprehend our own being at its core, then
we will grasp the substance of the wider universe that flows
through us. His preferred way to attain this self-knowledge is not
through scientific observation, as a doctor might study physiology or anatomy, but by introspection. A person's hand, for
example, appears objectively as a complex mechanism driven by
nerve impulses. To the person whose hand it is, it also appears
subjectively as a part of that person's body, apprehensible from
the "inside," unlike the table upon which the hand might rest,
and to which no one else has access. Schopenhauer regards this

---

[21] Fry, "Vincent van Gogh," p. 235.

[22] Schelling suggested such a vision in 1800 when he admitted the possibility
that "man is no more possessed of a history than the animal, being confined, on
the contrary, to an eternal circuit of actions, in which, like Ixion upon his wheel,
he revolves unceasingly ... " (Schelling, *System of Transcendental Idealism*,
pp. 202–3). Schopenhauer invokes the image of Ixion to describe our ordinarily
suffering condition, which aesthetic experience alleviates (*The World as Will and
Representation*, Volume 1, §38). Nietzsche's doctrine of eternal recurrence is also
foreshadowed here.

introspective access to physical objects as more metaphysically revealing than observing them from without, since it presents a dimension of physical objects that would otherwise remain unsuspected and unknown. He reasons that if our hand has a subjectively accessible interior, then so must the rest of the objects we perceive, since as a physical object or "representation," our hand is no different from any other object.

When feeling the inside of his hand (or any part of his body) with the hope of apprehending a metaphysical core appropriate not only to his hand, or his body, but to all objectively perceivable things – animals, plants, and inanimate matter included – Schopenhauer is led to disregard the rational quality of his bodily awareness, since this quality is present only in humans. At his experiential center and, as far as he can surmise, at the basis of everything else, he discerns nothing beyond a striving, or "will," that, in its pure condition, is an inner energy that is goalless, and merely pushes on. He experiences it as a "lack" that objectifies itself, always inadequately, in an effort to become self-fulfilled. To him, reality is like an immortal artist who never quite paints the perfect picture, forever condemned to paint in tantalizing frustration.

Schopenhauer's characterization of this unconscious drive might sound strange at first. It is, however, recognizable as instinctual energy, if we consider how newborn animals manage automatically to find their mother, food, shelter, and defenses, or as sheer biological drive, considering how plants seek water and light, while lacking self-consciousness and the capacity for rational deliberation. These beings have a vital force, but one that lacks a self-conscious rationality. In Schopenhauer's terms, they function through a sheer "will-to-live," and if Will involves any rationality, that rationality appears only at the most highly refined levels of its manifestations. As external observers, moreover, although we may imagine a conscious design that informs a vine's encircling movements around a tree trunk, the vine itself seems to have no idea of what it is so interestingly doing. Neither do newborn babies, kittens, puppies, or other such living things. Human beings that have moved beyond the stage of infancy appear to be the only instances of deliberative, self-conscious beings in existence.

Adding another dimension, Schopenhauer notices more disconcertingly how living beings survive by devouring other individuals.

This is the will-to-live being organized through our human lens into a vicious field of articulated self-consumption. As Schopenhauer surveys nature, he observes Will everywhere "feasting upon itself," where each plant, animal and human being, considered as individual manifestations of Will, is the graveyard of the other things it consumes to survive. When Schopenhauer surveys ordinary life, he sees perpetual war, battlefields, and carnage as the way of the spatio-temporal world.

Although we have the power to do so, our capacities for self-consciousness and rational thinking do not ordinarily serve to diminish this nightmare. Different parts of the mind conflict with one another, people eat themselves up over one issue or another, warfare continues, and society persists as a flow of multiple desires, many of which are selfish, and most of which remain driving and unsatisfied. Since ordinary life presents itself as a frustrating arena where people fight within and without, Schopenhauer maintains that happiness can only reside else-where, in minimizing one's desires and decreasing the intensity of one's instinct for competition and one-upmanship. As we can read in Hindu and Buddhist scriptures, less desire produces less frustration, less temptation, less conflict, less mundane involvement, and more tranquillity. At the extreme, and as an ideal, Schopenhauer accordingly describes true happiness as a painless and will-less state of peaceful transcendence, of utter stillness, and many of his references to this suspended condition arise in his discussions of aesthetic experience. Much of Schopenhauer's positive reputation stems from his therapeutic view that art can enlighten and relieve us from life's daily troubles.

2. AESTHETIC EXPERIENCE, IDEALIZATION AND ARTISTIC GENIUS

Schopenhauer believes that artistic awareness, in the best sense of the word, is based upon the *idealization* of some given subject matter. For any object, we can perform this idealization ourselves through direct perception and imagination, or alternatively apprehend an already idealized representation of the object in which an artist has rendered the object more flawless than it appears in daily life. Not all art aims at this visionary and consoling effect, but much art is of this idealizing kind, as we can see in traditional portraiture, classical Greek sculpture (Plate 3, *Discobolus*), landscape painting, drama, cinema, and photography. For Schopenhauer, the value of these idealized images resides in their capacity to convey the peaceful, timeless essences of the objects and themes portrayed.

Idealized images of minerals, plants, and animals are clear instances, since the ideal types involved are recognizable, definable, and naturally fixed. An image of a perfect palm tree, for example, reveals the form that every palm tree aims naturally to realize. Similar effects arise within the realm of human beauty, though less reliably. A person's portrait can remove the facial blemishes, warts, and disfigurations, and idealize the person's bodily contours to the point where the pattern that nature had ideally in mind presents itself to reveal, supposedly, a person's true character.

Since some people of bad character are physically attractive, the process of idealization in portraiture does not uniformly generate a trustworthy indicator of the quality of a person's inner being. This difficulty appeared at the end of our chapter on Kant, where we addressed the rhetorical use of beauty in connection with the beautification of criminal characters. The problem arises once again in Schopenhauer, owing to his position that beauty is revealed through the idealization of an object's physical appearance.

Schopenhauer nonetheless highlights two elementary aspects of aesthetic experience. The first refers to the knowledge that idealized images provide; the second, to the peace of mind that the contemplation of idealized images bestows. Both happen simultaneously, since according to this view, the state of pure knowledge, or pure knowing, produces a psychological state that dramatically minimizes willing and desire. Following a long philosophical tradition that pits desire against knowledge, or equally speaking, action against theory, Schopenhauer assumes that if we adopt a more detached, knowledge-seeking attitude, then our desires will fade into the background to become less pressing. This is especially so, since he believes that during aesthetic contemplation, we imaginatively disengage the object of our attention from all of its practical relationships, as we apprehend it as the embodiment of a timeless ideal.

Although it might seem that Schopenhauer's aesthetics is concerned primarily with art, the transcendent experience itself is its target. Artistic "geniuses" are catalysts for this experience, since (for Schopenhauer) they have the uncommon capacity to perceive the archetypes of things without further aid, just as the man in Plato's Parable of the Cave ascends from the world of shadows to perceive the Eternal Forms. The genius might likewise perceive a tree, and through the perception of that single tree, apprehend the universal being of all trees. In the same way, the genius would be able to perceive particular groups of people at war, or in social harmony, and immediately grasp the essence of all wars, or the principle of all ideal social arrangements. Such an apprehension lifts a person above the flow of mundane details, dissolves the feeling of time, and precipitates an outlook that transcends individual interests. Within Schopenhauer's aesthetics, the genius's function is to produce artworks that stimulate such timeless visions in others, and hence convey metaphysical insight to those who live in the world of mere shadows. It is not the artwork itself that is central, but rather the genius' aesthetic experience that the work communicates.

Schopenhauer assumes that the quality of a person's consciousness matches, or slowly grows to match, the type of objects that the person contemplates, just as one becomes what one eats, or as a person's attitude and behavior soon reflect the company that he or she keeps. In reference to the apprehension of ideal types, Schopenhauer accordingly holds that the universal quality of those archetypes will resonate in the person who attends to them, thus transforming the perception of the everyday sphere of changing, perishable, individual objects to reveal a truer, more permanent level of being. Insofar as these archetypes are inherently stable, they foster a profound and peaceful stillness as their presence infiltrates a person's awareness. The result is a universalistic, tranquil state of mind, where desire, frustration, and pain are reduced.

Here, highly idealized works of art that display universalistic content are called "beautiful." This usage is not standard, since a perfectly portrayed toad might not be beautiful in the ordinary sense, despite the image's suitability to reveal the underlying pattern of all toads. The tranquillity achieved in aesthetic contemplation does invite the term "beautiful," however, for even in those cases of animals or insects with a frightening appearance, we can overlook the initial repulsion for the sake of apprehending the thing's archetype in a detached way, as might an aesthetically sensitive biologist or entomologist. Depending upon the kind of object portrayed, though, this kind of natural beauty can disappointingly yield technical, formal, and exacting presentations that lack grace and animation. When we advance to human beauty and introduce grace, which Schopenhauer associates originally with humans, a more profound kind of beauty appears.

Emotionally complicating the experience of beauty in general, Schopenhauer reflects upon the experience of the sublime. As mentioned in connection with the dynamical sublime in Kant, the experience requires that we tear ourselves away from the apprehension, frustration, fear, or repulsion associated with the object or its surrounding context. To appreciate aesthetically an encircling thunderstorm with its nearby lightning strikes, booming thunder, and heavy rain, we cannot allow the fear of being electrocuted to overwhelm us. There are degrees of threat and fear, so one would speak properly of the sublime only in cases where the threat or fear makes it difficult to stay mentally composed.

Other types of aesthetic experience are cousins to the sublime, albeit like cousins who have been cut off from the family. In these stubborn cases, we must also resist the pressures of the will as a condition for having the aesthetic experience, but can rarely do so. Schopenhauer mentions here objects that are naturally repulsive in appearance or function, such as vomit, pus, or putrid flesh. He also mentions objects that are naturally attractive in their appearance or function, such as mouth-watering foods, or sexually arousing bodies. In such instances, we must self-consciously neutralize the pull of desire, either away from or towards the object, if we are to have a pure aesthetic experience of it. Schopenhauer believes that although we can achieve this detachment to experience the sublime, he doubts whether many of us have the power to detach fully from powerfully disgusting or deeply sensuous subject matters. He concludes that art consequently becomes self-defeating, when it is disgusting or pornographic, given that most people are incapable of detaching themselves from the nausea or sexual desire that it stimulates.

3. NATURAL BEAUTY AND THE ARTS

Schopenhauer's aesthetics does not portray the experience of beauty, either natural or artistic, as an end in itself, but treats beauty, sublimity, and aesthetic experience in general as a means to apprehend timeless essences and to cultivate a peacefully transcendent awareness. When he attends to natural beauty and the various arts, Schopenhauer begins by describing arts that provide knowledge of the less meaningful archetypes that underpin inorganic nature, and then, following the various grades and meanings of Will's objectification in an upward path, he considers aesthetic experiences related to the archetypes of plants and animals. He concludes with aesthetic experiences that express the more meaningful and sublime archetypes that relate to humans and their cultural life. We will describe the details of his hierarchy in the arts in the next section, and will focus presently on some broader relationships in this upward movement from inorganic nature to human beings.

Schopenhauer notes that the more closely we approach humans in the hierarchy of ideal types, the more obvious the blind, irrational, and constantly striving nature of the world as Will becomes. The human being displays the world's essence most clearly, not because Will's self-conflict is the most violent at this level, but because Will's subjective reality is here most explicit. If we start with natural beauty and pass through the successive levels of artistic beauty as they match the various grades of archetypes, the presence of subjective life, or consciousness, becomes more intense. This increasing explicitness of subjectivity leads Schopenhauer to locate natural beauty at the lower levels of his aesthetic theory for similar reasons as does Hegel, namely, because the quality of ideal types that it displays does not reflect a high intensity of subjectivity or metaphysical interiority.

Schopenhauer's estimation of natural beauty's value is accordingly mixed. He affirmatively maintains that aesthetically contemplating a tree (for example) can raise us to a level of universalistic awareness, free from frustrating desire, and produce a measure of transcendent tranquillity. The object of contemplation could be a rock, tree, animal, or human body, regarded as a pure form, and the resulting transcendence would be the same, as would the peace of mind that issues.

When Schopenhauer contrasts natural beauty with artistic beauty, however, especially in light of other forms of transcendent awareness that later play a role in his philosophy, such as moral awareness and ascetic awareness, his attitude towards natural beauty becomes disapproving. From this angle, he states that natural beauty can deceptively fix our attention upon mere appearances, as it fills us with joy in the presence of a sunset's bright colors, or a flower's soft petals and fragrance. Worse yet, such lovely experiences can suggest misleadingly that the world is governed by an intelligent, benevolent, and caring divinity that created beauty for our pleasure or moral education, as Kant believes. In disparaging terms, Schopenhauer refers to this attitude as "optimism," and asserts that natural beauty, insofar as it draws our attention to superficial physical appearances, reduces our capacity for empathy with the world's suffering-filled, *inner* being. His objection to this aestheticist and optimistic approach to natural beauty is essentially a moral one.

In this regard, we can recall the views of Plato and Kant, both of whom inspired Schopenhauer's metaphysics. According to Schopenhauer, Plato and Kant adopt the same devaluing attitude toward the daily world as does Schopenhauer himself, asserting that it has no intrinsic value, but value only insofar as it expresses a higher, transcendent reality. For Plato, this reality contains the unchanging Ideas, or archetypes – archetypes that are more real than anything that happens to be patterned after them. For Kant, it contains the thing-in-itself as the ground of all appearances and as the object of our idealizations. Yet unlike Schopenhauer, both Plato and Kant believe that natural beauty positively indicates that ultimate reality is good.

Schopenhauer rejects such optimism and admits no rational or moral being at the universe's core, although he importantly shares Plato's and Kant's view that the natural, daily world is not absolute, is more dreamlike than real, and is nothing more than the fluctuating appearance of a fundamentally stable, and hence truer, reality that is in itself spaceless and timeless. This reality is Will, which immediately appears to us as a set of timeless archetypes (that is, the set of natural kinds). Natural beauty can consequently direct our attention to realities such as these eternal archetypes and Will as the thing-in-itself. As noted, natural beauty's compelling sensory attractiveness can also mislead us either to value appearances beyond what they metaphysically merit, or to speculate mistakenly beyond those appearances to hypothesize an optimistic foundation to the world, as when we look hopefully at the stars on a beautiful night with a prayer-like mentality, and imagine a self-conscious and benevolent divinity of some kind who can deliver us from evil.

4. THE HIERARCHY OF THE ARTS

Schopenhauer's treatment of the various arts extends from natural beauty in a stepwise fashion starting with architecture, whose aesthetic purpose he believes is to express the conflict between gravity's downward pull and the architectural structure's gravity-defying rigidity. It proceeds to sculpture, painting, and the literary arts, which together reveal increasingly the nature of human subjectivity and universal Will. In the transition from one art to the next, Schopenhauer observes how the respective capacity for subjective expression becomes more pronounced. We have seen how Hegel presents a comparable hierarchy, beginning with architecture, and advancing to sculpture, painting, music, and the literary arts.

Schopenhauer's rendition of the hierarchy of the arts departs from Hegel at one crucial point, insofar as Schopenhauer locates music within its own independent sphere, which we will describe shortly. This leaves painting and literature as arts that proceed from architecture and sculpture to portray subjective states of mind more effectively, matching Hegel's conception of Romantic art. As we can recall, the wider purpose of Schopenhauer's presentation is to reveal how aesthetic experience embodies increasing degrees of subjective intensity as we approach the human archetypes, and how pure, and relatively empty, tranquillity slowly gives way to a tranquillity more meaningfully infused with the knowledge of suffering.

Schopenhauer's discussion of the various arts thus functions philosophically as the first stage along a path of spiritual development that takes us from aesthetic awareness to moral awareness and, finally, to ascetic awareness and mystical experience, which concludes his philosophy as a whole. Only ascetic awareness yields the richest tranquillity and wisdom – a type of wisdom that pain-free, empathy-lacking, pure beauty cannot provide. Since for Schopenhauer, universal empathy is necessary for moral awareness, and since moral awareness, in turn, is a precursor to ascetic awareness, aesthetic awareness marks a spiritual beginning that educates us towards moral sensitivity. Here, Schiller's notion of aesthetic education echoes within Schopenhauer's aesthetics.

The goal of attaining ascetic wisdom underlies Schopenhauer's claim that the finest works of art portray human subjectivity with detachment and tranquillity to reveal the universality of human suffering. In sculpture, he refers to the Laocoön Group (*c.*25 BCE); in painting, Raphael's and Correggio's portraits of Jesus and the Saints, which express a peaceful resignation; in literature, classical Greek tragedy. Beginning with a purely tranquil state of mind in the aesthetic experience of natural beauty, aesthetic experience slowly becomes more sublime, as pure beauty gives way to aesthetic experiences and expressions that the knowledge of suffering informs. Classically contemplative images of the Buddha are sublime in this sense as well.

This brings us to music, which Schopenhauer circumscribes within its own, unique sphere. His aesthetics culminates with reflections on music insofar as theatrical tragedy (as the highest visual-literary art) and then music (as the highest sonic art) reside at the summit of beauty's transformation from relatively superficial instances of pure, natural beauty to the more profound and sublime instances of beauty in painting and drama. With the exception of music, all genuine works of art fit the following Schopenhauerian description: when serving their primary spiritual purpose, artworks represent universal objects, or facilitate the perception of universal objects, such that the perception of those objects produces a metaphysically grounded, peaceful state of mind. Music differs in that its theoretical place is on the side of the universal subject that contemplates universal objects, rather than on the side of the universal objects themselves.

Schopenhauer believes that music expresses emotion in an abstracted, formalistic manner, as it simultaneously preserves the emotion's natural movement. Listening to music also compares to reading or hearing someone's words, for within the musical experience, we become one with a person's emotional flow, as when we experience through someone's writing or speech the same words and meanings that the person thought or said. Moreover, the tensions and resolutions of the musical notes, chords, melodies, and harmonies, as they unfold through time, mirror the tensions and resolutions of human feeling, and this isomorphism allows us to experience not this or that feeling of sadness, joy, melancholy, elation, or any other emotional instance, but sadness, joy, melancholy, and elation "themselves." We musically become one with the composer's or musician's experience, but also become one with the common experience of humanity insofar as we all feel sadness, joy, melancholy, elation, and so on. Corresponding to the aesthetic experience of universal objects in the visual and literary arts, Schopenhauer locates in connection with music the aesthetic experience of universal feelings on the side of the universal subject.

Unlike the actual emotions that people experience, music's emotional dimension is characteristically detached and pain-free. The sadness that some music expresses – as might be associated with the loss of a loved one – could be terribly painful if experienced in a concrete context and specific instance. As frozen and sublimated into a musical form, however, where emotions recollected in tranquillity appear abstractedly and independently of the painful or pleasurable circumstances in which they originally occur, we can experience those emotions in a universalistic way, more beautifully free from the pain that would ordinarily accompany them.

Since he conceives of music as reflecting the subjective side of aesthetic awareness, rather than that of the universal archetypes, Schopenhauer refers to music as a "copy" (*Abbild*) or direct presentation of Will. Music thereby brings us closer to experiencing the world's fundamental impulse than does any other art, since it allows us to experience another person's subjective interior, albeit abstractedly, given that Will is most characteristically present there as the inner nature of things. Music compares to a painting, photograph, or film, for just as these arts allow us to see through the eyes of the painter, photographer, or filmmaker, the experience of musical form allows us to coincide with the musician's emotional experience, along with the subjectivities of everyone who has felt similarly.

Insofar as music embodies forms of emotional experience, it has a closer contact with Will, for according to Schopenhauer's theory, the reality of everyone's subjective flow of experience is Will expressing itself distinctively as human being. This is one sense in which music is the most metaphysical art.[23] A second sense, and enhancing music's status as the highest art, is the metaphorical relationship that musical structure bears with the world's structure as a whole. Schopenhauer philosophically describes the hierarchy of timeless archetypes as the immediate and objective expression of Will, and he observes a correspondence between music's sonic structure and this metaphysical hierarchy's structure. The bass notes and fundamental tone metaphorically match the lower-level archetypes related to forms of inanimate matter. The middle-level notes and overtones match the intermediary archetypes of plants and animals; melodies and the higher-pitched overtones match the archetypes related to human beings. When sounding a single bass note, that note and its accompanying overtones metaphorically and microcosmically reflect the archetypal structure of nature as a whole. From this standpoint, music is an analogue to the universe's cosmic dance, as the various grades of timeless essences metaphorically reverberate in endless imaginative configurations as the music plays.

Schopenhauer also identifies music as the most metaphysical art in reference to a fundamental contrast between aesthetic and scientific awareness. Following Kant, he maintains that our scientific and mathematical thinking work well to organize our experience and to render it predictable and coherent, but that they do not provide any knowledge of how things are in themselves. Although the aesthetic, intuitive apprehension of timeless archetypes assists conceptually oriented scientific thinking in many cases, such as when we discern the perfect forms of biological types, listening to music directly presents the tensions and resolutions of subjective experience, and goes beyond the

---

[23] Since Schopenhauer characterizes Will as a continuous, ever-yearning urge, music that embodies this dynamic quality would be metaphysically exemplary, as in musical works that are constituted by lengthy, sustained sequences of tension-ridden chords that transform into further tension-ridden chords, perpetually deferring resolution. Richard Wagner's well-known and disorienting "Tristan chord" (F, B, D#, G#) upon which he grounds much of his music, is a leading element for musical structures of this unresolving kind, not to mention the germ of modernist atonal music.

objective, relational world of ordinary experience that mathematics and scientific, causal thinking describe so well.

Science may tell us exactly how objects and events stand in mechanical relationship to each other, but Schopenhauer insists that science cannot reveal the inner nature of those objects and events, or of the forces upon which its explanations rely. Subjective experience, and paradigmatically within the arts, musical experience, reveals these underlying realities, and Schopenhauer believes that if we are interested in metaphysical knowledge, it is more appropriate to listen to music than engage in physics, chemistry, biology, or mathematics, since the latter disciplines reveal only the world's outer shell, rather than its inner, driving impulse.

Like natural beauty, Schopenhauer regards science as limited to the metaphysical surface of things, no matter how spatially or temporally enormous or infinitesimal the objects of the scientific investigations happen to be. We might identify an elementary set of subatomic particles, but as objects, being aware of them is – from a metaphysical standpoint – no different from being aware of a rock, a book, a grain of sand, the moon, or someone else's hand as it rests on a table. Music and subjective experience alternatively provide access to the *interior* of things, and reveal the inner reality from which all objects, including subatomic particles, emerge into view as objects of awareness *per se*.

Since music is at the summit of the fine arts, musical composers and musicians enjoy a superlative status in Schopenhauer's aesthetic theory, for they either create new musical forms or newly interpret already existing forms through musical performance. Schopenhauer mentions that the artistic genius should create freely, without moral restriction, with an aim to idealize any subject matter for the sake of metaphysical knowledge and peaceful contemplation.[24] Composers should accordingly be free to write music that expresses any sector of the human emotional spectrum. In this way, the types of music that would consequently

---

[24] Nietzsche will reiterate this idea within his own idiom: "To represent terrible and questionable things is in itself an instinct for power and magnificence in an artist: he does not fear them … " (*The Will to Power*, §821 (March–June 1888), pp. 434–5).

come into existence would more accumulatively represent the quality of subjective reality that the human species has as a whole.

As noted, a particular advantage of having emotions presented within a musical form is the psychological distance and relative painlessness of the emotional expression. We could hear angry, violent, or aggressive music, understand more abstractly the vicious nature of these emotions, and yet not become consumed with anger, violence, or aggression ourselves. Conversely, a disadvantage to such abstracted expressions is that the abstractive process dilutes the emotions' disagreeable reality. It compares to how we can look at a photograph of a corpse or crime scene with great interest, or watch a war scene in documentaries with excitement, not realizing how we might be repulsed or terrified to the bone if we were to be in the physical presence of the corpse, crime, or actual firefight.

This ambiguity motivates Schopenhauer's departure from aesthetic awareness as a whole, as he regards musical experience as a stepping-stone to moral awareness. His philosophy is predominantly interested in advancing moral awareness and ultimately, a permanent, peacefully transcendent outlook on the world, as he turns away from the constant strife, fighting, anger, and aggression that the ordinary world contains. Schopenhauer champions artistic freedom, but this is for the sake of conveying the knowledge of what Will, the nature of the world, is like. He thus urges the moral independence of artists who, in their properly aesthetic portrayals of objectionable subject matters, paradoxically advance our awareness by allowing us to empathize with what is ordinarily distasteful, as if a door to an infernal realm were opened and we were allowed to gaze upon its interior from a safe distance. Hence follows the sublimity of the artistic genius, for, essentially siding with Aristotle, Schopenhauer believes that the aesthetic representation of horrible subject matters is beneficial, if it reveals those subjects sufficiently well to render their reality apprehensible.

On the other hand, Schopenhauer observes a deficiency – and one can say that this is a moral deficiency – in all traditional artistic representations insofar as they do not convey the full reality of the objects they portray. Even when actual objects, such as supermarket food items or human bodies, are presented as art, their ordinary meanings are transformed to a point where the impact they would otherwise have as ordinary objects is diminished. Although it is easy to believe that a corpse presented as a work of art (as some museums present Egyptian mummies) can allow us to contemplate the reality of death more effectively, what often happens is that the corpse is not seen respectfully as having been previously a living human being, but is regarded as a work of art to be contemplated with a measure of personal disengagement.

In such instances, the aesthetic distance that the artistic context generates does little to enhance our empathy, and this is particularly so for music: since the emotions musically expressed are detached from their concrete contexts, we do not experience love or anger, for instance, in relation to any actual person or event, but experience these emotions only as general forms. The larger philosophical and spiritual goal of Schopenhauer's theory, however, is to foster empathy for the sake of realizing what the nature of the world – and the nature of oneself – is violently like, and artistic representation can achieve this only to a limited extent. He consequently concludes his aesthetics and prepares his readers for an entrance into the more concrete realm of empathy – a disconcerting field where the torturer and tortured become one and the same person – with the image of Raphael's *The Ecstasy of St. Cecilia* (1514–16). Here, St. Cecilia, music's patroness, having set her musical instruments upon the ground to render them silent, looks skyward to a more sublime realm.

5. SCHOPENHAUER'S AESTHETICS IN HISTORICAL PERSPECTIVE

At the relatively young age of thirty, Schopenhauer published his views on art and beauty in 1818, as Book Three of *The World as Will and Representation*. This was almost thirty years after Kant's aesthetics (1790), twenty-three years after Schiller's (1795), simultaneous with Hegel's aesthetics, and at least twenty years prior to Marx's aesthetics (1840s and the decades following). Schopenhauer's irrationalist metaphysics of Will is nonetheless well ahead of its historical time, which renders his philosophy understandable as a successor to Marx in anticipation of Nietzsche – a philosopher known for his doctrine of the Will to

Power, and who, after reading Schopenhauer in the late 1860s, considered himself a Schopenhauerian for at least a decade thereafter. We can conclude our discussion with some reflections about how Schopenhauer's aesthetics not only looks forward into the twentieth century, but how it embodies earlier views, as it stands entrenched in the early to-mid-nineteenth-century mainstream. In these alternative respects, he is a fascinating and instructive transitional figure in the history of aesthetics.

Schopenhauer's inspiration is largely from Kant and Plato, and this lends a non-historical orientation to his philosophy, along with a traditional eye towards the apprehension of universal constancies that is common in the bulk of Western philosophy before the nineteenth century. We see this in the central place Schopenhauer assigns to the apprehension of Platonic ideas in aesthetic experience. This attention to Platonic ideas grounds a traditional account of art as the presentation of idealized images of things and themes, where the subjects appear rationalized in their best light. It remains that a large segment of fine art does not concern itself with the presentation of ideal types, and during the nineteenth century this preoccupation with ideal types slowly loses currency with the gradual emergence of modern art.

In accord with the spirit of his times, Schopenhauer retains a moral core to his philosophy, as do Kant, Schiller, Hegel, and Marx, not to mention an analysis of the arts that traces an upward path from inorganic nature, through the plants and animals, to the human being. He also conceives of art in a single-minded fashion, as if it had only one primary function that surpasses its many other possible functions. In Kant, Schiller, and Marx, art serves morality; in Hegel it serves metaphysics; in Schopenhauer, it serves the quest for salvation from suffering. Embodying a shared single-mindedness, the theme of aesthetic education operates in these theorists, where art and beauty are valued as a means to enhance people's awareness, whether it happens to be moral, social, metaphysical, or religious.

Despite his affinities with Kant, we also see in Schopenhauer an early challenge to the Enlightenment assumption that reason is the key to resolving every important issue. This finds expression as a resistance to any attempted assimilation of philosophy on the part of natural science. Schopenhauer overturns this naturalistic project by arguing that in conjunction with sheer introspection, aesthetic experience (especially the experience of music) provides metaphysical knowledge more effectively than could any science. Nietzsche would later develop the theme that art is preferable to science for doing philosophy.

Finally, Schopenhauer's irrationalist metaphysics of Will – one that he formulates a century before its time becomes historically ripe – only comes into fashion near the end of the nineteenth century and the beginning of the twentieth century. Contrary to Hegel and the nineteenth-century atmosphere of progress, Schopenhauer sees no historical development, no divine plan, no ultimate and glorious goal, and no grand narrative. His focus on irrational, metaphysical Will carries with it an attention to the unconscious, instinctual forces that drive us biologically and psychologically, and a door to theories such as Freud's.

It might remain an unfortunate aspect of Schopenhauer's aesthetics that, unlike Freud, and despite Schopenhauer's insightful association between genius and madness, Schopenhauer does not pursue the link to artistic creation and unconscious energies in his aesthetic theory sufficiently to dislodge the traditional account of art as a form of idealization. This is due to his having set Will's experiential turbulence directly against the peaceful stillness that he discovers in aesthetic experience. In this regard, Schopenhauer's aesthetics retains an otherworldly, non-historical emphasis consistent with the seventeenth-century spirit from which it emerges. This emphasis is a hardly blamable one, for this otherworldly aspect compares to how older parents' values infuse themselves into their young children, despite the differences in generations.

6

THE ART OF SUPREME HEALTH

Friedrich Nietzsche

1. THE PROBLEM OF NIHILISM AND THE WILL TO POWER

The perennial concern with how to live a meaningful life in the face of wars, suffering and death is among the determining features of Friedrich Nietzsche's philosophical outlook. We live, reproduce, and eventually die, creating more people that live, reproduce, and eventually die. Sometimes good, innocent people suffer terribly. Sometimes criminals enjoy comforts and riches. Wars do not conclude the violence or settle the fear and anger. At some point, humans, organic life, and the earth itself will physically disappear, rendering the question of life's meaning and the question of death's meaning essentially the same.

When taking the long view, a person might conclude that if there is no meaning or justification of human existence on an otherworldly, death-defying dimension, then there is probably no meaning at all, and that no ultimate and justifying end compensates for life's gamut of assorted joys, expectations, limited achievements, disappointments, and cruelties. Moreover, for someone disinclined to accept the presence of otherworldly realities, and who remains troubled by death's apparent emptiness, nihilistic despair can follow like a shadow.

Nietzsche's philosophy attempts to dissipate such hopelessness by prescribing attitudes appropriate to living in a continual springtime, carefree and inspired, in the absence of a grand, explanatory plan. His philosophy attempts to achieve a strong, healthy, and noble attitude in the midst of a losing battle against death, as it reflects upon life's inevitable return to the emptiness from which it emerged.

As a dedicated scholar of classical Greece – a culture that European intellectuals during the late eighteenth and nineteenth centuries admired as among the healthiest in human history – Nietzsche (1844–1900) is well placed to diagnose the source of the Greeks' supposed cultural health. After organizing his findings, he develops a remedy for the growing nihilistic despair he sees infecting his surrounding culture and himself. Throughout his career, the Greeks remain Nietzsche's model and inspiration for achieving a healthy attitude in the face of every kind of adversity, especially the metaphysical adversity of life's potential meaninglessness.

Nietzsche's preliminary account of the Greeks' cultural health – one that he formulates in the early 1870s – refers us to their fiercely competitive mentality, or *agon*, wherein one-upmanship, the thrill of battle, coupled with a sense of supreme self-assurance, if not self-glorification, are the ruling attitudes. This is not a bloodthirsty love for raw violence and heartless conquest, but a refined, athletic attitude where one values the game, the arena, and the opponents who competitively stretch their adversaries to their limits, pushing everyone to excel.

That health depends upon conflict is Nietzsche's steadfast conviction, but he transforms this idea as he matures, shifting its original focus on *agon* to an emphasis upon the quest, drive, passion, or will towards greater power. Nietzsche first employs the Will to Power to explain human behavior around 1880, in *Dawn*, and he soon uses it to account for all organic life around 1883, in *Thus Spoke Zarathustra*. Allowing his doctrine to express its own philosophical strength, he invokes it in 1885–86 in his notebooks and in *Beyond Good and Evil* to interpret the cosmos as a whole. It remains an open question whether Nietzsche believes that the Will to Power is the actual governing principle of things, or whether he accepts it merely as the healthiest way to interpret the world. With respect to understanding his aesthetics, these two options bear the same fruit.

A useful elementary image for understanding Nietzsche's notion of the Will to Power is that of any star, like our sun – a powerful entity from which light and other forms of energy creatively and constantly emanate. If we reiterate this image and draw an analogy, each individual would be like a small sun, and the set of individual things, like an immense collection of stars. Since individuals are physically situated close together in our daily lives, our immediate surroundings would compare to a set of closely packed stars, where each star's projection of energy inevitably and conflictingly comes into conflict with the projections of others.

The resulting world picture is a tension-filled domain of expanding, jostling, and conflicting forces, where larger, more powerful individuals outshine and overcome the smaller, less powerful ones, absorbing them into their spheres of influence, or pushing them out of their way. Each individual fades in power at some point, and gives way to others whose power has in the meantime grown. This exchange of energy establishes a great current of continual transformation, where particular loci of power intensify, weaken, and dissipate, only for the energy field to reconstitute itself into a new constellation of conflict. Beyond this powerful current, there is nothing.

Within this vision, being healthy is the expression of power's increase, and being sick is the expression of power's decline. Life-affirming attitudes are upbeat and healthy; life-negating attitudes are defeatist and infirm. Indeed, were a person to harbor doubts about life's meaning, the motivating feeling of emptiness would itself betray a lack of power to say "yes" to life, despite its pains, disappointments and death. Here, the very questioning of life's meaning is a manifestation of unhealthiness. Such is how we would interpret the world and people's perspectives in terms of Nietzsche's doctrine of the Will to Power.

Since Nietzsche's concern is with nihilism's debilitating effects on a person's total comportment towards life, it is natural for him to reflect upon the Greek art of tragic theatre to understand how the Greeks managed their experience of the world's existential terrors. He realizes how the realm of art is particularly significant for them, for, as Hegel observes as well, art does not reside at the periphery of their social life, but at its religious center. By examining ancient Greek tragedy, Nietzsche believes he can reveal the heart of Greek culture and of the problem of nihilism as they conceived it. Regarding the latter, he recites an exemplary Greek anecdote about the god Silenus, the voice of life's absurdity. Upon being asked what the best thing for humans would be, Silenus replies chillingly that it would have been best had humans never existed, and second best, if they were to become extinct as soon as possible.[25] In light of this paralyzing message, Nietzsche regards Greek tragedy as a supremely healthy reaction to the nihilistic death-threat that Silenus' attitude poses – a threat to which everyone must respond at one point or another.

2. NIETZSCHE'S THEORY OF ART AND TRAGEDY

Nietzsche presents his foundational account of classical Greek tragedy in his first book, *The Birth of Tragedy* (1872), situating it within an overall theory of artistic creation. He begins by describing art and the will to artistic creation as the fusion of two complementary ways to interpret one's experience and the world. The first is through an ecstatic psychophysical condition, where life's energies rise powerfully and expansively to generate feelings that are iconoclastic, unruly, and powerfully connected with our instinctual depths. The second is through a dreamlike mental state, where visions of more perfect, soothing, transcendent, and beautiful conditions render harsh reality's pain less disturbing. Introducing mythological representatives of these two attitudes, Nietzsche associates the ecstatic energies with the god Dionysus, and the idealizing energies with Apollo.

Nietzsche's characterizations tempt us to speak univocally of "the Dionysian" and "the Apollonian" energies and respective attitudes, as if each had a single meaning and value, but his presentations and valuations of each are internally tension-ridden,

---

[25] Nietzsche, *The Birth of Tragedy*, §3. The Silenus-Midas discussion to which Nietzsche refers appears almost verbatim in *Moralia*, by the Roman historian Plutarch (Vol. 1, "Consolation to Apollonius," section 27). The phrase also appears in Sophocles' *Oedipus at Colonus*, line 1224ff. The idea is found originally in Theognis' poetry (*Elegies*, line 425), which Nietzsche studied as part of his philological training at the University of Leipzig.

like aspects of a metaphor. Sometimes he prefers the Dionysian attitude over the Apollonian; sometimes he reverses his preferences. Sometimes he characterizes the Apollonian attitude in a positively soothing way; sometimes he presents it in a frighteningly violent way. He does the same for the Dionysian attitude.

The Apollonian attitude relates immediately to dreams and idealizations, but it also includes rationality. Part of the latter concerns how, for example, with respect to idealizing some given image, rationality operates in the process of artistically tempering the image's imperfections, smoothing out its contours, recomposing its elements to display a greater interdependency and organic unity. Rationality assists to beautify the image in accord with some ideal model. We can also beautify or "give style" to ourselves, as Nietzsche describes in §290 of *The Gay Science*, by minimizing what is unattractive, enhancing what is attractive, and composing the whole in accord with a single theme, namely, our ideal personality.

By associating rationality with the Apollonian attitude and by accepting Schopenhauer's description of rationality as a divisive force that produces the distinct, finite, and perpetually conflicting individuals of everyday experience, Nietzsche associates the Apollonian attitude not only with tranquillizing dreams, but with all that is individuated.[26] This links it to violence, suffering, pain, death, the threat of meaninglessness, and nihilism. The Apollonian attitude consequently has either angelic or demonic aspects, depending upon whether we refer to the soothing archetypes that rationality constructs in the process of idealization, or whether we refer to the daily world's logical articulation that rationality also produces, in conjunction with the world's suffering that follows in its wake. The first aspect parallels Schopenhauer's tranquil realm of Platonic ideas; the second, Schopenhauer's violent world of space and time as the objectified Will that feasts on itself – a world to which Schopenhauer also ascribes a dreamlike, unreal, status.

The Dionysian attitude has divine and demonic aspects as well, one of which we have mentioned, namely, the enthusiastically

---

[26] Schopenhauer's conception of rationality is presented in terms of the principle of sufficient reason, which for Schopenhauer includes mathematical, geometrical, and mechanical causality as structures of our daily experience.

expansive, feral, universalistic, creative, invigorating force of life that transcends an individual's death and redeemingly reabsorbs the individual into its universal overflow. This flood of life-energies also has a fiendish aspect insofar as it is chaotic and essentially meaningless. The latter truth is typically disturbing enough to require a veil, usually in the form of a meaningful, Apollonian, ideal-rich overlay that makes sense of the world and provides thereby a measure of stability, comfort, and security.

The result is a set of contrasts: the Dionysian attitude redeems in the form of life itself, into which we can ecstatically absorb ourselves, while it also debilitates as a meaningless flux; the Apollonian attitude redeems through its constellation of universalistic and inspiring idealizations, while it also debilitates in its rationalistic production of nightmarish suffering in the daily world. These tensions reveal the trickster-like quality of them both, and imply that discussions of the Dionysian and Apollonian attitude require some care to distinguish which aspect of the Dionysian or Apollonian attitude is under consideration. The image of the trickster is among the most fundamental in Nietzsche's thought, perhaps on a par with that of the energetic and overflowing sun, and it helps to explain why his views are often difficult to pin down in their conflicted quality.

Nietzsche accentuates a positive Dionysian dimension at its basis of Greek tragedy that relates to the tragedies' seasonal performance and musical content. These tragedies were presented during the springtime festival of Dionysus, and appreciating how the springtime atmosphere produces physiological and psychological elation, Nietzsche discerns a foundationally *life-affirmative* quality to the tragedies' seasonal context of performance. As winter passes into spring, the air becomes fresh, less chilly, more fragrant, and conducive to the feeling that life is once again on the ascent. The springtime strengthens the instincts, motivates reproduction, and instills a feeling of unity with the earth and its perennial life cycles.

Reinforcing this supportive natural atmosphere, Nietzsche identifies the tragedy's rhythmically voiced chorus as a further Dionysian element appearing within the tragic performance itself. The singers resonate expressively with the springtime resurgence of life, and operate as a unifying force that constitutes the theatrical base upon which the tragedy's particular, usually horrendous, details play themselves out. The overall theatrical result is the display of idealized, strong, larger-than-life individuals who suffer and die, often through bad luck, unfortunate character combinations and circumstances beyond their control, wherein the individuals' demise does not signify an ultimate end or defeat, as the entire scene floats upon the inspiring ocean of life itself.

Nietzsche conceives of the springtime atmosphere and musically attuned chorus as forces so reinforcing in their combination, that their expressive content consistently prevails over the suffering and death of the tragic heroes to lend an uplifting spiritual interpretation to the otherwise dreadful events. As individuals, we play the hero's role in our own ways, and death comes to us all. By witnessing the very best individuals' deaths on the tragic stage, with their great lives seeming so fruitless, while apprehending simultaneously how life's overwhelming presence flows supportively beneath their destruction, and appreciating thereby, or even directly feeling, how its rejuvenating forces underlie everyone's activity, we can experience a transcendent and redemptive awareness. This renders our personal finitude and eventual disappearance as individual personalities unproblematic, as we feel the continual inspiration that life itself imparts. The uplifting springtime quality is the Nietzschean key to Greek tragedy's therapeutic, life-affirming, nihilism-defeating value.

This experience compares in part to Schopenhauer's characterization of aesthetic experience during which we abandon our individuality and assume a universal personality in the contemplation of Platonic ideas. Within Nietzsche's rendition, the universality does not stem from the Platonic ideas, but from a more down-to-earth, naturalistic – but no less universalistic – notion of the world as a constantly recycling, living being. The latter is also reminiscent of Schopenhauer's conception of the totality of sentient beings with which we identify in moral experience. In effect, Nietzsche replaces Schopenhauer's aesthetic and moral experience with a nature-mystical union that yields a similar type of transcendence, and by doing so, he articulates an ecstatic aesthetics that inspires us to set aside our finite individuality to assume a universal aspect.

Concerned mainly with formulating a therapeutic alternative to his seemingly nihilistic surroundings, Nietzsche follows the neoclassical strategy – one that was more in vogue during the earlier part of the nineteenth century – of resurrecting classical Greek ideas for use within modern society as a way to invigorate the cultural environment.[27] Like a revolutionary leader, he calls out in the concluding sections of *The Birth of Tragedy* to institute a new, tragic culture and to celebrate, as a means to it, the healthy and inspiring music of Richard Wagner (1813–83), his then friend and father-figure.

Nietzsche's apothecary-like project of preparing remedies for his spiritually ailing culture prevails within his philosophical project as he matures, but as he approaches the end of the 1870s, his opinion of Wagner sharply declines, as does his confidence that modern culture's revival resides in a simple injection of Greek ideas. In the 1880s, Nietzsche advances the same health-related project, but more fittingly with the historical spirit of his own times. Instead of applying Greek mythology to inspire health, he creates his own mythology, and advances the health-inspiring doctrines of the Will to Power, Eternal Recurrence and the Superhuman.

3. ART'S REDEMPTIVE AND REVIVIFYING VALUE

As we have seen in earlier chapters, a leading feature of Nietzsche's nineteenth-century era is the more intense focus on history, on being down-to-earth, and on being incredulous towards other-worldly solutions to real-life problems. If we intensify this notion of being earthly, taking the idea of "otherworldly" to include even those solutions that aim to realize some ideal on earth, but in a distant, vaguely specified future or, alternatively, that try to reach back into times now past, then only the present survives as a possible scene of redemption. Once the present is regarded as

---

[27] Like Hegel, Nietzsche maintains that the best art – in Nietzsche's case, this is judged as the healthiest, rather than the most metaphysically appropriate art – was produced in ancient Greece, and that there was a decline thereafter. Both advance a "death of art" thesis whose versions can be informatively compared and contrasted. Unlike Hegel, Nietzsche believes that this supremely healthy art of the ancient Greeks can be resurrected.

pain-filled, accidental, and leading nowhere, however, it is easy to appreciate how nihilistic attitudes can emerge from the effort to be realistic, down-to-earth and focused ultimately on the here-and-now.

At this juncture, Nietzsche's characteristic philosophical problem is how to resist otherworldly solutions by remaining realistic in a strict, hardline sense, while not allowing his immersion in the contingency-filled present moment to stifle the production of an upbeat, healthy, life-affirming, if not redeeming, attitude. Since being realistic also entails preserving one's sense of individuality, and of acknowledging the presence of suffering and one's upcoming death, Nietzsche's earlier, metaphysically comforting and individuality-dissolving – and, according to his views in the 1880s, otherworldly – solution, inspired by Schopenhauer's aesthetics, no longer appeals to him. His love for Wagner and his music dissolves accordingly.

Part of Nietzsche's change of attitude towards Wagner's music issued from a harsh critique of Christianity that grew contemporaneously with his eroding friendship with Wagner. If one is intent upon affirming the world, and notices how unfair and violent it is, a dilemma arises: either we retain an allegiance to traditional moral values, recognize that they must be grounded on an otherworldly dimension and forego the effort to remain this-worldly, or we remain this-worldly, reject otherworldly dimensions and, with them, reject the only unconditional foundation morality seems to have. Taking the latter route, Nietzsche jettisons traditional moral values as expressed in the Ten Commandments, Judaism, and Christianity, and actively wages a "war" on them in the interests of health. Retaining his general style of evaluation in terms of health and sickness, now expressed in terms of strength and weakness, he attacks Christianity as an unhealthy and weakening outlook, portraying it as the leading source of the cultural ills that surround him.

Consistent with his earlier interest in stimulating a musical renaissance, although now favoring Rossini and Bizet in Wagner's place, Nietzsche distinguishes between healthy and unhealthy music, namely, music for the strong that invigorates and inspires, as opposed to "romantic" (that is, Schopenhauerian) music for the weak that pacifies, appeases, soothes, and consoles. Underlying this is the observation that creativity can issue from a sense of lack, hunger, and need, *or* from an opposing sense of powerful superabundance, where artistic creations overflow, like a shining sun or inexhaustible fountain. Assuming that an artist's motives are inevitably expressed in the artworks themselves, he presents the distinction between good versus bad art in terms of healthy versus sickening art, or as invigorating versus debilitating art.

Elaborating on a conception of the artist who creates from superabundance, Nietzsche states that such artists create from instinct, allow their sexual energies to flow freely, and are captivated by a creative frenzy. This inspired condition is compatible with being in pain, and with the idea that artists engage generally in a process of idealization. Nietzsche accordingly maintains that idealization is not a fundamentally rationalizing or mechanical process. Rather, it is visionary, where one imaginatively and intuitively draws out into explicit expression the meanings that an object or theme holds within itself implicitly, as in a process of midwifery.

During the 1880s – Nietzsche's final decade of intellectual activity – his vision of the world does not change dramatically from the nature-mystical stance he assumes in *The Birth of Tragedy*. He now theorizes it in terms of the Will to Power, continuing to recognize an extensive field of energy, structured in cycles, recurrences, and returns, and apprehending a creative, life-giving force within it that can be expressed in terms of circulating consolidations of power. The main difference in this later period is that Nietzsche attends more closely to life's details to the extreme point of peering concretely into every moment, with its sounds, textures, movements, colors, and feelings, all of which he infuses into the grand round of things. Life-affirmation amounts to saying "yes" to every experiential detail to include the sufferings, disappointments, unrealized potentials, and the rest of life's negativities.

This 1880s vision gives a greater weight to the more terrifying dimensions of the Dionysian perspective that Nietzsche first presented in the 1870s. He faces more explicitly that the universal field of energy has no intrinsic meaning, merely recirculates, and carries us along eternally in its mindless flow. Affirming life no longer involves the loss of individuality and absorption into the thrilling cosmic process, but involves embracing the never-ending presence of pain, suffering, death, birth, growth, strength and decline, triumph and failure, the great and the pitiful. To affirm life, we must affirm the good with the bad, without hoping to tip the balance permanently in favor of the good, without expecting wars to cease, without expecting starvation and disease, not to mention ordinary squabbling, domestic abuse, and petty crime to disappear in some ideal society to come.

Identifying with this hard and terrific realism is difficult, if only because it offends our hopeful sense of rationality. As evidence of Nietzsche's consistency, it is revealing that he does not frame this vision in rational terms, but presents it through *aesthetic* conceptions, saying that to affirm life's assortment of details, good and bad, is to beautify, that is, reinterpret, the world in one's own eyes. At the summit of life-affirmation, all of reality becomes beautiful in its eternal recurrence, not in a moral sense of beauty, but insofar as a holy, invigorating aura infuses into the world, extending to the world's most sickening features. Indeed, the aura must extend to these debilitating details if our world interpretation is to be absolutely health-inspiring. Everything that is touched by the supreme life-affirming attitude becomes sacred. Nietzsche's formula for life-affirmation consequently presents us with a religiously oriented and redemptive aesthetics, filled with mythological and alchemical associations to the Philosopher's Stone that changes lead into gold, and prisons into utopias.

Within this framework, Nietzsche identifies two grades of life-affirming aesthetics. One is for those with the most strength; the other is for strong people, but of a relatively weaker constitution. Those within the first group can wholly and joyously affirm the potentially depressing truth that the world, and one's life, is essentially hopeless and meaningless; those within the second can bear the difficult truth, but only through a thin veil that softens the nihilistic impact. The first group aligns with a purely Dionysian aesthetics; the second, with a Dionysian aesthetics tempered with an Apollonian veneer. Both involve idealization; both positively acknowledge pain.

Nietzsche's aesthetics of tragedy exemplifies the second, tempered aesthetic, since he claims that in the ideal artwork of this kind, the artist should maximize the Dionysian energies to the breaking point, bringing one to the very edge of the abyss, while adding, at that explosive point, a small dose of relieving rationality. The tragedies fit this sublime form, as they portray events in a theatrical, formalized manner – events that, if they were to occur in daily life, would be too terrible for most people to bear.

Nietzsche's prescription, mentioned above, that one should "give style" to one's character has the same tempered aesthetic form, since he suggests that we temper unsightly and distracting aspects, and accentuate attractive ones, so that one's personal character – whatever it might be – can shine through clearly as a matter of a single style. This is not a matter of psychologically repressing one's unsightly personality qualities – some of which might be difficult for a person to face explicitly – but of becoming aware of those aspects to render them tastefully within the context of an aesthetic whole. In this aesthetic, deceptions and lies are appropriate – for the lies constitute the aesthetic veil – as long as they contribute to a strong, invigorating, and inspiring appearance that reveals the deeper truth of one's character.

In the pure Dionysian aesthetic, we alternatively have situations portrayed or an attitude adopted where someone experiences a typically crushing degree of pain or suffering, with the strength to reinterpret the suffering to work in his or her favor. The suffering does not debilitate the person, but operates inspirationally to generate higher levels of achievement or endurance. The characters in Greek tragedies usually have their suffering produce further torment, often debilitating, as in the case of Oedipus. We speak here, however, and almost mythologically, of more superhuman characters who can absorb many polluted, weakening streams and yet remain clean, strong, inspired, and ambitious. Successful political, military, cultural leaders often approach his ideal, as did Caesar, Napoleon, and Goethe in Nietzsche's estimation. Such *relentlessly positive* people never give up, and fight hard to overcome whatever obstacle they face. Independently of his moral qualities and considered simply as a strong and steadfast character, Jesus would be a supreme example.

For Nietzsche, such powerful personalities are in principle capable of appreciating, and perhaps even adopting, the general aesthetic attitude that he advocates, which is to regard as beautiful what is necessary in things, to say "yes" to everything, to accept constructively what happens, as distasteful as it may be, and to make the world beautiful, acceptable, and welcome to oneself through this mode of interpretation. The aim is to appreciate what the world simply happens to be, and if it contains violence, weakness, degeneration, and death, the beautifying attitude would be to accept it wholeheartedly, rather than have it turn one nihilistically, bitterly, and unhealthily to stone, or to another dimension where redemption in a better world is imaginatively expected. This alienation-dissolving aesthetic attitude takes great strength, for whatever one finds difficult to digest about our world – whether it is the injustice, selfishness, greed, violence, weakness, complacency, foolishness, boredom, or suffering – Nietzsche prescribes that we adopt the attitude of the artistic genius, for whom no subject matter is foreign, and for whom no subject is absolutely resistant to an artistic, beautifying interpretation.

Nietzsche usually refers to this aesthetic attitude as a beautifying one, but it is more accurate to describe it as one that renders the world sublime, as he sometimes does, since the aesthetic experience includes suffering and pain. Neither, though, is sublimity the perfectly apt aesthetic category in this context, since in standard treatments of the sublime, the aesthetic experience arises from setting aside or ignoring the threat of death or pain. The concept of the sublime describes Nietzsche's 1870s aesthetic of tragic, metaphysical comfort reasonably well, but it does not capture the earthy spirit of his aesthetics of the 1880s. The latter does not expect us to set the pain or suffering aside, but encourages us more challengingly to confront and subsequently beautify the injustice, criminality, immorality, weakness, disappointment, or object of disgust. This aesthetic embrace renders the negative factors valid and legitimate phenomena within the world's train of ever-circulating events. This aesthetic – "terrific" in both senses of the word, one might say – is for the very few, as it maximally reintroduces the problem of beautifying immorality and, in effect, of overturning the prevailing tables of moral values.

4. NIETZSCHE'S AESTHETICS IN HISTORICAL PERSPECTIVE

Since Nietzsche is known as an iconoclast along almost every philosophical dimension, it is reasonable to expect his aesthetics to depart radically from the tradition he inherits. As we can see, his aesthetics of tragedy from the early 1870s nonetheless coheres with neoclassic attitudes, as does his long-lasting emphasis upon being down-to-earth, which accords with the nineteenth-century intellectual spirit in general, insofar as it anticipates later existential thought. Nietzsche's aesthetics is also one of idealization or perfection throughout, and this locates him within a centuries-long tradition where the presentation of ideal types is assumed to be aesthetic expression's goal. The peculiarity of Nietzsche's view is that he projects the perfection and satisfaction associated with idealized forms upon each and every (what would ordinarily be described as imperfect) detail of contingent existence.

To the extent that Nietzsche conceives of art in reference to whether it reinforces health or sickness, strength or weakness, his view remains as single-minded as the theorists we have examined so far, namely, Kant, Schiller, Hegel, Marx, and Schopenhauer, all of whom regard art as the means to some external end, whether it happens to be moral, social, or metaphysical. In each theorist we encounter distinctions along the lines of "good art vs. bad art," "true art vs. false art," or "genuine art vs. benighted art," where in each instance, the good art aligns with the favored moral, social, or metaphysical theory, and the bad art undercuts the favored theory's value system. Pure aesthetic values take second place to other values and render it possible within these theories for the finest art, judged exclusively in aesthetic terms, to become subject to sharp disapproval. Consistent with this, Nietzsche condemns Richard Wagner, Victor Hugo, George Sand, Émile Zola, Thomas Carlyle, Friedrich Schiller, and Dante Alighieri, among others, because he regards their art as unhealthy in various respects. This is similar to how Marxists condemn artworks that enthusiastically express capitalist values, no matter how high the works' pure aesthetic quality might be.

Despite his preoccupation with restoring, maintaining, and enhancing health, Nietzsche exhibits an art-critical sensitivity that counteracts this one-sidedness. His aesthetic judgments are impressively nuanced, and his usual approach to his subject matters is multi-aspected, as he reviews his given theme from alternative interpretive angles. This perspectivist attitude suggests a theory of interpretation – mostly implicit within Nietzsche's writings, since his nuanced and sophisticated art-critical observations always serve the external interests of health – that comes to fruition during the later twentieth century. His more independent thought is that there is no legitimately single and closed interpretation of any work, but only a cluster of intersecting and sometimes conflicting construals of meaning, each of which resonates with the others to generate more construals. We will see a temperate version of this in Hans-Georg Gadamer's theory of interpretation, and an extreme version in Jacques Derrida's.

We have already noted how this notion of multi-dimensionality of meaning appears in Kant's notion of an aesthetic idea, or rich aesthetic image. It also appears briefly in Schopenhauer's aesthetics, when he describes the complexity of the Platonic Idea of humanity, mentioning how its inexhaustible facets appear collectively in the variety of artworks and artistic media whose subject is the human being. It is also an artifact of Schopenhauer's philosophy as a whole, which he describes as a single thought examined through a series of different lenses, namely, epistemological, metaphysical, aesthetic, and moral.

The notion of interpretive multi-dimensionality has a more historically fruitful presentation in Nietzsche's theory, though, because he combines this idea with an understanding of artistic creation that emphasizes its instinctual quality. By associating instinctual expression with the production of multi-interpretable artistic displays, we have the seeds of a theory of art-as-dream-construction, suggested by Nietzsche's association of the Apollonian outlook with dreams, and which is more explicitly developed by Freud near the turn of the century.

In this Nietzschean connection with Freud, Schopenhauer's influence is stronger than one might imagine. The link between artistic creation and unconscious instinct resonates powerfully in Schopenhauer's metaphysics, where through us, unconscious Will objectifies itself creatively as the timeless world of Platonic ideas and of the daily world in space and time. By accepting Schopenhauer's metaphysics and by regarding reality itself as a kind of artist – and Nietzsche does both in *The Birth of Tragedy* – one arrives at the position that artists create through unconscious instinct.

This minor retooling of Schopenhauer's view precipitates within Nietzsche a departure from Schopenhauer's and the entire seventeenth- and eighteenth-century aesthetic tradition's emphasis upon disinterestedness as a necessary condition for a properly aesthetic attitude. As a standard feature of the disinterested aesthetic attitude, one encounters the directive to contemplate nude figures only after setting one's sexual desire aside, if one intends to appreciate the figures aesthetically. Nietzsche observes to the contrary that beautiful faces and bodies function fundamentally to inspire a desire to procreate, and that it is unnatural to regard them otherwise. He consequently associates art intimately with sexual desire, and if we add his emphasis upon multi-interpretability, we approach Sigmund Freud's psychoanalytic understanding of art, based on the model of dreams, which Freud conceives of in a multi-interpretable way.

Finally, and most radically, we should reiterate that Nietzsche's aesthetics legitimates as a matter of health and life-affirmation, the beautification of physically and morally repulsive subjects, for beautifying such subjects is a way of affirming them. Not only, then, does Nietzsche disrupt the tradition of aesthetic disinterestedness, he also breaks with the entrenched association between art and morality that pervades the eighteenth century and early nineteenth century. In its service to health, art forsakes its service to morality as it renders immoral and repulsive subjects holy. Again, the theoretical anticipation resides in Schopenhauer's avant-garde metaphysics that identifies an amoral, timeless, blindly striving Will at the basis of everything, much as Freud later describes the human unconscious, or "Id". As we have seen, what prevents Schopenhauer from amalgamating beauty with the nightmarish horrors of the Will's objectification in space and time, is his perception that aesthetic experience offers redemption on another, universalistic plane. Nietzsche's more earthly stance precludes this kind of transcendent aesthetics, and he accordingly replaces it with one that suffuses beauty directly into the very violence-filled world from which Schopenhauer seeks some spiritual relief.

The dance of death – an image seen frequently during the times of the plague – where skeletons dance the farandole, bear musical instruments, and sing happily along the path to their demise, is a characteristic image that expresses Nietzsche's amalgamation of aesthetic value and the world's nihilism-producing aspects. In its combination of song and death, it summarizes his Dionysian aesthetics, as it radiates the joy, laughter, and light-heartedness of the life-affirmer as it embodies the most life-negating point in human existence. Similar, and perhaps more disturbing, is the song-, sex- and death-fused image of the Sirens in Greek mythology, whose irresistibly beautiful singing, like a fire that fatally attracts an unsuspecting gnat, draws its admirers to their violent conclusion.

7

THE ART OF SUBJECTIVE INWARDNESS

Søren Kierkegaard

Søren Kierkegaard (1813–55) contrasts with the theorists we have described so far in at least three ways. First, he does not offer a traditional aesthetic theory that attends to the nature of the various arts and their interrelationships. Second, he is unlike traditional philosophers in how he signs his work: sometimes he signs his writings with a pseudonym, sometimes he uses a pseudonym in conjunction with his actual name, and sometimes he simply signs his actual name. Third, rather than expressing himself straightforwardly as a literalistic philosopher, he writes as a literary figure who, through an abundance of fictional constructions, creates a set of characters whose voices express alternative philosophical positions. Kierkegaard uses this more theatrical style to present competing outlooks on life, leaving it up to us to measure their respective values.

His writings seek to discover the meaning of Christianity as a kind of spiritual awareness, as this awareness contrasts with the socially instituted rituals, rules, and ministry of the established Christian Church. Recognizing a great difference between the masses of church-goers and the relatively rare, genuine Christians, he searches for an authentic Christian experience by exploring alternative lifestyles, wondering which will bring one closest to a true Christian standpoint. He aims for an attitude that approximates what Jesus might have experienced, which, if incorporated into oneself, would render one into a true Christian.

In the course of these investigations, three lifestyles emerge, all of which have an aesthetic dimension, and hence bear on issues in aesthetic theory. Since Kierkegaard's interests center mostly upon attitudes and lifestyles, his relevance to aesthetics is in the more subjectively oriented dimensions of aesthetics such as artistic creativity and the aesthetic attitude, although we will derive criteria for a "Kierkegaardian art" that will call to mind modern atonal music and jazz. These musical associations notwithstanding, his writings concentrate upon the literary arts, which lead him to reflect upon literature, literary creativity, and life's poetic dimensions. His field of interest is restricted, but he offers insights that resonate informatively with the aesthetic theories we have been examining, as well as with theories that emerge at the end of the century such as the "art for art's sake" movement and, more generally, modernism in the arts.

One of Kierkegaard's literary trademarks is his irony and wit. Having studied Hegel's dialectical philosophy when he was young, he assimilated the intellectual technique of constructing the opposite of any given position as a means to illustrate the limits of that given position. His discussions consequently develop by juxtaposing alternative views or contrasting interpretations of the same view. Kierkegaard never aims towards a dialectical synthesis, though, and he rejects the Hegelian project of developing a fullscale integration of opposites into any type of system. Instead, he mocks Hegel, his "System," and all systematic philosophy, content to perceive the world's disjointedness wherein perspectives remain clashing. When encountering a philosophical position, Kierkegaard frequently inverts the position through irony and comedy to remove its seriousness, and adopts a critical perspective on the position thereby.

An example is his treatment of the outlook made famous by Schopenhauer, which regards ordinary life seriously and pessimistically as a frustrating arena of unfulfilled desire, punctuated by brief episodes of satiation and ensuing boredom. Unlike Schopenhauer, for whom boredom is annoying, depressing, and debilitating, Kierkegaard presents boredom entertainingly as having a productive, comical, aesthetically interesting, and explanatory side. God was bored, and so God created the world; Adam was bored alone, and so God created Eve to provide some relief; Adam and Eve soon became bored as a couple and so they created their children; the resulting society then became bored, and so decided to build a tower to the heavens – a boring idea in itself, Kierkegaard submits, that soon bored everyone engaged in the architectural construction.[28] This is not exactly a philosophical argument against Schopenhauer, but it rhetorically leads us to question the truth of Schopenhauer's view as we lighten up on the oppressive atmosphere that Schopenhauer attaches to boredom.

In Kierkegaard's personally signed writings – these are his "religious" as opposed to his pseudonymously signed "aesthetic" writings – and also in his journal entries where we find him speaking more privately, he presents straightforward philosophical arguments, although they often remain touched with skepticism. With respect to the long-standing claim that art's purpose is to provide visions of eternal ideas or truths, he argues that the timeless cannot be portrayed in the temporal, precisely because it is timeless.

This relationship between the temporal and timeless is central to Kierkegaard's thought. In relation to the above argument, he observes that the painterly portrayal of the temporal is a falsifying activity, since the action that is momentarily frozen in the painting does not stop moving in reality. To make his point, he asks us to reflect upon the difference between perceiving someone blowing his nose, and a painting of that person blowing his nose. Whereas we can hear the sound of the actual nose blowing, the painting remains silent. While poking fun at the art of genre painting in the example, he also concludes soberingly that "all art is essentially involved in a dialectical self-contradiction."[29] The related, and paradoxical, assumption – again, Schopenhauerian – that a physical object can provide a vision of an eternal idea resonates with Kierkegaard's Christian concern about how paradoxical it is to assume that an eternal being (God) could instantiate itself in a temporally located human being (Jesus). Kierkegaard's argument against painting and sculpture is essentially the same one he advances against the coherency of Christianity.

We can appreciate Kierkegaard's talents as an author by recognizing his ability to regard any given perspective from an

---

[28] See Kierkegaard's *Either/Or*, Volume 1, "The Rotation Method – An Essay in the Theory of Social Prudence."

[29] This is from an entry in Kierkegaard's journals (A 88), dated 1847, when Kierkegaard was thirty-four years old (Kierkegaard, *The Last Years*).

objective distance, much in the way Kant describes the attitude of aesthetic disinterestedness, where we disengage from our personal involvement. Kierkegaard is inspired here by the image of the actor that he finds in a passage from Schopenhauer – an actor, who, having played his initial scenes according to a script that has his character dying during the last act, takes an interim seat in the audience to watch the play unfold towards his character's theatrical demise.[30] Like a playwright or director of a marionette theatre, as some have described Kierkegaard, he often presents his books and their respective characters through a variety of pseudonyms, sometimes with autobiographical content, as when he speaks of his own romantic relationship with his fiancée in real life, Regine Olsen, or through fictional characters, as if he were a playwright writing about his own life, or about what he called his "education in Christianity."

Kierkegaard mentions in his private journals that one of his pseudonyms – Johannes Climacus, the nominal author of *Philosophical Fragments* (1844) and *Concluding Unscientific Postscript to Philosophical Fragments – A Mimetic-Pathetic-Dialectic Compilation, An Existential Plea* (1846) (a text which contains a fundamental treatment of truth "as subjectivity") – expresses the true Christian standpoint. Along with Climacus, Kierkegaard lists himself as the editor of these two works, and one can discern their transitional, "coming out" nature as they stand chronologically between the earlier aesthetic writings such as *Either/Or* (1843) and the later, distinctively religious works that extend until his death in 1855. Despite these authorial contrivances, it remains that Kierkegaard often maintains a psychological distance from his writings' contents, as well as a playful attitude which includes self-parody.

This theatrical attitude contrasts with the other thinkers we have so far considered, and relates in a complicated way to

---

[30] The reference is from *The World as Will and Representation*, Volume I, §16. Regarding Schopenhauer's own character as an "actor," we can read that after a week of merrymaking with Schopenhauer when the latter was seventy years old, M. A. Weill concluded that Schopenhauer was no pessimist and that his pessimism was an "act" (Weill, "Schopenhauer Only an Actor"). Kierkegaard had a similar opinion, stating that Schopenhauer was "not a radical pessimist" (Kierkegaard, *The Last Years*, "Arthur Schopenhauer," XI^{1}A, 537, p. 171).

Schopenhauer, who also derives insight from the idea of adopting a theatrical distance from the world. For Schopenhauer, distancing oneself is nothing less than a life strategy for salvation, arising at one of the most profound moments of his philosophy. This is where he stands ascetically apart from life's daily events and regards the world at a supreme distance – a disengagement expressed by the Buddhist Wheel of Life, an image wherein the god of death holds up the daily cycles of suffering to view, advising us all to detach for the sake of enlightenment and the relief of suffering. In Kierkegaard's hands, the same thespian attitude has a more nuanced quality, as it provides him with a literary device to express a series of contrasting lifestyles or basic outlooks, while it also gives him the ability to step back from those perspectives for the purposes of critical evaluation.

The three perspectives that Kierkegaard sets against each other are aesthetic, ethical, and the religious. As is true of Hegel's conceptions of art, religion, and philosophy, Kierkegaard's aesthetic, ethical, and religious perspectives can be interpreted either as phases of a three-phase developmental sequence, or, more realistically, as mentalities that can be adopted at any particular time or place and that can be simultaneously operative within any particular person in different proportions and intensities.

His three perspectives coincidentally match Schopenhauer's own stepwise path to salvation, and although Kierkegaard refers to himself in his journals as an "inversion" of Schopenhauer (even going so far as to play upon their respective initials, "A.S." and "S.A." [Søren Aabye]), he did carefully study Schopenhauer's *The World as Will and Representation* near the end of his life – a book that begins its path to enlightenment with aesthetic awareness, advances to moral awareness, and culminates in religious asceticism. Working independently, Kierkegaard defines the three phases differently, emphasizing their *disjointed* relationship to each other, and does not recognize them as three aspects of a single thought, as does Schopenhauer. He also punctuates his expositions with a levity that reaches moments of hilarity, also absent in Schopenhauer. One is tempted to introduce Nietzsche here as a kind of dancing spirit, who always urges us to be lighthearted, but Kierkegaard's humorous approach renders Nietzsche relatively heavy and serious in contrast. His irreverence expresses a joviality and great sense of comedy, as mocking and ironic as it can sometimes be.[31]

The aesthetic, ethical, and religious outlooks correspond to the attitudes often associated with different chronological ages, namely, youth, middle age, and older age, and if we appreciate this, the decisions about which outlook to adopt will *prima facie* depend upon our own perceived psychological age. They will also depend upon our philosophical assumptions concerning the relative values of those age-related perspectives. Some will assume that youthful attitudes are preferable. The value accorded to staying young at heart is an example, also evident in the nostalgic desire to return to the ancient Greeks, or to return similarly to the days of the noble savage. Alternatively, others will assume that as one grows old, wisdom increases. Yet others will assume that middle age marks the peak of development, with youth as a prelude, and old age as a phase of organic decline into inevitable senility. Kierkegaard never wholly sacrifices the aesthetic and ethical lifestyles, but his interest in Christian subjectivity prevails, and this disposes him towards the outlook of an older person. It is remarkable that he expresses it so well in his thirties and forties, given his death at the relatively young age of forty-two.

The aesthetic outlook correlates well with a less mature, almost adolescent, fascination with sexual conquest, pure sensory experience, and the testing of one's social powers; the ethical outlook correlates with a more socially respectable and steadfast marriage, family, and rule-respecting domesticity; the religious outlook involves a more retired, reflective, mystical orientation towards God, seeking answers to life's philosophical questions.

Kierkegaard does not draw the connection, but the contrast between his ethical and religious outlooks resembles the difference between Confucian and Daoist attitudes in Chinese culture. After leading a respectable family-centered social existence during one's early and middle age as a good Confucian, one may

---

[31] To put Kierkegaard's sense of humor in perspective, it helps to recall that death loomed large in his consciousness. His early life was punctuated tragically by repeated deaths in the family, namely, at age six (a brother), age eight (a sister), age nineteen (a sister), age twenty (a brother), age twenty-one (a sister and his mother) and age twenty-five (his father). By the time he was twenty-five, seven members of his family had died, including his parents.

later retire to a peaceful forest, mountaintop, or similar retreat, to contemplate Daoistically the cosmos and one's universal place in the grand scheme of things. This cross-cultural comparison reveals that Kierkegaard's identification and discussion of the three outlooks is not idiosyncratic; it reflects basic issues that we all face as our lives unfold.

1. THE AESTHETIC OUTLOOK

As a matter of lifestyle, a person can be sensory-enmeshed and excessively this-worldly, where immediate and anticipated pleasures are of absolute value. Kierkegaard describes varieties of this aestheticist attitude, the predominant one of which involves a measure of selfish disengagement from other people's concerns, an underlying, if repressed, sense of hopelessness, a desperate aversion to boredom, a game-like approach towards social interactions, a love of devilish novelty, a premium upon connoisseurship in one's most mundane activities, and a condescending and manipulative attitude towards others. This aesthete is ultimately alone in his (or her) quest for enjoyment and, as a fundamentally unreliable character, is unwilling to develop long-lasting friendships, romantic relationships, or social commitments.

As Kierkegaard describes him, this selfish aesthete is a free spirit, and seems to have no need, and expresses no desire, to hold a steady job, lest this transform him into "Mr. Anybody." As such, the selfish aesthete is immune to the attendant pressures that require one to sacrifice a measure of freedom for the sake of adapting to the social order. The selfish aesthete also carries a subtle air of decadence, associated sometimes with those who are socially idle, where the need for entertainment and fear of boredom can become characteristic of people with empty time on their hands. Kierkegaard's own situation was financially comfortable, and he understood the temptations that such an aestheticist lifestyle presents.

Kierkegaard's selfish aesthete is also elitist, priding himself on his ingenuity and superiority in comparison to other, more ordinary, aesthetes. Whereas the ordinary aesthete changes his or her activities and locations as boredom sets in, the elitist aesthete exercises and cultivates his or her imagination to produce new and entertaining interpretations of the same setting. Kierkegaard gives the example of an unbearable acquaintance, namely, a philosopher who perspires excessively upon engaging boringly in his or her usual philosophical monologue, who the elite aesthete discovers how to render more tolerable. Finding it laughable to watch the beads of sweat slowly accumulate and drip down the acquaintance's nose, the aesthete encourages discussion upon every occasion to indulge in his or her privately mocking entertainment.

With respect to aesthetic theory, this method of relieving boredom illustrates a wider principle: our experience is inherently multi-interpretable. The elitist aesthete applies this principle to life, which bears equally upon artworks or texts. In every case, it requires imaginative effort to devise alternative interpretations to standardly encountered situations, especially if the new interpretations are to be innovatively meaningful, entertaining, or profound. Kierkegaard characterizes the imaginative efforts as containing an air of manipulativeness on the aesthete's part, as the aesthete prescribes rules for living that approach the world as if it were a toy with which one can play.

The aesthete's new interpretations nonetheless express new ways to appreciate one's surroundings, and this requires a disregard of established social meanings insofar as these obstruct more entertaining interpretations. The elitist aesthete is an *artist of life* in this respect, using surrounding events and people as materials to transform his experience into a personal theatre, as if he were the artistic director and manager of his surrounding social context. Implicit is an underlying theory of interpretation, where life – or, by implication, an artwork or text – has no single, intrinsic, true meaning, and where the critic, or reader, assumes as much interpretive power as the artist or author. This interpretive outlook respects no God's-eye perspective, or essential truth to the situation. Everything remains open to revision and interpretive manipulation, where the leading aesthetic criteria are ingenuity, enjoyment, play, and an avoidance of boredom.

This Kierkegaardian aesthete is ethically non-committed, and among the philosophical outlooks we have surveyed so far, this aesthete has made the greatest departure from recognizing a close association between art and morality – an association clearly upheld by Kant, Schiller, Hegel, Marx, and, to some extent, Schopenhauer. Nietzsche dissolves the connection, but he does so for the sake of health, which he regards as naturally more important than morality. The Kierkegaardian aesthete's moral offensiveness is more insulting, since morality here disengages from art for the mere sake of the aesthete's personal enjoyment. Displaying this well is the seducer – another of Kierkegaard's instantiations of the selfish aesthete.

In the first volume of *Either/Or*, Kierkegaard develops this character in "Diary of a Seducer." The seducer is a devilish beast of prey with the most civilized veneer, who, as the diary describes the episode, initially sets his eyes and desire upon a young woman who happens to pass him by on the street one day. Attracted, he immediately follows the woman to learn what he can. As the days follow, the seducer makes sure that he informally crosses paths with the woman, posing at first as an innocent and uninterested person. In a methodical fashion, he soon discovers her name, family situation, and overall social standing. Gradually increasing the frequency of his encounters and conversations to become a casual presence in her life, he eventually befriends her boyfriend, participates in the boyfriend's separation from the woman, only to locate himself in the boyfriend's place, slowly transforming the tone of his relationship to a more intimate one. As he advances the romance to solidify it in a formal engagement with the woman, the seducer then manipulatively changes his tone to play hard-to-get, expressing doubts about the engagement, hoping thereby to stimulate the woman's sexual desire. He then culti-vates her desire to the point where she becomes desperate to offer him her sexual favors for the sake of securing the contracted relationship and preserving her honor. Now in possession of her very soul, the seducer sexually consummates the relationship, breaks off the engagement the next day and moves on to his next conquest. The seduction lasts several months, all planned from the very start, including the final breakup.

This seducer does not derive his primary enjoyment from the sexual consummation, for this is only a brief experience within the elaborate, months-long seduction. His enjoyment derives from the detailed manipulation of other people and the sense of invasive power it involves. The seducer is not content with simply experiencing a sexual union with the young woman, as might happen more casually and with less personal commitment, but concentrates his energies upon securing her deepest confidence and trust in view of betraying her, which takes longer and is more of a challenge. The aims are more immoral, essentially hateful, spiritually intrusive and appropriative. As Kierkegaard portrays him, the seductive character is socially charming, pleasantly attractive, apparently inoffensive on the surface, while being, underneath, scheming in his inherent falsity towards everyone.[32] To complete the perfect seduction, the seducer aspires to escape smoothly from his complicated web of manipulations via legitimate excuses, without anyone discovering the stage-set upon which they had been his unwitting players.

The aesthetic quality of the seducer's pleasure stems from the personally disengaged attitude he adopts and his assumption of life as a stage, or as susceptible to becoming transformed into a work of dramatic genius, even if the constituent episodes are domestic and localized. Rather than using this aesthetic distance to generate wisdom, as one encounters in the Schopenhauerian or Buddhist applications, aesthetic distance offers an opportunity to plunder the world for personal enjoyment. This is not an aesthetic of "living exclusively for the present moment" in a pure sense, where considerations of future and past fall away from consideration to leave only the "eternal now." To the contrary, the seducer plans elaborately and looks months ahead as he constructs an enjoyable game for himself. The seducer's satisfaction resides in the game's manipulative meanings – as if he were a playwright, painter, or sculptor – that transform life into a work of art of which he is the author.

In contrast to the elitist aesthete and seducer, Kierkegaard describes yet another kind of aesthetic outlook, albeit briefly. We find this in *Repetition: An Essay in Experimental Psychology, by Constantin Constantius* (1843) where he portrays an aesthete, who, at one culminating point, enjoys a quasi-mystical aesthetic

---

[32] Kierkegaard's criticism of the seducer's personal falsity and manner of turning life into art bears some close similarities to the way Hegel criticizes the German romantic ironists (namely, Schlegel, Solger, and Tieck) in the introduction to his *Lectures on Fine Art*. Kierkegaard was familiar with these *Lectures* and one can read Kierkegaard's aesthetic writings as inspired by, and as a critique of, the same romantic ironists.

experience. This is being perfectly content with the present moment alone, feeling at home in the world, having a feeling of lightness and gliding in one's walk, and perceiving an agreeable transfiguration of all commonplace details, including those that are ordinarily disgusting.

As in the other varieties of Kierkegaardian aesthetic outlook, a traditional moral component is lacking, but its absence is not offensive in this instance, since an overwhelming holiness that permeates all of existence compensates for the lack, much as how Nietzsche's experience of life-affirmation informs his doctrine of Eternal Recurrence. This third, "life-transfiguring" aesthete contrasts sharply with the elitist aesthete and seducer, and illustrates a more appealing way to live aesthetically, namely, in the experience of perfect contentment, or of organically unified "perfect moments," as Jean-Paul Sartre describes the experiences almost a century later, almost verbatim, in his novel, *Nausea* (1938). Although attractive, this life-transfiguring aesthete ultimately suffers as the outlook betrays an underlying discontent. Exactly like Sartre's character, Roquentin, who falls subsequently into a state of nausea, Kierkegaard's transfiguring aesthete falls into an abyss of despair when his perfectly contented experience ends, leaving him to wonder sadly whether he will ever experience such an elevated moment again.

2. THE ETHICAL AND RELIGIOUS OUTLOOKS

Kierkegaard's own relationship to the aesthete's outlook is complex, since he neither abandons it entirely, nor disavows its magical attraction. He does realize its spiritual emptiness, however, and in the ethical personage of "Judge William," he observes how the selfish and seducing aesthete leads a loveless life. Speaking from the ethical standpoint, Judge William maintains that love is essential to happiness, and that true beauty aligns with love, especially a love embodied in a happy marriage. Such a marriage also stands allegedly as an absolutely satisfying endpoint to life, where love and beauty generate a sense of eternity that permeates one's world in an amalgamation of the timeless and the temporal. Kierkegaard reflects upon the illusoriness of such a perfect love, reciting once again his argument that a fusion of the eternal and the temporal is contradictory. He admits, though, that those couples who can create such an illusion for themselves are living in a truly poetic manner. Indirectly acknowledging the psychological appeal of traditional accounts of art that define it as the presentation of ideal types, he remains skeptical about their truth.

We can appreciate this skepticism – not only about the aesthetic validity of marriage in its dreamlike immersion in beauty and love, but also about the implied possibility of portraying eternal truths in the visual arts – in reference to Kierkegaard's own solution to the philosophical problem about how the eternal can mesh with the temporal. As mentioned, this problem is at the core of Kierkegaard's thought, and it is also the central Christian problem: how can an eternal God materialize historically into a human being in the form of Jesus, or more generally, how can an eternal God be present within any of us, such as to render us into Jesus-figures and true Christians? From an objective standpoint, Kierkegaard maintains that such an amalgamation is absurd, and he turns away from all philosophical-logical attempts to explain how this contradiction can make sense.

At the beginning of his discussion of "Truth as Subjectivity" in *Concluding Unscientific Postscript*, Kierkegaard insists that "God is a subject" and "exists only for subjectivity in inwardness." He maintains that it is an error to believe that God exists outside of us, objectively, as the moon exists at a distance from the earth, or even as we might hypothesize some unknowable mind-independent thing-in-itself to exist. In precisely this respect, traditional proofs of God's existence are misguided in their assumption that God is a mind-independent being.

The only way to apprehend God is to allow God's everlasting subjective presence to shine through from one's inner depths. This, for Kierkegaard, is the only way to touch the invisible and the intangible divine realm – a realm alien not only to the objective world that science describes, but to all forms of art that depend heavily upon material embodiments. Hegel describes the death of art as a consequence of the intensification of subjectivity, and Kierkegaard maximally intensifies the experience of subjectivity. If any kind of art can express true Christian awareness, it will be romantic art in Hegel's sense.

3. CONCLUSION

Kierkegaard criticizes the aesthetic outlook chiefly in reference to the elitist aesthete and the seducer, reminding us of its magical attractiveness and spiritually dangerous emptiness. At one point, he even associates the aesthetic outlook with sinfulness, not primarily on account of its immorality, but on account of its exclusive and misguided orientation towards the external world, which is the very opposite of where Kierkegaard believes one's spirituality and Christian consciousness should reside. To this extent, all views that ignore the importance of becoming subjectively self-aware are sinful in their external orientation. Although captivated by this inwardly religious outlook, Kierkegaard also realistically acknowledges that it is impossible to live in complete denial of one's physical urges, as if a sinless condition were possible. His realistic compromise is to keep the aesthetic outlook in control and to subordinate it to the religious outlook, rather than eradicate it.

Kierkegaard's brief and alternative characterization of the transfiguring aesthete's experience does, however, anticipate a position that develops at the end of the century. This calls for art's autonomy and absolute freedom from moral constraint and is expressed in the "art for art's sake" movement, much of whose original inspiration stems from Walter Pater's *Studies in the History of the Renaissance* (1873). Pater concludes that work by stating that the leading purpose of art, wisdom, beauty, and poetic passion is to stimulate an awareness where one extracts nothing but the highest quality from one's passing moments, simply for the sake of those moments. With respect to its intensity, individuality, and self-sufficiency, this can be appreciated as an objectively focused, sensory experience preliminary to the subjective inwardness that Kierkegaard defines as characteristic of the genuinely spiritual consciousness. It does, though, lack a dimension of anxiety, crucial choice, and paradox for it to count as an objective correlate to the spiritual experience Kierkegaard intends with his notion of truth as subjectivity.

Although works of art may only be able to express this truth as subjective inwardness in an approximate manner, we can nonetheless extrapolate a set of aesthetic values that such Kierkegaardian artworks would satisfy. We are thinking here of a

Kierkegaardian aesthetic, modeled along the stylistic lines of Kant, Schiller, Hegel, Marx, Schopenhauer, and Nietzsche, all of whom define ideal art in reference to values that stem from their respective epistemological, metaphysical, social, and psychological theories. It is noteworthy – not to mention surprising, given that Kierkegaard was writing mainly in the 1830s and 1840s – how Kierkegaardian aesthetic values transmit a distinctively modern tone, comparing well with how Schopenhauer's irrationalist metaphysics published in 1818 was similarly a century ahead of its time.

Kierkegaardian works of art would first of all employ more intangible artistic materials, such as sound or words, typical of literature, or perhaps more intensely, music, as opposed to the more palpable artistic materials of architecture, sculpture, or painting. These preferred materials and art forms would be intensely romantic in Hegel's sense, as noted. Such works would also embody paradox, if not contradiction, to confound our literalistic and scientific approaches to objective, truth-seeking interpretation, and aim to defy attempts to capture their meaning in a single conceptual and definitive sweep. Kierkegaardian artworks would accordingly be anti-systematic and highly individualized, and would self-consciously lack organic unity. This would preclude their beauty in any traditional, rationalistic, or idealizing sense. They would also convey a sense of human finitude, and would precipitate a feeling of anxiety in the face of profound uncertainty.

Good examples might be instances of non-harmonious, grating, difficult-to-follow modern music that puts its listeners into a state of emotional discomfort and inward reflection, as that of the early twentieth-century atonal music of the Second Viennese School. In the same vein would be the screeching, disturbing, and yet spiritually oriented jazz in the work of John Coltrane, as in the 1965 album, *A Love Supreme*. Such works are rarely associated with the "aesthetic" outlook, so frequently discussed in connection with Kierkegaard's writings, but they come close to expressing the genuine Christian consciousness that Kierkegaard spends his life attempting to discover and convey in these writings.

Despite the manifest dissociation between art and morality in Kierkegaard's writings in connection with the aesthetic outlook, this dissociation does not express his final standpoint. A stronger connection between art and morality derives from his association of the external, scientific, materialist outlook with sinfulness. Subjective inwardness relates to holiness, albeit an anxiety-infused type of holiness akin to a suffering Jesus-figure, and with subjectively oriented art, it stands opposed to science.

The Kierkegaardian subjective thinker would become an artist to himself by expressing externally what his genuine Christian consciousness calls forth in action. The subjective thinker lives poetically by becoming explicitly or manifestly what he implicitly or inwardly is. This reflects Schopenhauer's notion of acquired character, where one molds one's behaviors and attitudes in accord with the knowledge of one's character. Insofar as one realizes oneself well and becomes a good person thereby – that is, "good" in the sense of "self-realized" – there is a sense in which moral considerations are not foreign to Kierkegaard's religious rendition of living poetically, understood as the honest effort to express oneself as an authentic person. It amounts to constructing one's life to express a genuine Christian consciousness, as if one were an anxiety-ridden Jesus-figure.

8

THE ART OF UNCONSCIOUS DESIRE

Sigmund Freud

1. ART AND THE UNCONSCIOUS

In his *New Introductory Lectures on Psychoanalysis* (1933), Sigmund Freud (1856–1939) criticizes Marxist approaches to art by observing that detailed records of economic conditions do not capture long-term psychological continuities.[33] He accordingly prefers a psychoanalytic perspective that reveals mental structures and processes, most of which are unconscious, that hold steady across the ages and that inform our understanding of individual and social awareness. Earlier writers such as Jean Paul (1763–1825) and Eduard von Hartmann (1842–1906) had referred to the human unconscious as an "inner Africa," but Freud, an explorer in his own right, provided useful maps of its terrain. His subterranean path – one that runs beneath the rationalistic enthusiasm for progress and rational development popular during the nineteenth century – emphasizes instinct, irrationality, and the unconscious.

Like Marx, whose materialism emphasizes how we labor upon our natural environment to produce food, shelter, and basic goods for survival, Freud is keenly aware of our survival instinct,

---

[33] Freud, *New Introductory Lectures on Psychoanalysis*, p. 60.

and as one of its fundamental aspects, our interest in reproducing the species. The reproductive drive is natural, infused into our psychological and physical constitution, and powerful enough to precipitate aggressive territoriality and murder. It centrally pre-scribes the contents of entire life-projects, and is essential to the construction of the social fabric through the sexual attractions and intense pleasures it generates, as well as through feelings of human meaning expressed in the form of love and interdepen-dency. As a working psychiatrist, Freud specifically devotes his attention to understanding human sexuality and its relationship to mental disorder, but his investigations reveal more broadly how our instinct for survival involves the powerful drive to repro-duce ourselves, and hence our sexuality. Marx and Freud can accordingly be appreciated as complementary thinkers insofar as they both understand the human being in reference to survival-related activities: Marx attends to the acquisition of food, shelter, and material needs; Freud attends to sexual reproduction. Marx focuses on our outer, practical life; Freud focuses on our inner, instinctually expressed, psychological life.

In accord with the biologically oriented dimension of the nineteenth-century spirit, Freud adopts a developmental approach to sexuality that examines our sexual energies as they begin in infancy, extend through childhood, intensify in adolescence and transform into adulthood. Departing from his society's common belief, his conviction is that sexual energies and drives are present from the moment of birth as unconscious energies, desires, and drives. His conception of sexuality is non-historical in this respect, and he describes the central sector of the unconscious, which he calls the "Id," as having a timeless quality, where logic and morality are absent, and where conflicting impulses stand side by side in a chaotic amalgam.[34] As these primitive, infantile energies remain dynamically and unconsciously in place, we slowly mature, become socialized and, in the majority of cases,

---

[34] "Id" is the Latin word for "it" (that is, "object"), signifying an alien part of our psyche. Freud's earlier (c.1900) model of the mind has two main divisions, the "conscious" and the "unconscious," interfaced by a "preconscious" level of awareness; his later model (c.1923) has three divisions, the "ego," the "superego" and the "id," each of which has unconscious aspects. For a concise characteriza-tion of the Id, see Freud, *New Introductory Lectures on Psychoanalysis*, pp. 65–6.

focus our widely dispersed, or polymorphously directed, energies more narrowly and socially acceptably into the constellations of standard sexual behavior.

According to Freud, our infantile sexual energies are indiscriminate and amorphous, and do not distinguish between the sexes, humans and animals, animate or inanimate objects, or different parts of the body. Any aspect of the environment can become the object of infantile sensuous pleasure. Although in the mature adult, for example, sexual attractions between humans and animals are significantly unorthodox, infantile sexuality does not recognize such social restrictions. When such energies become expressive in the adult mind, the adult suppresses them, owing to their foreignness to civilized society's rules. The same holds for incestuous thoughts and, to a lesser degree, fetishistic and homosexual thoughts.

Like an inner fountain, our unconscious drives push for expression, but owing to their polymorphously sexual, morally problematic, and sometimes violent nature – as when one desires to kill a parent of the same sex to join sexually with the parent of the opposite sex, as Freud describes in the Oedipus Complex – they are constrained by psychological mechanisms whose function is to preserve a more civilized and morally governed condition. This more controlled state is also essential to our survival as we need to cooperate in group-related activities. On Freud's model, one aspect of the mind works against another to keep the unconscious energies from destructively and selfishly overflowing, and to allow for their healthy ventilation.

The process of dreaming is one of the leading psychological mechanisms that allow our instinctual urges safe expression. When we dream, we express unconscious desires – the majority of which involve sexual or violent content that would make us shudder, if apprehended in their raw, animalistic state – in a disguised form that is acceptable to our conscience, or superego, as Freud calls our self-critical, supervisory, society-respecting persona. The process of transforming such disturbing, anxiety-producing, content into a more acceptable form involves, for instance, (1) substituting symbolic imagery (for instance, towers or doorways) for explicit images of sexual body parts, (2) relocating troubling images to the dream's semantic periphery, and (3) connecting the dream events together into a pleasing narrative to render the experience more rationally constructed, coherent, and satisfying.

These techniques of disguise operate as a self-protective mechanism, effectively to deposit a candy-coating upon a distasteful and potentially upsetting psychological substance – a substance that would otherwise disturb our sleep and lead possibly to fatality if left unchecked. Freud's theory states that as part of our instinctual human constitution, we unconsciously desire to commit murder and incest, along with a wide variety of unacceptable social behaviors, and that for our health's and society's sake, the explicit versions of these desires need to be kept at a safe distance from our immediate consciousness.

Artistic production functions like dream production, and artworks are interpretable through the same methods that psychoanalysis uses to interpret dreams. It is common knowledge that artists have powerful imaginations, and Freud's specific understanding is that when an artist creates a work of art, he or she taps into the unconscious and allows its energies to come forth, much as occurs when dreaming. Artistic creation is for Freud a kind of daydreaming. The resulting images consequently have the disguising qualities of a dream insofar as they give the anxiety-producing unconscious content a more socially acceptable presentation.[35] Nietzsche speaks of how artists apply such a disguising or tempering veneer when he associates the Apollonian artistic attitude with dreams and refers to it as a veil that renders palatable the otherwise Medusa-like quality of raw, violent, and debilitatingly meaningless existence that plagues everyone, and which artists try to manage aesthetically. The Medusa-like quality that Nietzsche calls "Dionysian" and the true "witches' brew" corresponds to the Id's infantile, amoral, sex-and-violence-filled desires that Freud accentuates in his own theory.[36]

---

[35] Freud writes: "If a person who is at loggerheads with reality possesses an *artistic gift* (a thing that is still a psychological mystery to us), he can transform his phantasies into artistic creations instead of into symptoms. In this manner he can escape the doom of neurosis and by this roundabout path regain his contact with reality" (*Five Lectures on Psychoanalysis*, Fifth Lecture, p. 50).

[36] Foreshadowing Freud, Nietzsche also states that "the demand for art and beauty is an indirect demand for the ecstasies of sexuality communicated to the brain" (*The Will to Power*, §805 (1883–88), p. 424).

The artistic process' upshot is a work whose content fascinates and engages, owing to its amoral, socially objectionable, and frightening quality which we apprehend satisfyingly and safely with a subliminal sense of taboo-breaking. We remain on the civilized side, where the objectionable content does not force itself upon us upsettingly, as we derive satisfaction from the liberating contents it presents. From a Freudian perspective, this type of subliminal sexual satisfaction occurs daily, outside of the art world, as when we experience a dimly sexual satisfaction upon driving through a tunnel, riding a subway, or using an elevator. With a small artistic step, we can similarly apprehend the blended male and female qualities of iconic landmarks such as the Eiffel Tower and the Taj Mahal (Plate 5), whose exceptional balance of male and female symbolism renders them instinctually attractive and satisfying to behold, as they represent a perfect sexual union. In their fully explicit psychological form, these images would be pornographic. Other well-known and highly visited buildings such as the Empire State Building or the Sydney Opera House display more uniformly male and female resonances, respectively. When experienced in such terms, these buildings become attractive on account of the unconscious sexual satisfaction they imaginatively provide.

From a psychoanalytic perspective, the surreal 2001 destruction of the World Trade Center's twin towers can also be interpreted symbolically as an act of emasculation. Independent of the political context, Freudian dream analysis offers a supply of symbols for interpreting this event's indelible mark on our collective psyche, such as the flying airplanes, the airplanes' penetration into the towers, the fires, and the falling, all suggesting that an atrocity can be interpreted literally as an objectified nightmare, or, more repugnantly, as a work of art.[37]

Compared to the theories we have considered, Freud's account of aesthetic experience is more innovative and

---

[37] Kant's conception of adherent beauty (see Chapter 1) succinctly articulates the moral objection to appreciating 9/11 as a work of art. He states that "we could add much to a building which would immediately please the eye, if only it were not to be a church" (*Critique of the Power of Judgment*, §16). The parallel phrasing would be that we could destroy a building in an aesthetically dramatic way, if only it were not occupied with innocent people.

provocative, notwithstanding Nietzsche's brief foreshadowings in his mythologically expressed aesthetics of the complementary Dionysian and Apollonian energies. Freud's account also has a traditional and commonsense quality as an example of a "communication theory" of art. We discussed this kind of theory in connection with Schopenhauer's aesthetics, where the artistic genius envisions a timeless Platonic Idea and portrays that vision in an artwork for the sake of communicating the vision to others. Communication theories tend to dissolve the artwork's intrinsic value, since the work serves mainly as a functional intermediary between the audience and the subject portrayed.

This communicative quality weakens Freud's account of art, although his core analogy between artworks and dreams compensates for some of the drawbacks. Since the artwork functions not only to communicate an objectionable unconscious desire, but also to render the desire enjoyable while minimizing anxiety, the artwork's aesthetic qualities can be appreciated in how they function as a disguise: we can savor the mechanisms of the disguise and derive some intellectual satisfaction from how the disguise achieves its effects. Freud does refer negatively to the aesthetic pleasure – in particular, the pleasure derived from formalistic balances, symmetries, compositional arrangements, and such – as bribes or bait that the artist provides, which operate to render our assimilation of the artist's socially objectionable daydreams palatable, but the aesthetic disguise can be appreciated on its own account. This compares to appreciating a mathematical proof's elegance, or a battle strategy's efficiency, where the strategy itself aims not for elegance, but for winning. Psychoanalytic techniques of dream interpretation thus double as principles of art criticism.

Also worth noting is the kinship between Freud's negative attitude towards artistic formalism and the rhetorical use of beauty that we considered earlier in connection with Kant's aesthetics. We previously discussed how beauty can operate to legitimate immoral contents, as when one represents a criminal in an attractively composed, formal and expensive portrait. Freud acknowledges that unconscious artistic contents are immoral and he regards beauty as among the artwork's formal, disguise-generating qualities, and hence as having a positive rhetorical function. A strange, almost macabre, sense thus emerges in which we can say that Freud regards all art as analogous to beautiful portraits of horrible people, for this is precisely the result of attractively clothing an unconscious, morally repugnant content in an attractive, dreamlike way, as when a beautifully decorated shoe covers an unsightly foot, or as when a politically inspiring justification covers a war's dreadful reality, or as when a smiling and friendly demeanor covers a deceitful character. Aspects of Schopenhauer's vision of the world also have this character, as when the pleasing surface of natural beauty is said to mask an interior energy that produces horrendous suffering.

Two cases in point are works by Leonardo da Vinci and William Shakespeare that Freud discusses psychoanalytically. He interprets da Vinci's *Virgin and Child with St. Anne* (1507–13) as representing da Vinci's childhood memory of having been dually raised by, initially, his natural mother and his stepmother, and then by his stepmother and grandmother. The smiles (also appearing in the *Mona Lisa*) supposedly represent da Vinci's mother's smile, and his psychological attachment to his mother.[38] These are not morally objectionable contents as described, but they can represent da Vinci's unconscious desire to reunite with his mother, as within the context of Freud's Oedipus Complex – a fundamental psychological constellation of the Id – where in the male's case, there is a desire to murder one's father for the sake of uniting sexually with one's mother. The beautiful paintings would then be disguising da Vinci's essentially murderous and incestuous, albeit unconscious, motives.

Along similar Oedipal lines, Freud interprets Shakespeare's *Hamlet*, whose narrative framework is as follows. Hamlet's uncle, Claudius, murders his brother, the King of Denmark, who is Hamlet's father, and then quickly marries Hamlet's mother, Gertrude, the Queen, to become Hamlet's stepfather. Hamlet, after a visit by his father's ghost, vows to take murderous revenge upon his uncle, now stepfather, but spends the bulk of the play deliberating, reflecting, worrying, and hesitating to commit the crime. It dawns upon Hamlet to contrive a play (within the play) for Claudius' and Gertrude's benefit to illustrate the murderous deed, to confirm to himself Claudius' guilt, and to work through

---

[38] Freud, *Leonardo da Vinci*, p. 85.

his father's murder imaginatively. The tragedy unfolds where, at the play's end, the mortally wounded Hamlet kills Claudius in a fit of emotion. Much has been written and speculated about Hamlet's long hesitation.

According to Freud, Hamlet's hesitation is psychoanalytically explainable, and easily so. Hamlet cannot bring himself to kill Claudius without feeling inconsistent, for Claudius had succeeded in doing exactly what Hamlet unconsciously wished to do, namely, kill Hamlet's father and marry Hamlet's mother. Hamlet unconsciously concurs with Claudius' actions, and he cannot kill this kindred spirit without feeling that he would be enacting his own death in the process, which is indeed how the play ends. Shakespeare insightfully adds an episode in *Hamlet*, now famous, where Hamlet considers suicide ("to be, or not to be … "), that expresses the personal meaning of the murder-suicide that continually plagues him. To Freud, *Hamlet* presents the unconscious influence of the Oedipus Complex, and it stands as a testament to Shakespeare's intuitive grasp of the mind's unconscious motivations.

In the above examples from architecture, painting, and literature, the unconscious content is discernible either as symbols for sex organs or as sexual desires of an incestuous and murderous, sometimes patricidal and fratricidal, quality. Works of art are like dreams in that they incorporate such morally indigestible contents. Dream interpretation, however, does not typically involve a straightforward reading of a dream in reference to standard symbols that appear in a table of common dream symbols. Freud provides such a list, often cited, but only with the qualification that each dream is properly interpretable when we have on hand the dreamer's own associations. These can be idiosyncratic, as they express the personal nature of the unconscious contents, and without being able to consult them, the meaning of the dream can remain a mystery.

Within the realm of art, the same applies. It is optimal to know the artist's intentions, if we expect to interpret the work of art in an informative and reliable manner. Freud's analysis of Shakespeare's *Hamlet* is thus more of an exception to the psychoanalytic rule. In his book on da Vinci, Freud does assemble many details about da Vinci's life to set the latter's artworks into a personal context. It remains the case that da Vinci can no longer tell us what associations he made with his paintings, and we rarely have this information for any artist, living artists included, since many resist explaining what their works mean. From a psycho-analytic standpoint this resistance is unsurprising, owing to the socially objectionable nature of what the artists are actually expressing.

The psychoanalytic interpretation of art consequently gener-ates a good measure of frustration. Without having the artist available for psychoanalysis, there is always an uncertainty about what the unconscious contents of the artist's work happen to be. At the same time, only when the unconscious contents are more generally apprehensible and discernible through the more common dream symbols that operate similarly in everyone's mind, can the works trigger a popular appeal. All art may convey an unconscious meaning, but only psychologically non-idiosyn-cratic art can be effective in art museums and other public displays, since we do not need to psychoanalyse the artist to apprehend the artwork's unconscious meaning.

Artists' intentions are relevant as a rule with Freudian aesthetics, standing against any theory (for example, the New Criticism of the 1950s) which holds that to understand an art-work, we need only reflect upon the work in relative isolation and self-containment, without much need for background informa-tion. The anti-Freudian argument is that if the meaning has not been put into the work, then that non-present meaning is irrel-evant to the work, and if the meaning has been put into the work, then it should be evident by inspecting the work. The Freudian response is that if the meaning is present in the work, then due to the unconscious contents and the processes of disguise that operate, we usually need to know the artist's intentions and psychological associations to discern that meaning.

This response does not fully vindicate Freudian aesthetics, since the main problem resides less in what the psychoanalytic approach can reveal about works of art, but rather in what it leaves out in principle. The analysis of an artwork's psychological contents can tell us about the artist and the artwork's unconscious message, but just as Freud observes how the Marxist analysis of art in reference to economic and social considerations remains incomplete, and in need of a Freudian supplement, Marxist analysis itself relevantly complements the Freudian approach by adding the economic and political considerations that psycho-analytic considerations overlook. Moreover, exclusively Freudian analyses tend to ignore art-historical considerations, such as the reasons why this or that style emerges or appears in the work. These stylistic factors often have little to do with psychology, but more with fashion, technical discoveries, the work of artistic competitors, and sometimes merely chance. Rather than maintain critically that Freudian aesthetics is misguided, owing to its exclusive and reductionistic attention to unconscious content, we can appreciate it as an insightful style of artistic interpretation, but one that needs to be supplemented with other interpretive styles.

2. SURREALISM AND SEMANTIC RESONANCE

Freud's influence in the European artworld is most apparent in the Surrealist movement of the 1920s and 1930s. Surrealists sympathize with Freud's position that genuine artistic expression issues from the Id and they engage in artistic creation with that assumption in mind. For instance, surrealist poetry is inspired by the psychoanalytic technique of free association – a method of invoking automatic responses that Freud used with his patients to reveal the contents of the unconscious – where one writes without changing any words or elaborating upon further reflection, allowing the unconscious to present itself as authentically as possible, even though the contents undoubtedly suffer some censorship during the process.

Surrealist painters portray their fantasies with images that appear to be virtual photographs of their dreams. Again, this compares to Schopenhauer's conception of the artistic genius who paints visions of Platonic ideas, where the shared goal is to reveal truth through art, except that in the surrealist context, the visions are more dreamlike and psychologically charged. In Schopenhauer's case, the artist reveals a truth about timeless ideas; in the Surrealist's, the artist reveals a truth about the timeless and unconscious quality of the human mind, or of the artist's mind.

In contrast to theories that highlight art as the presentation of ideal types, we can experience how Freudian and Surrealist aesthetics comprehends the wide diversity and complexity of artistic forms, simply by surveying the imaginative quality of the leading artworks throughout history. Few of these works portray ideal types, as we might see in a biology, botany, or anatomy book, but in their endlessly fascinating forms, they appear more concretely to be products of freely creative, dreamlike states of consciousness, if sometimes nightmarish ones.

In further disengagement from the nineteenth-century tradition, the Freudian association between artistic creation and unconscious expression, given the morally objectionable contents of the unconscious, takes us a further step towards the separation of art from morality. In both Freud and in Surrealism, the only moral constraint on artistic contents resides in the techniques of disguise used to render the immoral contents socially acceptable. One acknowledges morality within the artwork for the sake of maintaining a civilized and psychologically assimilable aesthetic presentation, but this is not what the works are mainly about. Consistent with the nineteenth-century avant-garde conceptions of artistic genius, Freudian and Surrealist artists acknowledge that no content stands beyond the possibilities of artistic expression, even if it needs to be presented through a disguise.

By positively acknowledging the mind's unconscious province, we also step towards that sector of the psyche which, if allowed to erupt too forcefully and extensively, produces antisocial behavior, and in some cases, madness and self-destruction. This draws artistic creation closer to madness, and suggests a conception of madness that appreciates the psychologically troubled, often anxiety-ridden, person as a potential locus of otherwise inaccessible insights about our instinctual human condition. Expressed more reservedly, Freudian and Surrealist art blurs the line between waking and dreaming, along with the line between morality and immorality. Since the Freudian theory, like the weaker version of Nietzsche's Dionysian aesthetics that we identified earlier, recognizes how we inevitably filter the objectionable unconscious contents through an acceptable disguise of civility, Surrealism does not – at least in practice – allow unconscious energies to vent wildly, offensively, and destructively. At that extreme point, art would dissolve into the raw blow of the hatchet or the firing of the gun, notwithstanding how André Breton's second Surrealist Manifesto (1929) overstates that the supreme surrealist act is the very firing of that gun.

Surrealist art typically illustrates personal dreamscapes, but it is possible to combine Surrealist method with Marxist social interests to form an amalgamated, socially liberating art. If one psychoanalyses the society at large to reveal its repressed contents, bringing to light what the society fundamentally values, who it excludes, and for what it implicitly aims, and portrays this repressed content artistically, then art can serve a revolutionary purpose by attractively revealing social truths that no one can easily face. Following Freud, the psychological motivation would be to liberate by presenting the disturbing truth's more explicit, yet still psychologically digestible form.

Despite these emancipating features of Surrealism and its extrapolations, it remains that along with Freud's own view, the prevailing supposition of Freudian aesthetics is that art's main purpose and source of appeal is to reveal unconscious meanings and drives, where these are assumed to be psychologically difficult to acknowledge in their untempered form. The view is limited with respect to what it believes art is mainly supposed to convey, and its limitations compare to the ones we see in the theorists ranging from Kant through Kierkegaard. Each respective theory specifies some central content, usually moral or metaphysical, whose expression art is supposed to serve.

Freud's account of art can be extended beyond its standard expressions by retaining the idea that artistic presentations have a dreamlike form, and relaxing the claim that these presentations typically express sex-and-violence-oriented, morally objectionable contents of the unconscious. From a formal, structural standpoint, independent of their contents, Freud describes dreams as semantically-packed imaginative constructs, upon the analogy of packed ice, where layers are compounded and concentrated together to form a dense whole. Since works of art, in particular the great works, are semantically rich and are inexhaustibly interpretable, their semantic quality fits Freud's description of a packed-ice-style dream formation. Kant's notion of an aesthetic idea, or rich aesthetic image, has the same quality, with its density of metaphor-filled layers upon meaning-resonant layers.

When Kant discusses aesthetic ideas, his moral interests prevail, so we find him stating that rich aesthetic images best express the inexhaustible thoughts of heaven, hell, eternity, and the like. As noted earlier in that context, however, any subject matter can be portrayed artistically, with an accompanying depth of meaning, so if we incorporate Freud's ideas of art-as-dreamlike and as semantically packed with an open view towards the kinds of subjects that can be artistically portrayed, we arrive at a situation that allows for the application of psychoanalytic techniques in artistic interpretation, but without a commitment to searching for implicitly sexual, violent, or otherwise immoral contents. This may dissolve the natural thrill of venturing into the realm of sexual taboos whenever we interpret art, but it yields a wider conception of artistic expression, along with a more diversely applicable theory of interpretation that is effective for social critique.

This increased openness of subject matter preserves, and even enhances, the sense of liberation that art can provide. In the Freudian case, art provides a sense of freedom and release from society's civilizing and oppressive moral constraints, by allowing polymorphously sexual and sometimes violent contents to present themselves. This can be liberating, but in the more expanded case, art can provide a further sense of freedom by revealing society's repressive political and conventional rules – rules that often have little to do with prohibited sexuality – and by indicating an implicit escape thereby.

For instance, we can apply the psychoanalytic technique of interpreting a dream to elements that remain on the artwork's semantic periphery, but are of great significance nonetheless. Such contents could arise in an artwork that portrays a political theme, where the artist critically comments on the subject, such as a government's policies, but does so indirectly, as might be done by employing disguised images.[39] The socially critical content need not be from the human unconscious *per se*, need not be violent, and need not be sexually oriented, but it could be objectionable from the standpoint of a certain social class, privileged group, or prevailing value system. The critical content would be

---

[39] L. Frank Baum's 1900 book, *The Wonderful Wizard of Oz* (coincidentally published in the same year as Freud's *The Interpretation of Dreams*), has been read in allegorical terms where the "yellow brick road" represents the gold standard, and so on. See Littlefield, "The Wizard of Oz."

better described as stemming from society's outsiders, revolutionaries, or social avant-garde.

By expanding Freud's aesthetic theory beyond his original parameters, as do later theorists in fact, we take a qualitative step away from the single-theme conceptions of art's purpose that appear in Kant, Schiller, Hegel, Marx, Schopenhauer, Nietzsche, Kierkegaard, and Freud himself, and enter into a more diversified notion of what art can, or ought to, express. This expansion coincides historically with the gradual dissolution of beauty's primacy as an aesthetic category – a primacy that operates in Kant's aesthetics – as conceptions of the sublime, as well as the picturesque, emerge into the artistic scene as the nineteenth century progresses. By the time we reach the twentieth century, these categories are giving way to the notion of emotional expression, considered generally, which applies to any feeling and which precipitates a variety of artistic presentations. The requirement to be beautiful is no longer pressing; there is only a requirement to be expressive, as we find exemplified in the tribal art statues and masks that influenced German expressionist and Cubist painters and sculptors of the early twentieth century.

The social situation for artistic creativity becomes complicated at this point, owing partially to an ambiguity in how to construe the nature of dreams. Nietzsche expresses the ambiguity well: sometimes he describes the Apollonian artistic energy as providing a dreamlike veil that softens the violent presentation of Dionysian subject matters, much as Freud describes, and as we encounter in romantic art; sometimes he associates Apollonian art with the visionary portrayal of ideal types, as we find in Schopenhauer's aesthetics, and as we encounter in neoclassical art. The veil-like quality of dreams aligns them with the portrayal of objectionable or very emotionally charged subject matters; the purely idealizing quality of dreams aligns them with peaceful Platonic Ideas. Like a Janus-figure, dreams direct our attention to either hellish or heavenly panoramas, and art does likewise.

Upon accentuating the Nietzschean-Freudian conception of dreams, artistic creation steps closer to madness-producing energies – a connection that invites unsympathetic interpreters to regard surrealistic and expressionist artworks as akin to the presentation of madness, and, consequently, as unhealthy art. Emphasizing the more peace-generating conception of dreams, one can correspondingly pit the more expressionistic, or modernist, art that is consistent with Nietzsche's Dionysian energies, Freud and the Surrealists, against the idealizing, perfecting art that Kant, Schiller, Hegel, and Schopenhauer favor. In the most extreme expression of this division, the idealizing art that Greek sculptures exemplify, for instance, can be set against all artistic forms that do not respect naturalistic forms and ideal types. This is where modernist art becomes the enemy of supposedly healthy and sane art, contrary to Nietzsche's less rationalistic, Dionysian conception of health.

In light of this split in artistic preferences that issue logically from the ambiguity in the notion of a dream, we can see how theories that associate art with regions of the unconscious or subjective mind, as in Nietzsche's, Kierkegaard's and Freud's views, contrast with the earlier theoretical development that extends from Kant, through Schiller, Hegel, and Schopenhauer. The latter group's rationalistic emphasis upon the portrayal of ideal types does not allow much room for an irrationalistic, inner subjective reality to extend deeply into their aesthetics. Only in Schopenhauer's theory of music do we touch upon this dimension.

Given how the earlier aesthetic theories tend to associate moral content with the portrayal of ideal types, the beginning of the twentieth century crystallizes a cultural conflict between those who persist in closely aligning art and morality along rationalistic, neoclassic lines, emphasizing the necessity of using external forms as they naturally and ideally occur, and those who advocate a greater autonomy and freedom for art along more modernistic and expressionistic lines that emphasize the portrayal of inner states of mind, consistent with the wildest non-naturalistic forms. The conflict comes to a head in Germany during the 1930s and early 1940s, where in a purist and anachronistic effort to resurrect and enhance a form of nineteenth-century neoclassicism, the official Nazi position proscribed all forms of modernism. From a theoretical standpoint, this cultural tension can be understood in reference to the ambiguity in the nature of dreams, either as offering a vision of ideal types, or as expressing the wild energies of the unconscious.

Part II

1900–1980

Part II

9

THE ART OF ANTI-FASCIST AESTHETICS

Walter Benjamin

Walter Benjamin (1892–1940) was a natural intellectual, and he aspired to be a university professor at an early age. As a promising young scholar from an affluent Jewish family in Berlin, he attended excellent elementary schools and universities, married while in his twenties, started a family, and displayed a concentrated and imaginative intellect to all those who knew him. His hopes for a teaching career were cut short soon after he reached the age of thirty, but he maintained a scholarly life throughout his forty-eight years, socializing with many of Europe's leading thinkers, and referring to himself during his intellectual prime as "a man of letters."

After studying literature and philosophy, and receiving his doctoral degree from the University of Bern for his work on the concept of criticism in German romanticism, everything seemed on course for an academic position. The year was 1919, and Benjamin needed only to complete his professional qualification – the advanced habilitation manuscript – that would certify his entrance into university teaching. Publishing on Baudelaire (1923) and Goethe (1924) in the meantime, the University of Frankfurt decided to reject Benjamin's unorthodox manuscript on the origins of German tragic drama six years later, leaving him in 1925, at age thirty-three, disappointed and without the credentials to secure a university post. Focusing on translation work, independent writing projects, and short articles as a way to make ends meet, Benjamin never found a secure place in academia. Troubled by a sense of despair, he left Germany in 1932 following Hitler's ascent to power and planned to kill himself in southern France, but, after making out his last will and testament, decided to press on instead. His life ended eight years later, in what is said to have been a suicide while in police custody.

The rise of National Socialism in Germany accentuated Benjamin's personal difficulties after the rejection of his habilitation manuscript. The Nazis' efforts to force Germany's Jewish population to leave the country initially involved instituting laws that recalled the centuries-long history of the German principalities, long before Germany became a single state in 1871, in which Jewish people were prevented from holding most jobs, and were kept separate from the main population in gated communities. As part of this resurrected anti-Semitism, the Nazis stripped the Jews of their citizenship as part of the 1935 Nuremberg Laws and Benjamin, who had by then moved to Paris, was among those who officially lost their legal foothold in their native country.[40]

The need to avoid the Nazis cast a fearsome shadow over Benjamin's life, as they prepared their advance into France and other surrounding nations. With the start of World War II in September 1939, Benjamin's situation in France as an anti-Nazi writer became particularly dangerous. After being interned for three months by the French at the beginning of 1940, now approaching age forty-eight, he left Paris in June, a day before the Nazis entered the city. Resolving to leave Europe thereafter, he secured a visa to the United States in August, intending to arrive there via Portugal. The Nazi-sympathetic Spanish police at the small Spanish border town of Portbou blocked his escape, however, and arrested him on September 27. Before the night was over, he was dead.

The reports are that Benjamin committed suicide with an overdose of morphine, presumably as an alternative to facing torture or imprisonment by the German Secret State Police. Notwithstanding Benjamin's having been Jewish, his burial in a Catholic cemetery in Portbou makes one wonder whether his death was the result of suicide, since, as a rule, Catholic cemeteries

---

[40] The citizenship-stripping passage in the Nuremberg Laws reads: "A Jew cannot be a citizen of the Reich. He cannot exercise the right to vote; he cannot hold public office" (First Supplementary Decree of November 14, 1935 to The Nuremberg Laws on Citizenship and Race: September 15, 1935).

do not inter people who take their own lives. The exact circumstances surrounding Benjamin's death remain a mystery.

To understand the aesthetic ideas for which Benjamin has been most influential, it will help initially to characterize Nazi aesthetics, for the latter represents a reactionary trend against which many European intellectuals were critically responding during the 1930s and early 1940s, including Benjamin. The Nazis' use of aesthetics effectively inspired the German population, and, as Benjamin observed, formed a dangerous amalgam of fascism and art.

1. AESTHETICS IN NATIONAL SOCIALIST GERMANY

Nazi aesthetics and Adolf Hitler's attitude toward the arts go hand in hand, since Hitler ruled Germany with an iron fist and impressed his personal values upon most aspects of social life. Central to both Hitler's attitude, and the Nazis' in general, is an extremist and exclusionary form of nationalism, combined with anti-Semitism, where the latter reinforces nationalist attitudes as the Nazis defined them. Also playing an aesthetic role is Hitler's interest in architecture, which was established before he became a political leader.

Among heads of government, Hitler is notable for his having recognized the importance of instilling an appreciation for the visual and performing arts in the general population. Combined with his architecture-focused aesthetic mentality, this recognition was also instrumental to his rise to power and his maintenance of it. With this in mind, we can distinguish two dimensions of Nazi aesthetics. The first concerns Hitler's narrow conception of socially appropriate subject matters; the second concerns his use of aesthetic techniques – specifically architectural and ritualistic ones – to organize the German people and to promote his extremist and exclusionary nationalism. Determined to prevail, the Nazis removed from social participation those who openly disagreed with them, sometimes fatally. This included participation in the fine arts.

As mentioned at the previous chapter's end, the then prevailing European current of irrationalist-instinctualist aesthetic theory, modified in particular through Nietzsche's and Freud's influences, led to a loose conceptual association between artistic creation and madness, positively conceived as a revolutionary form of insight. This association stems from an understanding of artistic creation that links it psychologically to dreams, instinct, and wild, Dionysian or Id-derived unconscious energies. As far back as the 1790s and despite his neoclassic sympathies, we see hints of this amalgam in Kant's characterization of artistic genius, "nature's favorite," as an instinctive being. Given the subsequent historical overlap between the unconscious, instinct, madness, and dreams, and by exaggerating this informal association to a point where artistic creation becomes akin to madness, negatively conceived, an unsympathetic or merely ignorant interpreter can discern in the twentieth-century modernist rise of Dada, Surrealism, Cubism, and Expressionism, a corresponding and questionable loss of contact with the real world, and, following this, a dissolution of naturalistic, formally proportioned styles of representation.

Hitler perceived this supposed regression within the European cultural scene, as he criticized modernist paintings – German expressionist works in particular – for their non-natural coloration and radical departures from natural proportions. That Cubism's and Expressionism's fractured and distorted human forms were partly inspired by African tribal art only confirmed their dubious provenance in the Nazis' opinion. Profoundly antagonistic to modern art, and contrary to some of his subordinates, Hitler felt that his task was to restore health to German aesthetic sentiments by eliminating all modernist, so-called "degenerate," influences.[41]

Many of the painters in Germany who the Nazis condemned, forced out of work, or otherwise banished were not Jewish. Beyond Germany's borders, however, many of the modernist artists had Jewish backgrounds, and Hitler believed, accurately or

---

[41] From July 19 to November 30, 1937, the Nazis sponsored a large-scale art exhibition of "degenerate art" (*entartete Kunst*) in Munich. It included works by Ernst Barlach, Max Beckmann, Marc Chagall, Lovis Corinth, Otto Dix, Max Ernst, Lyonel Feininger, George Grosz, Erich Heckel, Alexej von Jawlensky, Wassily Kandinsky, Ernst Ludwig Kirchner, Paul Klee, Oskar Kokoschka, Wilhelm Lehmbruck, Franz Marc, Ludwig Meidner, Piet Mondrian, Emil Nolde, Max Pechstein, and Karl Schmidt-Rottluff.

not, that their influence was entering into and eroding the quality of German art. In his effort to remove modernist art and artists from exhibition venues and educational institutions, he was, though, acting from a personal conception of how healthy art ought to appear. For instance, he could not bear to look favorably at bright green dogs or at elongated, or otherwise broken-up, human faces and bodies. Misunderstanding them as failed attempts at realistic representation, he regarded such works as perverse venerations of physical deformity. The fundamental expressionist idea of visually portraying inner states through non-naturalistic coloration was beyond him.

Such attitudes are familiar in naive and unsophisticated individuals who often live outside of the artworld and remain unaware of the theories that motivate the newest styles of art. Among those well entrenched in the artworld, the attitudes also appear periodically among conservative critics who have identified themselves with established fashions, and, owing to this identification, resist radical change, lest it precipitate the loss of the artworld in which they feel at home.

Long before the Nazis assumed power, conservative art critics condemned the first modernist works. A famous case is the reaction to the 1913 Armory Show in New York, which initiated New Yorkers to modernist art, where the show suffered a now often-cited criticism from Julian Leonard Street (1879–1947), an art critic for the *New York Times*, who described it as an "explosion in a shingle factory."[42] Theodore Roosevelt, writing in the years after his presidency, referred to the Cubist works in the Armory show as "repellent from every standpoint," owing to their unnatural, distorted imagery.[43] After the Nazis were removed from power, comparable reactions appeared in the

---

[42] The artists represented at the Armory Show included George Bellows, Constantin Brâncusi, Georges Braque, Mary Cassatt, Paul Cézanne, Camille Corot, Gustave Courbet, Arthur B. Davies, Stuart Davis, Honoré Daumier, Edgar Degas, Eugène Delacroix, Marcel Duchamp, Paul Gauguin, Vincent van Gogh, Francisco Goya, Childe Hassam, Robert Henri, Edward Hopper, Ferdinand Hodler, Wassily Kandinsky, Ernst Ludwig Kirchner, Henri de Toulouse-Lautrec, Édouard Manet, Claude Monet, Edvard Munch, Pablo Picasso, Pierre-Auguste Renoir, Auguste Rodin, Georges Seurat, John Sloan, Joseph Stella, and James Abbott McNeill Whistler.

[43] Roosevelt, "A Layman's Views."

1960s and 1970s in reference to pop art, where ordinary objects – and these recall Dada works of the decades before – were set on display, praised by a number of leading artists, collectors, critics, and museum curators as innovative artworks, and criticized by many in the general population as artistic humbug.

It helps to appreciate the aesthetic mentality behind Nazi aesthetics in this broader light, namely, as a resistance to avant-garde art by either innocents or acknowledged conservatives who have difficulty apprehending or acknowledging its aesthetic value, and who experience alienation, or feel offended or duped, and are disposed to censor or otherwise dethrone the work. Although the Nazis were trying to create a new German society, the center of Nazi aesthetics has a proletarian and reactionary quality, independent of the Nazis' anti-Semitism, which rests on the assumption that works of art should be realistic, attractively idealizing, immediately understandable, and impressively meaningful as a matter of expressed talent and message.

Worth adding here is how the Nazi attitude towards modernism is in the same family as the Marxist reaction: both condemn modernism for being unrealistic. In a similar way, and also out of the mainstream, Jean-Paul Sartre criticizes poetry and poets in his post-war essay, "What is Literature?" (1948), maintaining that poetic expression renders decisive political action difficult, owing to the multiplicity and blurring – that is, confusion – of meanings that it embodies. This matches how Marxists condemn modernism for being too politically detached. The respective reasoning widely differs between the Nazis, Marxists, and Sartre, but the attacks on unrealistic works of art are in accord.

The Nazis nonetheless had some difficulty defining the style that should characterize officially German art, but amidst debates between neoclassicism, domestic realism, a kind of nostalgic throwback to a German tribal period, as well as some hesitant sympathy with modernism, the former two styles prevailed. In conjunction with imitations of classical Greek sculpture and plans for immense neoclassical buildings intended to rival those in Rome and Washington, D.C., we have family scenes, pastoral scenes, idyllic images of workers, almost communist in spirit, and art that represents ordinary people in a peaceful and sometimes inspiring way. Featured in this domestic realism were genre paintings of middle-class families listening to the radio, reading magazines, and the like.

There is little variation in the visual arts beyond the above neoclassical and domestic themes, aside from heroic political portraits and war images. In music, the Nazis preferred nine-teenth-century works, especially by Wagner, and discouraged modern atonal works and jazz.[44] As noted, they further deemed as "degenerate" almost all fine art, visual and musical, that fell into the non-naturalistic, abstract, category. In sum, the Nazis insti-tuted a narrowly defined, state-controlled conception of the arts, where they used art to stimulate and reinforce the society's health in accord with their political ideals. From a philosophical stand-point, this compares motivationally to a wide variety of efforts to use art as a path to social improvement and political solidifica-tion. These include Schiller's advocacy of aesthetic education that enlists classical Greek sculptural ideals, Nietzsche's early advocacy of theatrical tragedy, and Richard Wagner's operatic music, and Marx's advocacy of revolution-supporting art that emphasizes images of ordinary domestic life and social unity.

One might assume that owing to the Nazis' explicit support of Friedrich Nietzsche's philosophy, their aesthetic had a strong Nietzschean dimension. It was Nietzschean insofar as it aimed to produce the healthy attitudes Nietzsche advocated, but in some respects, Hitler's conception of art's social purpose fits more with Schopenhauer's conception of aesthetic experience, not to mention Nietzsche's unsympathetic characterization of roman-tic, Wagnerian, art in his later years, as the art of the weak-minded. Schopenhauer believed that art can offer some relief from the daily world's troubles and that it can inspire a more eternalistic attitude towards the world. Following suit, Hitler resisted closing the concert halls and opera houses during the extensive bombing of German cities, convinced that musical experience offered some escape and contemplative relief from the surrounding pan-demonium. His decision to keep the concert halls and museums in operation during wartime compares to those who would resist closing museums during a time of economic downturn.

---

[44] For a history of jazz in Nazi Germany, see Kater, *Different Drummers*.

Although Nazi aesthetics was neoclassical and realistic, as it tried simultaneously to gaze upwards towards eternalistic ideals and yet downwards towards an existential connection with the earth, nation, and family, such qualities do not fully capture the features that have led many to comment upon the role of aesthetics in Nazi culture. Benjamin and others attended mainly to Hitler's employment of aesthetics to organize the German population, not in connection with art museum and concert attendance, but in connection with political life on the street. The development of neoclassical architecture played some role, but Hitler also employed aesthetic techniques that are independent of the debate between modernism and neoclassicism/social realism. Prevailing here is the ritualistic use of aesthetics to organize large rallies, parades, and social events.

Along this aesthetic dimension, one of the less commented-upon features of Nazi German society was its sheer abundance of social events, many of which featured speeches by Hitler. These tended to be extravagant affairs with colorful parades, banners, uniforms, salutes, marches, and insignias, all arranged in the form of a quasi-religious ritual. It was part theater, part hallowed ceremony, and part mass event, much as we find today in the celebrations that initiate the Olympic Games. If we consider the exciting feeling of the Olympics, a large rock concert, or a major political convention, and combine this with the seriously reverent atmosphere of a religious ceremony reinforced by intense and menacing peer pressure, one can imagine the kind of aesthetic experience that the Nazis were trying to instill in the people, more or less as a constant, inspirational, mind-bending, social-political bombardment. Benjamin referred insightfully to this phenomenon as the aestheticization of politics, that is, the employment of aesthetic techniques to solidify dictatorial power, and he regarded the combination of aesthetics and politics to be a potent and dangerous amalgam, precisely because of its psychological ability to reinforce oppression.

Using his architectural sense, Hitler organized the participants in the large Nazi rallies into stadium-filling, square blocks of humanity, aiming to symbolize the unified German mentality of the population under a single ruler, ready for battle, and ready to sacrifice themselves for their leader. The materials of these grand compositions were masses of human beings themselves, socially organized into a religiously ritualistic, total work of art that expressed the Nazi version of the German spirit. Given the aggressive, intolerant, appropriating, domineering, and exterminating mentality that the Nazis extended towards the non-Nazi world, this created a sinister presentation outside of Germany. Within Germany itself, the predominant attitude was different: the combined effect of these social events was probably among the most inspiring and strength-generating experiences the country had had up until that time on the national and political level. Once World War II began, Benjamin became one of the early casualties of this artistically manipulated, mass-hypnotic hero-worship, as soon did millions of innocent others.

2. THE WORK OF ART IN THE AGE OF MECHANICAL REPRODUCTION

Benjamin published his best-known essay, "The Work of Art in the Age of Mechanical Reproduction" in 1936, four years before his death. The year also coincided with the start of the Spanish Civil War – a social conflict between republican and fascist forces that lasted until April 1, 1939, ending with a fascist victory only five months before Hitler instigated World War II in September. When he composed the essay, Benjamin had been living in Paris since 1932, surrounded by an atmosphere of emerging fascism on the European continent. In conjunction with the rigid governments in Spain and Germany, Italy had been adding to the repressive political situation, having stood under Benito Mussolini's leadership since the 1920s.

At the outset of Benjamin's essay, one cannot help but notice how concepts such as "weapons," "war," "fascism," "mechanism" (that is, technology) and "modernism" establish the rhetorical tone. Participating in the warlike atmosphere in a more theoretically centered manner, Benjamin conceives of himself as outlining a conceptual weapon against the fascist mentality, operating at the level of the sophisticated intelligentsia. The Nazis were, nevertheless, aware of his anti-fascist writings and this, combined with his Jewish heritage, gave Benjamin good reason to avoid being taken into custody by the Gestapo. Knowledge of the centuries-long history of persecution and social exclusion that the Jews experienced in Germany could only have amplified his worries.

At the beginning of the nineteenth century, it was common to encounter the belief that Europe was experiencing a new age of historical progress. Hegel, among others, expressed this view in his *Phenomenology of Spirit* (§11) in 1807. The same kind of belief appeared at the beginning of the twentieth century, although it was conceived differently as a dawning "modern" age that was sharply breaking away from the nineteenth-century days of the horse and carriage. World War I's amalgamation of old and new technologies marked a transition point for many, generating conflicting opinions about the value of inventions such as the airplane and motor vehicle. For many, these new mechanisms only made the prospect of war more horrifying, comparable to how we reflect upon the threat of nuclear and biological conflict today. Within the artworld, some artists condemned the new technologies, as did the Dadaists; some never ceased to praise it, such as the Italian Futurists.

Benjamin's conceptual relationship to the Dadaists and Futurists is mixed, since he believed that although the Dadaists adopted an anti-technology stance, their views anticipated the aesthetics of the motion picture, which Benjamin wanted to uphold positively as an avant-garde art form. The Futurists were sympathetic with fascism, which Benjamin abhorred, but they overflowed with positive sentiment for technological advances, which, contrary to the trend, Benjamin was trying to enlist against fascism. For him, the work of art in the age of mechanical reproduction is a welcome, anti-fascist phenomenon. Let us consequently turn to this aspect of his view, since it illuminates his position vis-à-vis the Dadaists and Futurists.

Until the beginning of the twentieth century, most works of visual art were unique items, as we encounter typically in architecture and painting. There is only one Eiffel Tower, only one *Mona Lisa*, and so on. In such cases, a single physical object embodies the artwork, often accompanied by copies, images, models, or reproductions of that object, where the copies are assumed to be aesthetically inferior to the original. In the complicated case of music, each performance is similarly a unique event, and it is a common assumption that there is an aesthetic difference between any particular live performance and an audio or audiovisual copy of that performance, such as a tape recording or video, although all are of the same "work."

As a way to identify an artwork, the notion of "original vs. copy" does not substantially enter into some arts, since the artwork appears in duplicates from the outset. Founding, stamping, woodcutting, printing, engraving, etching, lithography, and photography typically involve making a number of instantiations of the work, all of which count equally as "the work."[45] Book publishing is a familiar case; there is no original book among the sequence of books that a printing press turns out, as there contrastingly is an original *Mona Lisa*. No instance of the book, word-sequence-wise, is aesthetically better than another.

Inherent in the field of art in general, we thus have two contrasting kinds of being that an artwork might have: it may be in the "original vs. copy" mode, or it may be in the "many equal instantiations of the same work" mode.[46] For terminological simplicity, we can follow a phrasing established helpfully by Nelson Goodman in his 1968 book, *Languages of Art*, and refer to the former as "autographic" arts and the latter as "allographic" arts. Translated into these terms, one of Benjamin's key claims is that in the modern age of mechanical reproduction, allographic arts are beginning to take social and psychological precedence over autographic arts, with the result that the unique, autographic, quality of individual works of art – their "aura" – is becoming increasingly unimportant, if not straightforwardly representative of a negative throwback to an earlier age and outmoded conception of art.

With the term "aura," Benjamin refers to an object's unique physical presence. When people attend a stage performance or political speech, for instance, each actor or speaker is physically

---

[45] An exception would be the first photographs, namely, daguerreotypes done on a glass plate, which were unique, one-of-a-kind works. Polaroid snapshots are also one-of-a-kind images.

[46] Some stand in an intermediary position, as when the initial prints in a series are valued more highly than the later ones, even though every print in the series counts as a valid instantiation of the work. Similar cases arise in connection with prints made from a photographer's original negative, but by someone other than the photographer.

present before the audience's eyes and in this sense emanates an aura. The aura is a special quality of presence and distanced admiration, as one might experience upon bumping into a famous actor or musician in an airport or city street. According to Benjamin, an actor's image in a motion picture or photograph lacks this aura of immediate physical presence. The actor is not physically within the presentation, and there are many copies of the image in principle. The actual actor is elsewhere, and if deceased, perhaps nowhere. There is consequently, and supposedly, no aura to be apprehended in such images. In contrast, the original *Mona Lisa* – we refer now to the painting itself, rather than to the woman da Vinci portrayed – has an aura that impresses us when viewing the actual painting in the Louvre. Copies, images, photographs, or films of the painting accordingly lack this aura. One could say that an object's or person's aura lends it a fetish quality, that is, an enhanced value over and beyond what its ordinary image would convey.

Since photographs and motion pictures do not present people in actuality, as we would experience them if they were suddenly to walk into the room with us, and more crucially, since photographs and motion pictures have no single instance in principle, Benjamin believes that these new art forms – both of which are based on the mechanical reproduction of the images – are aura-lacking. We should add, though, that a portrait painting also dissolves a person's aura, if only because the painted portrait is a representation of the person, rather than the person him or herself. There can be many portraits of the person by different artists, or by the same artist on different occasions, as in Rembrandt's set of self-portraits.

As an artwork, the painted portrait has an aura as the unique, non-reproducible, physical object that embodies the work. Since, as a rule, standard photographs of the person printed from the same negative are aesthetically on a par with each other, Benjamin believes that photographs, as well as motion pictures, are artworks that lack an aura. Again, we refer here to the physical work of art's aura, rather than the aura of that which the work of art represents.

It is natural to assume that the aura's disappearance is regrettable, since we tend to value individuality, uniqueness, "this-ness," directly experienced reality, over and above copies, reproductions, indirect apprehensions, and such, if only because the latter usually provide a reduced amount of information in contrast to the original. On the other hand, it is also obvious that books have no original "copy," and that the same musical work can be performed time and time again. Whether it happens to be a nineteenth- twentieth- or twenty-first-century orchestra that performs Beethoven's *Fifth Symphony* in faithful accord with the musical score, the same work is being performed in each case, or so it would seem on the face of things.

In this case, the work of art is more of an abstract entity that can be instantiated at different times or in different places at the same time. Similarly, the filmic work of art does not reside in any particular reel of film, or in any particular DVD. There are no originals or copies in the traditional sense; there are only reiterations, duplications, or reinstantiations of the filmic work. Motion pictures, musical works, and literary works have no aura to begin with. With respect to auras, nothing has been dissolved or lost in these art forms, since what we thought might have been lost, was in fact never there.

Benjamin asserts that as a matter of general social consciousness, the age of mechanical reproduction transforms aesthetic perception to a point where most people develop a disposition to regard *all* artworks – whether they have an aura by nature or not – on the model of aura-less film, music, and literature. The emerging tendency is thus simply not to recognize originals, but to regard all physical works of art as reiterations or duplications, as we find in a stack of books, video cassettes, or DVDs. Every work of art is tacitly assumed to admit of duplication or, nowadays, electronic reiteration.

The replacement of an aura-focused, "original vs. copy" interpretive attitude with one that recognizes the ever-presence of reiterability – an attitude that presumably follows from the eventual prevalence of allographic art over autographic art – is a socially desirable transformation in Benjamin's view. He regards the very logic of "original vs. copy" as politically objectionable, not to mention the inherited cluster of concepts from earlier centuries that the distinction carries along with it. Among the concepts Benjamin includes in this network are ones we have seen operative in earlier chapters, such as "creativity," "genius," "eternal values", and "mystery" – all of which he associates with "aura," individuality, and an oppressive sense of authority. He recalls earlier views where the author/artist/genius was assumed authoritatively to determine the artwork's meaning, much as priests once dictated to their religious followers how the Bible should be interpreted.

Benjamin maintains that these traditional aesthetic concepts are aligned with a dictatorial mentality and should be replaced by new, modern artistic concepts that are antagonistic to fascism. For this reason, he champions photography and the motion picture which, by his lights, embody an aura-less aesthetic that is immune to fascistic manipulations. His view is that autographic arts are pseudo-fascist, bound to ritual, religiously toned, and tethered objectionably to past tradition, and that allographic arts are fascist-resistant, amenable to pure, evenly distributed exhibition, and symbolic of the twentieth-century modern spirit that makes a clean break from the past.

Benjamin formulates his position imaginatively and uniquely, but his attempt to develop a conceptual weapon against dictatorships is rooted in the very nineteenth-century traditions from which he aims modernistically to detach himself. His position also anticipates related developments in the history of revolutionary thought and avant-garde aesthetics that issue from the same nineteenth-century tradition. In particular, Benjamin implicitly repeats Nietzsche's proclamation of the death of God and anticipates Roland Barthes' and Michel Foucault's 1960s attacks on the notion of the "author." These conceptions all relate back to the Protestant Reformation and Martin Luther's ecclesiastical struggle to allow people to interpret the Bible freely, independently of priestly dictates. Their shared aim is to liberate people from the yoke of oppressive authority, whether the oppression stems from priests who represent a spiritually alienating Church, God's panoptic, soul-surveying eye, fascist politicians, authors who intend to control the interpretation of their texts, or conceptual systems that function to constrict the imagination.

In his expression of this perennial theme, it is noteworthy how Benjamin portrays technological advance as a savior from the types of forces that led Schiller, many years earlier, to propose aesthetic education as an antidote for tyranny. Hitler tried to achieve comparable social ends using tyranny itself. He likewise aimed to develop a stronger, forward-looking and more cultured society through a kind of aesthetic education, but did so by imposing exclusively upon the cultural and artistic scene well-proportioned models of the human body, healthy and homey domestic scenes, opera and musical performances in every major city, neoclassical architecture on a grand scale, and an assortment of museums with hand-picked, Nazi-consistent works.

Both Benjamin and Hitler hoped for, and theorized about, better societies and regarded art as the means to social improvement. Hitler brutally instituted classical aesthetic images from a recently bygone age, and in its anachronism, his project was probably doomed from the start; Benjamin advocated the peaceful dissemination of mechanically reproduced styles of art whose presence would supposedly undermine the harsh and oppressive mentality of his reactionary cultural opponents in Germany.[47]

The promotion of mechanically reproduced art runs against the social atmosphere of the early twentieth century in one respect, though, despite its harmony with the modernist idea of breaking away from the past. Issuing from the times of Kierkegaard, Nietzsche, and Dostoevsky, and flourishing during the 1930s and 1940s, existentialist thought constituted a steady undercurrent to intellectual life in Germany and France. Like Benjamin, existentialists emphasized the importance of personal freedom, as evident in Jean-Paul Sartre's and Albert Camus' philosophies. Existentialism, however, also put a premium upon individuality, uniqueness, self-authorship, and sharp differences

---

[47] The anachronism in Nazi art is most evident in its efforts at resurrecting neoclassical painting in the art of the nude. Across the nineteenth century and into the twentieth, the cultural temperament became more historically, existentially, and realistically centered, eventually reaching a point near the end of the nineteenth century where the portrayal of nudes in academic art – an art form that had once been inspiring – had become so palpable as to enter into the spheres of kitsch and soft pornography. The work of William-Adolphe Bouguereau (1825–1925), for example, *The Wave* (1896), is exemplary. By the 1930s, the strong spirit of existential palpability rendered the possibility of rendering inspiringly idealized nudes in the old style almost impossible. This accounts for the mildly comic reaction that inevitably occurs upon apprehending the painting over Hitler's mantelpiece in Munich, Adolph Ziegler's *The Four Elements* (1937). It also accounts for the daringly realistic quality of Gustave Courbet's provocative 1866 work, *L'Origine du Monde* (The Origin of the World).

between things and people. It highly valued what Benjamin calls "aura."

Benjamin's belief that mechanical reproduction disposes us to interpret the world in terms of duplications, reiterations, and reinstantiations is distinctively anti-existentialist in spirit, and instead conveys a more communist quality: insofar as we are all for one and one for all, our personal identity derives from the social whole, rather than from our individual personalities. Although we need not conceive of ourselves as minor variants of the more important, general human book, where each person is essentially the same rational being, much like interchangeable parts in a social mechanism, it would run against Benjamin's view to consider oneself existentially as one of a kind, and as an importantly irreplaceable kind.

3. CONCLUSION AND CRITICISM

Invoking the Marxist idea that a community's social consciousness necessarily echoes changes in the society's economic structure, Benjamin observes that in the age of mechanical reproduction, we will inevitably begin to perceive and interpret our surroundings in terms of duplications, reiterations, and reinstantiations. Simply put, if our lifestyle locates us in front of a computer screen or television set for an extended period of time, it will dispose us to interpret off-screen reality as a universal computer screen or television presentation.

Benjamin consequently anticipates that autographic arts will lose their importance as mechanical reproduction increases its cultural presence and allographic arts take their place. We can expect future generations to live in an age where music, the motion picture, photography (and now, digital photography), and the printed page (and now, webpages) prevail as the socially leading art forms. We can include mass-produced architecture as well, for example, buildings where the designs are minor variations on a basic plan. Individual paintings, sculptures, and unique architectural works will accordingly fade from social importance, at least insofar as they are perceived as irreplaceable, non-reproducible works. This is one way to understand Benjamin's remark that in

Plate 1 Design from the Lindisfarne Gospels manuscript (*c*.700)

Plate 2 Tukaroto Matutaera Potatau Te Wherowhero Tawhiao, Second Maori King – d. 1894 (G. M. Preston Collection, Alexander Turnbull Library, Wellington, New Zealand)

Plate 3 *Discobolus* (Discus Thrower), copy of original statue by Myron, *c*.460–50 BCE

Plate 4 Carl Wilhelm Hübner, *The Silesian Weavers* (1846)

Plate 5 Taj Mahal, Agra, India

Plate 6 Sergey Prokudin-Gorsky, *Nomadic Kyrgyz Family on the Golodnaya Steppe in Uzbekistan* (1911)

Plate 7 Alexander Gardner, *Lewis Thornton Powell* (a.k.a. Lewis Payne), 1865

Plate 8 Diego Velázquez, *Las Meninas* (1656)

Plate 9 Vincent van Gogh, *A Pair of Shoes* (1886)

Plate 10 Honoré Daumier, *Third-Class Carriage* (1862)

the age of mechanical reproduction, the artwork's aura will erode, dissolve, or disappear. It will vanish supposedly because the kinds of art forms that naturally have an aura will either fade from social prominence or will no longer be practiced. We can call this a genuine sense of aura-dissolution, since the allographic arts that will dominate the art scene and general culture will indeed have no original instances.

As noted earlier, sometimes Benjamin speaks of aura-dissolution in a second sense, where although a work of art has an original instance and embodies the "original vs. copy" mode of being, the social disposition will be to ignore that autographic mode of being, and instead interpret the work *as if* it had the allographic being of a photograph or film. Under these conditions, we would begin to believe that a copy of the *Mona Lisa*, assuming it were accurate enough, is just as good, or as aesthetically serviceable as the original. If the original were lost in a fire, it would make no significant aesthetic difference to such a technology-saturated mentality, for it would compare to losing a copy of a book in a fire, assuming hundreds or thousands of other copies were to remain.

Along the same interpretive lines, a photograph of a person would be perceived as substitutable for the real person in many relevant ways. This is not a strange idea. Consider how we can pass someone on a crowded city street momentarily for the first and possibly last time in our lives, and apprehend nothing more than their passing profile. Consider how much more information we would obtain about the person if we had photographed him or her when walking by, and later studied the photograph, with its details far in excess of whatever we might have perceived in the originally passing moment. In such a case, the reproduction of the event could be more aesthetically useful and rewarding than the original event. If one only knows a person through images, as most of us only know movie stars or television personalities, when the person dies and the many images of the person remain, the sense of loss is thinned. One can learn about a movie star's funeral on a news report, and then watch that celluloid hero a few hours later on television or in a cinema.

Benjamin's thought is that the age of mechanical reproduction – now exponentially enhanced by computers and electronic photography – subconsciously leads us to interpret copies of originals as if they were reiterations, possibly even enhanced reiterations, of the original. In this respect, he compares photography to psychoanalysis in its ability to reveal aspects of perceptual experience that would otherwise remain overlooked. The questionable side-effect is that one might see a film about Paris, or scan through an electronic database of Parisian images, and assume self-deceivingly that the imagistic experience is an acceptable substitute for visiting Paris itself. After experiencing the film or set of images, one's desire to visit Paris or know more about the city may dissolve.

The irony is that part of what makes such experiences and attitudes possible – and this is a feature of traditional photographic imagery that Benjamin does not closely examine – is the causal, information-conveying relationship between the original scene, person, or object, and the photographic image of that scene, person, or object. When we look at a photograph of some past event, knowing that the event caused the image, it is easy to imagine that we are looking at the event through a window in time. The light rays from the event touched the photographic plate, and now the light rays from the plate touch our eyes, preserving for us the original event's visual form. When perceiving photographs, it consequently seems as if one is looking directly into the past, and this evidentiary quality preserves the object's aura to some extent. Contrary to Benjamin's assertion, the object's aura never dissolves in traditional photography, but only fades, assuming we look at photographs as people once looked at religious icons, where one was brought into the deity's very presence.

Two dimensions of "aura" thus remain blurred in Benjamin's discussion. The first is the aura of the person who is photographed and that the photograph preserves via the causal sequence; the second is how photographs do not have auras as works of art, since in connection with the photograph's artistic being, there is no "original" photograph of which there are merely derivative copies, but simply reiterations of the photograph. Benjamin claims that photography dissolves a person's aura because the photographic process produces no originals, but the causal or evidentiary quality of the photograph can make us feel as if we are looking directly through time at the person who is photographed. Photographs are aura-preserving in that respect, even though photography is an allographic art. Traditional photography and film dissolve the notion of aura only formally, one can say, but they preserve it in terms of their content, that is, in the subjects to which they refer and reveal.

The situation changes in electronic, or digital, photography, since this medium erodes the image's evidentiary quality. Electronic images can be manipulated to a point where the work represents little of the original events that caused the image. Digital photography is more like painting, or lithography, where the imagination can construct the image from scratch. Electronic images are nonetheless mechanically reproducible, and so digital photography remains an allographic art. Since digital photography tends to lack the evidentiary quality of traditional photography, and hence is not necessarily tied down to any original or authoritative event, the aura is dissolved more effectively in this electronic medium. So, wonderfully enough, Benjamin's arguments from 1936 about photography's dissolution of the aura apply more effectively to digital photography than to traditional photography. His insights were so far ahead of their time that no one could then imagine how well future developments would conform to his projections.

In digital photography, though, we experience not the aura's full dissolution, but the substitution of a virtual, or imitation, aura for a genuine one. This is due to digital photography's intriguing capacity to substitute an illusory aura – or the mere "form" of an aura – in place of the traditionally caused aura. Since digital photography can preserve and replicate the high resolution of detail experienced in direct perception, it has the ability to construct a digital image of fictional quality that, owing to its realistic detail, appears to represent an actual object or scene. In this production of a virtual reality, the realistic form of directly perceivable objects has been extracted and detached from its original context, and applied to a fictional construction. The resulting representations can be of single objects or of entire scenarios and environments in a moving, filmic form, as in video games.

This reality-replicating quality of digital photography and digital film structurally matches a phenomenon we observed in Kant's formalistic conception of beauty, namely, that the form of beauty can be detached from actually beautiful objects, and added rhetorically to any given subject to lend it an evidentiary and moral quality, even if the subject is misrepresentative and/or immoral. The problem of beautifying misrepresentative or immoral subjects arose within this context, and it parallels the rhetorical use of virtual reality (that is, aura-projection) onto a given subject matter. Through the latter, we render a subject more tangible as a virtual reality, even if it is purely fictional. Beautifully painted portraits of criminals thus compare rhetorically to digitally constructed (that is, fake) documentary photographs of supposed news events. A false objectivity, or *logos*, is added in the two instances.

Benjamin might have anticipated digital photography without realizing it, but these reflections bear negatively on his political purpose in promoting photography and film as a means to combat fascism, which was his essay's aim. We can question his success in light of how both traditional and digital photographs carry an evidentiary quality, either genuine or apparent. Causal processes underlie both kinds of photography and preserve an appearance of aura, which Benjamin was hoping would dissolve. In effect, Benjamin rested his main argument too heavily upon the allographic, aura-absent, formal quality of photography and film, and did not take into account their evidentiary quality that remains aura-preserving.

Further detracting from his essay's political plausibility, Benjamin also did not sufficiently explore film's hypnotic quality – a dimension that is independent of the notion of aura around which the essay revolves. Films are psychologically hypnotic owing to their basic link to visual perception and information processing. In tension with this, Benjamin argues that as an artistic medium, film, quite unlike live theatre, is distanced from the actual events owing to its being a mere representation of those events, and concludes that film is inherently criticism-stimulating. There is some truth to his observation, but film's hypnotic power to absorb and capture people's attention tends to overpower its criticism-stimulating aspect.

Ever since Leni Riefenstahl's *Triumph of the Will* (1935), it has been obvious that film's combined evidentiary and hypnotic quality allows it to serve as a powerful propagandistic device for fascist politics. The motion picture might lack an aura as a work of art, but the way it presents its subject matters retains a sense of aura that can operate contrary to Benjamin's thesis about the liberating quality of photography and film. In the worst-case scenario, film and photography – and one can add television – can become the opium of the people, and can render large populations complacent and insensitive to revolutionary issues. Our chapter on Gilles Deleuze focuses on cinema theory to extend Benjamin's core insight, and we will see how Deleuze describes ways to construct motion pictures that resist this propagandistic outcome.

The combination of film's hypnotic and evidentiary qualities provides a potent rhetorical tool that is essentially surrealistic in its imaginative blend of dream and evidentiary reality. This surrealism is one of the motion picture's basic, formal qualities, so whatever subject matter we happen to film, the presentation will be framed surrealistically, and this framing will automatically render the subject psychologically attractive and captivating. Had Benjamin appreciated the inherently surrealistic quality of the motion picture, he might have hesitated to define it as an intrinsic weapon against fascism, but rather more neutrally and instrumentally, like a knife or gun that might work either for or against liberation.

10

THE ART OF ATONAL AUTONOMY

Theodor Adorno

1. ART AND *THE DIALECTIC OF ENLIGHTENMENT*

To avoid persecution by the Nazis, Theodor Adorno (1903–69) fled Germany in 1934 for England, and, after a move to New York, settled in California, where he found himself amidst the newly emerging American culture of advertising, mass marketing, and the movie industry of the early 1940s. In Los Angeles, with his colleague-in-exile, Max Horkheimer, he co-authored *The Dialectic of Enlightenment* (1944), which became one of Adorno's and Horkheimer's most influential books. Having developed personally as sophisticated European intellectuals, much like Walter Benjamin, and although relieved to have escaped the terrors back home, neither Adorno nor Horkheimer was particularly comfortable with American culture, mainly due to a tastelessness, showiness, vulgarity, and veneration of mere entertainment that they perceived at the core of Hollywood's film-making industry. Unlike Benjamin, they regarded motion pictures – especially the widely distributed ones that Hollywood was producing – as a threat to human freedom. The films were so captivating and entertaining, while being so kitschy and implicitly propagandistic, that the attitudinal damage they could inflict upon their audiences became obvious.

Adorno's and Horkheimer's observation did not stem from an uninformed or naively immediate aesthetic experience, but from a cultivated aesthetic perception that had been tempered by the awareness of the seventeenth- to twentieth-century efforts to develop an enlightened culture, that is, a culture based on reason, where reason is held up as the sole intellectual light. Their critical views recall Friedrich Schiller's insofar as the latter perceived how the initially inspiring French Revolutionary attempts to install reason alone as the foundation of religion, and arbiter of justice, transformed into a social-political disaster. As Schiller learned about the Reign of Terror from neighboring Germany, he struggled to understand how such initially fine thoughts could have such terrible results.

Tracing the course of reason's history since the French Revolution, Adorno and Horkheimer maintain that what happened to the French Revolution within the short span of a few years has been happening within Western culture during the longer term. They interpret Germany's barbaric behavior during World War II as yet another Reign of Terror, except that by the time we reach World War II, we are experiencing the effects of how reason has slowly turned against itself. For them, reason – the god of the Enlightenment – contains self-destructive factors that inevitably lead to totalitarianism. World War II's display of inhumanity was not an aberrant phenomenon that started and ended with the Nazis; it was part of a wider historical process that had been brewing for over 150 years, expressive of Enlightenment reason's "dialectic," or turning to its opposite, in which an initially divinely-conceived reason becomes plagued by its own inherent demons.

An intellectual resource for Adorno's and Horkheimer's assessment of Western culture is their reading of Kant's philosophy of the 1780s, from which they extract a conception of reason based on Kant's notions of "understanding" and "reason," along with the principles of his theory of knowledge. As we know, Kant describes our understanding and human finitude as grounded in logic, mathematics, and geometry. He further describes reason as an integrating drive for systematicity and unconditional comprehension. His theory of knowledge characterizes us as beings who process data in our own rational, and yet finite, spatio-temporal image, such that our knowledge always bears the stamp of our cognitive processing. We apprehend an objective, mind-independent reality, but it appears to us as a world that carries the form of our own image, as if we were always looking into a mirror.

These assorted dimensions of understanding, reason, and knowledge do not obviously indicate a sinister force, but Adorno and Horkheimer observe that when we comprehend human beings in a purely logical, mathematical, and geometrical way, a dehumanizing effect is unavoidable. People appear as objects that one can add or subtract, like numbers on an accountant's balance sheet, or they appear as mere units in space that absorb and expend measurable quantities of energy, or similarly, simply earn and spend money. Since mathematical thinking closely aligns with instrumental thinking, as when we formulate natural laws for the sake of controlling nature, it can foster an aggressive and manipulative attitude by those who apply mathematical reasoning too rigorously to the human context. The very concept of causality, moreover, involves one event pushing deterministically into another event, as if it were giving orders to move.

If we add, to the above picture, the disposition to achieve thoroughgoing systematicity in the management of social organizations, we end up facing collections of controlling individuals who are disposed to regard their fellow human beings as objects to use, and who are preoccupied with achieving power over others. This generates governmental structures that dictate laws and control the economy and most citizens' movements, activities, and thoughts, all of which, brick by brick, work towards building a panoptic dictatorship, typically with good social intentions.

Adorno and Horkheimer conclude that reason harbors a sinister dictatorial side, that it is not the entirely positive, godlike, redeeming force it was first believed so inspiringly and naively to be, and that the Enlightenment mentality intrinsically gravitates towards a police state. They are accordingly on the lookout for social situations, cultural trends, and media phenomena that display a systematic and controlling quality. Among the social spheres in which they perceive this suffocating quality is in the "culture industry," as they witnessed it paradigmatically in California, although they apprehended reason's totalitarian tendencies long before they arrived in the United States.

Taking the notions of "system," "totality," "wholeness" – key ideas from Hegel's philosophy, and constitutive of his famous dictum that "the truth is the whole" – to be among rationality's *objectionable* features, Adorno and Horkheimer discern rationality's influential presence in the large commercial organization of mass media and popular culture.[48] They specifically have in mind the film industry, the music industry, and the radio industry, which soon became the television industry. One can add the sectors of large-scale publishing, in connection with the numerous newspapers and magazines that fill many people's minds and absorb their spare time. The guiding thought is that owing to the potentially widespread distribution of mass media commodities, there follows in suit an underlying business motivation to entertain as many people as possible, principally for the sake of reaping the most profits from the sale of the films, music, books, broadcasts, and the like. Adorno and Horkheimer associate with this commercial interest a constrained notion of artistic style that is disposed to reiterate successful commodities, and is hesitant to take intellectual or artistic chances by departing from already proven formulas.

The culture industry's capitalist interest in perpetuating widespread social appeal and commercial success leads to a leveling, schematization, and easy absorbability of artistic content, and hence a rigidification and formulaic predictability of the artistic productions. The result is a self-reinforcing cycle where the culture industry produces the sort of entertainment it expects will be profitable, and where its successful productions, upon being reiterated and re-injected into the society, serve in turn to mold people's tastes to prepare the way for yet further reinforcing instances of the same artistic kind. An example and descendent of the early movie serials is the practice of making sequels to successful movies, such as the *Rocky* boxing saga, the 1976 original of which was followed by five further movies of the same kind in 1979, 1982, 1985, 1990, and 2006, earning over a billion dollars in gross revenues. Similarly, the horror movie *Halloween* (1978) had sequels in 1981, 1982, 1988, 1989, 1995, 1998, and 2002,

---

[48] Recall that Kierkegaard also objected to Hegel's "system." It is no accident that both Kierkegaard's and Adorno's aesthetic ideals resonate with the grating expressive qualities of modern atonal music.

with remakes of the first two in 2007 and 2009. Although the artistic quality of the sequels varies, the aim of each sequel is to duplicate the entertaining qualities of the original movie for commercial profit.

Adorno and Horkheimer maintain that this dominance of the profit motive leads to a pervasive decline in aesthetic quality across the culture. They refer in this context to "aesthetic barbarism," to the artworks' calculating and manipulative quality, and to an objectionable "sameness" in the artistic productions. They also despair over the loss of content that occurs when, in film or popular music, artistic masterpieces are simplified for easy consumption. The prescribed counter-reaction is to insist on a strong resistance to the presence of sameness and reiteration within the field of artistic creation and appreciation.

Not only does the degradation of taste – a situation where people enjoy as intellectually satisfying and illuminating, artistic productions that are provably superficial and formulaic – emerge as one of Adorno's and Horkheimer's leading concerns, they note with unease how the lack of taste plays into the hands of manipulative and ambitious political leaders. Since the culture industry's artworks are superficial by nature, their form renders them amenable to propagandistic, sloganeering, ideological, and stereotype-reinforcing use. Adorno and Horkheimer convey the message that since totalitarian leaders have a vested interest in keeping the population's taste unrefined through such mass media productions, the social situation would improve if there were more critical reflection upon these modes of mass entertainment and, echoing Schiller, a greater cultivation of taste.

Having developed sharp eyes for this phenomenon after seeing how the Nazis used art and propaganda to solidify their regime, Adorno and Horkheimer observe similar tendencies in the United States' culture industry, insofar as the productions share a structural consistency and amenability to political manipulation. There is also a suggestion that the California-based culture industry is even more ominous, since the ideologically charged artworks are presented with an air of relaxed freedom, good-naturedness and joyful entertainment, without stimulating the suspicion that anyone is being held under a manipulative hand.

Such ideas are familiar to contemporary culture criticism, and the salient feature of Adorno's and Horkheimer's analysis of the culture industry is their rendition of the industry's pervasive quality to the point of evoking a sense of hopelessness. They outline instance after instance where superficiality, formulaic thinking, propagandistic messages, reflection-numbing captivation, fantasy fulfillment, and distraction from pressing social issues are present in the artworks made for mass consumption, and they give the impression that the culture industry has succeeded in imprisoning millions of people in an aesthetic quagmire, from which extrication is either unlikely or extremely difficult. Their vision is dire, and they sound a cultural alarm tempered with the sobering tone that the presently existing damage might already be so debilitating that the situation might be unsalvageable. Over a century earlier, Schiller expressed similar frustrations in his effort to identify contemporary poets who were still natural and naive; Nietzsche was likewise overwhelmed by the debilitated culture that he perceived all around him.

Despite their tone of alarm, despair, and unrelenting fault-finding, Adorno and Horkheimer were not the first to argue that the prevailing state of the arts has suffered extensive downgrading, and that a more liberating alternative is required to set the society on a more productive path. At the end of the nineteenth century, Leo Tolstoy's short book, *What is Art?* (1899), offered a similar diagnosis. Reporting on the cultural scene in Russia, Tolstoy distinguishes authentic from counterfeit art, where the latter is held to be superficial, formulaic, and a waste of time, money, and people's careers, much in the way Adorno and Horkheimer describe the productions of the culture industry.

It is instructive to mention Adorno and Horkheimer in connection with Tolstoy, since their argumentative form, estimations, and complaints about their respectively surrounding cultures is essentially the same, while their critical contents are the reverse of one another, since their respective conceptions of authentic, liberating, higher art are at the opposite ends of the spectrum. Tolstoy distinguishes authentic, universally appealing art from counterfeit, elitist art, argues that the former is preferable, and specifically expresses a strong preference for simple Russian folk songs as opposed to Beethoven's symphonies, precisely because the folk songs can unite all people with a positive, emotional bond. He regards the symphonies as socially divisive, given their complex structure and educated aesthetic awareness that informs their composition, not to mention the exclusively high cost of attending concerts. Adorno criticizes the economics of theatre and concert tickets as well, but Tolstoy's celebrated folk songs are the kinds of musical productions that Adorno regards as superficial, uncultivated, and lacking in taste. To appreciate Adorno's position and criticism of popular art, it will help to consider his views on music, to which he devoted a large part of his writings.

2. ADORNO'S WRITINGS ON MUSIC

Among Adorno's most frequently cited essays is his "On Jazz" from 1936, written almost a decade before *The Dialectic of Enlightenment*. In this earlier essay, Adorno displays a comparably critical attitude towards mass culture, regarding jazz music through a cluster of negative associations to popular music, mass marketability, rational predictability, and the standardization of form, in addition to claims about jazz music's mere illusion of spontaneity, improvisation, and originality. Referring to Duke Ellington (1899–1974) as a principal representative, Adorno's essay dates from a time when jazz was at its beginnings, prior to its transformation during the 1950s and 1960s into less standardized and more free-form modes. Adorno's intellectual approach casts a suspicious eye upon popular culture as a breeding ground for fascism, and this illuminates his discontent with jazz.

Adorno's particular dissatisfaction with jazz music revolves around its pretention to avant-garde status, while being mainstream in fact, and, as a mainstream phenomenon, exemplary of the principles of popular music that are supposedly consistent with a totalitarian social enterprise. Jazz presents itself as spontaneous and new, but rests upon traditional and popular musical formats; jazz presents itself as musically complex, but from a music-theoretical standpoint, it is relatively simple; jazz presents itself as rebellious, but its leaders compare well with the more amenable Benny Goodman and Guy Lombardo; jazz presents itself as original or primal African-American music, but its roots to such music are relatively distant and tenuous. Adorno accordingly perceives jazz music as a hypocritical art and a pretender to the aesthetic throne, which plays into the hands of a manipulative and taste-degrading mass culture more than it tends to realize. In this respect, jazz is more objectionable than popular culture's straightforward kitsch, since the latter does not pretend to embody a revolutionary or avant-garde quality.

Objections can be mounted against Adorno's estimation of jazz and jazz musicians, for there are counterexamples to his analysis that date from the time of his essay (such as Louis Armstrong), and counterexamples that issue from later times (such as John Coltrane). Adorno's assimilation of jazz into the category of popular music, thereby saddling it with the latter's problems, is also questionable, if only because for most of its history, jazz has not been a leading popular art form.

It is fair to add, though, that musicians such as Louis Armstrong, Duke Ellington, John Coltrane, Charlie Parker, and Miles Davis have become cultural icons, and in the case of Miles Davis, have sold millions of recordings to secure a lasting and respected place in popular culture and musical history. If the assimilation into popular culture indicates an artist's consistency with the status quo and prevailing market values, then it is worth considering whether the art is unconsciously supportive of the totalitarian forces that Adorno fears, for there is a sense in Adorno's view where sheer success in marketability and mass appeal renders an artist or art form suspect. One can also reflect upon the number of people who buy musical recordings merely for their status value rather than pure aesthetic value, given how the commodity form dominates contemporary music and how status symbols are mainly commodities.

Since Adorno is critical of rationality's claim to ensure social progress, his disapproval of the various arts highlights their rationalistic structures, as he questions whether those structures are implicitly dominating and constraining. This is partially why he criticizes traditional music for its foundation in intuitively comprehensible architectonic structures that rest upon chord sequences, harmonies, and melodies that logically develop and satisfyingly resolve. His critique is not limited to contemporary popular music, but includes much classical music, among the most prominent of which is Richard Wagner's, which Adorno regards explicitly as a repressive voice that speaks the language of fascism. By discerning the striking similarity between Wagner's music and the top-quality scores that often accompany feature

Hollywood films – Wagner is a forerunner of John Williams – it becomes easier to appreciate Adorno's resistance to popular music of even the more complicated and accomplished sorts.

To formulate how Adorno conceives of an artistic resistance to such musical forms, we can enumerate the correspondingly opposite qualities to those characteristic of the popular art and music that he tends to condemn. This indicates a kind of art that is not easily marketable, that cannot make a profit, that does not seek mass appeal, that is not rationally structured, that does not lend itself to easy listening, that is unfamiliar, that is antagonistic to beauty, that is essentially incomprehensible and resistant to psychological processes of simplistic reduction, that breaks away from past traditions and is completely new, that defies totalities, and that thereby resists appropriation and use by political manipulators. For Adorno, one of the best examples of this kind of modern art is Arnold Schoenberg's atonal music, or more broadly, that of the Second Viennese School, which defies traditional harmonies and has never enjoyed widespread appreciation. More generally, Adorno celebrates modern art insofar as it is intellectually challenging and self-consciously divorced from past traditions. He espouses arts that are autonomous, that define their own rules, speak in their own terms, indicate a realm beyond fixed and regimented totalities, and express freedom from oppression thereby.

3. ADORNO'S *AESTHETIC THEORY*

Adorno's writings conclude with the monumental work *Aesthetic Theory*, which was close to completion at the time of his death in 1969, and was published a year later. This is a complex, non-systematic study that, in a lengthy series of short sections, addresses aesthetic topics that range from natural beauty, to ugliness, to the nature of artworks, to the role of art in society. Guiding the work is Adorno's concern with combating totalitarianism in its many forms, and he composes it within a discourse inspired by the thought of Kant, Hegel, Freud – against which Adorno reacts – as informed by his extensive knowledge of modern art and his battle against the leveling trends of contemporary mass culture.

Underlying many of Adorno's analyses in *Aesthetic Theory* is his critique of Hegelian dialectical reason from *Negative Dialectics* (1966), where he portrays Hegel's dialectics as an objectionably totalizing form of reason, and hence as politically totalitarian. At the basis of his critique is a rudimentary idea and common observation that an abstract general concept, precisely because it is an abstraction, must disregard many details of the specific objects that are subsumed under it. If we decide to refer exclusively and abstractly to a car in general, for example, then for any car referred to, we must disregard the car's size, shape, weight, power, and color, among its other qualities. The cars' concrete details are lost in the process of abstraction. By confusing a description of a musical performance with the music itself, or a biography with the actual person, or a totalizing network of concepts that form a philosophical system with the physical, social, and concretely complicated reality that the system aims to characterize, one disregards the distinction between concept and actual thing. Individuality, however, always outstrips conceptual formulations, no matter how specifically the latter may reach. Concepts and objects, or essence and existence, never fully coincide. Contrary to how Hegel's dialectical thought tries so powerfully to fix the concrete truth, Adorno's appreciation of how objects and existence refuse to be conceptually nailed down informs his philosophical writing.

As we have seen in the chapter on Hegel, his systematic thought aims to comprehend everything in the world that is considered to be important, without remainder, such as to grow into a condition of absolute knowledge. His developmental progress of increasingly rich and comprehensive concepts by means of continual opposition and reconciliation presents a magnificently integrated pattern of thought that presumes a capability of absorbing every important detail. Here, exactly, is where the interpretive difficulties reside, namely, with respect to what one regards as significant or important for inclusion within a theory. If one were to argue that all of the world's perceptual details are important, then Hegel's, or any, system would face immediate defeat, for no system of abstractions has room enough to include the world itself.

When Adorno describes the philosophical will to system in *Negative Dialectics*, he likens the mind to a hungry stomach that desires to consume everything, stating, "the system is the belly turned mind, and rage is the mark of each and every idealism."[49] This rage is a "rage against nonidentity," where thought appropriately aims to grasp, comprehend, or hold fast the overwhelmingly detailed reality that continually stands before it, such as to achieve an identity between concept and object. Adorno's analogy characterizes philosophical systematizers as thinkers whose intention is to categorize, rigidify, render with a structure of necessary relations, and hence *control*, reality itself. His position is that this essentially scientific project is not only impossible, but is politically repugnant in light of the totalitarianism and megalomania it implies.

Adorno's characterization of the will to philosophical systematization as a rage against non-identity bears a thematic affinity to the "nausea" that figures centrally in the existentialist thought of Jean-Paul Sartre, and, by implication, to Sartre's notion of jazz music that compares in reference and contrasts in value with Adorno's. By considering this dual relationship, we can situate Adorno's aesthetics in a sharper light.

In his novel *Nausea* (1938), Sartre draws our attention to a disconcerting way in which the overwhelmingly rich, contingent, incomprehensible, material, extensively overflowing details of the perceptual world are sometimes experienced. The experience is partially caused by the realization that the perceptual details of ordinary things defy the capacity of conceptual definitions to capture their palpable presence. This generates the feeling that one's ability to comprehend the world is weak and ineffective, and that complete philosophical understanding, especially when it assumes a systematic or mathematical form, is impossible. As the incomprehensibility, absurdity, meaninglessness, and blunt materiality of the perceptual world become evident, the upshot is a terrible feeling of nausea and alienation from both self and world. Under these conditions, looking at one's face in the mirror yields not much beyond the raw apprehension of a fleshy mass, as one might apprehend a piece of meat in the supermarket.

Sartre's main character in the novel who experiences this nausea – a biographer named Roquentin – eventually finds release

---

[49] Adorno, *Negative Dialectics*, p. 23.

from his feelings of anxiety, weakness, meaninglessness, uncertainty, impotence, frequent boredom, and lack of purpose, upon listening to a phonograph playing a jazz piece, "Some of These Days," sung by a woman of African descent, that defines for him a "perfect moment." The music's organic unity, necessary thematic development, firmness, consistency, transcendence of everyday details, meaningfulness, and communication of strength all combine to create a redeeming, enlivening, and yet knowingly illusory presentation. This, if we recall Nietzsche's theory of tragedy, closely parallels how Nietzsche describes the experience of the ancient Greeks, who allegedly used tragic theatre to relieve themselves of nihilistic and debilitating feelings. In both Sartre and Nietzsche, art provides strength as it obscures the difficult truth of the world's meaninglessness.

Adorno's account of jazz music as a product of the culture industry works in opposition here, since the qualities that Sartre's Roquentin finds attractive in the jazz, such as its organic unity, necessary development, and firmness, are features of the rationality that Adorno characterizes as totalitarian and contrary to social liberation. As does Sartre, Adorno hopes to preserve the recognition of life's concrete details, but rather than seeking redemption in a security-providing system – for one can see the quest for system not only as an expression of rage *simpliciter*, but as an initial strategy for combating fear, whose frustration often leads to rage, or, in the case of Sartre, leads to nausea – he regards the flight into the arms of such a comforting system as a most unattractive solution. Sartre's choice of jazz music as an aesthetic mode of redemption is thus disappointing from the standpoint of Adorno's aesthetics, for in terms of Adorno's critique of jazz music, Sartre's celebration of jazz is not redemptive, but is exemplary of a mentality that invites totalitarianism.

The particular song in question, "Some of These Days," was written in 1910, and is considered to be the first twentieth-century popular standard. It was recorded in 1911 by Sophie Tucker – a Jewish-American singer who sang in blackface until 1909 and who studied with African-American singers to absorb their style. It was also recorded by Louis Armstrong, Bing Crosby, and many others. These details are revealing, since it supports Adorno's view that early jazz and popular music went hand in hand.

Instead of upholding popular jazz music as an ideal, Adorno, as mentioned earlier, features the atonal music of the Second Viennese School as aesthetically more valuable and paradigmatic of authentic art. His appreciation of Schoenberg's music tends to be more formalistically oriented, as he describes in detail how atonal music does not adhere to the structure of traditional classical music. Adorno also notes, though, that the expressive properties of atonal music are ideal for communicating feelings of tension, suffering, confusion, anxious inwardness, violence, and irrationality – feelings characteristic of the twentieth-century spirit as Adorno apprehends it, as anticipated by Kierkegaard. Adorno is particularly sensitive to the immensity of human suffering and, echoing Schopenhauer's antagonistic attitude towards optimism, has little respect for art that jovially ignores it or makes light of it.

Adorno's enthusiasm for art and music that coheres well with Schoenberg's paradigm, expresses an appreciation of *autonomous* art, namely, art that self-consciously tries to remain separate from the influence of the culture industry or the accepted aesthetic mainstream. This can be achieved only as a matter of degree, since some commodification is inevitable, but Adorno believes that the least commodified and least rationally structured kinds of arts are optimal for the cultivation of taste and corresponding social resistance to regimented, hierarchical forms. He thus champions early twentieth-century modernism, which, in its focus on "the new," tries to sever its ties to nineteenth-century art forms. Just as modernism tries to divorce itself from the academic art of the past, the best modernist artists also try to divorce themselves from the contemporary culture industry of the mainstream.

It is tempting to criticize Adorno's strong attraction to modern art as a fatal flaw in his aesthetics, since the modernist period was arguably a passing phase and is no longer socially prevalent. If we survey the past centuries, however, and note that at the end of the nineteenth century and the early twentieth century there were breakthroughs in geometry, physics, logic, visual art, and music – we refer here to visionaries such as Lobachevsky, Riemann, Einstein, Frege, Picasso, and Schoenberg – who dramatically and irreversibly changed the face of cultural life, and if we wonder whether any advances since then have been comparably influential, one might pause before rejecting Adorno's attraction to artistic modernism.

In light of such reflections, the question naturally arises for Adorno's aesthetics whether the subsequent era of pop art and postmodern art represents an advance, stagnation, or even degeneration of artistic sensibilities, for its incorporation of advertising imagery in pop art, along with the postmodernist reintroduction of nineteenth-century decorative forms in an amalgamated pastiche, presents a confusing picture. On the one hand, these art forms intend to be rebellious and antagonistic to traditional, ladder-like, or systematic structures, while on the other, they paradoxically express this antagonism through an artistic heteronymy that incorporates images that are entrenched in the culture industry. The art may intend to be socially critical, but it is not self-enclosed and aesthetic monadic in accord with Adorno's aesthetic ideal.

A way to form a critical judgment of postmodern art from the standpoint of Adorno's aesthetics is to assume that rebelliousness against the status quo, or perpetual quest for "the new" *per se*, does not quite capture the uniqueness and specificity of Adorno's view. We find this idea in Nietzsche's philosophy as well, where he advocates the creation of new values and a war against traditional morality. Artists throughout the ages have arguably been operating with this fertile idea, which is to say that every society has its chaos-introducing, taboo-breaking, artistic avant-garde, if we use the latter term broadly. Paolo Veronese's 1573 trial before the Inquisition in Venice for having depicted the Last Supper with "buffoons, drunken German dwarfs and other such absurdities" is an example. To say, then, that Adorno's aesthetics is simply an aesthetics of the avant-garde would characterize it too generally.

Salient in Adorno's theory is a more historically centered view that directs our attention to issues that concern contemporary totalitarianism, the capitalist culture industry and the degenerative qualities of the pre-twentieth-century artistic tradition, as this tradition has been subsequently incorporated by mass media, as we have seen in the extreme case of the Nazis' efforts to reinstate neoclassicism during the mid-century. The question in judging postmodern art, then, involves estimating the extent to which it reinforces the culture industry's values, while it simultaneously aims to express a social critique in its resistance to consistency in traditional style.

Adorno's view is that the more an art is entrenched in the culture industry, the more difficult it becomes to escape its clutches, and hence that the optimal position would be as disengaged from that industry as possible. Autonomous art is distanced art, and by adopting a thematic distance from the oppressive status quo, it is in principle a less corrupted, and hence freer and truer, art. The verdict on pop art and postmodernism would be to regard its attempts at self-conscious ironic and playful mocking of tradition, in comparison to modernist art's serious and more literalistic detachment from tradition, as a less socially enlightened and less effective approach.

Adorno's critique of the French existentialists of the 1940s, and, by extension, the Beatniks of the 1950s, can apply here to the pop artists and postmodernists: the French existentialists wore beards, "acting like cavemen who refuse to play along with the cultural swindle, while in fact they merely don the old-fashioned emblem of the patriarchal dignity of their grandfathers."[50] The same can apply to the early jazz musicians in Adorno's perspective. The pop art and postmodernist situation compares to writing obscenities in scare quotes, such that one simultaneously does, and does not, utter profanities. The modernist would simply not mention them.

This interpretation of the core of Adorno's aesthetics renders his concern with totalitarianism a monolithic concept that compares with the aesthetic styles of many earlier thinkers, all of whom were dominated by one or another overriding preoccupation that established the contours of their aesthetic theory. Kant, as we have seen, was concerned with securing universally valid knowledge; Hegel, with a dialectically structured metaphysics; Freud, with the exposure of repressed psychological contents; and Marx, with social reform. Benjamin similarly regarded the very distinction between original and copy as a fundamentally negative way of thinking.

Like Marx, Adorno addresses the role of art as a means of social critique or rebellion, even though he takes his principle a

---

[50] Adorno, *Negative Dialectics*, p. 123.

step higher. Upon using the quest for non-systematicity and disruption of oppressive totalities as the leading idea of his atonal philosophy, this idea itself assumes an oppressive quality as it permeates his entire vision of art. It remains, though, that for Adorno, since "art may be the only remaining medium of truth in an age of incomprehensible terror and suffering," the oppressiveness of his anti-totalitarian principle might be justified on the grounds of our living during an oppressively desperate historical situation where consumerism has become the people's opiate.[51] Once again, one can appeal to the situation's desperation and the subsequent atmosphere of crisis as a reason for adopting exclusive, hardline, freedom-restricting remedies. The rationale, as we can see today, is perennial.

There remains a dilemma in Adorno's position with which we can conclude. If reason becomes increasingly unreasonable, and if pure reason is a fantasy, then we have rationally nowhere to turn. We cannot turn towards the irrational, since this is the force that has infected reason to render it unreasonable. Neither can we turn towards reason, since it has now become diseased. How an art can be socially critical, and be neither the embodiment of irrationality nor the embodiment of irrationality-infected reason, would be the crucial and residual question for Adorno's aesthetics.

---

[51] Adorno, *Aesthetic Theory*, p. 23.

11

THE ART OF POETICALLY DISCLOSING TRUTH

Martin Heidegger

1. THE ORIGIN OF THE WORK OF ART

One of Martin Heidegger's most influential essays in aesthetics is "The Origin of the Work of Art," which he completed in 1936.[52] Its timing is historically noteworthy, since it issues from the same year as Walter Benjamin's "The Work of Art in the Age of Mechanical Reproduction" and Theodor Adorno's "On Jazz." It also precedes Jean-Paul Sartre's novel, *Nausea*, by only two years – a work we described above within the context of Adorno's critique of the culture industry. During this time, Heidegger (1889–1976) was a philosophy professor at the University of Freiburg and was a member of the Nazi party. The year 1936 also saw the Olympic Games in Berlin, when the Nazi regime had gone a long way towards coalescing its power and, although known to be oppressive and aggressive, had not yet become the notorious instigator of a World War. These assorted facts invite us to consider the contents of Heidegger's essay in light of the anti-fascist writings of Benjamin and Adorno, and to ask whether

---

[52] Heidegger first gave a lecture entitled "The Origin of the Work of Art" in November 1935 in Freiburg, repeated the lecture in January 1936 in Zürich, and presented an enhanced version in November and December 1936 in Frankfurt.

the essay resonates or conflicts with the freedom-seeking attitudes that Benjamin and Adorno expressed against the Nazis.

Heidegger's essay represents an effort to reveal the basic philosophical structure of "the work of art," considered in a broad-ranging sense to include ancient Greek temples as well as nineteenth- and twentieth-century paintings such as Vincent van Gogh's *A Pair of Shoes* (1886) (Plate 9), to which Heidegger refers.[53] Using the term "art" honorifically, he considers more precisely the philosophical structure of genuine or true art. Starting from the self-evident, Heidegger observes initially that works of art are typically embodied in media such as stone, paint, sound, or ink, and are physical things that people display in museums, hang on walls, locate on bookshelves, or listen to in concert halls. This preliminary inquiry examines the thing-like quality of artworks, insofar as this quality might reveal the nature of the work of art *per se*.

When reaching into the reservoir of past philosophical concepts for some illumination of the thing-like character of artworks, Heidegger encounters a difficulty, for he perceives that the leading philosophical concepts of a thing, or, similarly, of a perceptual object, do not connect well with what we ordinarily understand to be an artwork's artistic quality or artistic being. In fact, they seem to obscure it. These conceptions of a "thing" are familiar from philosophers such as John Locke, George Berkeley, and Aristotle, who respectively describe a thing in literalistic, objective terms, as a blank substance in which perceptual qualities inhere (Locke), as a mere set of perceptual qualities (Berkeley), or as an amalgamation of matter and form (Aristotle).[54] Noting that the latter concept of "formed matter" prevails in the history of Western aesthetics, Heidegger concludes that this history rests on some fundamentally misleading concepts that need to be rethought. The traditional philosophical conceptions of a thing are literalistic and amenable to scientific descriptions of the world, but they fail to touch the *poetic* nature of works of art.

Looking further into the Aristotelian concept's original meaning, Heidegger adds that the conception of a thing as formed

---

[53] We will examine Heidegger's interpretation of this painting in Chapter 15.
[54] This sequence from Locke, to Berkeley, to Aristotle is inspired by Hegel's discussion of the perceptual object in *The Phenomenology of Spirit* (§§119–23).

matter issues from a yet more basic attitude towards physical objects as things that we use. As "equipment," things have purposes, and these purposes are what lend them their physical configurations and define their substantial form. Items such as cups, hammers, and books all appear as they do because their forms follow their respective functions, and the functions embody their respective definitions. The concept of formed matter has scientific affinities, but it more fundamentally has pragmatic roots. Even these roots, however, do not shed light on the artwork's status as a thing, for Heidegger maintains that the poetic being of genuine artworks surpasses any equipmental role that they might have.

These preliminary considerations allow us to pause briefly to observe how Heidegger shares with Benjamin and Adorno an attitude towards scientific thinking that questions its appropriateness for expressing truth, and in the present case, for expressing the truth about the nature of art and artworks. This attitude, as we have seen, appears earlier in Nietzsche's assertion in *The Birth of Tragedy* (1872) that the logical, scientific spirit that has been dominating Western philosophical thought from the times of Socrates, Plato, and Aristotle has been stifling human creativity and cultural strength. The association of reason with technological developments in weaponry that occurred near the end of the nineteenth century and beginning of the twentieth, not to mention the French Revolution's rapid turn for the worse at the end of the eighteenth century, only rendered reason more suspicious in light of World War I's destruction. Benjamin and Adorno, writing well into the 1930s at this point, continue with this suspicion of rationality – conceived mainly as scientific and instrumental reason – and advocate, as did Nietzsche, the replacement of reason with their choice arts as a means to express philosophical and cultural truths. Benjamin upholds mechanically reproduced art; Adorno applauds atonal music; Nietzsche celebrates classical tragedy and the music of Bach, Beethoven, and Wagner; Heidegger emphasizes examples of poetry and poets that fit his philosophical vision.

To express the thing-like quality of artworks more effectively and truthfully, Heidegger formulates and invokes a rich and imaginative conception of the "earth." The earth is the physical foundation of things, but Heidegger conceives of it in a more poetically resonant manner that recalls primeval notions that, in more contemporary terms, suggest the ideas of "mother earth" or "mother nature." A person who works in the fields, for instance, directly connects with the earth, and may conceive of the earth not as an impersonal scientific thing, but as a sustenance from which the plants grow yearly, and as that from which he or she works to derive personal meaning. Heidegger accordingly conceives of the material, thing-like aspect of artworks as based on the earth, in a way that resonates with the array of allusive, mythological, and existential associations that emanate from this supporting-and-nurturing-focused, poetic conception. At the point where literalistic conceptions fail to capture the philosophical subject at hand, Heidegger introduces a poetic conception to cover the terrain.

Heidegger's innovative introduction of the poetic conception of earth as a more human replacement for the traditionally scientific, rationalistic, literalistic notions of a thing, reveals a poetic consciousness and poetic method at the foundations of his own philosophizing. In this essay on the origin of the work of art, he tends to speak in the literalistic voice of traditional philosophy, but when his train of thought arrives at foundational philosophical terms and insights, these receive distinctively poetic presentations. A question naturally arises about whether these presentations are well grounded themselves, since there are other poetic characterizations of the earth that conflict with Heidegger's.

Complementing the Heideggerian poetic conception of the earth is the idea of a "world" that a genuine artwork portrays. With respect to the atmosphere of rural life described above, the person's world would include his or her worries about growing enough food, raising children, and facing death, in addition to more mundane day-to-day concerns, many of which remain simply lived-through and never explicitly thematized or brought into extended reflection. The purpose of a genuine or true work of art is to reveal such a world, which in this case is a personal world. A world can also be conceived more broadly as the spirit of a culture or time period, or as the spirit of a more localized social group.

Heidegger's main thesis is that works of art reveal worlds by opening up a quiet space amidst the clutter, absorptions, and preoccupations of daily life. By disclosing worlds for reflection, works of art reveal the essence of a thing, person, group, or general cultural situation. We have seen Schopenhauer offer a version of this kind of theory, where he describes the artistic genius as someone capable of apprehending a thing's or person's essence and portraying that timeless Idea with greater clarity and intensity in an artwork, so others can apprehend universal realities that would otherwise remain hidden or overlooked. Along the same lines, Heidegger replaces Schopenhauer's Platonic Ideas with worlds in an effort to formulate a more down-to-earth, existentially richer philosophy of art. Both theories describe art as a means to reveal meaningful aspects of life that people usually overlook or that remain only subconsciously present.

Associated with Heidegger's conception of art is a concept of truth, wherein truth is experienced as a kind of disclosure or revelation. For example, a work of art can express truth by revealing a cultural world, as a Greek temple can reveal the ancient Greek love of rationality in conjunction with their religious practices, architectural knowledge, and social values. The worlds that genuine artworks reveal are not fully describable, and their meanings emanate inexhaustibly. Heidegger intends this notion of "truth as disclosure" (*aletheia*) to contrast with the more familiar notion of truth as correctness, as when we say that *2 + 2 = 4* is "true." He regards the sphere of truth as correctness as well represented by scientific and mathematical perspectives, but sees this mechanical kind of truth as parasitic upon the more profound, insight-producing truths that emerge when we experience new, reorganizing disclosures within ordinary experience. Art, politics, or philosophical reflection typically generate such insight-producing truths by revealing new worlds.

Heidegger is adamant that genuine art issues from a poetic consciousness, and he asserts that poetry – as a kind of visionary projection – is the foundation of all good art, considered in the broadest sense of the word. Again, the core of this idea is already present in Kant's aesthetic theory, where Kant conceives of beauty as the expression of aesthetic ideas. As we know, Kant understands these ideas to be images – they are essentially poetic images – whose metaphoric content renders them so semantically rich that they stimulate a great deal of thought that resists precise definition and intellectual containment. In their semantic multiplicity, Heidegger's concepts of "earth" and "world" are like resonant aesthetic images, and this renders his philosophy of art as a literary work of art itself, whose aim is to reveal the nature of art and artworks.

2. HEIDEGGER AND NAZI ART

Judging from a traditional philosophical standpoint, the poetic quality of Heidegger's philosophizing is a mixed blessing, as it appeals inspiringly to our sense of humanity while it rests questionably on arbitrary grounds. Supposing one were to interrogate the philosophical legitimacy of Heidegger's poetic concepts of earth and world (and in his other writings, the associated notions such as "sky," "divinities", and "mortals") by seeking their poetic ground. One would perhaps ask how Heidegger himself distinguishes good poetry from bad poetry, to judge sympathetically his poetic presentations on his own terms.

As a start, he mentions that poetry is not an aimless imagining of whimsicalities or a flight into the unreal, but is grounded in revealing worlds. If we accept this, and ask whether this world or that world, as revealed in some given artwork (or philosophical text), reveals the world accurately, *or* whether, as in Riefenstahl's propagandistic masterpiece, *Triumph of the Will*, it arguably presents a distortion of truth. We presently recognize the film as brilliant propaganda, and yet it also partially discloses the reality of the 1934 Nazi Party Congress in Nuremberg. This film, released in Germany in 1935, immediately before Heidegger began his essay on the origin of the work of art, fits well with Heidegger's definition of truth-as-disclosure. It does not help to add, as Heidegger does, that in any disclosure of truth, other truth is thereby obscured, for our hindsight about the Nazi regime's unattractive realities renders suspect the judgment that this film discloses much truth. Rather, it seems to present a terrible illusion. Works of art manifestly present fictions, and understanding how fictional forms can present truth beyond the fiction remains unclear.

We can also note that when Heidegger lists some main ways in which truth is disclosed, namely, through art, through politics, and through philosophical reflection, he awards politics a leading metaphysical role. This would be innocuous, if he did not add that the act that founds a political state discloses truth, as that state transports a people to its appointed task, as an entrance into that people's endowment. This particular phrasing coheres too well with Nazi descriptions of their new state and political purpose, and if we recall how Hitler conceived of himself as primarily an artist, if not a poet, it is difficult to avoid the observation that the essay's verbiage at these several junctures positively resonates with the German spirit of those times.

The theory of art-as-revelation that Heidegger expresses in "The Origin of the Work of Art," however, is not a Nazi theory of art. It avoids criticizing Nazi values, and sometimes it appears to be self-consciously adhering to them. For example, it contains two leading artistic examples – an ancient Greek temple and a van Gogh painting of a pair of shoes – both of which could have come paradigmatically from Nazi aesthetics. The temple reflects neoclassical values and the painting of the shoes, especially as Heidegger describes it specifically as a painting of a female farm worker's shoes, instantiates socialist worker sentiments. Together the examples represent the two poles of Nazi aesthetics, as we have seen. The painting of a worn pair of shoes fits well with the Nazi aesthetic endorsement of peasant and farming scenes insofar as it (for Heidegger) glorifies rural, hardworking farm life, and does not involve the painterly traits for which van Gogh's work was later condemned.[55]

The more interesting problem with Heidegger's essay does not reside in any inherent quality, passing statement, or artistic example that coheres with Nazi aesthetics and politics; it resides rather in the essay's high level of generality. Heidegger describes the nature of the artwork abstractly, leaving his readers to decide whether this or that given work of art fits his characterization of true art. This is because almost any artifact, for instance, a plastic pen, can disclose a world, if one were to explore the cultural meaning of the artifact, and if one were to conceive of a "world" vaguely enough. In the case of the plastic pen, one could regard it as an anthropologist might, as an item that discloses a world

---

[55] Van Gogh's works were later removed from German museums, but in 1936 one could not have foreseen this. In the 1937 Degenerate Art exhibition, there were also no works by van Gogh.

littered with mass-produced throwaways. A painting of a plastic pen, or perhaps of a box of soap pads as we find in Andy Warhol's art, would disclose our contemporary world even more effectively, following Heidegger's thought.

Part of the theory's obscurity and atmosphere of arbitrariness stems from the difficult-to-pin-down quality of Heidegger's poetic conceptions of earth and world, in conjunction with the self-contained way he characterizes poetry itself as the ability to disclose a world. New aspects of Being are revealed through poetry, as it discloses a world, and poetry is that which reveals new aspects of Being by disclosing a world. Poetry that does not reveal a world is not genuine poetry, and so art – which is defined as fundamentally poetic – that does not reveal a world is not genuine art. Since Heidegger's definitions of art and poetry are honorific in this manner, the theory is self-reinforcing. To render it more objective, one would need an account of non-art and of non-poetry that imply determinate criteria of aesthetic evaluation. We will encounter some indication of this below, albeit vaguely, when we consider Heidegger's criticisms of contemporary technological culture.

On the positive side, Heidegger's introduction of poetic discourse at crucial philosophical junctures coheres with anti-scientific notions of truth that stem from Nietzsche's and Freud's views. In this respect, his intellectual method inspires later French theorists who arrive at similar methodological conclusions by exploring the Nietzsche–Freud pathway through surrealism and structuralism. Heidegger's method also inspires the French poststructuralists of the 1960s, precisely because he resorts to poetry at critical philosophical moments, rather than to scientific or literalistic conceptual definitions, in an effort to fix his thoughts.[56] This identifies Heidegger as a leading figure within the wave of thinkers who question scientific approaches to truth. In addition to Nietzsche, the group includes Adorno, who associates reason and science with fascism, and whose thought poses a dilemma in connection with Heidegger. If Adorno is correct that instrumental and mathematical reason harbors a fascist

---

[56] The same occurs within Maurice Merleau-Ponty's phenomenology, which invokes poetic phrasings when literalistic characterizations fail to capture the phenomena under investigation.

dimension, and if Heidegger prefers poetry to instrumental and mathematical reason, then we can ask whether there is any sense in which poetry harbors a fascist dimension as well, given the affinities between Heidegger's advocacy of poetry and the Nazi ideology. If poetry, as well as instrumental and mathematical reason, plays into the hands of fascism, then an easy escape from oppression will be difficult to find.

3. HEIDEGGER'S PHILOSOPHY OF ART IN LATER YEARS

After having written "The Origin of the Work of Art" while the Nazis were enjoying their political and cultural strength, Heidegger later wrote "What are Poets For?" amidst the rubble that was once Germany. Banned from lecturing and teaching by the French Occupation Authorities for his Nazi sympathies and living amidst the war's devastation, Heidegger reflected upon the immense task of rebuilding the culture. His leading question in 1946 is: who shall be the new spiritual leaders during destitute times?

Consistent with his earlier thought, as well as with Johann Georg Hamann's remark in "Aesthetica in nuce" (1762) that "poetry is the mother-tongue of the human race," Heidegger maintains that *poets* are the visionaries to whom we should look, for they can inspiringly present the "holy" as a cure for spiritual depression. Heidegger characterizes the spirit of destitution in close association with those whom he regards as the uninspired souls among the modern population. These are individuals whose minds are preoccupied with mercantilistic, exchange-related and appropriative concerns, and who lack the poetic capacities and insight to appreciate the deeper meaning of things and human life. This translates revealingly into an image of bankers, businessmen, and petty hagglers as the main culprits, and it sounds distinctively like Marx's condemnation of capitalism. We should note that Heidegger's 1946 essay cites American culture as a locus of this modern attitude, and that Horkheimer and Adorno's 1947 work, *The Dialectic of Enlightenment*, which was written during the early 1940s, uses similar terms to characterize American, especially Hollywood, culture.

Among the redeeming poets, Heidegger identifies Friedrich Hölderlin (1770–1843) and, within the early twentieth century, Rainer Maria Rilke (1875–1926) as exemplary, quoting Rilke extensively to illustrate the Heideggerian vision of the world that he espouses. Along with philosophy such as Heidegger's, poetry such as Rilke's can supposedly help inspire the holy, and reinvigorate a depressed culture. In both thinkers, a religious spirit struggles for inspirational contact with an ineffable divinity, while being held down by a context of struggle and anxiety.

Forming a dramatic and memorable point in the essay, and resonating with his earlier image of the Greek temple that truthfully discloses the ancient Greek world, Heidegger pronounces that "language is the precinct (*templum*), that is, the house of Being," adding accordingly that all redemptive, visionary efforts require linguistic clothing, and that poets are especially able to do this daring work.[57] Heidegger's own essay is itself exemplary, as he fuses poetic and philosophical discourse evenly and impressively, unlike his earlier essay on the origin of the work of art, where he speaks literalistically for the most part, and introduces poetic discourse only at critical points.

Complementing his reflection that poetry is the most revelatory linguistic mode, Heidegger introduces a further observation regarding the infusion of language in general into our daily experience. He states that when we walk to the well or through the forest, for example, the semantic resonances of the words "well" and "tree" cannot but enter our minds, if only subconsciously. This is a fertile, anticipatory observation for the 1940s, for it coheres with the structuralist idea, soon to become popular, that cultural expressions are essentially linguistic expressions. It also foreshadows the 1960s poststructuralist outlooks, Derridean in particular, that distinctively appreciate how the unconscious aspect of the mind operates in accord with linguistic structures, and how one can experience the daily world as an immense and inexhaustible text.

If we turn now to the attitudes associated with contemporary culture that align with an anti-poetic spiritual condition, we find Heidegger discussing them in "The Question Concerning

---

[57] Heidegger, "What Are Poets For?", p. 132.

Technology," originally written in 1949, three years after "What are Poets For?," and published in 1954. Here, Heidegger describes an ignorance-generating force, namely, a technological attitude that considers nature exclusively as a resource to exploit, and which is accompanied typically by a calculating and objectifying standpoint. To illustrate this idea, he compares how several generations ago, a forester cut down trees innocently, without the thought of producing commercial woods for megabusinesses that manufacture paper, and that reinforce the distribution of newspapers and magazines. He also contrasts two conceptions of the Rhine, the first of which conceives of it as a resource that we can dam up into sectors to create and store electrical energy, and the second of which regards it poetically, as we find in Hölderlin's poem entitled "The Rhine." The examples of the modern forester and dammed-up Rhine reflect, more generally, ways in which one can regard a human being inhumanly – as a capitalist would financially regard a wage-laborer – as a mere means to secure profit, as opposed to regarding the person humanly, as one's brother, sister, mother, father, son, or daughter.

Matching how Horkheimer and Adorno describe the culture industry as a threat to aesthetic taste and human freedom, and how Nietzsche portrays excessive reason as stifling our creative energies, Heidegger characterizes the technological environment and technological attitudes as impeding the development of philosophical-poetic insight and human freedom, and hence as inhibiting a more inspired, holy attitude towards the world. Both Adorno and Heidegger echo Marx, as in the first chapter of his *Communist Manifesto* (1848), when he describes how the capitalist mentality has "drowned the most heavenly ecstasies of religious fervor, of chivalrous enthusiasm, of philistine sentimentalism, in the icy water of egotistical calculation."[58] Heidegger describes the decline of contemporary culture in the same terms, observing the loss of meaning along with the alienated and objectifying distance that people adopt towards nature and each other, and he warns of the great spiritual danger that the technological attitude

---

[58] Marx, *Manifesto*, p. 475.

represents. This appears to be inspired by Heidegger's citation of a 1925 observation by Rilke in "What are Poets For?":

> To our grandparents, a "house," a "well," a familiar steeple, even their own clothes, their cloak *still* meant infinitely more, were infinitely more intimate – almost everything a vessel in which they found something human already there, and added to its human store. Now there are intruding, from America, empty indifferent things, sham things, dummies of life ... A house, as the Americans understand it, an American apple or a winestock from over there, have *nothing* in common with the house, the fruit, the grape into which the hope and thoughtfulness of our forefathers had entered ...[59]

As in the 1946 essay, Heidegger concludes his essay on technology by referring to poets and poetry as the primary means to cultural salvation, despite having underscored the powerful and demonic counterforce that technological thinking embodies and having suggested bleakly that we might never emerge from its grasp. As Adorno despairs of the difficulty in extricating ourselves from the influence of the culture industry and the clutches of instrumental reason, Heidegger is distressed by the death-grip that technological thinking exercises on the general population, as it implies that, in the worst-case scenario, genuine artistic production might no longer be possible. Both thinkers describe an aesthetic nightmare and atmosphere of desperation – apparently stemming from America – where art degenerates into kitsch, as we enter a dark night of the cultural soul.

Just as Adorno commemorates atonal music, Heidegger holds out the possibility that art may rise redemptively to the spiritual occasion, owing to its common roots with the technological attitude. He indicates the appropriateness of poetry's role and potentiality to achieve a revision of attitudes towards nature in the shared etymology of the words "art" and "technology" in the Greek word "*technê*," whose semantics once amalgamated the ideas of handicrafts, fine art, and practical know-how. As he looks back nostalgically to a lost world where technological thinking did not dominate – and this compares again to how Marx recalls

---

[59] Heidegger, "What Are Poets For?", p. 113. The letter from Rilke is cited from *Briefe aus Muzot*.

a feudalistic mode of production where workers were far less alienated than in their capitalistic condition – Heidegger offers some hope. This, as we have seen, is again via poetry and poetic thinking, as he asserts that despite all, human beings dwell in the world poetically as a fundamental condition.

Through poetry and the temple of language, Heidegger envisions the resurrection of an outlook that embodies more holiness, as the Greek gods once inhabited and enlivened the temple sculptures of ancient times. His position amounts to nothing less than asserting that art-as-poetry is the potential cultural savior, and that poets can play the role of the Redeemer in a refined echo of the nineteenth-century conceptions of the artistic genius as a creative, godlike being. As Schopenhauer's aesthetics inspires musicians in its alignment of music with metaphysical truth, Heidegger's philosophy of art inspires poets in its alignment of poetic inspiration with truth as disclosure. As Nietzsche's aesthetics upholds classical tragedy, Bach, Beethoven, and Wagner as culturally redeeming forces, Heidegger's philosophy of art rests everything upon the insights of the poetic consciousness.

4. HEIDEGGER'S POETIC AESTHETICS

With respect to their philosophical form and their spiritual content, Heidegger's writings on the nature of art are arguably far ahead of their time. As a matter of form, some of his later writings infuse literalistic philosophical presentation with poetic discourse to the point where one can no longer separate the two. To those who find exclusively literalistic expression within the philosophical realm to be one-sided and limited, if not oppressive and boring, Heidegger's writings will come as a great relief and long-awaited accomplishment. Their attractive rhetorical quality is enhanced even further through his references to poets as the key participants in the great task of achieving profound philosophical insight for the sake of preventing cultural disaster and the worldwide spread of ignorance.

To reinforce these themes, Heidegger employs poetry along with references to artists and artworks of his own choosing, all of which illustrate and help communicate the task he sets, which is to save humanity from its emerging, modern self. Although one may hesitate to question such a great task, it is important to wonder about Heidegger's criteria for selecting his exemplary artists and artworks, since it is possible to choose from many artists, many kinds of art, and many messages that art can communicate. There is also a question of whether, assuming these artists, arts, and artistic messages are genuine, they all aim for the same end. Heidegger refers in the above-mentioned essays to van Gogh, Greek temples, Hölderlin and Rilke, and in each instance, they appear as the artistic voices of his philosophical principles. If one were to describe this intellectual approach unsympathetically, it could be said that Heidegger's attitude towards works of art is appropriative, for they appear in his writings as resources to advance his philosophical program, language and style of thinking.

This is evident from how Heidegger does not present the artworks to which he refers in a way such that they can speak easily on their own. Rather, he presents them steeped in his unique philosophical language. Neither does he engage in art-historical or literary-historical interpretation of the works, where other works by the artist would be compared and contrasted, where the artist's possible intentions would be considered in some depth, and where the art or literary cultural context would be explored. Heidegger presents his own interpretations of the works, conceived in art-historical isolation and as they are absorbed into his philosophical vision.[60]

If one accepts Heidegger's vision, then his philosophical appropriation of artworks might appear unobjectionable, since *a priori*, he would then be interpreting the works in light of the truth. If one is suspicious of Heidegger's philosophical vision, his rhetorically powerful literary and philosophical modes of expression, and the psychologically captivating power of the intellectual and cultural tasks he calls upon us to engage with, then his renditions of the artworks, along with his pronouncements that

---

[60] Maurice Merleau-Ponty refers to Cézanne's paintings in a similar way, albeit more convincingly, as an illustration of his own phenomenological orientation towards perception. See his essay, "Cézanne's Doubt," which appears in his book, *Sense and Non-Sense*.

art – defined as grounded in a poetic consciousness – is the savior of Western culture, will stand in need of further substantiation.

Questions often arise in reference to Heidegger's specific description of van Gogh's painting of a pair of shoes as belonging to a female farmer, when van Gogh appears to have been representing his own shoes.[61] The latter suggests that the painting communicates the world of a city-dweller, and that of a man, rather than a hard-working woman in the fields. As the painting stands, one cannot say which interpretation is correct, since its meaning remains underdetermined between these two options, and leaves Heidegger's interpretation questionable as a disclosure of the world he imagines.

A technological device, or even a simple tool, can be used for constructive or destructive, good or evil, illuminating or ignorance-generating purposes. So can poetry. If so, then the employment of the poetic consciousness *per se* provides no guarantee or conclusive reason for hope, for it remains as underdetermined as the meaning of van Gogh's painting of a pair of shoes. Heidegger's writings on art stirringly elevate the poetic mind and masterfully fuse poetic and philosophical language, but his discourse is pitched at such a high level of abstraction that different kinds of poetry – for example, propagandistic as opposed to revolutionary – are not well distinguished. This leads to the issue of whether Heidegger's own poetic discourse, since we have seen how he can exclusively adopt one side of an ambiguous situation, carries an objectionable propagandistic quality of its own.

One can discern this quality in his key idea that language is the house of Being, wherein language is honored as a temple from which holiness promises to rise again, phoenix-like, from a destitute culture. It is easy to present a counter-image of language as a prison-house whose fixed concepts, valuations and implicit oppressiveness demonically keep us from realizing our freedom. This counter-image transforms Heidegger's reverent and quasi-religious temple of language into a house overpopulated with contradictory ideas and in-fighting between competing

---

[61] This is in light of art-historical evidence cited by Meyer Schapiro. This will be discussed further in Chapter 15.

discourses, each of which clashes with the others in a competition for power. If the unconscious is structured like a language, and if language embodies the unconscious dimensions of society, then a conflict-filled conception of language would be more plausible than one filled with unifying and redeeming religious inspiration.

Heidegger's philosophy of art thus leaves us with the following problem: when a theorist, whoever it might be, locates poetic imagery at the root of his or her outlook or argumentation, a myriad of alternative poetic construals immediately arise to cast doubt on the specifically chosen poetic vision. If a theorist who believes in an afterlife grounds his view of death upon the metaphor of a caterpillar that transforms into a butterfly, this opens the way for another theorist, who disbelieves in an afterlife, to ground his or her view on the metaphor of the flame that is blown out. Judging the aesthetic difference in the expressive qualities of the metaphors brings us no closer to deciding intelligently upon whether there is an afterlife. Heidegger defines truth as disclosure, but since both of the above metaphors and their corresponding worlds disclose a new way to regard death, they are both true, and this renders their respective philosophies arbitrary, if the final ground is the metaphor itself, and if poetic consciousness is its own judge.

The point can be expressed positively by saying that Heidegger is a leading spiritual thinker whose outlook amalgamates art, religion, and philosophy into a single vision, reminiscent of what Hegel called absolute spirit. Heidegger does not offer art *per se*, religion *per se*, or philosophy *per se*, but a fusion – a fusion more in tune with Schiller's amalgamating style of thinking – of the three during a historical time when he believes that philosophy and art have reached dead ends. He answers to the nineteenth-century calls for new religions and mythologies that can replace traditional Christianity and revivify the culture, and it is probably best to conceive of Heidegger's philosophy of art within this historical context, as a feature of his larger, spiritually rejuvenating project.

12

THE ART OF INTERPRETATION

Hans-Georg Gadamer

1. GADAMER'S CRITIQUE OF KANTIAN AESTHETICS

We now arrive at the thought of Hans-Georg Gadamer (1900–2002), and can begin to appreciate how a line of leading thinkers, from the beginning of the nineteenth century onward, oppose the presumption of scientific thinking's unquestionable authority. This is not only in matters properly amenable to quantitative analysis, but in social and philosophic spheres, where human feelings, moral values, and metaphysical insights are at stake. Although Gadamer appeals to art as a preferable vehicle of truth, as do others in this line, he extracts from artistic experience a general theory of understanding, and subordinates scientific understanding to this more fundamental hermeneutics. Like Kant, Gadamer is interested in truth, but he rejects Kant's logical and scientific way of conceptualizing it, and accordingly rejects Kant's aesthetics, whose governing interest in universal validity rests upon a seventeenth- to-eighteenth-century scientific image of the world.

As we have seen, the motivating concern in Kant's aesthetics is to establish how any single person's judgment of an object's pure beauty, recognizing that the judgment is based on the person's feelings alone, can have a persuasively objective, rational respectability for other people. This is to ask how someone's aesthetic judgment can have universal validity, akin to how a moral judgment can oblige others to follow its dictates, or how a mathematical or geometrical judgment can command universal assent. To establish universal validity in judgments of beauty, Kant appeals to a non-historical, highly abstracted, detached, impersonal quality that knowledge and truth share.

Kant's view is that judgments of pure beauty stem from feeling the rudimentary operations of the cognitive mechanisms that he defines all humans as having. This feeling arises in its purity, only when we contemplate an object's abstract, spatio-temporal design (or, more generally, its scientifically relevant perceptual properties), disregard the object's cultural meaning and sensory content, and allow that design to resonate exclusively with the universal quality of the human cognitive faculties that we embody. If two people – the individuals could be an ancient Egyptian and someone from the twenty-third century – perform the requisite abstractions, then presumably both will feel cognitively the same way about the object, and will judge similarly about the object's beauty. According to Kant, only if we conceive of judgments of pure beauty in this rarefied, depersonalized, culture-independent manner is it possible to avoid the relativistic conclusion that everyone has their own taste, as well as the disruptive idea that given any person's judgment of beauty, no one else is obliged to agree.

Gadamer observes that to sustain this abstractive, homogenizing, universalistic approach to judgments of pure beauty, Kant requires us to make some sacrifices, the first of which is to accept an uninformative conception of aesthetic experience. Since Kantian judgments of pure beauty require that we take no cognizance of the kind of object we are aesthetically appreciating (that is, we must disregard the object's meaning), there is nothing to experience beyond an indeterminate pleasure in reference to the object's uninterpreted scientific structure. The problem is that this pleasure provides no determinate knowledge, and hence no *understanding* of the object.

Nature and art become indistinguishable at this rarefied and formalistic level of contemplating only abstract forms, and Gadamer maintains that this renders it impossible to do justice to art, with its rich density of suggestive meanings. He accordingly concludes that Kant's theory of judgments of pure beauty, since it is preoccupied with establishing a universal validity for judgments of beauty, is misguided in its primary attention to an object's formal design, for this removes from consideration the extensive semantic qualities that constitute great art. As Kant states himself, when we judge any object's pure beauty, knowing what kind of thing we are appreciating is irrelevant:

> In order to find something good, I must always know what kind of thing the object is supposed to be, i.e., I must have a concept of it. In order to find beauty in a thing, that concept is not necessary. Flowers, free drawings, lines aimlessly intertwining which go by the name of foliage, have no meaning, do not depend upon any determinate concept and are nonetheless pleasing. The satisfaction in beauty must depend upon the reflection upon an object, which leads to some concept or other – it makes no difference which – and is thereby distinguished from the pleasant, which rests entirely upon sensation.[62]

In light of Kant's quest for universal validity and adherence to scientific form, the second sacrifice that his theory requires is a disengagement from all historically grounded, contingent qualities of human understanding and judgment. Flatly rejecting this proposition, Gadamer states as a self-evident truth that judgments about the beauty of any particular landscape, for example, depend upon the artistic taste of the time. In such evaluative situations – and Gadamer regards these as typical – an ahistorical, universalistic theory of judgments of pure beauty is unrealistic and distortive, given how a historically determined notion of taste constitutes our artistic evaluations. If we set aside this historical factor, he believes that artistic judgments would be impossible.

This all reveals how Gadamer and Kant are talking at cross-purposes. The theory of pure beauty that initiates the *Critique of the Power of Judgment* is not concerned with artistic judgments and historical matters; Kant's initial aim is to characterize the most fundamental, universal form that judgments of beauty can assume. Gadamer's criticism is not directed at this leading conception of pure, formal beauty, however, but to culturally informed artistic judgments, which Kant treats in a different part

---

[62] Kant, *Critique of the Power of Judgment*, §4.

of his theory, many sections later. The difference between the two theorists is that Gadamer's outlook rests upon artistic judgments, rather than upon judgments of pure beauty, and so he criticizes Kant for grounding this aesthetics on judgments of pure beauty, which does not immediately concern artistic judgments.

Once we recall how Kant's theory of pure beauty eventually tries to accommodate the semantically richer realm of fine art via the notion of aesthetic ideas, however, Gadamer's criticism cuts more deeply. In this artistic context, Kant maintains that beauty – and presumably this is pure beauty – is itself the expression of aesthetic ideas. Since an aesthetic idea, or rich aesthetic image, is a meaningfully resonant image that is constituted by a set of figurative relationships, where, for instance, the image of a king can suggest thoughts of power, domination, aristocracy, and the like, difficulties for Kant's view immediately arise. In a society where there are no kings, such an image would be meaningless. Regardless of how effectively the notion of aesthetic ideas illuminates the artistic dimension of fine art, the equation of rich aesthetic images with beauty undermines the universal validity that Kant hopes to establish and preserve in judgments of pure beauty. It is common knowledge that people with different linguistic, cultural, and psychological backgrounds can read artistic images and metaphors in different ways, so it becomes quite implausible to expect the rest of humanity to agree with one's judgments of beauty, when these concern artistic meaning. Metaphors make sense only from a historical standpoint, and once the historical and linguistic variability in their meanings is acknowledged, one cannot invoke aesthetic ideas and preserve the universal validity in judgments of beauty. The same metaphor, as understood by a native German speaker as opposed to a native Chinese speaker, or by an ancient Greek in contrast to a modern Greek, will carry different associations. This discrepancy will hold, even if the German speaker learns Chinese, or vice versa – this assuming one can understand the metaphor at all.

To express the point more generally, even if Kant succeeds in identifying the grounds for universal agreement in those cases when we aesthetically appreciate objects according to their uninterpreted form, once the object's meaning enters into consideration, the meaning cannot be rendered ahistorically stable. We either have a theory that establishes universal validity for judgments of beauty, but fails to comprehend artistic meaning, or a theory that comprehends artistic meaning, but fails to establish a universal validity for artistic judgments. Either we establish universal validity with very lean and skeletal aesthetic judgments, or we admit a degree of relativism with semantically rich and interesting ones, and thereby sacrifice the universal validity. Kant cannot have it both ways.

Acknowledging historically saturated judgments as the foundational condition, Gadamer himself faces the struggle to avoid radical relativism, as he resists theorists who insist that artworks have definite, objective, potentially definable, unchanging meanings. To achieve a theoretical balance between these extremes, Gadamer invokes as ballast the established linguistic tradition in conjunction with a disposition towards open-mindedness and honesty in interpretation, none of which are quantifiable or easily specifiable ideas.

2. ARTISTIC UNDERSTANDING AND HERMENEUTICS

Gadamer's approach to art assumes that works of art speak to us, invite us into a dialogue, and call for our personal interaction and understanding. Insofar as they speak to us, our understanding of them is linguistically grounded, and insofar as they require understanding, the philosophy of art presupposes a theory of interpretation, or hermeneutics. The most appropriate approach to art must consequently be grounded upon historically dialogic, rather than the purely aesthetic, pleasure-centered considerations that we find in Kant, notwithstanding the latter's universalistic characterization of the pleasure in pure beauty in reference to cognitive, truth-related sources, namely, in the felt harmony of the cognitive faculties. Gadamer believes that the latter feeling, universally valid as it might be, cannot do justice to art, for it self-consciously disregards what the work of art has to say to us as a cultural expression. It requires us to ignore the kind of object we are contemplating, as it aesthetically differentiates an object's purely formal qualities from its semantic qualities.

To phrase a Kantian reply in Gadamer's terms, it remains that Kant is concerned with what, in an object, can speak in exactly the same way to all of humanity. This is the object's purely rational import as conveyed by its formal design. The number of such abstractly beautiful configurations is uncountably many, and each expresses a rationality that transmits a feeling of its own. Every snowflake, for example, is unique in its aesthetic impression. Moreover, although there may be no known divine author of natural beauty, Kant interprets such naturally-occurring rational forms symbolically, as formal analogues of moral ideas, and intellectually, as speculatively suggestive of an unconditional rationality underlying nature that speaks to us through beautiful forms. He theorizes consistently with Gadamer's communication-related concerns, but does so at such an abstracted, semantically lean level, that he transcends the variabilities of historically determined presuppositions, values and cultural exchanges. In contrast, Gadamer's hermeneutics does not recognize any non-historically determined meanings or interpreters; even our conceptions of rationality are subject to historical change, contrary to Kant's belief that human understanding is constituted fundamentally by a finite set of universally valid forms of logical judgment, as defined initially by Aristotle.

Despite this disagreement with the scientific assumptions of Kantian aesthetics, Gadamer's positive account of art is inspired, as was Schiller's, by Kant's notion of "play," which Kant used to characterize the relationship between the cognitive faculties in the experience of pure beauty. According to Kant, the faculties are in a condition of harmonious free play in relation to each other and within themselves, when the pleasure in pure beauty is experienced. Given his primary interest in art, Gadamer alternatively associates play with art, and, echoing Wittgenstein and anticipating Derrida, speaks more generally and concretely about how play can be serious, how it involves a self-sufficiently satisfying activity, how it is creative, how it is relaxing, how some works of art (as in music) are "played," how they involve "players," and so on, exploring the notion of "play" along associative lines, and combining these into a conception of "art as play" that differs from anything we find in Kant.

Continuing with his philosophical play upon the notion of play, Gadamer considers Aristotle's theory of tragedy, recalling how ancient Greek tragedies were performed during times of religious festivals, and pointing out how within such a social situation, the spectators' appreciation of the plays presupposed an established tradition of meaning that the Greek playwrights embodied in the works when composing them. At the basis of the tragic plays – and, Gadamer adds importantly, of all artworks – there is always *a tradition of linguistic meaning* that the works incorporate, and which allows the works to speak to the human community. He does not conceive of the spectators as passive recipients of pre-established, timelessly fixed meanings. Rather, the spectators' interpretive presence completes the artwork insofar as the work functions to generate meaningful experiences, and, as such, stands as one pole of the artistic interrelationship between artist and audience. This relationship is dialogic in that understanding involves a social interplay that tends towards agreement or harmony between one person and another, and requires, within the context of art, a focus upon an artwork's meaning as opposed to its abstract perceptual form.

As time widens the gap between the artist and the audience, as when we now read or perform ancient Greek plays, the common background between artist and audience becomes increasingly diluted, as newly emerging meanings enter into and reconstitute the perspectives of generation after generation of new audiences. Although the common human background of meaning, transmitted through history, language, and culture, never disappears, and while this commonality establishes the standing possibility of understanding, the new perspectives that interact with the artist's work also generate novel significances for the work.

We can formulate this process of understanding as follows. The audience or interpreter of an artwork is a person (or persons) whose consciousness is constituted by the language he or she inherits, and this language embodies an established tradition that is infused into those who assimilate that language. The study of etymology reveals this tradition, where the meanings of our contemporary words display their historical roots. The interpreter consequently apprehends his or her surrounding world through the inherited linguistic medium, and this medium allows meaningful objects to appear, especially at the more complex levels of meaning beyond basic, physiologically centered apprehensions such as raw pains and pleasures. These meanings radiate from the objects in our world and are like persons who speak to us. Some of the objects and their associated meanings are contemporary; some are more historically distant. In the most contemporary item, there is always a history behind it. In the most ancient item, there is always a common horizon that we share as humans and as living beings.

The immediate experience of the meanings that objects radiate is clearly presented and expressive of a rudimentary truth, as when we see a cup on the table, appreciate what it is mainly for, and recognize the cup as having a mind-independent quality. In daily experience, we apprehend the meanings that radiate from surrounding objects and we eventually ask questions about these objects in an effort to understand them better – questions whose form reflects our inherited prejudgments and linguistic tradition. In asking such questions, we anticipate answers – answers that appear to issue from the meaning-laden objects themselves – and that therefore present themselves as objective, insofar as we appreciate that despite our prejudgments, we nonetheless do not simply determine the answers to our questions implicitly through the very forms of those questions. We open ourselves to the meanings that the objects radiate with the assumption that these emanations of meaning contain more than what we could ever determinately imagine or constrict.

In this dialogic process of inquiry – a process of question and answer – we engage in a conversation with the object, and this conversational process produces a measure of communion, or fusion, between our own set of semantic anticipations, and those that the object itself presents. As we obtain further elaborations of the answers that the object provides through our process of inquiry, we experience greater truth in our relationship to the object. As time goes on, more of the object is revealed through our questioning and we come closer to grasping the object's radiating meaning more comprehensively and multi-dimensionally. The process can involve reformulations of our questions, new projections of anticipated meaning, along with revisions of earlier assumptions, all in an effort to arrive at some satisfying agreement and consistency between how we perceive the object and how the object presents itself to us of its own accord. In later generations of interpreters, the projected questions will be different, as will the correspondingly revealed aspects of the object in answer to those new questions. Some of the object's aspects that are now revealed to us through our questioning might be incorporated into existing tradition to be transmitted to future interpreters; some aspects that we now enjoy may be lost forever with our passing. There is no single, true interpretation of a work, but there are many informative and legitimate ones.

Gadamer employs some specific terminology to describe the above process. Inspired by the discussion of the interpretive situation in *Being and Time* (§32) where Heidegger identifies three preconditions for all human understanding, Gadamer likewise acknowledges that we must always bring to bear, on any interpretation, our prior knowledge and expectations, which he refers to as influential "prejudices" or "prejudgments" (*Vorurteile*).[63] Supposing, for instance, that as a native speaker of English one intends to learn ancient Greek, the only way to learn it is through the meanings of English that constitute one's interpretive consciousness. These English meanings are laden with prejudgments which obscure certain meanings as well as revealing others. Upon learning ancient Greek, one will be enabled to read Plato's or Aristotle's original texts, but in certain respects one will remain precluded from fully understanding what their cultural atmosphere was like.

No matter what one's prejudgments happen to be – including the scientific prejudgment that one should have no prejudgments – the resulting understanding involves a fusion of horizons (*Horizontverschmelzung*), where a kind of melting, amalgamation, or merging of meanings into a new understanding occurs, as one's own projections of meaning merge with those radiated by the object one is interpreting. On this model, which is inspired by Hegel's conception of a dialectical synthesis, meanings have properties comparable to metals that can be blended into an alloy. Each generation will consequently understand differently some given object from the past, such as a prehistoric cave painting, given their different prejudgments and associated interests that are brought into a conversational blend with the object.

As mentioned, Gadamer's hermeneutics recognizes a sense of better and worse interpretations, and the difference depends significantly upon the intensity and breadth of one's own

---

[63] Heidegger's three preconditions for understanding are "fore-having" (*Vorhabe*), "fore-sight" (*Vorsicht*) and "fore-conception" (*Vorgriff*). There is presupposedly a given context, a general point of view, and a specific preconception.

historical self-awareness: if one knows more about the past, about the artwork's background tradition, and about the history of the kinds of artworks in question, then the interpretation will be more truth-oriented. When using artistic masterpieces as philosophical illustrations, for example, one would resist introducing the masterpieces out of context, in relative abstraction, and independently of the knowledge of other works by the same artist, the qualities of the genre, the cultural concerns of the time, and such.

Gadamer's theory of interpretation offers no mechanical, scientific way to arrive at a truth-oriented interpretation. One must be honest, open-minded, subject to self-correction, comprehensively oriented, and cognizant of one's own interests as much as possible. A certain wisdom and balanced judgment is also required, as well as a tolerance for change and multiplicity, all of which is to say that for Gadamer, the hermeneutic revelation of truth is not subject to scientific stabilization. Even when there is a wide consensus about the meaning of some artwork, the consensus remains open to criticism and revision in light of the need to maintain an open-mindedness to alternative questions that can be asked about the work. In this way, situations where ideological or otherwise distorted interpretations of works that prevail within a large population will eventually give way to more informed interpretations.

3. CRITICAL DISCUSSION

Gadamer's hermeneutical approach to art introduces historical considerations that, in contrast to our previous theorists, have a more pervasive role. After reading Gadamer, it becomes difficult to interpret art in a naive manner, such that someone could believe, as it once was thought during the nineteenth-century era of romantic hermeneutical theorizing, that it is possible to set aside the distortive influence of one's own time period and cultural heritage, such as to understand some artwork as it is, or was, in itself. One might try to recreate a Shakespearean play in the most authentic manner, but some feature or other will be inevitably overlooked, and will reveal where our contemporary view has entered quietly into the picture. Such a theatrical effort might at first appear to be successful, but perhaps one will eventually realize that plastic buttons were used inadvertently on the old-style costumes, or that the actors did not have a sixteenth-century set of odors on their bodies and clothes, or that their accents were too contemporary.

More pointedly, if we could replicate the exact sound waves that Elizabethan musical instruments once produced, such as to hear exactly what the original players heard, present-day interpreters would still assimilate those sounds in light of their accumulated experiences of contemporary music. The same holds for any words in an artwork that have since assumed a new or added meaning, such as "heart of gold," which, although coined by Shakespeare, became a well-known title in the popular music of the 1970s. Similarly, if the standard format for motion pictures eventually transforms into a three-dimensional or virtual reality format, accompanied by olfactory and tactile inputs, one can expect that the now fashionable DVDs and home theatres will soon be experienced with a psychological distance and nostalgia comparable to how we now regard early black-and-white photography. Gadamer's position is that such interpretive changes are unavoidable, and reveal the historical and dialogic nature of the interpretative situation.

An unsympathetic reaction to Gadamer's hermeneutics can be advanced from a position that adheres more closely to a scientific notion of truth, where meanings are believed to be more fixed and exactly repeatable, as the meanings of numbers and formulae seem to be. Unlike Gadamer, who claims that understanding always goes beyond recreating someone else's intended meaning, a more ahistorically oriented position could maintain that an artist's or author's intentions absolutely define a fundamental aspect of the work's meaning, and that our task is to discover, recreate, resurrect, replicate, or reinstantiate this fixed authorial meaning in any valid interpretation.[64] We are always free to add significance to the work that was not originally there, but such enhancements – as when we interpret *Hamlet* through a Freudian lens – are independent of both the work's fundamental meaning

---

[64] This is the position of E. D. Hirsch in his book, *Validity in Interpretation*.

and the truth-oriented project of understanding the work on its own terms.

Suppose, though, that Gadamer is correct that our historical situation and background are always infused into any interpretation that we might offer. A relevant question is whether it nonetheless remains desirable to uphold, as an ideal, the project of resurrecting the artist's intention, or, if not the artist's intention, the work's original cultural meaning. Characterizing such a supposedly fixed meaning is difficult, but it will at least rule out anachronistic readings, and will direct our attention towards the work, the artist, and the work's own historical context in an effort to understand it faithfully. Admittedly, given the nebulous quality of the author's intention or original cultural atmosphere, such a standard is unlikely to determine effectively the validity of any particularly well-researched, art-historically centered interpretation over another. We have here only a principle that excludes radically anachronistic interpretations and fosters more historically faithful ones.

The analogy of the metallic alloy, if representative, indicates that Gadamer is not a radical historicist who believes that understanding the past is impossible, and who is subject to the criticism that his theory leaves no way to adjudicate between interpretations. We have access to past meanings, just as when one apprehends a piece of brass, one is automatically and directly in contact with the constitutive copper. The interpretive difficulty resides in the demanding expectation that one should be able to apprehend the copper transparently, by itself, which is impossible. It is only apprehensible through its co-presence and amalgamation with the tin that the brass also contains. Analogously, this resulting *translucency* of apprehension produces the nebulous quality that past meanings have when they present themselves to us, for it is as if past meanings must always be perceived through a kind of frosted glass, which, although it renders them vague, does not render them invisible, as if they were set behind a brick wall. Gadamer's theory rather precludes a perfect understanding or exact replication of those past meanings within our contemporary context, because our present historical and linguistic condition always infuses itself constitutively into the interpretations of those meanings, as water soaks into a dry sponge.

From an opposing, skeptical direction, Gadamer can be criticized as advancing a theory that relies too optimistically upon the ideas of fusion, amalgamation, coming-into-harmony, consensus, continuity of meaning, and stability of linguistic tradition. If we consider a word such as "play," mentioned above within the context of Gadamer's extrapolation and transformation of Kant's notion of the free play of the cognitive faculties, and consider its set of possible associations at any one time, the resonances will be potentially endless, and become especially so when the word is combined with others, often metaphorically, that carry their own associations. In principle, the full semantic resonance is unmanageably dynamic, and it becomes doubtful whether an artist's or writer's intended meanings are ever closely comprehended by apprehending the artworks or texts.

Rather than understanding interpretation upon analogy to the simple amalgam of how metals form an alloy, we instead face a set of incessantly, variably, and alternatively ringing bells whose sound is potentially cacophonous. In such a situation, it soon becomes an issue whether anyone could effectively understand anyone else to a replicable extent. If we introduce a theory of linguistic meaning that accentuates how words dynamically resonate with one another – Jacques Derrida's understanding of language offers a good example – and if we add that the passing of time complicates this resonance and differentiation between linguistic expressions, then the common ground of linguistic tradition, upon which Gadamer relies as the precondition for understanding, begins to soften, and with it, the possibility of substantial fusions of horizons and a sense of genuinely understanding others.[65]

In the same regard, we can question the supposed unity of linguistic tradition, if only because the world's linguistic field contains at least five thousand languages whose semantic parameters are sufficiently incommensurate, considered as a whole. This suggests more of a mosaic, or tangled, or dispersive structure that is constituted by various traditions, instead of a single,

---

[65] This frustrating difficulty in acknowledging a common conversational ground is exemplified in the 1981 meeting between Gadamer and Derrida at the Goethe Institute in Paris. See Michelfelder and Palmer (eds), *Dialogue and Deconstruction*.

all-embracing human tradition – an assumption that itself echoes the seventeenth-/eighteenth-century Enlightenment attitude that Kant espoused. Once we recognize a set of conflicting discourses instead of a single one, the possibilities for genuine communication and agreement begin to diminish.

To defuse the communicational corrosiveness of such considerations, Gadamer can direct our attention to our experience of artworks and texts that have been written in earlier centuries, and to the kinds of interpretations that have been advanced through serious historical research, many of which reveal continuities and stabilities of meaning. Going back to Plato and Aristotle, for example, we can discern from their times to the present day, the influence of the subject–object distinction, the distinction between the perceptual order versus conceptual order, and the distinction between fluctuating versus stable conceptual situations, which together indicate a more stable linguistic tradition than is suggested by the view that each word compares to a ringing bell, or, more dramatically, a volatile explosive or morphing virus.

If we accept that there is a unified linguistic tradition that, like a singly-flowing cultural river, underlies our interpretive efforts, it remains that this flowing tradition could nonetheless suffer from what one might call "semantic drift." Just as red passes into orange, orange into yellow, and yellow into green, we might presently (say, as green) believe that we share a common tradition with the ancient Greeks, whereas what has happened is that the linguistic meanings have transformed so significantly since that earlier time, and unbeknownst to us, that our prejudgments and efforts to understand that earlier culture are mostly distortive. It is difficult to determine the extent to which this has already happened.

Adding to the thickness of the translucent glass through which we interpret the past – even if we admit the relative stability of linguistic tradition – the multi-dimensionality of the dialogic components in the interpretive situation does not suggest that genuine understanding is an easily achievable goal, for there are many layers of hermeneutical circles and spirals throughout the interpretive situation that complicate and enrich the experience of understanding. To begin with, with respect to texts, one cannot understand any individual word in a sentence without making a projection of what the entire sentence could mean, and then having that projection reflect back upon one's subsequent interpretations of the sentence's words. Similarly, the constitutive sentences and paragraphs of a longer text cannot be understood without an anticipation of what the whole text might mean, and understood again in relation to how one's projection of the whole text's meaning later reflects back upon the meanings of the earlier sentences and paragraphs, for example, as when a surprise ending of a novel reorients the entire interpretation of the work.

Furthermore, there is a reciprocity between how one understands a text initially, and one's awareness of the genre concepts to which the text belongs. There is also a reciprocity between one's *prima facie* understanding of the text, and what one might later discover or hypothesize about the author's intentions. This understanding again must further react with one's conceptions of the broader social context, ranging from concepts of the family, to that of the local community, country, and overall spirit of the times. On top of this, one must take into account the position that one self-consciously ascribes to oneself as a reader with a certain background, either psychologically, socially, or as a member of a certain historical period, which again introduces factors that can modify the understanding of the text, or artwork.

When Gadamer speaks of a fusion of horizons, the situation is consequently not as simple as it might at first seem, as when we were invoking the reference to metallic alloys. There are many dimensions of semantic amalgamation. Since we are always interpretively involved in a many-layered condition of accumulated and interacting fusions, as described above, one might wonder about how translucent our access to past meanings in fact happens to be. It remains, however, that we do read classical texts with great profit and sometimes share a deep sense of intimacy, as in the experience of Plato's dialogues, where the logical awareness displayed is surprisingly familiar, at least if we compare these Greek dialogues to earlier texts from Egypt and Mesopotamia.

The most acute problem with Gadamer's hermeneutics might arise at a different level of inquiry, though, in relation to a Kantian question: how is it possible for Gadamer's theory to have validity as a general hermeneutics? It would contradict Gadamer's purposes to assert that his theory is plausible only for those living in the later twentieth century and early twenty-first century. Just as Kant offers a theory of human knowledge that intends to be valid for all humans, Gadamer, like Heidegger, offers a theory of human understanding that purports to describe how all humans interpret their surroundings. He is not speaking exclusively about the interpretive processes that twentieth-century individuals employ. Neither can he be interpreting the human situation through his twentieth-century lens, and then fusing his twentieth-century presuppositions with whatever the timeless truth of human understanding might be. Gadamer's understanding of human understanding presents itself, if implicitly, as a hermeneutical theory that is true to how we all – ancient Egyptians reading hieroglyphics and contemporary teenagers surfing the internet alike – understand our world and each other, and this generates a contradiction: it cannot be that all understanding is historically based and involves the fusion of horizons, except for the very understanding of understanding. If Gadamer's theory is accepted as a universal hermeneutics, then it compares in its philosophical aim to Kant's theory of judgments of pure beauty, which similarly required an ahistorical standpoint.

13

THE ART OF PAST APPEARANCES

Roland Barthes

1. PHOTOGRAPHY'S EVIDENTIARY QUALITY

Long before the invention of photographic techniques in the early nineteenth century, one of the leading functions of artists was to paint or sculpt portraits, often of wealthy or otherwise influential people. Although this tradition lives on, the portrait artist's original purpose was not only to idealize and flatter his or her subjects, but to record for posterity how the individuals actually looked. For instance, the confusing variety in the set of portraits that are supposedly of William Shakespeare, and the difficulty in deciding which portrait is the most faithful, attests to the persistent interest in how people and things which are now visually inaccessible in fact appeared. For the bulk of human history, there are relatively few kinds of records that approach the sort of reliability that photographs instantiate, such as fossil records and death masks, and this leaves us with a profound sense of vagueness about our human history's past perceptual realities. In *La Chambre claire* (*Camera Lucida*), the final book written by Roland Barthes (1915–80), published posthumously in the year of his death, 1980, this evidentiary, documentary, history-preserving quality of photographs marks, for him, the essence of photography.

When we look at the stars, or at anything located at a great distance, reality and illusion mix together inextricably. The light from our sun takes about eight minutes to reach us. Light from the closest stars arrives here in about four years, and light from some of the most distant celestial objects appears to have taken several billion years to enter our planetary vicinity. When we look at ourselves in the mirror, or look at our hand, the reflected light also takes a bit of time to reach our eye. Our immediate visual field and sense of what is now happening in the external world thus compares to the large lobby of a train station, where through numerous doorways, people continuously enter from different trains after having travelled for different distances and lengths of time. We see the large assembly in the lobby all at once, and succumb to the illusion that every individual has the same travel history, since we apprehend the collection of individuals immediately as "this group of arriving travelers." The temporal orientation and perceptual angle of our visual field compares also to a person who walks in a forward direction while facing backwards, whose body continually moves forward, but blindly, with a gaze fixed always towards the rear, as if saddled backwards on a horse. As we move into the future, we always look into the past at the external world. Expressed most extremely, we see only dead things, or phantoms.

Perceiving some constellation in the night sky also compares to glancing through a set of photographs that were taken each on a different date, with some being very recent, some starting to age, and some very old. More precisely and generally, we can imagine our visual field as a set of simultaneously-running, realistic motion pictures that blend into one another. Some of the films were taken a few seconds ago, some a few minutes ago, some yesterday, some several years ago, some decades ago, and some eons ago. To appreciate how these various images fuse together into a single visual presentation (that is, as our retina fuses them), consider looking through a nearby tree's swaying branches to watch the sun setting through the clouds, and reflect upon how each of these objects of our simultaneous attention are set at different distances, how the light from each has correspondingly taken different times to reach our eyes, and how we thus perceive, in a single apprehension, events that have happened objectively at *different* times.[66]

---

[66] The semantic field is analogous. As we speak or write, words originating from different times and cultures are amalgamated into the meaning of a single

Since the "motion pictures" of our own bodies and very immediate surroundings were made, so to speak, only milliseconds ago, and continue to be made, we experience as a practical matter, no spatio-temporal difficulty navigating our bodies within and about our immediate environment. Since the time-lag between our willing to move our hand and our perception of our hand's moving is practically non-existent, we experience the entire sensory presentation as if it were all happening right now. It remains, though, that only some of the events and objects that we visually perceive – namely, those objects and events that are in our spatially immediate surroundings – are most likely to be in the condition in which we are perceiving them.

As the spatial distance between ourselves and any directly perceived object increases (imagine that we are looking at the sun or at a star), the more likely it becomes that that object's own present condition does not correspond to how we are directly and presently apprehending it. As the distance between ourselves and some perceived object increases, the more our directly perceived reality is likely to be transforming into an illusion. Looking at a star compares to now hearing the rumble of thunder, let us stipulate, twenty-four seconds after a lightning bolt has just struck far in the distance. By the time the sound reaches us to create the present impression that the lightning strike is now doing its damage, the explosive effects of the lightning strike five miles away have already taken place close to half a minute ago.

Like an artificial retina, a photograph records a pattern of light. Catching a pattern in its tracks, a photograph allows those light patterns to be perceived at some later date, as if the later perceiver were located in the place of the light-sensitive, photographic paper at the moment when the photograph was taken. This, for Barthes, is the essence of the photographic medium. It is an idea he extracts from contemplating photographs of his recently deceased mother, whose persona and immediate presence he tries to apprehend and resurrect for himself through the images in his aging photographs. In principle, a photograph of someone can capture what the person looked like in a revivifying

---

sentence or paragraph, presenting the illusion that the words all originated semantically in the same place.

way, and it can imaginatively allow us to re-enter that person's environmental reality, almost as when we look into the distance and see a star that might now no longer exist.

Since photographs do not replicate the object itself, but mechanically and reliably replicate its appearance, the object itself can transform or be destroyed, while its appearance survives in the photograph. By allowing an object's appearance to survive, and insofar as that appearance once coincided with the object's perceived presence, the photograph makes us feel as if we directly perceive the object as it once was, like time-travel. Barthes argues that this evidentiary, documentary, non-fictive quality distinguishes photography from painting and the other arts. Although art might be a window to the human imagination, photography is a window to the actual past, or to the "that-has-been," as Barthes puts it. For him, the fictive quality of art conflicts with photography's documentary quality, and this leads him to question the idea of characterizing photography as a fine art.

Despite photography's evidentiary quality, photographs always involve some pigmentation, sizing, cropping, or distortion that varies from what one would otherwise perceive in the object's immediate presence. Just as a color-blind person might perceive a landscape with an alternative coloration than would be normal, a photograph preserves the appearance of what is objectively present, but with some inevitable departure from the perceptual norm. Admittedly, such distortions open up artistic possibilities insofar as they can be used for expressive purposes, as one might use a black and white or sepia coloration in a more contemporary photograph to suggest an earlier photographic era.

For Barthes, though, such expressive or fictionalizing distortions conflict with photography's nature, which is supposedly to present that, and how, this or that object or event once actually existed. He is fascinated by the way photographs provide a direct perceptual knowledge of the world's prior condition, as when we appreciate an old photograph of a street scene in Paris, study the lines on some now-deceased actor's face, or contemplate the devastations of war through photographs. To emphasize this evidentiary quality, Barthes mentions that within photographs, color acts as a mere cosmetic that is superadded to the image, and that has the effect of rendering its appearance artificial. He has in mind how, before color photography, images were hand-colored to give them a more intense lifelikeness, and how this practice confused photography with painting.

Inaccurate as it is, Barthes' remark about the presence of color in photographs bears a coincidence with Kant's claim that as far as pure beauty is concerned, colors are merely charms that offer only individual-relative as opposed to publicly objective aesthetic qualities. Barthes seems to appreciate that objectively speaking, light waves are energy-concentrations that have no color in themselves, but only cause color-experiences when they touch our retinas. It is these energy concentrations, however, that are active in the causal sequence that chemically creates the photographic image. Just as Kant disregards colors to highlight the objective spatio-temporal qualities of things, Barthes similarly appreciates the monotone photographs that were common at photography's outset as more purely presenting the essence of photography.

If we acknowledge Barthes' fundamental concern with apprehending exactly how things used to appear – the optimal way to perceive some object "that has been" – one would nonetheless expect to reproduce the original colors as well as the original form. The scientific notion of objectivity might lead us to distinguish between subjective colorations and objective forms, but the phenomenology of experience blends them together. We can appreciate this power of color in the photographs by Sergey Prokudin-Gorsky (1863–1944), taken during the early twentieth century, which transport us back into the Central Asian world more effectively than do any black and white photographs of similar scenes (Plate 6). A related desire for more intense perceptual fidelity lies behind the practice of colorizing black and white films that were made when the technology for color films was either unavailable or impractical.

Barthes' account of photography nonetheless runs thoughtfully against his own contemporary cultural grain, especially since it dates from 1980, after advances in photographic technique had taken effect, and efforts to transform photography into a fine art had made significant progress. For Barthes, these artistic so-called developments are in fact retrogressive, since he maintains that the essence of photography is the very feature that renders it resistant to becoming an art. While many twentieth-century writers argue how photography harbors creative possibilities that rival painting, Barthes insists that we should attend to photography's evidentiary quality and its ability to provide a "certificate of presence" for objects that once existed.

2. PHOTOGRAPHY AND DEATH

Death is the hallmark of *Camera Lucida*. Barthes describes photographers as agents of death, photographs themselves as the embodiments of death, and the art of photography as an effort to counteract photography's death-centered essence. The immobile quality of the photographic image symbolizes the fixity of death, not to mention Henri Bergson's[67] and Nietzsche's philosophical antipathy towards concepts and conceptual thinking, where fixed definitions and essences are regarded as falsifying and obscuring the living, flowing nature of things. This attitude towards concepts reflects Barthes' style of thinking across his writings, as he subscribes to the position that fixed concepts should be broken up whenever possible. Indeed, Barthes' aesthetics of photography that we will describe below emphasizes how the best photographs defy their own fixity and undermine the status quo in the same kind of fixed-concept-breaking way. His interest in photography and death, however, goes beyond these iconoclastic themes as he concentrates on how photographs freeze the appearances of things for future perceivers to render the present perceivably accessible to upcoming generations.

With such thoughts in the background, Barthes feels that when his own photograph is taken, he experiences a micro-vision of death, as his appearance is absorbed by the camera – almost as would a soul-robber – and as he becomes a ghost, or specter, that will inhabit the consequent photograph for future generations of perceivers. Those who later see the photograph will see him as he is right now, at the moment he is being photographed, as he sends his appearance into the future. To them, the perception of his image will signify a "return of the dead," since Barthes himself

---

[67] Henri Bergson (1859–1941) was one of the most influential French philosophers of the early twentieth century. In Chapter 16, we will describe his views in more detail as an influence on Gilles Deleuze.

inevitably, at one point, will have been long deceased. This macabre return of the dead that inhabits every photograph is, for Barthes, a "rather terrible thing."

At a more penetrating level, Barthes articulates a peculiar phenomenology that resides at the core of photographic perception – one that, mentioned above, is also revealed by our experience of seeing celestial bodies. As an example, he contemplates an April 1865 photograph by Alexander Gardner of a young man named Lewis Payne (aKa Lewis Thornton Powell), shown imprisoned, in arm shackles, and condemned to death for having attempted to assassinate the American Secretary of State, William H. Seward, two weeks earlier (Plate 7). We perceive the photographic image, place ourselves imaginatively within the photograph's original time-frame (that is, as if we were the photographer) and say to ourselves, "This twenty-one-year-old man is going to die." We simultaneously recall our present position and say to ourselves, "This man is dead, and he has been long dead," thus blending the experience of two different time-frames to create the paradoxical feeling of "shuddering over a catastrophe that has already occurred." The perception of a star similarly amalgamates two different time-frames: we experience the star twinkling quietly above us at the present moment, and yet know that, as we see it, the star might no longer exist, thinking of its imagined explosion as a catastrophe that has already occurred. In principle, every external perception is like this.

In such a situation, what happened in the past happens imaginatively before us right now, as we look at the past traces in the present, where those traces are of a quality sufficient to display the past as a present reality. We see the past-in-the-present, much as we perceive photographs. Just as an object, such as a star, that we see in the distance remains too far away to touch with our hands, it remains that we directly apprehend it visually. The difference between the star and the photograph is that the star's appearance conveys a more lifelike quality, as does the sun that we see and feel burning our skin on a hot summer's day, whose rays had left its surface eight minutes ago.

Barthes' observations about how our perception of photographs involves a merging of the past and the present time-frames, also apply in a more compressed way to our immediate experience of "now," which does not occur within any infinitesimal "punctual present," but which more complexly involves a fusion of dovetailing events that smoothly blend the immediately-passing-past and the punctual present together into a time-span, or "duration" as Bergson would call it. In this respect, the living present, or "now," itself embodies what Barthes perceives as salient in the phenomenology of looking at photographs. In the latter case, as in that of looking at stars, it is only that the present and past are more obviously distinguishable, as we experience their amalgam.

In his reflections on photography, Barthes distinguishes photography from cinema by asserting that photography's documentary quality contrasts with how cinema involves actors, narratives, and fictionalizations that depart from and distract us from the film's photographic qualities. This aspect of cinema is especially evident in movies typical of Hollywood and television that present a straightforward narrative.[68] It remains, though, that Barthes' definitive references to the documentary and evidentiary quality of photographs apply equally to pure documentary film, as well as color film. The presentation of color documentaries of World War II episodes is revealing in this regard, since they contrast vividly to most of the films from that conflict, which were still being done in black and white. Hitler, when seen in a color documentary, appears as a far more threatening figure, precisely because the film lends a more tangible reality to his photographic presence, as well as to our memories of the damage he caused.

It may be true that the immobility of the classical photographic image invokes an association with death, but the canonical photographic experience that Barthes illuminates for us, namely, the mixture of experiential perspectives, as in, "he will die and he is now dead," occurs in both photographs and film. It takes little imagination to look at ourselves in the mirror, project our perspective into the future, and imagine ourselves and everyone we

---

[68] In narrative-based movies, the film image's documentary qualities are significantly overridden by the film image's representational qualities. In certain shots, for example, an anonymous stuntperson (that is, a particular documentary reality) might be used to replace a leading actor during filming. The film-as-artwork, however, expects us to maintain a continuous illusion, and to see only the leading actor represented when we are actually seeing the stuntperson.

know as having been long dead. What Barthes discerns in photographs is not unique to photography, but is a more global awareness of human finitude and the passing of time that photographs happen to capture well.

This structure of Barthes' photograph-centered awareness has wide applicability. Not only does he show a paradoxical dimension of ordinary experience through his analysis of the photographic experience, he reveals a constituent of nostalgic perception that involves similar amalgams of past and present. We can watch a film of a past musical performer, or perhaps listen to favorite music from years past, and re-experience past events thorough a contemporary lens. Duplicates of past sound waves and light waves stimulate the same experience as before, but this is overlaid with present memories, interpretations, and knowledge that have been gained in the meantime. We watch a *YouTube* video of a concert that we attended years earlier, imagine ourselves present once again while recalling, as an interpretive overlay, the time that has since passed. The same experience occurs when we visit places where we have lived in the past, see old friends once again, reread books that were once so exciting, and so on. Barthes's reflection upon our perception of stars and photographs thus reveals how the amalgamation of different time-frames is a feature of everyday experience.

3. BARTHES'S PHOTOGRAPHICALLY GROUNDED AESTHETIC

From the above, we can extract a *way of seeing* that embodies a photographic approach to our experience. Using the example of "he will soon die/he is already long dead" from Barthes' discussion of Lewis Payne's photograph, and applying it to some painting, for example, the upshot would be to appreciate the work – let us assume that we are in a museum of fine art – as something we watched being painted by the very hand of da Vinci, Michelangelo, or Picasso, but additionally as a present object that we understand in light of contemporary information and past history. We would consequently appreciate da Vinci's *Mona Lisa* (1503–19) – among the many possibilities – imagining ourselves to be at da Vinci's side during the early sixteenth century, while simultaneously appreciating the work knowing how it has become the subject of many imitations and degradations. In the same way, we would look at the photographic images of the Pearl Harbor attack, imagining ourselves perhaps in the place of someone living in Honolulu a week after the attacks, fearful of how America's entrance into a world war might entail death within the upcoming year, while simultaneously appreciating the present-day peace in the Hawaiian Islands, many decades later. Like the light from a distant star that we see, both past and present amalgamate within our consciousness.

This photography-inspired attitude is neither universalist nor historicist. It is not historicist, because we acknowledge some direct access to the past that remains independent of any of our historically-centered interpretive projections. It is not universalist, since neither do we acknowledge an absolute God's-eye position that can be disengaged from our temporally conditioned perspective. The position resides between the two, as we acknowledge our historical situation's influence, while grasping more comprehensively how the work, object, or event in question was perceived by individuals at various times and places. We would not consequently assert, analogously, that when we look at a star, we are either directly experiencing the past, or that we are experiencing nothing more than our immediate sensations. Rather, we apprehend the past in the present, as we simply see a spatially distant object at a non-touchable distance from our bodies, acknowledging that what we see is situated in a public world that allows the present and the past, or the close and the distant, to merge, as if the objective reality in itself were an ever-present, higher-dimensional one that includes the present and the past, and the near and the far.

A noteworthy aspect of Barthes' photographically inspired perspective is its tension with the commonly held view, now canonical, that photography can be a fine art, and might even be essentially so. It also conflicts with the presently entrenched view that since the end of the seventeenth century, our prevailing cultural atmosphere involves an overwhelming sense of historical awareness. It is difficult nowadays to advance seriously any philosophical position without including some proviso about how our contemporary times necessarily affect our interpretations, and how this prevents us from having an objective standpoint, and so on.

Historical considerations certainly have their impact, but Barthes suggests through his account of photography that we can significantly lift ourselves out of our own time period to re-experience what happened in the past, as when we look at nineteenth-century travel photographs that present the Pyramids, or Notre Dame Cathedral, complete with visitors who, as we perceive the photographs, imaginatively become our contemporaries for a moment. This history-defying phenomenon is unusual insofar as photography's beginnings coincide with the increase in historical awareness whose onset is usually located during the early nineteenth century. Although the 1820s saw the full realization of Hegel's system of historically enmeshed, dialectical philosophy, which itself foreshadowed the more radically historicist outlooks to come, the 1820s also included the development of photography, whose defining quality is history-transcending.

Although the experience of celestial bodies – or more generally, the kind of experience of the visual field that they imply – remains a paradigm for understanding Barthes' multiperspectival approach to understanding art and experience, he does realize in 1980 that his own paradigm of photography, understood in this evidentiary, documentary sense, is in danger of disintegration. He speaks of how photography is being regarded canonically as an art, and how this attitude introduces a fictional quality into the photographic image that conflicts with its documentary nature. Barthes also observes how mass media imagery is reaching the point where we no longer appreciate the imagery *prima facie* as documents of the past, but unreflectively accept the immediate presentations and content. It is easy to forget that the images of the shirts, cars, houses, or hamburgers that populate contemporary magazines were taken at some past time, and that through such imagery, we are able to apprehend things that were, but which might no longer be as they were.

Since Barthes' death, the disintegration of the documentary image has been intensified with the more recent dominance of digital, or electronic, photography. It is now difficult to perceive a photographic image without suspecting that it might have been enhanced, sharpened, filtered, cropped, or otherwise altered to the point where fictionality predominates. Such artistically modified electronic photographs, or *electronic paintings* as they should now be called, are replacing the documentary quality of traditional photographs with the mere illusion of documentary quality, as we find in many narrative-based films. The transformation compares forebodingly to the substitution of superficially convincing logical fallacies – what Aristotle called "logical illusions" – in place of valid logical argumentation, as one often finds in corrupted legal and political reasoning. The idea and the basic techniques of such photographic deception are nonetheless not new. In the 1860s, a photograph of John C. Calhoun was modified to produce an often-reproduced image of Abraham Lincoln by removing Calhoun's head and putting that of Lincoln in its place.

4. *STUDIUM* AND *PUNCTUM*

As already noted, Barthes' effort to distinguish photography from other modes of artistic expression is unconvincing, since the evidentiary quality that he associates uniquely with photography is also characteristic of documentary films. Other kinds of direct-contact representations have this documentary quality as well, such as the plaster casts of human figures from Pompeii made *in situ*. Betraying this recognition, Barthes reflects upon the frustration that attends the experience of photographs: they naturally dispose us to seek further details of the photographed object for the sake of experiencing the evidentiary quality more intensely, but as we bring ourselves closer and closer to the photograph to discern more detail, the details dissolve into a blur.

This desire for greater palpability calls for increasingly sharper detail, more realistic coloration and movements, three-dimensionality and, ultimately, an increasing number of engaged sensory modes (for example, motion pictures with olfactory additions, seat movements, and such). Black and white documentary photography thus gravitates into color photography, and photography itself gravitates into motion pictures, which themselves point the way towards high-definition imagery and virtual reality. If we follow these evidentiary lines, it would be best to qualify Barthes' characterization of photography to say that in conjunction with its evidentiary quality, photography typically captures some particular moment's meaning, as opposed to that of some longer episode. We can appreciate this in Robert Capa's well-known and always disturbing image, *Loyalist Militiaman at the Moment of Death, Cerro Muriano, September 5, 1936*, that shows a soldier falling backwards, with his weapon dropping from his hand, just as a bullet appears to be striking through his head.[69]

A misleading upshot nevertheless arises from the psychological quest for photographic detail, namely, the fallacy of physiognomy: people naturally try to discern personality characteristics in an individual's physical presentation. Some might study photographs of the Dalai Lama's face to discern the extraordinary spirituality that is believed to be there, and that is hoped to be emanating. Some, like Francis Galton in his development of composite photography in the 1870s, might study police mugshots to discern the essence of criminality. Some, like Barthes, might look carefully at photographs of loved ones to discern the quintessence of their personal presence. The disappointing aspect of these efforts is that the faces usually do not reveal what we seek. Many people coincidentally look like famous or infamous individuals, but their personalities and abilities differ.

A similar pattern of hurried theorizing arises in connection with the interpretive principle Barthes introduces to distinguish successful, as opposed to unsuccessful, photographs. Here, he suggests a principle supposedly unique to photography that, upon reflection, also applies to other arts. This is based on a fundamental contrast between a photograph's given, easily-perceived general theme, as it stands in relation to some detail that disrupts that theme in an illuminating way. Barthes refers to the former as the *studium*, and the disrupting detail as the *punctum*.

The *studium* is constituted by a set of familiar themes and information, along with standard modes of expression, rhetorical manipulation, and artistic strategies, all of which mesh easily with typical expectations about what is interesting, valuable, salesworthy, publishable, socially interesting, or desirable. The *studium*

---

[69] There have been some questions about whether the fatal shooting took place during the heat of battle or during an organized photo shoot in dangerous territory, so the image presently embodies a mixture of fact and fiction for many interpreters (Rohter, "New doubts").

expresses the status quo and the established and expected content of artistic practice. We might have before us, as Barthes describes memorably, a photojournalistic image of some Nicaraguan soldiers patrolling a street in 1979, which, at first sight, appears to be a typical "war photograph."

Perennially unfriendly to arbitrarily established norms and rules, Barthes also notes that the *studium* also lends validity to the propagandistic and objectionable qualities that often attend photographs. In his early work, *Mythologies* (1957), the chapter entitled "Photography and Electoral Appeal" comments upon how photographs can express propaganda-friendly values such as country, army, family, honor, and reckless heroism, and how they can quietly support the "interests of Order." Barthes gives voice to the same idea four years later in his essay, "The Photographic Message" (1961), where, noting the oppressive weight of tradition, he negatively associates with our historical entrenchment the interpretive factors that we commonly bring to our perception of photographs. Introducing thereafter a measure of hope, he discovers a point of liberation in "absolutely traumatic images" that break through social myths by suspending our ordinary ways of thinking, writing, and speaking. This early interest in traumatic photography foreshadows the notion of *punctum* that Barthes sets forth two decades later.

The *punctum* is a detail within the photograph – sometimes intentionally situated in the image, and sometimes there by accident – that undermines, disrupts, and challenges the *studium*, and consequently opens up alternative fields of interpretation. In the photograph of the patrolling Nicaraguan soldiers mentioned above, the *punctum* is a group of nuns crossing the street next to the soldiers, whose religious symbolism undermines the soldiers' violent presence amidst the piles of rubble. Not every photograph has a *punctum* according to Barthes, but all good photographs have one. Run-of-the-mill photographs and, more problematically, the commonly presented images that perpetuate contemporary myths and alibis, such as the no-longer-deceptive image of a corrupt politician kissing a smiling infant to confirm his innocence, are fundamentally *studium*-oriented.

We can observe that Barthes' *studium/punctum* account of good photography is independent of photography's documentary quality and of photography in general. It applies equally to highly artistic digital photography, painting, and most arts: one needs only an initial composition that reflects a standard and recogniz- able theme rendered according to commonly accepted techniques, punctuated by some disturbing or interruptive factor that desta- bilizes the work's manifest thematic and technical foundation. Edgar Degas' *The Absinthe Drinkers* (1876), for instance, appears to be an ordinary, if sad, painting of a solitary couple in a tavern, until one notices that the tabletops lack supporting legs and appear to be floating in the air. Marcel Duchamp's *Fountain* (1917) initially appears to be an ordinary ceramic sculpture, until one realizes that it is a urinal set on its side. Grant Wood's *American Gothic* (1930) appears to be a standardly posed painting of a farm couple in front of their church-like house. It appears to be so, that is, until one's aesthetic complacency is disturbed by the quasi-diabolic pitchfork in the farmer's hand.

Barthes' *studium/punctum* account of good art (we can now say more generally) expresses, among many ways, only one way in which artistic quality can be embodied. This is in terms of surprises, thought-provoking structures, or challenges to the status quo. Like many French and German theorists of the time, Barthes here participates in a shared countercultural interest in disrupting totalities, undermining frozen definitions, identifying manifestly peripheral features as crucial in an overturning of values, and in advocating, in general, a visionary iconoclasm that can serve revolutionary interests.

Barthes' 1977 Inaugural Lecture for the Chair of Literary Semiology at the Collège de France is exemplary, as he speaks of language itself as a fascistic system of fixed concepts, and advocates, for the sake of remaining open-minded and creative, the constant need to question, revise, loosen, and shift our ground as we think and speak. That is, established rational forms must always be creatively questioned. Barthes' theorizing is often imprecise, but he remains intriguing in his heartfelt atten- tion to one of the most objective and fixed modes of artistic expression – the photograph, as if this were the toughest nut to crack – developing upon its basis an aesthetic of the *punctum* that celebrates flux and disruption, just as the nuns quietly parade religiously and defiantly behind the menacing group of soldiers.

14

THE ART OF SELF-DISCIPLINE

Michel Foucault

1. ARTISTIC CREATIVITY AND THE BOUNDARIES OF LANGUAGE

Michel Foucault (1926–84) received his initial training in psychology, and by the time the revolutionary 1960s arrived, he had developed into a historian with interests in social critique and the nature of mental illness. He accordingly established his intellectual reputation during those turbulent years through writings on the histories of madness, medicine, and the social sciences, rather than in art criticism or the philosophy of art. Foucault's interest in art, especially in literature and theatre, nonetheless traces back to the mid-1950s, when he was teaching in Sweden as a member of the Department of Romance Studies at the University of Uppsala, and then in Poland, when he was the director of the French Center at the University of Warsaw. In Uppsala, he taught a course entitled "The Conception of Love in French Literature, from the Marquis de Sade to Jean Genet," and in Warsaw, a course on contemporary theatre. Foucault's more manifest interests in psychology, medicine, and the social sciences were augmented and moderated by these interests in literature and theatre, in part, because they contain a sexual undercurrent – a theme Foucault later embraced more explicitly in his multivolume *History of Sexuality* (1976–84). His interest in art reveals a continuing concern with the transgressive and revolutionary potential of artistic expression, similar to what Barthes was discussing in his conception of the *punctum* in connection with photographs.

Foucault's attitude towards his own reflections on art was nobly tempered with a good proportion of modesty. In a 1984 interview, he stated that he was not a great author.[70] In 1982, he mentioned that he was not capable of talking extensively about music, and in 1980 he admitted that he did not know anything about the aesthetics of motion pictures.[71] [72] In 1975, he described his interest in literature as only a matter of passing theoretical interest, and in 1971 he acknowledged that he was not a specialist in painting.[73] [74]

Foucault nonetheless often appeals to artworks, artists, aesthetic themes, and aesthetic theories when he expounds his subjects from philosophical, sociological, psychological, culture-critical, and literary angles. These references are integral to his outlook, for at bottom, he is convinced that social structures, values, institutions, and practices are all artificial. As fundamentally artistic constructions authored by the society at large, they are subject to change, and subject to no higher authority. On Foucault's view, our social structures, values, and practices do not embody eternal or timeless truths about people; they are fictional works of social artistry.[75] He harbors a thoroughgoing skepticism towards "anthropological universals," aiming to reveal in careful

---

[70] Foucault, "An Aesthetics of Existence" (interview with Alessandro Fontana, April 25, 1984), in *Politics, Philosophy, Culture*, p. 53.

[71] Foucault, *Politics, Philosophy, Culture*, p. 307.

[72] Foucault, "What Is an Author?," in *Aesthetics, Method and Epistemology*, p. 241.

[73] Foucault, "The Four Horsemen of the Apocalypse and the Everyday Worms," in *Aesthetics, Method and Epistemology*, p. 233.

[74] Foucault, *Manet and the Object of Painting*, p. 27.

[75] We have seen the idea of social artistry assume some diverse forms, none of which have been attractive as of yet. Kierkegaard's seducer was a social artist who orchestrated the heartbreak of his innocent victim over the course of several months. Hitler was a social artist who tried to mold the German population to fit his oppressive nationalistic vision. Foucault speaks here at a more neutral and elementary level, indicating that social forms are in themselves highly manipulable, and hence amenable to socially artistic projects of whatever kind.

detail how artificially imprisoning our social worlds happen to be, and, in association with this artificiality, how implicitly free we are to change those worlds. He shows us how our prison is constructed, how it arbitrarily incarcerates us, and how we can escape.

Foucault's recognition of a permeating contingency, artificiality, and consequent malleability within the cultural sphere stems partly from the influence of Jean-Paul Sartre's radical conception of freedom and its negatively correlated notion of "bad faith." Writing in the midst of World War II, Sartre similarly expressed an aversion to fixed definitions, essences, universal laws, and conceptual structures that purport to determine how one, or the world, must unchangeably be. Sartre was particularly critical of personal definitions that resist revision, as when someone affirms essentialistically "I *am* an accountant," or "I *am* an artist," or "I *am* a responsible person," or "I *am* a soldier" as if this were to say, "I am a soldier necessarily, so I cannot question orders." These definitions compare in their fixity to ones such as "a circle is the set of points equidistant from any given point on a plane." The difference is that we are not speaking here of mechanically governed geometrical figures that simply are what they are, but of humans who always have a choice, who can always question authority, who can always question the labels that society projects upon them, and who can always question themselves.

Sartre emphasized how it is possible to make different fundamental choices and alter one's personality, and he cautioned against imposing ossifying definitions upon oneself, others, social values or customs. A person might be raised in a tradition that values honesty, hard work, and conjugal community only with others of that tradition, but Sartre would condemn a person as self-deceptive if he or she were to assert that that tradition dictates the absolute word.

Freedom thus characterizes both Sartre's and Foucault's philosophies. In his aversion to fixed social categories, Barthes intends to foster freedom as well. The heart of Adorno's outlook is also freedom-centered, insofar as he continually resists the oppressiveness of instrumental reason. Coincident with these thinkers, Sartre accentuates our freedom of choice and develops his philosophy by concentrating upon the individual's power of self-determination.

Although likewise acknowledging our power to choose, Foucault is more oriented towards understanding social phenomena, in line with Barthes' interests. Focusing outward into the public world, his project is to show how social and cultural qualities are thoroughly contingent. As such, and despite their frequently oppressive quality, Foucault regards them always as subject to the reformative exercise of human choice and the introduction of new interpretations. Here, in connection with the possibility of offering new visions of the world, he attaches a liberating value to art and artists.

Our natural languages are relatively stable systems of signification which, even though they enable us to communicate effectively with each other, also prescribe how communication must transpire through their vocabularies, grammatical forms, and general word usages. To appreciate this prescriptive quality in its elementary form, we can recall how some languages ascribe a gender to nouns. The nouns in Spanish and French, for example, are either masculine or feminine; in German, they are either masculine, feminine, or neutral. If one speaks such a language, it can be difficult to disengage oneself from the language's inherent and implicit patterns of evaluation. In a language where most of the words that designate high-ranking governmental positions are male-gendered, for instance, as is true in French, it becomes impossible to speak about women in political office without giving voice to a mismatch between the women and their described roles. The language itself tacitly questions the legitimate placement of women in those positions.

With a similar type of bias, some languages are more literalistically oriented than others. Yet others conceive of the world in terms of things or substances, while still others are more action-focused. Some embody a conception of time that would be disorienting to anyone who speaks a European language, and so on. In short, as we know from Gadamer's hermeneutics, one's native language powerfully influences how the mind-independent world presents itself, and despite Foucault's optimism, the degree to which it is possible to transcend the limitations of that native language remains open to philosophical dispute. Among the most stable languages are the scientific languages, which aim to capture fixed truths about the world using precisely defined mathematical forms. If we associate stability with truth, as did

Plato, then the scientific languages would seem to be among the most reliable, truthful, and authoritative, and, by implication, among the most difficult to transcend. As such, and when seen from a different angle, they are also among the most oppressive languages.

With respect to transgressing any given set of linguistic boundaries – and this is usually done by advancing new linguistic forms, rather than by mystically leaving language behind altogether – Foucault looks primarily to literature, for he appreciates how it can revise linguistic patterns and present alternative visions of the world. In reference to this rule-breaking capacity he refers enthusiastically to Jean-Jacques Rousseau (1712–78), the Marquis de Sade (1740–1814), Stéphane Mallarmé (1842–98), Raymond Roussel (1877–1933), Antonin Artaud (1895–1948), Georges Bataille (1897–1962), Pierre Klossowski (1905–2001) and Maurice Blanchot (1907–2003), for whom he has a special regard. Foucault's appreciation of literature matches Heidegger's high estimation of poetry, which has similar revolutionary potential. Both thinkers note the ossifying and imprisoning quality of the status quo, and advocate the development of new linguistic forms as a way to achieve a measure of liberation.

2. FOUCAULT'S USE OF ARTISTIC EXAMPLES

In a more typically academic manner, Foucault also invokes artists and their artworks to illustrate his philosophical and historical theses. Some of these illustrations have generated some controversy, since, although initially persuasive, closer examination has revealed their implausibility. Consider how Foucault sets the stage in the first chapter of *Madness and Civilization* (1961) with a set of artworks centered upon the theme of the *Narrenschiff*, or Ship of Fools, that was popular during the 1400s. There are several versions of this subject, ranging from a ship filled with mentally handicapped individuals who are benevolently sent away from their home towns to disembark at other shores, to a ship filled with ordinary people playing cards, thinking about sex, and so on, whose activities are so engaging that they remain oblivious to their ship's direction and destination.

The latter allegory has been popular in its suggestion of the human condition: we sail through space and time, remain unaware of any particular destination, and are consumed in everyday activities to the point of neglecting to reflect upon our more universal situation and the meaning of our upcoming death.

Foucault employs the Ship of Fools image from the 1400s to illustrate, through the contrast it creates, how the prevailing attitude towards mentally handicapped people took a major turn for the worse in the 1600s and 1700s, with the Age of Reason. Whereas the Renaissance treated these difficult-to-fit-in people with impressive tolerance, where they were often appreciated as having an odd type of wisdom, it did not take long before they were incarcerated in asylums and treated like criminals. Foucault symbolizes this downturn with the establishment in Paris of the *Hôpital Général* in 1656, where people who were mentally ill, elderly, physically handicapped, or unemployed were indiscriminately herded into this institution, since all were supposedly "unreasonable" and consequently perceived as misfits in this Age of Reason. According to Foucault, the ostracism of the mentally ill occurred partially because society's former pariahs, the lepers, were becoming fewer in number owing to medical advances, and the mainstream society needed a new marginalized population against which to coalesce itself.

To illustrate the Renaissance attitude – when a greater benevolence towards mentally handicapped people appears to have prevailed – Foucault introduces the Ship of Fools to suggest that popular attitudes were more humane than those that became the norm in the 1600s. Unfortunately, the existence of such ships has become questionable, rendering idle Foucault's reference to these vessels in support of his historical claim.[76]

Five years later, Foucault commenced *The Order of Things* (1966) using art similarly to portray the book's main theme, which is to investigate a historical sequence of distinct knowledge-styles (*epistemes*), conceived on a parallel to revolutions in artistic styles. Specifically, the book begins with an elaborate art-critical analysis of Diego Velázquez's *Las Meninas* (1656) (Plate 8) – one of the finest masterpieces in the history of Western painting – which,

---

[76] See Maher and Maher, "The Ship of Fools."

according to Foucault, paradigmatically encapsulates visually the "classical" theory of representation and associated *episteme* that prevailed during the 1600s and 1700s. Foucault believes that the 1656 establishment of the *Hôpital Général* in Paris conveys the spirit of those Classical times, and since *Las Meninas* was painted in the same year, one can imagine that he was inspired to use it as a representative of the Classical way of thinking, tacitly assuming that Paris and Madrid were of a historical piece with regard to the Classical style of representation's prevalence during this period.

As is true for his Ship of Fools example, Foucault's analysis of *Las Meninas* has drawn some scholarly attention from those who question the validity of his account. We will take a brief look at Foucault's art-critical analysis of Velázquez's painting, since the problems exemplified by his analysis expand into difficulties that critics associate with Foucault's theory and use of artworks in general.

The Order of Things aims to characterize the different *epistemes* that prevailed respectively during the Renaissance (1400s–1500s), Classical period (1600s–1700s) and Modern period (1800s–1900s). According to Foucault, the Renaissance conception of knowledge operates by establishing resemblances that issue from analogical thinking, as when someone might expect a cupful of brain-shaped walnuts to cure a brain ailment, or might believe that piercing a person's image with a needle will cause a piercing pain to the person him or her self. The Classical *episteme* reflects our more familiar scientific attitude that relies upon detached observation and the imposition of mathematical orderings upon any given subject matter. The Modern *episteme* involves a stronger sense of historical reflection and an awareness, often multi-dimensional, of the contingent influences that compose our societies and the sense of individual selves. Within this context, Foucault argues that Velázquez's *Las Meninas* represents Classical representation insofar as it displays, in a pictorial form, the idea of an observer who adopts a wholly disengaged attitude towards his or her subject matter, just as the classical scientific attitude prescribes for objective inquiry.

Las Meninas is officially a portrait of the five-year-old Spanish princess, Margarita Teresa (1651–73), who was the daughter of the then reigning Spanish monarch, King Philip IV (1605–65), and his wife, Queen Mariana (1634–96), who was also his niece and junior by twenty-nine years. At the time of the painting, Philip was fifty-one years old and Mariana was twenty-two. The young princess Margarita is shown accompanied by her entourage that includes a pair of ladies-in-waiting (or "meninas"), a governess, an accompanying soldier, a female dwarf, and a male midget. The Queen's chamberlain, standing in a distant, light-filled doorway, along with the King's chamberlain, who happens to have been Velázquez himself, are also present. Velázquez depicts himself looking at us, the viewers, perhaps as his artistic subjects, while at work on a large canvas whose surface he has hidden from our direct view. On the back wall, a mirror reflects the images of Philip and Mariana, and crucially so in connection with Foucault's interpretation of the painting.

Foucault perceives the background mirror's reflection as situating the King and Queen outside of the painting as its main viewers and subjects, at the center of attention of most of the people in the painting, such as Velázquez, the female dwarf, the young princess, and the Queen's chamberlain, who gaze outward from the painting's surface, at us, but also fictively at the observing King and Queen, as we stand in their place. On the basis of this mirror's reflection, Foucault claims that the painting is primarily about the King and Queen. Since the royal pair are not explicitly in the painting, but appear only as shadowy mirror-images within it, he interprets their physical absence as illustrating a key feature of Classical representation, namely, that the representer is never thought to be involved in the representation that he or she creates. It classically makes no difference who measures the height of some building, for instance; the height remains the same for every correctly done measure. The one who measures is not thought to be part of the measure itself.

Independently of contemporary relativistic physics, where this classical hypothesis is brought into question, a problem with Foucault's interpretation is that the background mirror is located off-center, and from a geometrical or compositional standpoint, does not reflect anyone who might be standing directly in front of the painting. In terms of the painting's geometry, its vanishing points and such, the mirror actually reflects the contents of the hidden canvas upon which Velázquez is working, and it reveals to the audience that Velázquez is working on a portrait of the King and Queen.[77] From a compositional standpoint, Foucault's reference to the mirror image in *Las Meninas* consequently does not support the idea that the painting is the representation of classical representation.

From a naive or ordinary observer's viewpoint, the background mirror does look nonetheless as if it is reflecting the King and Queen as if they were standing outside of the painting as the audience. Foucault is correct here. The difficulty is that this ordinary, or phenomenologically grounded, interpretation of the mirror reveals only one dimension of the painting's complicated quality as a representation; its geometrical composition reveals another. The tension between these opposing phenomenological and geometrical readings contributes to the painting's intriguing quality, and Foucault's analysis does not capture this dynamic oscillation.

There is yet another weakness in Foucault's account. It has been argued that *Las Meninas* is significantly about Velázquez himself, insofar as he used *Las Meninas* as a self-portrait to display his worthiness to be awarded a coveted knighthood.[78] If so, then Foucault's analysis must be implausible, since one of the painting's main subjects, Velázquez, as depicted, is explicitly *present* in the painting. To make matters worse, Velázquez is also outside of the painting, in his real-life role as the actual artist.

A third difficulty resides in Foucault's implicit suggestion that *Las Meninas'* artistic classicality compares well to the *Hôpital Général*'s social classicality. In contrast to the French cultural situation, Spanish society during the mid-1600s was still steeped in the Renaissance style of thinking, so the cultural parallels between France and Spain, or Paris and Madrid, are not as solid as Foucault's interpretation would have us believe. Furthermore, *Las Meninas* contains multi-dimensional aspects in its meaning and composition which lend it a more Modern guise.[79] If we combine these factors, we reach the conclusion that although

---

[77] See Snyder and Cohen, "Reflections on '*Las Meninas*'." For a detailed analysis of the angles of incidence and reflection involved, see Moffitt, "Velázquez in the Alcázar Palace."

[78] See Brown, *Images and Ideas*, Chapter 5, "On the meaning of Las Meninas," pp. 87–110.

[79] See Wicks, "Using Artistic Masterpieces as Historical Examples."

Foucault's analysis of *Las Meninas* may have been imaginative, ingenious, influential, and exciting, it is unconvincing on a number of counts, much like his Ship of Fools example.

Foucault once admitted that much of his work – and this would include his interpretations of the artworks that he uses as artistic examples – was fictional.[80] If we read the remark severely, as some do, then this creates a problem of how to interpret his historical analyses and use of artworks in his writings, since the admission could suggest that his presentations more realistically serve political, rather than philosophical, ends.

More sympathetically, we can say that Foucault was convinced from the start that the bulk of our cultural forms are artificial. His consequent mission is to reveal the artificiality of those forms, one way of which is to describe the accident-permeated processes of their genesis. Foucault's historical analyses might have some noticeable inaccuracies, but even if the details of his analyses are inaccurate (that is, fictional) upon closer examination, the mass of evidence that he collects suggests that sequences of events, similar to those he describes, probably took place. His works tend to assume a more fictional quality when considered in their microscopic detail, but they are more convincingly non-fictional when appreciated along their general contours. In varying degrees, this quality attaches to all historical works, if only because historians are either temporally too close or temporally too far from their subject matters to interpret them without introducing some distortion. The Ship of Fools and *Las Meninas* examples may have been regrettable choices, but Foucault's observations about the essential qualities of the Renaissance, Classical and Modern *epistemes* remain viable and informative.

---

[80] He stated, "I am well aware that I have never written anything but fictions. I do not mean to say, however, that truth is therefore absent" (Foucault, "The History of Sexuality," in *Power/Knowledge*, p. 193). This suggests a comparison to how great novelists write fictions that nonetheless express a great deal of truth. Commenting upon these sorts of projects approximately forty years earlier, Ernst Bloch (1885–1977) stated that "Many a pen becomes helpless by writing fiction while wanting to write the truth, or by looking for subjects that do not only let themselves be described or even narrated, but, in an honest way, let themselves be colored in an imaginative way or their story be continued" (Bloch, *The Utopian Function of Art and Literature*, "Marxism and Poetry" (1935), p. 156).

Just as Foucault regards Velázquez's *Las Meninas* as illustrative of basic principles that define the intellectual temperament of the Classical period, he discusses the surrealist paintings of René Magritte (1898–1967) as indicators of the general mentality typical of Western cultural thinking during the twentieth century. According to Foucault, two principles have ruled Western painting from the fifteenth to the end of the nineteenth century: first, words and images have usually been kept distinct, and when they have been both present in the same painting, one of these has tended to be subordinated to the other in artistic importance, and second, whenever a painted image resembled an object in the world, the image usually served to direct the viewer's attention outside the painting to that object's presence in the world. Words tended to be subordinated to images within paintings, and painted images themselves tended to be subordinated to the actual objects they represented.

Foucault argues that Magritte's 1926 painting *Ceci n'est pas une pipe* (*This Is Not a Pipe*), is structured in a manner that controverts both these assumptions.[81] The work contains a realistic and straightforwardly rendered image of a pipe, but it includes the painted sentence "*Ceci n'est pas une pipe*" in large letters directly below the pipe's image. In passing, Foucault notes that within this sentence, the word "*Ceci*" ("This") is ambiguous – it could refer to the image of the pipe, or to the sentence "*Ceci n'est pas une pipe*," or to the entire painting – and he concludes that the painting is intrinsically ambiguous and resists any singular and exclusive interpretation. This capacity for multiple interpretations is also a key feature Foucault assigns to twentieth-century art.

Foucault further asserts that Magritte's painting disrupts the traditional expectation that either the image or the text constitutes the painting's primary message. Rather, he notes that the total composition generates an interpretive oscillation between word and image, much like the experience of perceiving a calligram (an image constructed with the shapes of words whose meanings themselves refer to the kind of object represented by the image). It is also comparable to the experience of perceiving an ambiguous geometrical configuration that stimulates

---

[81] See Foucault, *This Is Not a Pipe*.

perspective-switches in the viewer, such as the Necker cube. In multiple interpretable imagery of this kind, none of the projected points of view is given precedence.

Magritte's compositions depart also from the second feature of the fifteenth- through nineteenth-century Western attitude towards words and images mentioned above, namely, the assumption that realistically rendered images refer the viewer naturally to the corresponding objects in the world. In Magritte's own words, his paintings, despite their realistic style, are "farthest from trompe-l'oeil."[82] Magritte intends no deception, and no reinforcement of the relation, or of any assumed priority, between image and object. In this way, his work questions philosophically the traditional conception that words and images refer primarily to actual objects and events. Foucault, in his discussions of Magritte's work, appears to see expressed artistically in the paintings he considers, a general view of meaning which closely approximates that of the linguist, Ferdinand de Saussure: the idea that the meaning of a word is established primarily by the semantic network of associated words within which it operates linguistically, as opposed to an initially clear, unambiguous, and independent reference to some specifiable object in the world.

Foucault interprets the imagery in Magritte's paintings as relatively self-enclosed, as essentially self-referent, and as displaying the dissolution of static hierarchies and meanings that are derived from things which straightforwardly present themselves in experience. When, in the perception of a painting such as *Ceci n'est pas une pipe*, a person's interpretive focus shifts from image to word, and from word to image, back and forth continuously, this experience of shifting from one interpretation to another becomes literally the key point to which Foucault aims to draw his reader's attention. Although this point of interpretive transition has no substance of its own – it is a non-entity – the entire dynamism of the ambiguous presentation depends upon this point. He writes, "[Magritte's] incisions that drew figures and those that marked letters communicate only by void, the non-place hidden beneath marble solidity."[83]

---

[82] Foucault, *This Is Not a Pipe*, p. 43.
[83] Foucault, *This Is Not a Pipe*, p. 41.

As we shall see in the next chapter, Jacques Derrida's notion of *"difference"* bears close affinities to Foucault's analysis of Magritte's surrealist painting insofar as Derrida emphasizes the centrality of transitional and differentiating points within the field of linguistic phenomena. Also, Jean Baudrillard's notions of "simulacra" and "hyperreality" are foreshadowed by Foucault's analysis of Magritte. The self-contained, and self-referential aspect of the imagery that Foucault emphasizes within his interpretation of Magritte's paintings anticipates Baudrillard's thought that contemporary representations convey the impression that they are "always already reproduced."[84]

Foucault's multi-aspected analysis of Magritte's surrealism coincides with the spirit of the 1960s and 1970s post-structuralist intellectual times during which it was written. He reveals, however, that the principles heralded during those decades as distinctly post-structuralist and postmodern were already culturally operative during the 1920s. In this respect, Foucault differs from theorists such as Jean-François Lyotard, who identifies the idea of multifacetedness as a distinctly postmodern phenomenon.

Foucault does not limit his examples of historically exemplary works of art to the visual arts. His early reference to Francisco José de Goya y Lucientes' well-known etching, *El Sueño de la Razón Produce Monstruos* (*The Sleep of Reason Brings Forth Monsters*) (*c*.1797) in the conclusion of *Histoire de la Folie* (*Madness and Civilization*, 1965), and his later, more extensive discussion of Velázquez's *Las Meninas*, are complemented by an acknowledgment in *The Order of Things* of Miguel de Cervantes' *Don Quixote* (1605/1615) – a literary work which, for Foucault, expresses the transition between the Renaissance and Classical intellectual temperaments. Additionally, and with great significance, he regards the work of yet another figure within the Spanish-speaking tradition, Jorge Luis Borges (1899–1986), as embodying the contemporary principles referred to in connection with Magritte. Employing one of Borges' passages as almost a microcosmic description of the contemporary world scene, Foucault prefaces *The Order of Things* with a brief discussion of a passage

---

[84] Baudrillaud, "Symbolic Exchange and Death," in *Jean Baudrillard: Selected Writings*, p. 146.

from Borges' short story, "The Analytic Language of John Wilkins." The story mentions a:

> "certain Chinese encyclopedia" in which it is written that "animals are divided into: (a) belonging to the Emperor, (b) embalmed, (c) tame, (d) sucking pigs, (e) sirens, (f) fabulous, (g) stray dogs, (h) included in the present classification, (i) frenzied, (j) innumerable, (k) drawn with a very fine camelhair brush, (l) et cetera, (m) having just broken the water pitcher, (n) that from a long way off look like flies."[85]

The categories of this encyclopedia, in sharp distinction to the standard practice of formulating clearly partitioned categories of classification (as in biological taxonomy), are sometimes overlapping in scope, sometimes incongruous with each other with respect to their meanings, and sometimes contrary to typical ways of classifying animals. As a whole, they operate without, and defy the postulation of, any underlying conceptual space in relation to which they can be organized into a coherent scheme. The kind of array here is nonetheless not altogether unfamiliar: it expands the more elemental, double-aspected style of incongruity characteristic of Magritte's painting into a multi-sided incongruity, and it displays what Foucault recognizes as a general principle of the twentieth-century mentality. It is that the world invites characterization and understanding in a multi-faceted way which can run contrary to logically grounded and scientifically interested styles of classification. In its nineteenth-century bud, Foucault apprehended this outlook in the paintings of Édouard Manet (1832–83), who he believed made possible "all the painting after Impressionism … [and] all the painting of the twentieth century … from which, in fact contemporary art developed."[86]

There are two upshots of Foucault's discussion of works of art as exemplars of historical principles. The first is his observation that, as noted, it has been during the entire twentieth century, and not simply during the 1960s and later, that the field of human experience has been perceived as multi-faceted, many communitied, and filled with incommensurabilities. Many Cubist paintings, as

---

[85] Foucault, *The Order of Things*, p. xv.
[86] Foucault, *Manet and the Object of Painting*, p. 28.

well as numerous examples from the Futurist, Surrealist and Dada movements, display this multi-dimensional awareness in the history of art; in literary theory, Mikhail Bakhtin's conception of "heteroglossia" exhibits this tendency as well.

The second upshot of Foucault's discussion concerns his broader interest in drawing our attention to the limits of any given perspective. Those of a traditional mind might find Magritte's paintings to be confusing, and could very likely regard the Chinese encyclopedia as only light-heartedly comical, or, if taken seriously, intellectually indigestible. Yet the very experience of conceptual disorientation that such artistic constructions can generate under-scores an important way in which they can reveal the limitations of logically structured thinking of an Aristotelian sort, and pave the way for a more conceptually prismatic outlook.

3. ARTISTRY AND DISCIPLINARY POWER

Discipline and Punish: The Birth of the Prison, Foucault's 1975 book, reveals another dimension where we can appreciate his interest in artistic creativity and social artistry. Foucault is concerned here with how societies form people into subjects through the power of their ruling authorities. He observes that in earlier soci-eties, soldiers, for example, were found, rather than made: men with originally strong, large bodies and a courageous personality were naturally chosen for participation in the army. By the late 1700s, however, it became a common assumption that most anyone could be shaped into an effective soldier by subjecting the person to the right kind of training, or discipline.

Salient for Foucault is the emerging assumption that the human body and person are manipulable materials, capable of being fashioned into whatever form the society needs. This ren-ders human organizations akin to works of architecture that require both artistic and engineering skills for their construction and maintenance. It also renders social leaders – dictators, in many cases – as analogous to architects, and the people who they manipulate as analogous to the architect's materials. In the case of dictators, the relationship to the people is domineering and controlling, and the social organism envisaged amounts to the dictator's living work of art. Germany during the 1930s and early 1940s displayed this quality, as we have discussed in the chapter on Walter Benjamin.

Accompanying this conception of human malleability is the idea that people's self-conceptions are significantly impressed upon them by their society; if the society, through its various labels, locates a person in the "in-group," or alternatively in the "out-group," then the person is likely to take that definition to heart. The definition is merely an arbitrary social construction on the one hand; on the other, it is psychologically driven-in and difficult to disown.

Foucault observes that the forces combining to manipulate and control any given population are, in fact, more varied, impersonal, accidental, unintentional, and disorganized than would arise from any conception of perfect social planning, dictatorial or democratic. Realistically considered, the "artist" of the living social organism who is regarded quasi-fictionally as manipulating the population's values and self-conceptions has, in fact, no centrally governing intelligence. There is no leading figure and no genuine control over the long-term course of events, for the most unexpected and apparently trivial event can change the course of history. Each day is filled with millions of accidental and coincidental human interactions, any cluster of which can reverberate to alter the direction of history's main path.

This renders the manipulative powers that organize social institutions and their rules not much more than a "they," or *das Man*, as Heidegger expressed the idea. If we are to speak of "the social artist" who manipulates the subjectivities of the population at large, then this artist must be conceived of as an anonymous and collective being, that is, as no one in particular, with no one specifically accountable. An aspect of this "artist's" mentality might be called "tradition" or the status quo, side by side with a tangle of contingencies.

Foucault, writing in the 1970s, and growing up during and immediately after World War II, can be appreciated as offering a theory like Theodor Adorno's to the extent that it identifies a highly permeating, dominating power at the core of contemporary society. For Adorno, this was instrumental reason, conceived of as a faceless force. For Foucault, it is a faceless cluster of power/knowledge constellations distributed across and within the leading social institutions – institutions whose constraints eventually need to be broken, if one is to realize freedom, undermine oppression, and offer alternative values. The upshot is a hard confrontation between two kinds of artists, namely, (1) impersonal social institutions whose activity involves the imposition of prejudicial and exclusionary labels upon people and (2) individuals who prefer to define themselves. The image of the sadist from Sartre's philosophy is useful here – a master of discipline who is motivated by power, not sex, and who attempts to control every movement of his or her victim's body and mind, only to realize, through the victim's defiant look and interiority of intangible freedom, how futile these manipulative efforts in fact are.

Foucault's various characterizations of our contemporary society coalesce in the model of a penal colony, concentration camp, or prison, where manipulative efforts are exerted against a relatively corralled population. A typical prison has a set of constituent institutions – educational, labor-oriented, corrective, health-related, and so on – all of which impose disciplinary structures that determine how its inmates can legitimately act. Some of the constituent institutions present a benevolent façade; some do not. All operate on a principle of maximum surveillance and control, where the individuals under observation are led to believe (for example, through the effective positioning of law enforcement personnel, cameras, one-way mirrors, microphones, controlled passageways, and such) that they are under constant view, and hence are led psychologically to stay in line.

This situation's panoptic atmosphere recalls certain kinds of theism, when it is supposed that God – the artistic creator and moral judge of the world – observes all activity and punishes those who do not behave appropriately. Such lack of privacy is maintained in a prison, as the godlike figure is transformed into the collectivity of institutional surveillance mechanisms that put people under constant judgment. We have here an unexpectedly traditional aspect to Foucault's vision of society, since his image of the prison resonates with the medieval Christian conception of the world as a kind of moral testing-ground, where those who behave properly are rewarded by a release into heaven, and where those who do not conform are transferred to a location that imposes an even more severe disciplinary scene, namely, hell.

There remains a positive side to this quasi-sadistic social scenario. Just as a person can be manipulated and disciplined by external authorities, a person can alternatively manipulate and discipline him or herself, by imposing strict and detailed regimens in an effort to become a self-made person or self-created work of living art. Foucault characterizes this as an "aesthetics of existence" that attends to matters of lifestyle as expressed through self-discipline. By means of such self-imposed regimens, a person works on his or her values, character, and plans, as bodybuilders work on their bodies, or as artists work on their paintings and sculptures. Social control thus shifts over to self-control.

Important here is the thought of becoming an artist to oneself, and the recognition that changes do not happen immediately, as if one could radically change oneself by merely exercising a new fundamental choice of character, as Sartre imagines. Change happens through self-discipline and hard work, echoing how Nietzsche pays tribute to the idea of being hard on oneself. The expected result is a greater measure of autonomy that issues from the long-term activity of self-determination. In effect, one frees oneself by creating as a matter of self-expression, a personal world that runs according to a set of self-imposed rules. Kant's ethics institutes this idea for humanity at large.

Since these rules are in themselves public vehicles, others can adopt the same kinds of regimen towards the same stylistic end. Foucault's aesthetics of existence is not consequently an exclusively individualistic enterprise, but implicitly contains the wherewithal to generate new subcultures, communities, and institutions, coincident with Nietzsche's, Benjamin's, Adorno's, Heidegger's and Barthes' aims. In this respect, the very manner that one reforms oneself through a set of rules implies the Sartrean idea that as one chooses for oneself, one chooses the way for others as well. The difference in Foucault is that there is no obligation for others to follow any given regimen; the regimental structures may be objective, but they stem from personal visions of self-determination.

Finally, bearing further on artistic and aesthetic issues, another aspect of Foucault's writings concerns his methodologies for understanding historical phenomena, namely, "archaeology" and "genealogy." The archaeological inquiries reveal underlying principles, or structures, that govern some historically defined subject matter, for instance, the respective *epistemes* of the Renaissance, Classical and Modern periods, as we have discussed. The genealogical analyses display the detailed mechanisms of historical emergence that give birth to leading cultural concepts. For any given concept, Foucault identifies when it first came into currency, when and why it faded (if it has faded), and, in the course of this, reveals the mazelike variety of overlapping and crisscrossing lines of discourse and power relationships that feed into the construction and/or decline of the concept under consideration. This kind of genealogical inquiry can be implemented for almost any concept.

Among his well-known applications of this genealogical approach is his discussion of "author" and "work" in "What is an author?" (1969). Foucault points out that these concepts are difficult to define, observing they have changed over time, and that they are composed of economic, literary, psychological, and cultural dimensions that transform at different speeds. The concepts are more akin to densely packed, complicated, and essentially unstable conglomerates of meaning, rather than univocal, evenly constituted entities. Their multi-dimensionality and transformations along only some dimensions at any particular point in time, while remaining constant along others, speaks against there being any essential definitions or timeless forms that accompany, or simply are, the concepts' meanings.

Given the thematic contents of his works in general, Foucault maintains unsurprisingly that the socially constructed idea of "an author" is an "ideological product" through which "one limits, excludes, and chooses; in short, by which one impedes the free circulation, the free manipulation, the free composition, decomposition and recomposition of fiction."[87] He also supports the position set forth a year earlier by Roland Barthes in the essay "The Death of the Author,"[88] namely, that the concept of the author ought to be minimized, because it carries with it a fundamentally authoritarian and oppressive conception of literary criticism. Nietzsche's proclamation of the death of God in *Thus Spoke Zarathustra* reverberates here into the realm of

---

[87] Foucault, "What Is an Author?," in *Aesthetics, Method and Epistemology*, p. 221.
[88] Barthes, "The Death of the Author," in *Image, Music, Text*, pp. 142–8.

contemporary literary criticism, where it transforms itself into a critique of monologue-centered conceptions of literature. Foucault himself anticipates the "death of the author" simply as a matter of cultural change, and echoing his famous last lines of *The Order of Things* – "one can certainly wager that man would be erased, like a face drawn in sand at the edge of the sea"[89] – he states correspondingly that "at the very moment when [our society] is in the process of changing, the author function will disappear."[90]

Foucault's and Barthes' joint questioning of the author's authority led to significant developments in literary theory in the decades that followed, especially in reference to "reader-oriented" approaches to criticism advanced by theorists such as Hans Robert Jauss, Wolfgang Iser, and Stanley Fish.

Although Foucault did not develop a detailed aesthetic theory *per se*, he developed a powerful *methodology*, namely, genealogy, that can be used to illuminate concepts such as beauty, sublimity, the picturesque, artistic representation, artistic expression, or authenticity, among many others, that play key roles in aesthetic theories. This method assumes that essentialistic definitions are misrepresentative, and that we must instead examine tangled interplays of power to understand social concepts more truly.

4. CRITICAL DISCUSSION

There are parallels between Sartre's and Foucault's interests in developing a theory that inspires people to realize their freedom. Both contain modernist aspects insofar as their expository tone suggests that when we genuinely express our freedom to create ourselves anew, we can leave most of what we were behind. In Foucault, this is expressed in the opposition between the manipulative/artistic forces that the society at large exerts upon us, and the manipulative/artistic forces we can exert upon ourselves, as we shape ourselves into a new form. It is as if we must set ourselves squarely against the disciplinary activities of the prevailing social institutions to establish our personal autonomy.

---

[89] Foucault, *The Order of Things*, p. 387.
[90] Foucault, "What Is an Author?," in *Aesthetics, Method and Epistemology*, p. 222.

His method compares to building a dam against an onrushing current, or cutting away a patch of forest to build a log cabin in the clearing, or looking defiantly back into the face of an aggressor, or painting an image in a style contrary to all commonly accepted styles in an attempt to be new.

This remains an unrealistic way to conceive of our freedom, since we must inevitably use the language we inherit, project our assumptions whenever we interpret any subject, and define ourselves against a set of given values which themselves set limits upon what we can imagine as alternatives. The problem of realizing our freedom involves the paradox of having to speak within the very language, the validity of which one is trying to question. Since one must be a creature of tradition as a condition for questioning tradition, this tends to undermine sharp distinctions between the society's perspective and the individual's perspective, since the former significantly constitutes the latter from the outset. There is a substantial chance that a person's efforts to break free of institutional values will end up reinstating them under a new description, and that rebellion against a fascist state will result in reiterating that state's own disciplinary style. Arguments against oppression often become the very voices of oppression, as occurred during the French Revolution.

Along a different dimension, the ineffectiveness of Foucault's use of artistic examples such as *Las Meninas* and the Ship of Fools reveals a difficulty that is not unique to Foucault. It is the problem of using artistic examples without investigating the meanings of the examples adequately, for it is an unfortunately common practice in philosophical aesthetics to refer to works of art within one's theorizing without considering the art-historical context, and, in particular, other works by the same artist. In the case of *Las Meninas*, if we consider other works that Velázquez painted before and after it, new dimensions of *Las Meninas'* meaning emerge, and these meanings conflict with Foucault's use of the painting as a philosophical example.[91] Had Foucault included reflections on how *Las Meninas* fits into Velázquez's total *oeuvre*,

---

[91] Relevant works for comparison would include *Prince Baltasar Carlos with the Count-Duke of Olivares at the Royal Mews* (1636) and *The Spinners* (1657). The former work, for instance, has a similar compositional arrangement. The room depicted in *Las Meninas* was also that of Baltasar Carlos (1629–46), Philip

he might never have referred to it as a representation of Classical representation, since its main subject matter is more obviously either Velázquez and/or the young princess, and since it contains Renaissance and Modern, as well as Classical, aspects. *Las Meninas* is not clearly a representation of Classical representation, once we consider the significant array of art-historical factors.

More favorably, Foucault's genealogical analyses of artistic concepts present a strong case against the more common way of understanding them essentialistically. At first, this strength might seem doubtful, since one can argue that even if Foucault's gene-alogies are correct, they reveal merely when a concept historically emerged, and have no implications for the concept's metaphysi-cal being and truth. For instance, it could be said that circular things, and hence the concept of a circle, existed long before there were any human beings to reflect upon that concept, and so genealogically articulating the historical processes that account for how people first conceived of circles has no bearing *whatso-ever* on whether there is a Platonic Form of circularity.

The above argument retains its plausibility only when we overlook the details of Foucault's genealogies. Their remarkable features reside in their multi-dimensionality, dynamic quality, and complexity. Concepts such as "art," "author," "work," "beauty," "sublimity," among many others, can be shown to have semantic dimensions that are interdisciplinary and that involve multiple forms of discourse. Insofar as they are complicated, prismatic, tension-ridden concepts, as Foucault's analyses display, they are not amenable to the kind of simple, one-dimensional definitions that fit standard notions of Platonic ideas or fixed definitions. They compare more closely to the packed ice that Freud uses as an analogy for the semantic quality of dreams. It is not, then, Foucault's mere tracing of a concept's historical genesis that renders his skepticism towards anthropological universals con-vincing; it is his multi-dimensional presentation of these concepts that renders futile any attempt to supply a fixed definition. This complicated historical understanding of aesthetically relevant concepts is, ultimately, Foucault's outstanding and enduring contribution to aesthetic theory.

IV's deceased son of a decade before, whose ghostlike presence – far less visible than that of the King and Queen – permeates the painting.

15

THE ART OF FREE INTERPRETATION

Jacques Derrida

1. MARTIN HEIDEGGER VERSUS MEYER SCHAPIRO

Jacques Derrida (1930–2004) wrote often about literature and the visual arts, and we can appreciate his approach to these subjects through a characteristic example from his extensive body of publications. This is his interpretive treatment of Vincent van Gogh's painting entitled *A Pair of Shoes* (1886) (Plate 9), which appears as the 125-page-long final segment of his 1978 book, *The Truth in Painting* (*La Vérité en peinture*).[92] The book's title is inspired by an October 23, 1905 letter from Paul Cézanne to Émile Bernard where Cézanne states, "I owe you the truth in painting and I will tell it to you," and it presents, within the context of artistic expression, the general Derridean question of whether absolute truth is a valid value, in painting or anywhere else. His chapter is entitled "Restitutions of the truth in pointing" ("*Restitutions de la vérité en pointure*"), since he is concerned about whether the depicted shoes in van Gogh's painting point to some timeless truth that the work is about, and whether determining who the shoes belong to can reveal this supposed truth. Derrida adopts a skeptical attitude towards these questions, but

---

[92] Derrida reflects upon Kant's aesthetics in the first half of this book. For other examples of Derrida's discussions of artworks, see his *Memoirs of the Blind*.

believes that an examination of them can nonetheless be enlightening.

In response to a 1968 critical attack on Heidegger by the art historian Meyer Schapiro (1904–96), Derrida attends carefully to van Gogh's painting to preserve as a possibility Heidegger's interpretation of the work that appears in "The Origin of the Work of Art" (1936).[93] Schapiro, aiming straightforwardly to invalidate Heidegger's interpretation, claims that the historical evidence surrounding van Gogh's artwork contradicts Heidegger's reading. Citing some facts about van Gogh and the painting's origins, Schapiro develops his criticism in detail, although not without becoming victim to some of his own unsubstantiated assertions about the painting, as Derrida reveals. We will consider these contrasting interpretations of van Gogh's work, not mainly to decide on whether Heidegger's or Schapiro's conception of the painting most accurately reflects van Gogh's intentions, but to illustrate Derrida's linguistic approach to the work and to reveal some basic qualities of his unusual style of thought as they bear on aesthetic matters.

As we have seen in our discussion of Heidegger's aesthetics, Heidegger invokes van Gogh's painting in the course of developing the broad-ranging idea that a work of art discloses truth by revealing a world. He refers to the painting not by title, but as "the one by van Gogh that represents a pair of farmer's shoes" and as "a well-known painting by van Gogh, who painted such shoes several times." With respect to the world of shoes, Heidegger reflects that as a rule, shoes are most genuinely themselves when they are being worn and used, and when they are forgotten as we engage in other activities while wearing them. This is true for most equipment; a tool usually functions best when it does its job invisibly, as when we overlook a telescope or a pair of eyeglasses while attending closely to the objects they help us see more clearly.

Heidegger observes that a good, artistic portrayal of the shoes will set the shoes apart from their ordinary use, detach them from their practical context, and hold them up for contemplation.

---

[93] Schapiro, "The Still Life as a Personal Object," pp. 203–9. Heidegger's essay took shape during the year-long time span from November 1935 to December 1936.

In doing so, the portrayal will reveal the shoes' world more perspicuously. He expresses this by saying that the work of art transports us out of the ordinary and discloses the nature of the object portrayed – a nature that was previously concealed in the sense that it had been present, but overlooked. The experience compares to what happens when a piece of equipment malfunctions, as when a pair of eyeglasses breaks. As they break, the eyeglasses immediately move to the center of attention, their role as equipment comes to light, and along with that significance, the network of practical relations or "world" in which the eyeglasses are embedded presents itself more explicitly. Heidegger states that works of art reveal a world in this respect, so any good work of art that has shoes as its main theme will reveal the equipmental, or practically centered, world of those shoes. The artistically portrayed shoes of a king, peasant, city-dweller, ballerina, soldier, businessperson, or surgeon would ideally reveal the respective worlds that those shoes inhabit. Heidegger's idea of how works of art reveal worlds does not reflect every consideration that would be artistically relevant to our judgments about works of art, but it does draw our attention to some important features.

The van Gogh painting to which Heidegger refers shows two worn shoes, apparently a pair, rather thick and heavy – one could equally call them boots – set within a nondescript background. We have only the shoes to contemplate, rather than the streets, fields, paths, rooms, or vehicles through which the shoes may have traveled, or any other symbolic qualities that the shoes might have, as would be more manifestly the case with the shoes of a ballerina or tribesperson. Neither does the painting provide clues about who specifically might have worn the shoes, or where or when the shoes were made. The generic image shows them as heavily worn, ordinary and perhaps a bit forlorn, with no discernible origin.

The point of dispute is that Heidegger refers to these shoes as belonging specifically to a female farmer (*Bäuerin*). In light of the painting's generic content, one is left wondering why Heidegger believes that these heavy-duty work shoes are farmer's shoes, let alone women's shoes. Given how they look, these could be the shoes of a trainman, or miner, or perhaps a soldier. Further assuming that they originate from a rural context, Heidegger imaginatively describes the world that the shoes supposedly reveal, attending in particular to the "dark opening of the worn insides of the shoes." He asks us to look into the dark opening – we should probably recall Freud's psychoanalytic interpretation of art here – and while doing so, to imagine the female farmer's "toil-some tread," her "slow drudge," the wind-swept fields in which she works, the soil's richness, the loneliness of the paths during her evening homeward walk, the earth's call, the ripening grain, the fields' emptiness in winter, her anxiety in the face of hunger, her joy upon the occasion of sufficient nourishment, all framed emo-tionally by the fear of death. Heidegger envisages this world through the dark openings of the shoes, poetically appreciating the world of the shoes within their greater environmental, personal, and equipmental context – a world that the actual shoes during the course of their ordinary use would probably not reveal, but which can be revealed well through the shoes' artistic portrayal.

These inspired passages in Heidegger's essay are brief, as is Schapiro's critical commentary. Challenging Heidegger's inter-pretive line, Schapiro notes that in 1886, van Gogh was a *city-dweller* living in Paris, that the shoes in the painting were likely to have been van Gogh's own, and that there is nothing tangible in the painting to suggest that the shoes are those of a farm woman, or that van Gogh painted them to express the reali-ties of living close to the earth. Schapiro is confident that the shoes belong to van Gogh and were bought in Paris, and that Heidegger's rendition of their meaning is a dreamlike invention to suit his philosophical, and possibly political, purposes.

Such is the argumentative situation at the point when we encounter Derrida's treatment of this dispute. On the face of things, Schapiro presents some convincing historical evidence against Heidegger's interpretation and suggests that Heidegger badly mis-understood the painting. In reaction to this attempted invalidation, Derrida's own text is a puzzling curiosity, for although he admits that Heidegger probably misconstrued the painting's meaning, he would like to allow Heidegger's interpretation all the same.

2. DERRIDA'S DEFENSE OF HEIDEGGER

At first sight, Schapiro's well-informed, rationally and factually grounded interpretation of van Gogh's painting renders rather pointless the prospect of defending Heidegger's rendition of the work. Like a lawyer enthusiastically representing a plainly guilty defendant, this is precisely what Derrida appears to be doing, for as he leaves Heidegger's views mostly intact, he injects doubt into Schapiro's position at every turn. To achieve this, Derrida employs a method – and highlighting this Derridean method is our main reason for attending closely to this Heidegger–Schapiro exchange – that attaches a set of supplementary associations to the details of the Heidegger–Schapiro dispute. These supplementations modify the exchange's background meaning and thereby shift the context away from one within which Schapiro's claims can take root.

Derrida states initially how an "essential indeterminacy" surrounds this dispute from the very start, since both Heidegger and Schapiro assume that the two shoes in van Gogh's picture constitute a matched pair of shoes. Derrida questions whether in fact the shoes are even a pair, presenting this as a viable interpretive possibility.

Given the abundance of evidence to the contrary, it is surprising to find anyone doubting that the shoes are a pair, since shoes usually come in pairs and are usually painted in pairs. Van Gogh himself also painted other pairs of shoes. Reminiscences from François Gauzi (1861–1933), one of van Gogh's fellow students at Fernand Cormon's art school, the *Atelier Cormon*, further suggest that the painting shows a pair of shoes that van Gogh purchased in a Paris flea market, as Schapiro reports.[94] This information accompanies the contemporary presentation of the work at the Van Gogh Museum, where the work is accordingly entitled *A Pair of Shoes* (as opposed to a title such as *Two Right Shoes*). If one looks carefully at the painting by itself, however, it does appear that the shoes have been portrayed very strangely, almost as if they *could* be two left shoes or two right shoes. If one looks beyond the borders of the painting, as Derrida's own method itself prescribes, and considers the historical evidence, there is little question that van Gogh painted a pair of his own shoes.

Derrida nonetheless asks whether the shoes are indeed a "pair," and notes that the painting itself *does not preclude* that we

---

[94] Gauzi, "Vincent van Gogh," pp. 33–4.

could be looking at two right shoes or two left shoes. He says sharply that we cannot "prove" that they are a pair, which is to say that the image itself is ambiguous. If one allows this doubt to set in, Schapiro's attack against Heidegger, along with the significance of any debate between the two over the shoes' proper owner – an owner now rendered non-existent – loses its significance. Of course, if we allow ourselves to speculate in an uncontrolled way, it is *possible* that van Gogh owned two pairs of shoes, and chose to paint two left shoes, one from each pair. If this were true, then the shoes would still belong to van Gogh, contrary to what Derrida is trying to establish by suggesting that the shoes are not necessarily a pair. Not only can one not prove that the shoes are a pair, one cannot prove that they are not a pair.

This unexpected strategy of questioning whether van Gogh painted a pair of shoes does not assist Heidegger's interpretation, although it does well illustrate the inherent ambiguity of the painted image. Derrida shows that there is an alternative to both Heidegger and Schapiro, and that if this alternative is legitimate, then neither Heidegger nor Schapiro has an absolute hold on the situation's truth, which is Derrida's main concern. Derrida aims to deny that Schapiro has the truth of the painting in his hand, since Schapiro's success in this matter would close the discussion about what the painting can and cannot mean, at least as far as the possibility of its depicting a pair of female farmer's shoes is concerned.

Derrida adds that even if we admit that van Gogh painted a "pair" of shoes, the word "pair" itself remains indeterminate. If so, then the meaning of what we are asserting about van Gogh's painting remains vague, and hence the basis for the debate between Heidegger and Schapiro finds itself on unstable ground. From yet another angle, Derrida introduces doubt by reminding us that since van Gogh identified with the peasant life and often painted peasant women, the shoes depicted in Paris in 1886 *could have* been intended to be those of a peasant woman. He states once again that we cannot prove otherwise. We should add, though, that if one admits that van Gogh's paintings of rural folk count as evidence that the 1886 painting could be of a female farmer's pair of shoes, it would be inconsistent to overlook how van Gogh's other paintings of pairs of shoes count as evidence that the 1886 painting is also of a pair of shoes.

The core of Schapiro's criticism is that Heidegger treats van Gogh's painting in isolation. It fails to consider its wider art-historical context and consequently presents a misinterpretation that lacks sufficient factual backing and contradicts the existing documentary evidence. Turning the tables on Schapiro, Derrida maintains that Schapiro commits the same intellectual sin, since he ignores the wider philosophical and textual context within which Heidegger situates the van Gogh example within his own essay. Let us then consider Derrida's claim.

When Heidegger mentions van Gogh's painting in "The Origin of the Work of Art," Derrida emphasizes that Heidegger is at that point engaged in providing a preliminary account of how ordinary things (such as shoes) function as equipment. Quite correctly, he points out that this discussion comes before Heidegger explains how paintings function as works of art *per se*. Nonetheless, within that more mundane, preliminary section about equipment, Heidegger describes the painting and the world that it artistically reveals in anticipation of his general account of the work of art – one into which the characterization of the woman's trudging back home, the empty fields, and such, fits retrospectively as an example. If we do not regard the passage in this way, there would be no reason for Heidegger to be asking us poetically to imagine the woman's fear of death and hunger, the wind-swept fields, and the long trudge, if he is concerned merely with how shoes, hammers, doorknobs, and other such tools function rudimentarily as equipment.

Derrida also notes that for Heidegger's philosophic purposes, there is no need for Heidegger to mention the van Gogh paint-ing, and its presence in the text is not crucial to the general argument. This may be so, but neither does this erase Heidegger's description of the painting as depicting a female farmer's shoes, and as revealing a female farmer's world. With respect to Heidegger, the question is how much leeway one should allow a philosopher who invokes works of fine art to illustrate his or her philosophical principles. This question arose in the last chapter in reference to Foucault's use of *Las Meninas*, which we noted was used without Foucault's having explored the art-historical situa-tion to any substantial extent.

Speaking with greater imaginative resonance, Derrida con-tinues his defense of Heidegger by stating that Schapiro's primary aim, metaphorically and almost psychoanalytically speaking, is to return van Gogh's shoes to van Gogh, after Schapiro had become uneasy about how Heidegger had given the shoes to a peasant woman after having stolen them away from their rightful owner. These phrasings generate a cluster of associations around the word "ownership" that leads to Derrida's charge that Schapiro tries interpretively to transform van Gogh's painting into van Gogh himself; for if the shoes are "returned" to van Gogh, then the shoes in the painting, symbolically considered, would "be" van Gogh. Derrida offers this interpretive assertion as a rhetorical expansion of Schapiro's claim that Heidegger overlooked the essential presence of the artist, van Gogh, in his work.

A more balanced response would be that Schapiro intends to indicate, as would any art historian, that to discuss the painting in a respectably scholarly way, we should respect the artist's intentions, style, and overall *oeuvre*, along with the relevant historical context. Contra Derrida, Heidegger agrees with this, for he states in his own essay that an essential characteristic of appreciating something as a work of art is to appreciate it as having been created by the artist, that is, as embodying the essential presence of the artist, as Schapiro himself points out. Finally, Derrida confronts Schapiro for having presented himself as an academic authority who feels obligated to bring Heidegger to trial, and who, by prosecuting Heidegger for the restitution of van Gogh's shoes, is acting in an oppressively police-like, authoritarian manner.

As we can see in a variety of ways, and particularly in connection with Derrida's likening of Schapiro to a legal prosecutor, Derrida can be depicted in this conflict as Heidegger's defense lawyer, as he aims to deposit doubt upon Schapiro's case. This advocacy is confirmed by Derrida's *ad hominem* argument that portrays Schapiro as a representative of academic policing and as an antagonist to freedom. The import is that Heidegger should be free to interpret van Gogh's painting as he sees fit, since no one can "prove" that Heidegger's interpretation is wrong.

We have not yet made explicit one of the most characteristic features of Derrida's efforts to allow Heidegger's interpretation. A distinctive feature of Derrida's writings is the abundance of associative discourse with which he free-flowingly envelops the topic at hand, weaving into it layer upon layer of context-shifting overtones, suggestions, connotations, unexpected relationships, semantic nuances, vague insinuations, poetic allusions, symbolic references, and other types of linguistic reverberations.

In the present instance, Derrida responds to the subject of van Gogh's painting – a pair of shoes – and offers extended side excursions into the topics of fetishism, sexual symbolism, ownership, feet, the figures of Heidegger and Schapiro as standing for the different factions who fought in World War II, the significance of shoes in the Bible, along with reflections on how other painters have depicted shoes. Noting in the essay's concluding pages how Schapiro allegedly tries to identify van Gogh himself with the painting, Derrida introduces the Freudian notion of narcissism to supplement his originally presented association of the shoes with fetishism, and suggests that the discussion of van Gogh's shoes could be extended even further by using the idea of narcissism as the basis. His associative approach reveals a process of continual, and potentially endless, thickening, supplementing, and overflowing of the meanings that reside more simply, superficially, and definitively in the officially framed debate about whether Heidegger's interpretation of van Gogh is defensible.

It is worth observing that some of Derrida's layers of associations function as an argument-like structure where the association itself works rhetorically to support the position for which Derrida is arguing. The first of these attends to the shoes as ambiguous sexual symbols: shoes have an opening into which accommodates a solid foot, and hence display a female quality; shoes also have a rigid outer form, and hence display a male quality. Using a more familiar image, we can ourselves compare the shoes' "bisexual" (as Derrida describes it) structure to the Eiffel Tower, which has a female-suggestive base and a tall, male-suggestive tower, thus semantically assimilating the Dutch painting into a paradigmatic French context, as Derrida might do.

With the shoes' bisexual meaning in view, Derrida upholds this ambiguity as symbolizing the two perspectives in the debate, namely, where Heidegger appears to be correct from one angle, and where Schapiro appears to be correct from another, and where we oscillate back and forth, arriving conclusively at neither pole of the debate. For Derrida, the shoes in van Gogh's painting symbolize the inability to decide between Heidegger's and Schapiro's interpretations of the shoes, or more precisely, the inability of Schapiro to affirm that he is definitely correct.

The other argument-like association is in Derrida's claim, mentioned above, that the two shoes in van Gogh's painting might not be a pair, but could be two left shoes or two right shoes, standing either as duplicates or as shoes from different pairs. From the perspective of this possibility, as noted, he adds that since the two shoes might not be a genuine pair, then there is no definitive owner of the couple of shoes, no "subject" to whom we should be assigning the two, and hence no genuine debate between Heidegger and Schapiro. This alleged non-pairing of the shoes reflects the remote possibility that the assumption under which Heidegger and Schapiro stage their disagreement is itself unfounded. The non-pairing also symbolizes the basic idea of denying the validity of a conceptual "pair of oppositions."

In these examples, Derrida sets forth associations to the shoes that serve symbolically to support the interpretive angle he has been developing along more straightforward lines; he uses metaphors to support and add rhetorical weight to the conclusions of his standardly styled arguments. In light of the line of defense that Derrida mounts, we must now ask whether his attempt to defend Heidegger, which is often rhetorical, has a serious rationale and philosophical depth.

This is an appropriate place to mention parenthetically that some writers still continue to defend Heidegger's interpretation of van Gogh's painting. One recent attempt (2010) maintains that Heidegger discerned a hidden picture of a woman carrying a hoe in front of a fire, and that Heidegger's reference to the female farmer has a phenomenological basis, namely, in this hidden image. Ian Thompson writes:

> ... if one attends carefully to what emerges from "[o]ut of the dark opening of the well-worn insides of shoes" ... – attending specifically to the lighter patches of color that emerge from the dark opening of the shoe on the right – one can in fact discern the head (hair bonnet and face in profile), torso, and arms of what could easily be a woman, carrying a hoe (a small shovel), with what could even be a small orange-brown "fire" smoldering behind her.[95]

Heidegger does not mention any hidden images in van Gogh's painting, so we should immediately pause. Since hidden images

---

[95] Thompson, "Heidegger's Aesthetics."

are difficult to discern, and if they remain difficult to discern when explicitly pointed out (as done above), their meaning can only remain vague. More importantly, though, Heidegger's own *style* of interpretation does not bring hidden images into play, and this would remain true, even if van Gogh had hidden some images in the painting. If we consider how Heidegger reads the painting, it becomes obvious that he is not interpretively geared towards pictorially symbolic elements of an obscurely discernible sort. Heidegger instead consistently refers to concrete features of the shoes as expressive of rural life.

Heidegger states in particular that "from out of the dark opening of the well-worn insides of the shoes, stares the toil of the worker's steps." Heidegger refers here to the act of walking; he refers to the traces of the laboring feet that fill the dark openings when the shoes are being used. His perceptions are concretely and existentially oriented. The next lines confirm this when he states that the shoes' "heaviness" expresses the woman's slow trudge, and that the "leather" shows the dampness and richness of the soil. Heidegger continues by referring to the space "under the soles" which makes contact with the lonely path upon which the woman walks. This is an area of the shoes that the painting does not display, and which indicates that Heidegger is also not phenomenologically pinned down to what the painting literally shows. In sum, there is nothing in Heidegger's own description of the shoes that suggests that he was attending to hidden pictures within the painting. This is not to say that one cannot find, or imagine, hidden pictures there.

3. DERRIDA, AESTHETICS AND LANGUAGE

Let us return to Derrida. Derrida's strongest argument shows that the painting's appearance, if considered in isolation, does not support an inference to either a peasant woman or to van Gogh as the shoes' rightful owner. This is not the same as saying that the depicted shoes can legitimately be ascribed equally to either. Such an allowance would compare to asserting that although we know that X is of some color, but cannot say which, we can therefore speak as if X is blue and X is associated with blue skies, blue blood, blue feelings, and blue hats, all consequently understood to be revealed by X. This is also like knowing only that a person has some coins in his or her pocket, and then asserting that the person's pocket contains exactly thirty cents.

To appreciate why Derrida offers a set of arguments that are embellished and enhanced with an overflow of rhetorical associations, it will help to interpret his discourse's rhetorical dimensions from a less traditional angle. The ancient Greek Sophists were known as relativists, maintaining that right and wrong, truth and falsity, being and non-being, are what we decide them to be. "Man is the measure …" as Plato cites Protagoras.

If one accepts this position, it becomes tempting to put it into practice by challenging any expression that purports to convey unchanging, absolute, unassailable truths. This amounts to rejecting any positively formulated metaphysical foundations such as God, eternal Forms, or any proposed referent that transcends linguistic systems and contingent human conditions. It is to assert that nothing concrete or describable answers to the idea of a "transcendental signified," "thing-in-itself," or ultimate truth. The position is also difficult to express, since it asserts foundationally that there are no foundations.

When Nietzsche proclaims the death of God, he advocates the same idea that there are no ultimate foundations, which he refers to collectively as the "shadows" of God. As a future task, he calls for the eradication of these shadows as well, once people come to acknowledge superficially that there is no God and the prevailing culture becomes atheistic. The project involves not only expunging the idea of "God" from serious discourse; it involves *challenging the pretensions to absoluteness* that others might have, and involves rejecting every kind of absolute authority, whether it presents itself in the form of a dictatorial political leader, an absolutist doctrine, or a set of eternal facts. It involves challenging the metaphysical substance of what, at some level, we must acknowledge as the resistance of "brute reality," as embodied, for instance, in the bus that barrels heavily down the street, since no one can stand before it and remain unharmed.

Derrida's defense of Heidegger against Schapiro's criticisms occurs within this broader context. Although both Schapiro and Heidegger offer absolutist perspectives (for example, the notion of "Being" is an absolute foundation within Heidegger's philosophy),

Schapiro – by Derrida's lights – is the more manifestly totalitarian thinker of the pair. Derrida thus aims to undermine Schapiro's authoritative arguments as a leading and respected art historian, making some impressive rhetorical headway in rendering the weaker argument, namely, Heidegger's argument, as the stronger.

When one advances art-historical arguments that purport to reveal the facts surrounding a painting, one assumes that there are fixed limits to what the painting can legitimately mean. If van Gogh intended to paint exclusively his own shoes, rather than depict those of a female farmer, then the claim that they depict a woman farmer's shoes is false. It is still possible that van Gogh intended both meanings, which would be an upsetting proposition for Schapiro, for Heidegger's alleged misrepresentation of van Gogh's painting through an association with workers, earthiness and, implicitly, the 1936 Nazi German culture, holds a personal importance: Schapiro's good friend, the neurologist and psychiatrist Kurt Goldstein (1878–1965) – to whom Schapiro dedicates his 1968 refutation of Heidegger – had to flee from Nazi persecution. From Schapiro's standpoint, it is as if Heidegger – one of the most powerful philosophical authorities of the twentieth century – appropriated van Gogh's shoes, renamed them, and then donated them to the Nazis to use in their propaganda efforts, lending support to their activities. It is difficult to say, though, whether or not the meaning van Gogh ascribed to his painting ended with the shoes' origination in the Paris flea market. He did paint many rural scenes and rural folk, and he did live out in the country at times. So one might allow Heidegger's interpretation.

With a skepticism reminiscent of Descartes, Derrida questions whether *any* word's meaning is univocal, and as we have seen, he asks within the Schapiro–Heidegger context whether the ordinary word "pair" has a stable meaning. Since any word's meaning can be questioned, one is immediately put on the defensive when intending to make any steadfast assertions. Like Socrates, who, among his many definition-seeking adventures, approached authoritative military generals in an effort to define the word "courage" (since they, of all people, he expected would know its meaning) and who repeatedly ended up unsatisfied with the definitions offered, Derrida defies anyone to be definitive about what their words mean.

Convinced that clear, well-circumscribed, well-framed, uni-vocal and timelessly true expressions are pointless to assert, it is easy to appreciate how Derrida would be unlikely to rest his entire case against Schapiro on logical argumentation, since such argumentation itself supposes foundational forms of validity, uni-vocal meanings, and a clear separation of fixed and reliable logical form from variable semantic content. This paves the way for the rhetorical use of argumentation, where distinctions between valid and invalid logical forms are not firm, and where persuasive power is the last resort. Such methods of persuasion include the use of arguments from authority, *ad hominem* arguments, invalid lines of thought that appear to be intact, and essentially, the tech-niques that are often effective in winning a legal case, irrespective of whether one's client is guilty or innocent.

Interpreting Derrida in connection with the Sophists and legal rhetoric can be appreciated in a constructive manner within the traditions established first by Descartes in view of the ordi-nary notion of factual, literalistic, or scientific truth, and later by Heidegger and Sartre in view of a different kind of truth, namely, the truth of what it means to be a human being. All three thinkers employ extreme means to display their kind of truth. Descartes, as we know, introduces a method of doubt that regards as false any proposition that can be doubted. Heidegger, in reference to his conception of human being as that whose existence is always "an issue" for it, calls for constant self-questioning. Sartre, fol-lowing suit, asks us to question ourselves the moment we begin to define and falsify our free, living presence by conceiving of ourselves as things or fixed beings. With Derrida, whose primary interests reside in language and its meanings, the Sartrean, free-dom-loving spirit translates into a sensitivity and aversion to ossified meanings, definitions and eternal truths. Barthes' antag-onistic and demythologizing attitude towards fixed concepts is close kin.

Along with the existential truths of Heidegger and Sartre with which Derrida's approach resonates, Derrida's style of think-ing and writing also coheres with the surrealist and Freudian truth that authentic human being springs from the unconscious. Following Jacques Lacan, once we accept that the human uncon-scious is itself linguistically informed, it follows that the impressive variety of logical, associative, metaphor-laden, conversational, and narrative forms that Derrida employs, express not a scientific truth, but the kind of truth that the Surrealists were seeking when they chose to write poetry from the uncensored standpoint of free association. When Derrida writes about works of art, one can understand him as expressing, through a style of free association inspired by Freud's methods of revealing the unconscious, his authentic and instinctual reaction to the works, with few holds barred. In sum, Derrida speaks more like a psychoanalyst than a lawyer.

In *Being and Time* (1927), to recall, Heidegger argues that all of our interpretations are launched under the influence of some background anticipations; we are always already filled with prior conceptions, anticipations, expectations, habits, associations, all of which work together to inform how we interpret our surroundings, the things we encounter and ourselves. For Derrida, these underlying assumptions include our language as well, which implies that when we intelligently perceive a chair, rock, telephone, or cup, we cannot but submerge that item in our inner, and mostly unconscious, sea of language. The language is typically one that we share with others, but since we each absorb and embody language differently with respectively different mental capacities, not to mention a diversity of contrasting educational and cultural experiences, we variously interpret and speak about things.

In connection with aesthetics, Derrida's outlook *submerges every work of art into an ocean of flowing language*, so it is impossible to reflect upon any painting in a museum without implicitly immersing oneself into the cultural discourse on the history of painting, the history of interpretations of the painting, the history of museum practices, and the other paintings on display, since, to begin with, the very distinction between painting and frame is not solid. Thus considered, the painting – along with everything else – automatically exudes linguistic associations, many of which will be commonly appreciated, and many of which will issue more idiosyncratically from our own personalities as interpreters. As we have seen, Derrida associates van Gogh's painting not only with Heidegger's and Schapiro's interpretations, but with paintings of shoes by other painters, and, by implication, all of the writings devoted to these paintings and individuals.

The storehouse of linguistic associations is endless, impossible to specify in advance, potentially rich in meaning, flowing in innumerable directions, and always subject to one's imaginative and creative power. We can appreciate a painting and consider it initially and superficially in reference to the standard history of painting, some common ideas about art, perhaps in conjunction with the few details that we have on hand about the artist and the style. On the next level – and as exemplified by Derrida's style of writing about the work – we can experience a gradual thickening and expanding of the work's meaning by adding layers of associations, like repeatedly dipping a string into hot wax to make a candle. Derrida's treatment of van Gogh's painting exemplifies this, where the manuscript's train of associations starts with Freud's notion of fetishism and continues to a wide variety of themes. At the manuscript's end, Derrida notes that we could press on, presumably for the same impressive length, by considering van Gogh's painting in connection with Freud's notion of narcissism. Other concepts will then extend from that of narcissism, of both a psychological and mythological sort.

Herein resides the *positive* value of Derrida's approach to art, and to the world at large. Like Heidegger, who advocates a notion of truth as the constant unveiling of new perspectives on what is, and like Sartre, who advocates an attitude of constant self-questioning and creative advance where we willfully break out of habitual, well-worn ways of experiencing the world and ourselves, Derrida advocates, in connection with any object or theme, that we allow ourselves to engage in an open and uncensored stream of associations that respect only the most limited of constraints, consistent with the freedom to interpret in the most interesting and semantically rich ways that we can imagine. Although from a more standardly academic and authoritatively institutionalized approach to artistic interpretation, Derrida may appear to be irreverent, sophistic, inconsistent, and unconcerned with the raw facts and the truth of the matter, he can also be appreciated as someone who accepts such facts as mere starting points for further questioning and meaningful reflection, rather than as endpoints that close the discussion.

Given how, on Derrida's vision of things, our perception of ordinary objects is always resonating within a sea of language, how everything we perceive, conceptualize, and imagine is linguistically informed, how consequently we cannot apprehend anything that is completely independent of language – there is, as he says, no being "outside of the text" in any absolute sense – it is still open to ask about the status of this linguistic sea that informs everything around us. Either it is contingent, or it is necessary, or it is some combination of the two, or it is neither.

The Derridian perspective assumes that language and its meanings are variable, fluctuating, endlessly resonant, impossible to circumscribe, and all-permeating. Neither is language's being metaphysically necessary within this outlook, as would be a God, although language may be socially necessary for us. This lands us in the position of either accepting that the most solid ground that we can discern is a mere contingency, since language is "just there," or accepting, more mystically and alternatively, that beyond what we can discern, there is an unspeakable ground – one which, if we do try to refer to it, as this sentence now does, transforms quickly to a non-entity, or mere differential. Thus perhaps resides the deeper meaning of Wittgenstein's remark that "whereof one cannot speak, thereof one must be silent."

To appreciate how the above situation issues historically, we can compare and contrast Derrida to Hegel. A similarly holistic thinker, Hegel appreciates each and every subject matter as an integral aspect of a great rational whole which is the universe; the real is the rational and the rational is the real. Writing over a century later, Derrida takes Hegel's conception of the world as a systematically organized, rational, inevitably growing organic unity, and replaces that conception with "language," regarded as an all-encompassing, unmanageable, semantically overflowing being: there is no being outside of the text. Everything is steeped in language for Derrida, just as for Hegel everything is an ingredient of the rational world system. The difference concerns the respective structures and metaphysical status of their encompassing totalities; Derrida's linguistic world has the surrealistic structure of a Freudian dream, with its inherent contingency, multi-dimensionality, unpredictable dynamism, and semantic packed-ice quality; Hegel's dialectically structured world is well-organized, necessary, articulate, and growing in a clear direction with increasing self-consciousness, rationality, community and freedom.

As we thus jump from the nineteenth century to the later twentieth, and notice how the earlier visions of a necessarily organized world transform into a contemporary mass of contingencies and conflicts, we can observe that theories of interpretation such as Derrida's accordingly adopt a more individualistic approach to freedom. Hence, Derrida defends Heidegger's right to interpret paintings along idiosyncratic lines, and is antagonistic to the ideal of universal consensus at the basis of Kant's aesthetics. In contrast, insofar as Gadamer's hermeneutics upholds consensus as an ideal, he can be appreciated as a twentieth-century effort to retain, within a more historically aware context, the nineteenth-century philosophical spirit of community that we find in Kant, Schiller, Hegel, and Marx.

It is unfortunate that Gadamer perceived himself as being in disagreement with Kant vis-à-vis scientific thinking, for in view of the sharper differences between Gadamer and Derrida, one wonders whether Gadamer should have distanced himself so self-consciously from Kant. In reference to the broader history of aesthetics, a mutual respect for consensus is more telling than a difference of opinion regarding the value of scientific thinking. Gadamer and Derrida take sides against science, but their contrasting views on interpretation reflect a more fundamental tension between thinkers who value reason in general (in Gadamer's case, rationality takes the form of honest and open dialogue) and those who are antagonistic to reason, as is Derrida in his efforts to undermine logocentrism, or exclusively reason-based thinking, in favor of an amalgam of literal, associative, and metaphorical modes of expression that he considers to be expressive of language itself. By understanding Derrida in contrast to Hegel, the reason-friendly affinities between Gadamer and Kant emerge more clearly, along with Derrida's connection to the anti-rationalistic, surrealistic tradition that extends from Nietzsche and Freud.

16

THE ART OF THE TIME IMAGE

Gilles Deleuze

1. IMAGE, MOVEMENT-IMAGE AND TIME-IMAGE

Gilles Deleuze's approach to the cinema, and the kind of aesthetic awareness that accompanies it, requires that we abandon some entrenched philosophical assumptions about how to analyse, not to mention apprehend, the objects of human perception. It is natural that perceptual illusions invoke a distinction between how something is in itself, versus how it appears to us, for example, how a wooden stick, known to be perfectly straight, appears bent when immersed halfway into a container of water. Under such circumstances, the distinction between "reality and illusion" is obvious to draw. With some sustained philosophical reflection, one soon wonders whether items that convincingly appear to be intact, palpable, and "real," such as the chair upon which one comfortably sits, the fireplace in one's room that warms the air, the paper upon which one is writing, and the nightclothes that can be felt directly upon one's skin, are as palpable as they seem to be. In contemporary culture, we are familiar with this disconcerting situation from the movie *The Matrix* (1999), large segments of which are set within a computer-simulated reality that mimics ordinary experience, and where the majority of the population remains unaware that they are participating in a mere simulation.

Taking seriously the above uncertainty about what our perceptions actually represent, some highly reflective individuals – Galileo and Locke, for example, during the 1600s – questioned whether the ordinary objects that we apprehend are appearing, by and large, as they are in themselves. Noticing how one and the same bowl of room-temperature water feels warm to a previously cold hand, and cold to a previously warm hand, or how an object's weight remains the same, whether or not the light that illuminates it is bright or dim, green or yellow, it became common to assume scientifically and philosophically that when we perceive an object, only its extension, figure, and motion convey how the object is mind-independently, or in itself, and that the object's color, taste, texture, sound, and odor represent only how it appears to us. The distinction is clear upon appreciating how the face-puckering taste of lemon juice does not itself reside in the cup of lemon juice in our hand, that is, in the liquid itself, although its volume and weight does. We say "the juice is sour," as if the juice itself were sour, but this is misleading. It is equally misleading in the same sense to say that "the sunset is beautiful."

A tempting way to account for our perception of objects that immediately present us with a mixture of mind-dependent and mind-independent qualities, as when we look at a bright, full moon, is to maintain that we perceive external objects only *indirectly*. Instead, we directly and immediately perceive our mental images of external objects, where these mental images, like photographs, represent those objects. On this view, the things in the external, material world are constituted only by extension, figure, and motion, where supposedly these qualities act upon our sense organs to produce common side-effects such as colors, odors, tastes, sounds, and textures that appear only in our mental imagery.

Upon arriving at this philosophical point, it is a short step to infer that each of us is confined within a field of private mental images, stuck in the precarious position of considering how, merely by examining the contents of those images, it can be known that there is, in fact, an "external world" that is supposedly causing them. The situation compares to being presented with a photograph of a person whom one has never seen and about whom one has no information, and being asked to determine, from examining the photograph alone, whether the photograph is a good likeness.

Despite how the distinction between mind-independent qualities (such as extension, figure, and motion) and mind-dependent qualities (such as color, taste, odor, sound, and texture) logically gravitates us into an awkward theory of perception, the immeasurable value of that distinction's scientific utility continues to make it worthwhile to formulate a theory of perception that can accommodate it. We nonetheless have, at one philosophical extreme, the position that physical objects are nothing more than sets of mental images, and at the other, the position that the mind-independent world is completely unknowable as it is in itself. Both extremes run contrary to common sense.

Henri Bergson (1859–1941) inherited this philosophical predicament and, hoping to formulate a resolution that would preserve common sense, he presented an alternative way to understand the objects of human perception. This alternative admittedly creates other kinds of conceptual tensions, but for Bergson, they are less unsettling ones. According to him, the external world – or "matter" as he refers to it – is composed of "images" that are self-sufficient and yet vary from person to person. Within a theatre audience, for example, each person sees the stage from a different angle. Each person also apprehends the stage, that everyone else presumably sees, as a self-sufficient object – an object that, while remaining in a condition roughly akin to how one perceives it, would continue to exist if one were to leave the theatre. Bergson conceives of these "images" as having in themselves the colors, tastes, sounds, odors, and textures that they appear to have, even though their qualities vary from person to person, as when two people taste the same wine, but have different opinions about the taste's quality.

Bergson's conception of images requires us to accept an uneasy philosophical amalgam, since it is puzzling how an image can be both mind-dependent and mind-independent at the same time. His response is that we acknowledge this conflict every day in our common sense thinking. Whether we should accept Bergson's answer is not our immediate concern in connection with Deleuze, and we need only note that Bergson's conception of an "image" indicates a tension-ridden condition where qualities that we tend ordinarily to distinguish and theoretically separate are blended together to constitute a philosophical alloy, almost like a metaphor in its amalgamation of opposing qualities, upon which an entire world view is built.

This Bergsonian style of thinking suggests, by extension, that it might be a good idea to admit similar kinds of philosophical alloys into our theorizing, and recognize conditions that are blendingly both inner and outer, present and past, moving and static, conceptual and perceptual, real and imaginary, or aesthetic and non-aesthetic. With respect to sensory modes, one can also admit synesthetic amalgams, where one recognizes blendings of the visual and the tactile, or the visual and the sonic, or the sonic and the gustatory. Deleuze's thinking is fundamentally of this amalgamating kind, and it cuts against much traditional philosophical theorizing, just as Bergson's notion of "image" defies and denies the sharp distinction between mind-independent vs. mind-dependent qualities.

Adopting Bergson's understanding of our world as being composed of images in the above sense, along with Bergson's view that the flow of time is metaphysically basic, Deleuze describes our typical, daily-life images as finite and abstracted "movement-images," namely, chunks of movement that bear relationships to each other and transform into one another, all of which are immersed in the single, underlying movement which is the world, or most fundamental movement-image. When interpreting our surroundings in such terms, an analysis of our field of ordinary activity emerges, as when we experience an object, react to it with some thought or feeling, and then act in relation to the object. We might see some food on the table, for instance, smell its attractive aroma, perhaps also savor its visual presentation, and then move towards it with the intention to consume it, assuming we are hungry and that it is socially appropriate to eat the food within the context.

In Deleuzian terminology, this sequence is describable as one of "perception-images" (the food), "affection-images" (the smell and associated feelings), and "action-images" (the eating), to form a mini-story out of chunks of framed-time, almost as if the real-life world were itself a movie. This kind of sequencing characterizes a large portion of our daily behavior, and as the basis of the traditional narrative format, it underlies the structure of literary and filmic presentations that adhere to an Aristotelian conception of organic unity. Aristotle mentions in his theory of tragedy, for example, that the tragic narrative has a beginning, middle, and end that occurs with a comprehensible space of time.

Within this space, the action unfolds in a specific, inevitable direction, as a plant would grow, or as a chemical reaction would occur, such that all of the episodes are integrated in a rationally satisfactory way, one entailing the next.

Filmic representation, like ordinary perception, contains breaks, shifts, changes of focus, variable speeds of attention, and such, and it can mimic the phenomenological structure of experience. Within the traditional narrative format mentioned above, there is a broad spectrum of possible filmic instantiations, since film can incorporate variabilities in its structuring that go far beyond what ordinary experience contains. Shots can be taken at different times, or can represent different times, and yet they can be artistically set into a close, meaningful, narrative sequence. A filmic biography can encompass a person's eighty-year lifetime within the span of two hours. We can jump from the ground-level to the top of a building, to another city, within the space of a few seconds. All of this, and more, is possible within the parameters of the traditional narrative. In terms of this Deleuzian approach, films are themselves constituted by Bergsonian images of various kinds, and consequently present to us another world that blends into our present one, as a passing daydream while walking within the grocery store blends into the ordinary activity of buying milk or bread.

It is possible to organize films taxonomically according to whether their overall aesthetic atmosphere centers upon one of Deleuze's three main types of movement-images, although for any particular film, it would be a rarity not to encounter all three types in good measure, along with their subtle variations and intermediate versions. In his specific film analyses, of which there are many, Deleuze identifies these movement-type ingredients with great sensitivity, as a food critic employs the elementary tastes and their variants to characterize the experience of this or that dish of fine cuisine. The upshot of Deleuze's analyses is to reveal further image-types whose character transcends the standard, organic-unity, beginning-middle-end, "sensory-motor-based," "perception-affection-action imagery," Aristotelian narrative format with which we are naturally familiar and which has been described above. This effort to identify structures that step beyond classical cinema commences at the end of Deleuze's first volume of his two-volume study, *Cinema 1: The Movement Image*

(*Cinéma I: l'image-mouvement*, 1983), and foreshadows the next volume.

In *Cinema 2: The Time Image* (*Cinéma II: l'image-temps*, 1985), Deleuze identifies filmic situations – the majority of which arise in the post-World War II period – where the aesthetic atmosphere is less bound to the narrative form and in some important instances is more quietly reflective. This contrasts with films that bear a simpler, directly perceptual orientation towards objects, or focus on straightforward actions (as in combat scenes), or focus on the direct expression of emotions (as in close-ups of people who smile or cry unreflectively) while immersed in some activity. In the postwar instances, a film might show an ordinary sequence of mundane events, except that at one point the main character looks for a pausing moment at an ordinary object, such as an injured hand, or a slightly protruding stomach (as when pregnant), or perhaps a curiously shaped scar, that, within the film's context, is steeped in an imaginative depth and complex meaning that extends beyond the significance of the immediate surroundings. The character may take no subsequent action – the mundane sequence may continue evenly as before – but the situation contains a psychological break in the action that conveys an intensification of subjective feeling, usually of a reflective, mentally suspended sort.

Deleuze's uncovering of such succession-interruptive images explores how the familiar narrative form, which his theory describes as a "sensory-motor" centered structure, can become upset, disordered, and largely disintegrated. One way is noted above, as when a film introduces psychological factors to a point where their interruptive breaks weigh heavily to dominate the film's meaning. This leaves us in an action-suspended mode that invites us to contemplate the feelings of the characters themselves, as the characters themselves contemplate them. A similar kind of narrative dissolution occurs when a series of shots constitutes an aggregate whose accumulative effect conveys a more amorphous and confusing atmosphere, owing to the choppy, unpredictable transitions from shot to shot combined with the juxtaposition of diverse meanings.

Employing such techniques, the film experience can alter how it conveys a sense of time; in the more traditional, action-oriented kinds of film composition, one shot intrinsically suggests the next, and the subsequent connectedness of the events portrayed produces a sense of artificially constructed time intrinsic to the narrative sequence; in the postwar styles, the shots do not narratively cohere in a tightly knit way. Each image stands more on its own in the absence of a forced, or represented, sense of time that would otherwise have been inscribed into the filmic sequence as a whole.

This alternative to the types of movement-image – we now have varieties of "time-image" – can be understood by analogy to how, at the beginning of the twentieth century, the art of painting reached a level of abstraction where it presented pure, expressive forms, as opposed to forms that represented ordinary objects.[96] In both the filmic and the painterly instances, the natural link between an image and some object that it represents is severed, such that the image is presented to be contemplated for its own sake. Along yet another comparative dimension, the change from movement-image to time-image also relates to how atonal music – music that emerged historically at the same time as did non-objective painting – defies the rational structures of the traditional system of musical composition. Within the register of the time-image, the film composition does not proceed according to a pattern of natural unfolding, but, in the spirit of aggregation and collage, embodies sequences of incommensurable images, unexpected cuts and, corresponding to this, an inexplicable and undecidable meaning.

Although Deleuze does not accentuate this, the above analogies suggest that the development of the cinema in terms of the prevailing film-composition style – and this is what Deleuze's cinema theory is fundamentally about – lagged behind that of painting and music by a couple of decades. Whereas the purely sensory image appears significantly in painting and music just

---

[96] In his book on Francis Bacon's painting, *The Logic of Sensation* (1981), Deleuze emphasizes how painting should be appreciated fundamentally as an artistic medium for revealing non-representational, viscerally oriented realities. Just as Merleau-Ponty employs Cézanne, as Foucault invokes Velázquez, and as Heidegger relies on van Gogh, Deleuze uses Bacon to illustrate his philosophical view. Deleuze adds that "modern painting begins when man no longer experiences himself as an essence, but as an accident, always with the risk of fall" (*The Logic of Sensation*, p. 87).

after World War I (for example, as in Kandinsky's non-objective painting and in the Second Viennese School's atonal music), Deleuze maintains that the analogous kind of purely optical image in film – which is here an awareness of some object or scene simply for its own sake, as if it were a painting in itself, without its being the announcement of some inferred and subsequent image – appears significantly just after World War II, and, not surprisingly in relation to this Zen-like quality, in Japan, in the films of Yasujirō Ozu. Deleuze's prime example is Ozu's film, *Banshun* (*Late Spring*, 1949).

2. FILM AND SOCIAL CRITICISM

Deleuze's two volumes on cinema attend mainly to highlighting formal matters, most of which concern the differences in the filmic presentation of time, as they issue from two distinct styles of film composition, namely, the standard, straightforward, arguably natural, organic-unity-focused, narrative style of film organization, and the more expectation-defying, dispersive, reflection-centered, and subjectivity-exuding style. The former is grounded on the movement-image; the latter, on the time-image.

The time-image style involves a greater volume of self-sufficient imagery, image-to-image, where one aesthetically and semantically self-sufficient image is set next to another in a merely additive, collage-like sequence to yield a filmic presentation whose overall meaning remains relatively indeterminate, as compared to the narrative style. This time-image method serves well to express more intangible, difficult-to-comprehend ideas that are typical of imaginative philosophic visions, poetic moods, and inward reflection. It also has the power to open up new horizons of meaning, and in this capacity it can serve to challenge existing social values, even if these new horizons do not flatly contradict established norms.

At one point in his conclusion to *Cinema 2: The Time-Image*, Deleuze sympathetically refers us to the German film director, Hans-Jürgen Syberberg, known for his *Hitler, ein Film aus Deutschland* (1977), stating that "if Hitler is to be put on trial by cinema, it must be inside cinema, against Hitler the film-maker, in order to 'defeat him cinematographically, turning his weapons against him.'"[97] We can interpret Deleuze as taking up that challenge to defeat Hitler cinematographically in *Cinema 2*, in accord with Serge Daney's observation that the very cinema of the movement-image was rendered doubtful by the effective use of filmic effects for propaganda and mass rallies, as occurred in Nazi Germany.[98] Hollywood and Hitler become kindred spirits of the movement-image within this view, echoing Adorno's and Horkheimer's negative estimation of reason in *The Dialectic of Enlightenment*, which we discussed earlier.[99]

Just as Adorno refers us to non-rationalistic, atonal music as an antidote to fascistic rationality, Deleuze's characterization of the time-image in film does the same, where the "rationality" to be undermined is assuming the pragmatic form of the sensory-motor-based, organically-unified, beginning-middle-end, movement-image-based narrative structure. Deleuze's primary and respective historical assignments of the movement-image to pre-World War II cinema, and the time-image to post-World War II cinema, cohere with this perspective on Deleuze's two volumes, since the notions of atonality and loss of narrative resonate expressively well with a world that has recently fallen apart, as we can envisage in the cities devastated by World War II bombing raids. This is the landscape that motivates the emergence of the time-image in cinema. As is commonly observed, Hitler's defeat in World War II inflicted the *coup de grâce* to nineteenth-century theories of history that embody the grand narrative of humanity's march toward the perfect society. Having himself matured within the context of this grand narrative's ruin – Deleuze was aged fourteen to twenty during World War II, and it helps to recall that his older brother died on a deportation train to Auschwitz – it comes as no surprise to find Deleuze consequently ushering in a film theory that rests on the

---

[97] Deleuze, *Cinema 2*, p. 264.

[98] Deleuze, *Cinema 2*, p. 164.

[99] Michel Foucault believed that "the value of Syberberg's film is precisely in saying that horror is commonplace, that the commonplace bears dimensions of horror within itself, that there is a reversibility between horror and banality" ("The Four Horsemen of the Apocalypse and the Everyday Worms," in *Aesthetics, Method, and Epistemology*, p. 234).

idea that post-World War II cinema presents us with a disintegration of narrative structure. The disintegration of the grand historical narrative coincides with the disintegration of the narrative form in film.

When interpreted through this social-critical lens, a variety of questions and objections arise with respect to Deleuze's effort to identify a set of liberating, anti-fascist, filmic techniques inherent in the time-image. The first question – a preliminary one – is whether it is more revealing to read Deleuze as outlining a history of filmic style based on a model that roughly divides the history of the cinema in half, using a basic "pre-" versus "post-" World War II division, or alternatively, as extracting a general set of film techniques that can be used at any time or place, as one might encounter in a traditional structuralist project, notwithstanding how, at a more specific level, Deleuze denies that film is a language in the structuralist sense.

Although both dimensions are present in *Cinema 1* and *Cinema 2*, the more non-historical interpretation is the more intellectually sustainable from our present vantage point, if only because as counterexamples we have experienced how, over the past twenty-five years since the publication of Deleuze's volumes, films continue to be composed according to movement-image-emphasizing techniques, and how their cultural instances have not diminished in frequency, popularity, or influence. Most Hollywood movies employ this movement-image style, and the contemporary movies with the most social presence and marketing exposure are of this Hollywood kind. The historical situation does not consequently compare to how neoclassical art gave way to romanticism during the tail end of the eighteenth century and beginning of the nineteenth century, with the change reverberating through almost all areas of cultural life.

There is also some uncertainty surrounding Deleuze's implicit claim – at least if we are to judge by the respectively prevailing film composition styles – that pre-World War II culture was less reflective, less subjectivity-oriented, more pragmatically engaged and action-oriented, and post-World War II culture was more reflective, more subjectively focused, and less pragmatically engaged, typically set in a kind of existential limbo. One difficulty here involves the stunning variability in philosophers' opinions about which historical periods are more or less subjectivity-oriented than others. Hegel maintained that European culture became more subjectivity-oriented two thousand years ago, with the decline of Greek culture and the rise of Christianity, owing to Christianity's distinctive focus upon the quality of a person's inner character, as opposed to the appearances of a person's external behavior. Some identify Descartes' *Meditations on First Philosophy* (1641) as the point where Western philosophy and culture becomes more subjectivity-oriented, due to Descartes's exemplary method of doubt and extreme speculation that our daily experience could be nothing more than a dream. Foucault identifies Kant's *Critique of Pure Reason* (1781) as Europe's cultural turning point into a condition of deeper subjectivity and self-awareness, owing to Kant's theory that space and time are forms of the human mind. One could also say that in certain artistic spheres, a more intense sense of subjectivity arose at the beginning of the twentieth century, partially owing to the assumption of literalistic depiction by photography, which allowed painting to liberate itself from this task. Expressionist portraiture portrays inner emotional states using non-naturalistic forms and coloration, for example.

Deleuze's choice of films also reveals much about how we are to understand his analyses and value his conclusions. Of the over 500 movie titles that appear in the two volumes, only a relative few are popular, Hollywood films. At the basis of his analysis resides rather a more sophisticated, avant-garde subculture that he uses as a cultural thermometer. This is justifiable, if we compare his filmic examples to the paintings in the Louvre, Prado, or Metropolitan Museum of Art, for instance, which, as cultural exemplars, surpass in significance one-for-one the millions of photographic images that presently populate magazines.

Deleuze treats filmmakers such as Orson Welles, Alain Resnais, Alfred Hitchcock, and Yasujirō Ozu, among others, on a par with the leading thinkers of the age, and from their films he draws implications about the prevailing cultural conditions within which they live, as one might do by considering Picasso's and Braque's Cubist works as revelatory of the modernist period's values. Despite this, it stands that if one is interested in developing an account of the contemporary society's mentality – and this is a prerequisite for advancing any social critique – it is essential to consider carefully the contents of the prevailing popular imagery, and in the case of film this involves the contents and structure of Hollywood movies. It is notable that of the approximately 170 films that Deleuze mentions in *Cinema 1: The Movement Image*, only about twenty are in the popular mainstream. The rest are likely to be familiar only to academics, members of the artworld, and a variety of elite subcultures.

Beyond these qualifying considerations, there are two penetrating criticisms of Deleuze's study of cinema, both of which question its capacity to offer useful avenues for social critique. Although he appears to have believed otherwise, the first is that the technique-oriented, quasi-structuralist, formalistic approach that Deleuze adopts remains in itself too neutral, and hence politically non-committal. Contrary to Daney's perceptions, it does not follow – and this is reminiscent of the same kind of one-sided deprecation of rationality that we find in Adorno – that if a film is composed according to a traditional narrative structure, that, owing to its very form, it thereby plays self-defeatingly into the hands of a potentially fascist, ruling elite.

The movies *The Last Samurai* (2002), *Erin Brockovich* (2000), *The Insider* (1999), *Philadelphia* (1993), *Dances with Wolves* (1990), *Missing* (1982), *The Color Purple* (1982), *The China Syndrome* (1979), *Norma Rae* (1979), *All the President's Men* (1976), *Guess Who's Coming to Dinner* (1967), *Dr. Strangelove* (1964), *Gentleman's Agreement* (1947), and looking back further, *Modern Times* (1936) are based on the traditional narrative form, and although they are commercialized products, they provide a powerful social commentary. Adding to this list is how Charles Dickens' socially critical novelette *A Christmas Carol* (1843), with its capitalist miser Ebenezer Scrooge, has been rendered into a filmic form in 1901, 1908, 1910, 1913, 1916, 1923, 1935, 1938, 1951, 1953, 1970, 1971, 1983, 1988, 1992, 1994, 1997, 2001, 2006, 2008, and 2009, not to mention into versions for television, theatre, and radio.

Similarly, if a film is non-traditionally structured, amorphous in its meaning, quietly reflective, and composed according to collage-like principles, it does not follow that owing to its very format, it will work against the imposition of oppressive or questionable ideologies. At one point, Deleuze refers to Kubrick's *2001: A Space Odyssey*, indicating how the black monolith "presides over both cosmic states and cerebral states," presumably bridging both the inner and outer worlds.[100] This may be so, and the meaning of the black monolith may remain a mystery in the movie, fitting nicely into Deleuze's perceptions of time-image-based cinema. Beyond this coincidence, *2001: A Space Odyssey* can still be read as an advertisement for the space industry, and moreover, with its speculative journey into and through a black hole, as a quasi-religious, scientistic inspiration to those who remain unsure of our place in the universe.

These examples collectively indicate that if a theory of cinema devotes the bulk of its attention to categorizing film-composition techniques, then the theory's capacity for social critique is going to be diminished, for it is difficult to see how any one fundamental technique, grounded, in Deleuze's case, either on the movement-image or the time-image, can be aligned with this or that side of the revolutionary or culture-critical debate. The films' ideological contents are essential to consider, and Deleuze's impressively long, detailed, complicated, and imaginative study does not emphasize this dimension.

Deleuze, inspired by Bergson, is intellectually attuned to theorize in a manner where the foundational quality of standard philosophical distinctions is undermined through the introduction of an alternative, in the form of some kind of amalgamated condition. This positive disposition towards conceptual alloys stems from Hegel's presentation of dialectical reason, it is worth observing, but in Deleuze, distinctions are overcome in an amalgamated, synthesis-centered situation without the indication or implication of any further development.

We thus have Deleuze describing the time-image as merging the inner and the outer, the true and the false, the past and the present, and the real and the imaginary. If we add moral dichotomies to this list, such as right and wrong, just and unjust, good and evil, fair and unfair, virtuous and vicious, and so on, and extend this Deleuzian logic, there will be no unambiguous standpoint from which one can launch a social critique, if only because the world becomes thoroughly ambiguous, both metaphysically and morally, on this vision of things. There is consequently a contradiction between having an interest in social critique and

---

[100] Deleuze, *Cinema 2*, pp. 205–6.

adopting a Bergsonian metaphysics of amalgamation. If the underlying point is to scramble and merge every foundational distinction within the Western philosophical tradition, then the distinctions required to launch a determinate social critique will be scrambled as well, rendering social critique ineffective.

Integral to Deleuze's notion of the time-image is the idea of blurring the distinction between an object and its double, as in a mirror image. The underlying motive here is to challenge the traditional narrative form, where beginnings and endings are distinguished and separated by an obvious time interval. By blurring the distinction between an object and its double, where its actual image blends with its virtual image, Deleuze introduces a circular structure, where after a long journey, for instance, the hero ends up where he or she started, as if nothing had developed or transpired, with no real point to the journey. The often-cited filmic example that contains a brief illustration of an object and its double blending together is Welles' *The Lady from Shanghai* (1947), which culminates in a hall of mirrors, wherein the main characters face multiple images of one another, finding it impossible to determine within the splintering confusion which images are the flesh-and-blood ones.

Although one can appreciate Deleuze's interest in identifying structures that dislodge the traditional narrative format – this reminds us of how Benjamin highlighted art forms that dislodge the "original versus copy" distinction – the assimilation of subject and object does run contrary to the differentiated, disjointed, collage style of film composition that constitutes another aspect of the time-image film composition style. It also conflicts with the strong current of twentieth-century, anti-dialectical, French theorizing, where, as in Sartre and Lacan, emphasis is placed upon how we are inscrutable to ourselves, that is, how when we reflect, we never return to ourselves, but instead create a false, imaginary, idealized, and over-stabilized object that never coincides with the nature of the dynamically thinking subject. Much of Deleuze's thought emphasizes disjointedness and differentiations of this latter kind, so it is surprising to discover as a basic constituent of his account of the time-image, a vision of a pure subject–object amalgamation.

Again, this stems from the Bergsonian influence that gravitates Deleuze's theorizing away from atomization and differentiation into the themes of pure flux, duration, flow, and deep continuity. He is thus in an unsteady philosophical position, as he resides in the middle of a French tradition that, as its hallmark, emphasizes difference, opposition, conflict, failure of consensus, and icono-clastic disagreement, while standing committed to a Bergsonian vision that is continuum-based. The upshot is an intellectual atmosphere where the theory displays a "scrambled eggs" quality, such that scores of imaginative and insightful distinctions are recognized and drawn, only to shift and drift within an unruly, undependable, somewhat sticky theoretical mix that lacks a tele-ology, systematicity, or theoretical skeleton, and where one easily becomes lost within the irregular conceptual mass.

This style of thinking provides an intriguing aesthetic, as we apprehend the things in the world as being perpetually ambigu-ous and flowing within a broad field of interacting forces, where the distinction between aesthetic and non-aesthetic dissolves, and where essential distinctions between the arts that tradition-ally constitute a "system" of the arts melt away. The lava-like flow upon which this style of thinking rests, however, causes it to fall short of helping advance a social critique beyond advancing a basic and superficial objection to fixed social categories, in what-ever form they might take.

3. THE TIME-IMAGE AND PERSONAL LIBERATION

Deleuze's observation that the time-image never appeared more clearly in film than in the work of Yasujirō Ozu (1903–63), whose disconnected spaces, minimalistic cinematographic style and quiet suggestiveness – much like Japanese haiku poetry – leads us to the idea that the time-image is well-geared to revealing the present, perpetually flowing moment in a nearly Zen Buddhistic fashion. The Zen-enlightened attitude contrasts with being involved in the more common, survival-oriented, forward-looking, present-escaping, instrumental, acquisitive mentality that depends more upon sensory-motor links and their associ-ated movement-images, as Deleuze conceives of them. This connection to Zen suggests that Deleuze's film theory may be more useful for the project of personal enlightenment, rather than social critique, given Deleuze's underlying Bergsonism and the resonance between Bergson's flux theory of time and Buddhism's comparable metaphysics of flux, in addition to Zen's specifically practical emphasis upon experiencing the immediate presence of things in the flow of time.

Bergson maintains that metaphysical truth resides in the direct experience of time's flow, or pure duration, and criticizes accounts of time that conceive of it fundamentally as a set of atomic points or fixed segments, where those points are believed to add together mathematically to constitute a whole. Bergson and Deleuze reject this "spatialized" or atomized conception of time, along with the mathematical/scientific mentality that underlies it, in favor of theorizing in terms of conceptual blends, amalgamations, dissolutions of distinctions, and fusions that undermine our usual categorizations.

In Bergson, this attitude generates an antagonism towards fixed concepts as a whole, at least insofar as such concepts are presumed to reflect metaphysical knowledge. Zen Buddhism is also critical towards fixed concepts, asserting that they interfere with experiencing the true being of time, or "time-being," as Zen Master Dōgen (1200–53) calls it. Almost identically to Bergson, Dōgen states that "because flowing is a quality of time, moments of past and present do not overlap or line up side by side."[101] Fixed concepts form only a useful map of the rich and fluctuating sensory terrain, and to grasp what is truly happening, we must avoid mistaking the map for the terrain, the definition for the thing supposedly defined, the abstract concept for concrete reality, the box score for the actual baseball game, the music criticism for the actual musical performance, or the autobiography for the actual life.

The Sanskrit word "yoga" stems from the root "*yug*," which means "to join together or to yoke." The English words "joining," "junction" and "union" issue from this root as well, and at bottom, the etymology presents the idea of yogic liberation as a condition of being joined together, or being at one, with the universe as a whole. Deleuze refers to the apprehension of the universe as a whole as the "gaseous" state of "flowing matter" and

---

[101] *Moon in a Dewdrop*, "The Time Being – Uji," p. 78.

as the unified movement-image, that is, reality. Bergson describes it as pure duration, prior to our dividing this flowing unity for the sake of pragmatic considerations, or as Deleuze would say, into perception-images, affection-images and action-images.

The Japanese word *"Zen"* expresses the Chinese word *"Ch'an,"* which in turn stems from the Sanskrit *"dhyana,"* which signifies "meditation" or "meditational state," as in yoga. Zen, or meditational, Buddhism – now known popularly as a kind of Japanese Buddhism, but which developed in China centuries earlier as Ch'an Buddhism – is itself a down-to-earth, eyes-open extension of the yogic tradition, situated in the more time-flux-focused, Buddhist metaphysics. In light of how Deleuze's own theorizing resides within a Bergsonian/Buddhist time-flux, it is worth considering whether Deleuze's theory of the cinema implicitly conveys a Zen vision of personal enlightenment. If so, then this could replace the effort to implement a social critique that is less successful in his theory.

The dissolution of distinctions that the time-image cinematic style fosters (for example, distinctions between inner and outer, past and present, and real and imaginary) is close to what Buddhist thought prescribes, where thought in terms of fixed concepts, as noted above, and more specifically, the accompanying "either/or" thinking style, is regarded as a misguided mode of awareness, both metaphysically and existentially. An exemplary text from the Ch'an tradition is *Relying on Mind* by the Third Patriarch, Sengcan (d. 606), which states that "dualistic constructs don't endure, so take care not to pursue them; as soon as positive and negative arise, the mind is lost in confusion."[102]

Deleuze's image of the world, which we have described as being expressed through an intentionally scrambled-and-flowing conceptual construction, both in terms of phenomenology and the very structure of Deleuze's theorizing, where objects and distinctions are discernible, but are mixed into their surroundings as one would toss a salad, provides a realistic version of a Zen Buddhistic perception. We are not here describing a condition of perfect Zen enlightenment, but what a person reasonably on the way to such an enlightened condition would be experiencing.

---

[102] Foster and Shoemaker (eds), *The Roaring Stream*, p. 12.

In the latter, physical objects are recognized in their plain, everyday form, but are not taken to be rock solid. Dynamic inter-relationships between things are appreciated, accompanied by an awareness of one's inextricable immersion in the world in the present moment. The distinction between subject and object is mostly dissolved, and there is a feeling of liberation and release from the more fixed, ordinary world of people, politics, and money. Mostly lacking in Deleuze's vision, however, is the Zen Buddhist's exclusive savoring of the "this-ness" or "suchness" of the items within one's perceptual field, accompanied by only the very thin-nest layer of interpretation, as might be stimulated by mediation in a quiet rock garden. In its place, Deleuze offers an immersion in a rich concoction of novel, essentially unstable concepts.

With respect to the time-image, Deleuze's cinema theory might be unimpressive in its short supply of tools that are useable for direct social critique, but if we follow the pregnant sugges-tiveness of Deleuze's key reference to Ozu's filmmaking, the theory shows the potential to foster a Bergsonian/Dōgenian appreciation of the time-being of things. The end result is a French-Japanese theoretical amalgam that has a French theoreti-cal flavor mixed with an inspiring air of Zen, and which exemplifies neither French nor Japanese thought in a pure way.

Of the few examples of this kind of French-Japanese amal-gam, we can mention Kuki Shūzō (1888–1941) as having formulated a more Japanese-centered version of a similar cross-cultural mix. Theorizing with a set of French and German philosophical concepts – he traveled from Japan and studied in Europe from 1921 to 1929, meeting with Bergson, Sartre, Husserl, and Heidegger – Shūzō analysed the Japanese aesthetics of *iki* (quiet refinement; restrained chic; urbane, plucky stylish-ness) which was popular during the late eighteenth and nineteenth centuries in his homeland, and thus blended European theoriz-ing with Japanese aesthetics. If we were to search for an example in the visual arts that displays a similar French-Japanese amal-gam, we might turn to some of van Gogh's images of blossoming trees or of Japanese prints. Another example might be Whistler's *Nocturne in Black and Gold: The Falling Rocket* (1875), which dis-plays Whistler's absorption of both French and Japanese artistic styles, and which provides an image of Deleuze's Bergsonian world of flux and indeterminacy.

Deleuze's time-image style of cinema does not provide a determinate approach to a condition of Zen enlightenment, though, for in addition to Ozu's contemplative films, despite their exemplary status for Deleuze, other aesthetically different kinds of films also exemplify the time-image. Syberberg's film on Hitler, mentioned above, is an example. Another complicating factor is that time-image-constructed films (as well as movement-image ones) can have a negative ideological content, since their themes are open.

Suppose we have a time-image-constructed film that exudes the Zen spirit extremely well, and suppose for the sake of argument that the Zen style of enlightenment is desirable or genuinely enlightening. Even in a case like this, there is an inherent danger that the involved dissolution of personal identity and sense of individuality could work too agreeably with the ruling, and presumably self-serving, elite. Zen-trained Samurai warriors unconditionally offered their services to medieval warlords; Zen-trained soldiers fought bravely, nationalistically and single-mindedly to sustain the Japanese empire during World War II. There may be an underlying antagonism to fixed concepts that the Zen awareness advocates, but these two examples involve individuals who accept the legitimacy of their surrounding political situation, serve it, sacrifice their lives for it, and subordinate their Zen awareness to these political interests.

Although Zen awareness is ideally conceived of, and is perfectly realized as a kind of universalistic awareness, its subordination to the fixed concept of a feudal lord in the days of the Samurai, and later, its subordination to the fixed concept of the Japanese empire during the 1930s and 1940s, undermined its moral integrity. Kant's ethical theory suffered a similar fate in Germany. Although that ethical theory is officially based on a conception of universal reason and human respect, that is, a conception presumably inherent and equally binding in everyone, its subordination to the fixed concept of nationalistic duty undermined the thought of one's unconditional duty to humanity. With less intrinsic theoretical defenses than either Zen Buddhism or Kant's ethics, which in their pure forms can precipitate a positive social critique – for example, one would not commit oneself to any warlike government agenda in the case of Zen, and one would not recognize any "duty" to follow the orders of a military

superior to kill innocent people in the case of Kant's ethics –
Deleuze's analysis of the time-image in film contains a liberating
potential, but it has no intrinsic guarantees. It needs to be applied
with a measure of wisdom that the theory itself does not contain.

CONCLUSION: THE ARTS OF TRUST AND SOCIAL CRITICISM

In the wake of the French Revolution's descent into bloodshed and confusion that opened the way for Napoleon's rise to power, European aesthetic theories during the nineteenth and twentieth centuries were shaped by a pressing need to reassess the value of reason. The French Revolutionary interest in fostering social progress was typically shared by the aesthetic theories' respective authors, but conflicting estimations of reason's value generated a divergence of opinion regarding fine art's place in this effort. Extended reflections upon the positive social value of natural beauty fell mostly by the wayside. Depending upon whether reason was considered to have preserved its authority, or whether it was judged to inhibit the quest to secure freedom and social harmony, fine art either continued to be conceived in the service of reason, or it was regarded more iconoclastically as a promising counterforce to rationalistic systems of social planning and development.

On the side of respecting reason's authority, consistent with the French Revolution's original vision of 1789, we began our study with Kant, whose theory of pure beauty from 1790 emphasizes beauty's immediately satisfying systematicity and purposiveness, manifestly to reinforce Enlightenment ideals relating to the pursuit of scientific knowledge. More fundamentally, his theory highlights beauty's capacity to symbolize a rationally grounded, universal morality. Aiming socially to instill that universal morality more concretely as a matter of character development, we find Schiller writing in 1795 immediately after the Reign of Terror, following the Kantian line and appealing to fine art and graceful beauty as a constructive liaison between raw sensuality and conceptually abstract determinations of duty. Within a couple of decades, and convinced that the real and the rational coincide, Hegel presents fine art as a mode of supreme cultural expression within a sweeping logical development of humanity and of the universe at large. In the mid-nineteenth century, Marx formulates a materialistic conception of social movements upon a mathematically definable economic basis, assigning a supportive, if essentially propagandistic, place to art in general as a catalyst for realizing communally organized societies.

During the 1930s, Walter Benjamin expands the Marxist social vision by welcoming the mechanical reproduction of artworks as a way to undermine the totalitarian worship of powerful individuals. In the 1950s and 1960s, Gadamer presents a self-consciously humane conception of reason as a dialogic fusion of horizons that aspires ideally to achieve a communicative consensus and universal social inclusion, as it preserves a stable respect for tradition. At odds with mathematical and instrumental reason, Gadamer's hermeneutical notion of dialogic reason bases itself on the revelatory experience of art.

Notwithstanding the theoretical diversity in these attempts to present reason's better side, the above thinkers remain consistently inspired by the rationalistic attitude that characterizes the best moments of the French Revolution, or, speaking more broadly, the project of the Enlightenment that aims towards democracy and political emancipation through reason. In each case, art and aesthetic experience retain a strong connection to reason in one of its forms.

Among those resisting reason's fundamental legitimacy, whether it happens to be mathematically, dialectically, or dialogically formulated, we encounter Schopenhauer in 1818, whose search for ultimate tranquillity leads to a kind of aesthetic experience based on the apprehension of fixed, universal archetypes as a way to transcend the mechanical and pain-producing rational determinations of ordinary experience.[103] Likewise privileging aesthetic experience over traditional, Aristotelian reason, Nietzsche advances a hypothesis in 1872 that Heidegger later reiterates, namely, that since the times of Plato and Aristotle,

---

[103] Predating Schopenhauer by at least fifteen years, we should add Schelling's name to the list of early-nineteenth-century theorists who initiated this irrationalist trend. György Lukács describes Schelling's irrationalist aspects in his *The Destruction of Reason* (1952).

logical thought's definitiveness and automatic rigidity has been stifling our creative insight and naturally poetic dispositions. Kierkegaard, Freud, Adorno, Barthes, Foucault, Derrida, and Deleuze emphasize, as well, the need to appreciate art as an essentially non-logically grounded way to reveal important dimensions of the self, language, or the surrounding culture. When we set these individuals in contrast to the aforementioned reason-respecting group, and view them from a height sufficient to reveal basic historical contours, we can discern two families of theorists whose thought gravitates either towards or away from reason in its various guises, where their views on the nature and value of beauty, fine art, and art in general follow suit.

These efforts to advocate or criticize reason tend – and we speak here generally – to associate the oppressive, debilitating, dehumanizing, exploitative, or narrow-minded qualities of the self, language, or the surrounding society with one or another fundamental style of thought, either predominantly rational or non-rational. Witness the work of Adorno, who, with insistence and exhausting perseverance, single-mindedly attacks all forms of instrumental reason, alleging that they intrinsically harbor and precipitate totalitarianism. Derrida's antagonism towards reason-centered (or "logocentric") modes of interpretation and analysis is equally resolute. Heidegger's criticism of technological modes of thinking carries comparable suspicions with respect to their dehumanizing qualities. From the opposite camp, but also exemplifying a tough and dominating attitude, Hegel deprecates mere feeling and immediate intuition in his advocacy of dialectical reason, claiming that they are superficial modes of awareness. Hegel and Gadamer also strictly subordinate traditional Aristotelian logic to their preferred forms of dialectical and dialogical rationality.

To appreciate the confusion in assuming that one can effectively project the distinction between free versus totalitarian ways of thinking onto the difference between rational versus non-rational modes of expression, it is easy to observe in retrospect that either style can be used for or against the establishment of freedom-nurturing institutions. Reason offers objective criteria for adjudicating disputes and provides greater scientific control over nature, while its technological application often relieves us of tiresome and repetitious work. Once it begins to serve aggressive and selfish values, however, reason can be employed technologically to survey, incarcerate, starve, and destroy people.

When conceived as a fundamentally non-rationalistic mode of expression, art, once again, can be a vehicle for revolution, revelation, and liberation, but it can also operate propagandistically to play upon feelings, false authorities and factual misrepresentation in the interests of oppression and demagoguery. Each style is two-faced, and, as such, neither can be accorded prime responsibility for social ills, as if the simple insurance for freedom would be either to muzzle instrumental reason and mechanically oriented modes of rationality to let instinct show through more effectively, or, alternatively, to keep at bay all intuitively based and authority-based modes of knowledge for the sake of allowing objective decision making and rational planning to reign.

One way to reformulate this situation consistently with our theorists' interests in social reform, is to focus upon the personal qualities, or characters, of the individuals or institutions that would employ these alternative means of expression. In this respect, Schiller, among all of our theorists, blazes a promising trail when he reflects upon the deterioration of the French Revolution and observes that reason – and we can now add art, in opposition to reason, when art is conceived of non-rationalistically – will work well to improve a society only when the people who employ it are morally developed. This shifts our attention from a pair of ambiguously valued means to the characters of the people and institutions that employ them, and to perennial questions about whether aesthetic experience can function effectively as an educator of character.

Jean-Paul Sartre's existentialist philosophy of the 1930s and 1940s, although morally incomplete, pays close attention to issues of personal character and bad faith by accentuating the importance of avoiding excuses and taking full responsibility for oneself in light of one's inherent freedom. Two decades later, Gadamer acknowledges a moral requisite, comparably underlying, when he locates at the basis of his view the realization that a dialogue-transcending attitude of openness, or adoption of good will in view of our common conversational ground, is necessary for achieving consensus.

With respect to the kinds of attitudes the contemporary cultural atmosphere reinforces, we can ask whether it tends to fortify the use of reason and art for emancipating ends, or whether it tends to bolster their use for oppressive and propagandistic purposes. If we consider the earlier years of the present trend during which the home computer became a commonplace in the 1980s, we can recall how Jean-François Lyotard aptly encapsulated the emerging atmosphere in 1982: "eclecticism is the degree zero of contemporary general culture: one listens to reggae, watches a western, eats McDonald's food for lunch and local cuisine for dinner, wears Paris perfume in Tokyo and 'retro' clothes in Hong Kong."[104]

Lyotard here describes postmodernism, which by the end of the 1980s becomes tied to globalization, where styles from radically disconnected cultures gradually amalgamate into a multi-cultural concoction, accompanied by a certain degree of alienation, cultural homogenization, and loss of original context and tradition. In the 1960s, Marshall McLuhan spoke of the "global village" with comparable anticipations. In conjunction with Lyotard's term "eclecticism," we can also refer to a spirit of "amalgamation," "bricolage," "aggregation," "hodgepodge," "mishmash," "medley," "jumble," "assemblage," "polystylism," "collage," "pastiche," "miscellany" and "confusion," to capture the general atmosphere of the thematically discordant, psychologically ambivalent amalgam that characterizes this globalizing epoch.

Reinforcing this attitude is the internet, whose presence has been penetrating daily life in the industrialized world since the mid-1990s. Any person with internet access can retrieve a wide variety of subject matters within minutes, where the set of possible retrievable subjects within the system as a whole extends beyond any individual's imagination. Although any particular internet user might retain an exclusive interest in one or another kind of subject matter, the background informational reserve in which that subject is embedded is a multi-dimensional, international, encyclopedic aggregate.

---

[104] Lyotard, "What Is Postmodernism?" (1982), in *The Postmodern Condition*, p. 76.

Relevant to our interest in European aesthetics, we can observe that tensions abound within the indiscriminately encyclopedic quality of the internet's information structure, and that these tensions reverberate to constitute contemporary aesthetic sensibilities. Among its attractions, the internet provides increased freedom and access to an overwhelming variety of information, increased social opportunities for countercultural movements to coalesce, increased speed of communication between physically distant parties, and increased public exposure for any given individual. Among its more sinister aspects, it increases the power of institutional forces to observe and record any user's behavior, it intensifies the social divisions between computer-literate and computer-illiterate populations, it reduces the motivation for face-to-face social exchanges, and it intensifies the confusion between reality and image. In the present cultural condition, we thus have uneasy and discordant Barthean and Deleuzian amalgams at almost every turn: freedom combines with slavery, compassion with callousness, community with alienation, intimacy with isolation, spirituality with profanity, legitimacy with illegitimacy, truth with deception, immediate gratification with frustration, and revolutionary informativeness with manipulative propaganda. When persistently confronted with such tensions as a daily phenomenon, one is tempted to become indifferent or insensitive to the distinctions they embody, if only to avoid becoming too confused.

The contemporary world of museum-exhibition art mirrors the above situation insofar as many recent works are multi-media constructions, performances or installations that recognize few restrictions on the materials employed, and self-consciously cross boundaries between art and non-art, between traditional forms of art, and between opposing values. The expressive qualities of the constitutive items in the artworks are the leading consideration, for it is acceptable to use any materials or themes that seem appropriate to one's expressive ends. As is true for the structure of the internet surfer's imagination, the contemporary artist is limited only by his or her capacity to discern, and to amalgamate, meaningful sets of expressive properties in the world's surroundings.

As we know from Marcel Duchamp's contribution to art history, it was once aesthetically challenging to assert that any artifact can be regarded as a work of art. Not only did this render the difference between artworks and ordinary artifacts a matter of interpretation, it introduced a blur between the special and the ordinary, and between the meaningful and the meaningless. Almost a century later, that situation has been extended to the point where any set of common artifacts or social episodes can be assembled acceptably into a meaningful artwork, sometimes through their positioning alone, as when one sets on top of one another a series of professional-quality golf bags to create a traditional-looking totem pole.[105] Such works embody the ambiguity of contemporary times, since they can be interpreted as both celebrating and condemning the world of mass marketing in the same breath. Moreover, as noted, computer technology can digitally replicate the realistic texture of any object, allowing artists to use these textures within computer-reliant constructions to create a virtual reality, just as paints were used by previous generations of artists.

Among the theorists we have surveyed, Martin Heidegger's theoretical style foreshadows the postmodern, globalizing age using older, established, traditional terms, as it presents a noticeably disconcerting, culturally disruptive kind of amalgamation by integrating poetry, religion, and philosophy into a seemingly homogenous blend, the result of which is neither exclusively poetic, nor exclusively religious, nor exclusively philosophical. Heidegger presents a new kind of theoretical amalgam that defies standard categorizations, and in its self-conscious mixture of philosophy, poetry, and religion, it can be perceived – as one might also read Nietzsche's philosophy – either as a logically retrogressive, artificially mythopoeic, politically dangerous throwback to pre-philosophical thought, or as an insightful premonition of the future's distinction-melting cultural shape and as a doctrine that will replace religion for upcoming generations of intellectuals. Whether we assess it positively or negatively, his outlook is a forefather of the contemporary cultural atmosphere.

If we keep in mind these contexts that generate tradition-breaking amalgams, such as Heidegger's vision of the world,

---

[105] The 2006 work of the Canadian installation-artist, Brian Jungen (b. 1970), ingeniously arranges golf bags in this manner, expressing the contrast and uneasy integration of contemporary and indigenous cultural forms.

postmodernist eclecticism and the globalizing internet, where the definitive and common phenomenon is the uneasy amalgamation and implicit dissolution of forms that have been customarily kept distinct and intact, and if we recall the definitive problem around which our presentation of European aesthetic theory from 1790 to 1990 coalesces, namely, that of ascertaining reason's status in light of an interest in art's socially productive role, we can set that 200-year history of aesthetic theorizing into perspective.

Once it is clear how rationalistic and non-rationalistic modes of expression are two-faced, the strategy of opting too enthusiastically for "reason" as opposed to "non-reason," or vice versa, reveals itself as a non-starter. As our study indicates, the perceived need to make such a single-minded choice has been misleading theorists for at least two centuries. The historical transition in global culture that took a definite shape in the 1980s, as confusing as it is, has helped reveal the one-sidedness of these earlier approaches, as we now live self-consciously in a world where amalgamation, ambiguity, and double-messaging are in the spirit of the times.

With respect to the contemporary cultural situation, if one appreciates scientific developments while remaining reticent about the technological walls, weapons, and incarcerating violence that are imposed on people, if one appreciates new and expressive art forms while complacently accepting frequent propagandistic bombardment, if one appreciates the freedom to surf the internet while knowing, but repressing, how one's keystrokes can be recorded by an observing institutional authority, and if one accepts a conception of international violence framed in the alibi-like terms of just-and-criminal wars that combine justified combat with war crimes, then it is fair to expect an increasing personal tolerance for contradictory, and potentially socially numbing, conceptual amalgams.

Within such a contradiction-indifferent cultural atmosphere, it can become difficult to draw the distinctions required to improve the state of society, either globally or locally, despite the atmosphere's tolerant quality, especially since the latter is including an ominous tolerance for oppression. One of the main distinctions required is not that between rational versus non-rational modes of expression around which most of the theorists we have considered have aligned themselves during the past two centuries. It is rather the distinction between the freedom-and-respect-enhancing faces of both rational and non-rational modes, as opposed to the freedom-denying, propagandistic, and terrorizing faces of them both. The operative choice is not between rationality and its opposite, but between decency versus degradation. One can speculate that the variously formulable nineteenth-century disputes between classicism and romanticism, between academic art and avant-garde art, and between drawing versus color, and so on, have permeated nineteenth- and twentieth-century theorizing about art to the point of establishing a misleading set of basic polarizations, for by cutting in the wrong conceptual direction, they overlook the two-faced quality of rational and non-rational modes of expression.

If fine art is to serve as a civilizing force in accord with the socially constructive interests of the theorists we have here considered, then, as always, taste will be required to amalgamate appropriate materials into an expressive whole. Just as the word "pastiche" extends originally from the idea of a pie that contains many ingredients, there will analogously be a need to reject the slacker-like, immediately gratifying, mere mixings or combinations of any arbitrary set of ingredients, as we have before us in Lyotard's characterization of the postmodern atmosphere, and as we see in Deleuze's style of thought as a whole. Taste is required, as displayed in fine cooking's careful choice of ingredients, in musical arrangement's considered choice of ingenious instrumentation, in painting's imaginative choice of fascinating coloration, and in sculpture's sensitive choice of expressively potent materials. These characterizations lead us back to the concepts upon which Kant centered his aesthetic theory, namely, those of taste and aesthetic judgment.

Beyond Kant's specifically formalistic aesthetics, the powers of taste and aesthetic judgment that might be enhanced through aesthetic education nonetheless need to be informed by wisdom, if we are concerned with social improvement and social critique, for wisdom is required for effectively implementing the proposition exemplified by most of European aesthetic theories from 1790 to 1990, namely, that of putting art and beauty into the service of social and/or moral values. Moreover, the contemporary implementation of this kind of project requires an awareness that avoids the retrogressive return to debates between rational versus non-rational modes of inquiry. As is evident from our survey, this opposition needs to be transcended to understand how multifaceted values such as liberty, justice, responsibility, compassion, honesty, trust, and integrity can be fostered by either rational *or* non-rational modes of expression. Such an appreciation appears to be a precondition for instantiating genuine political freedom, as Schiller understood it, along with its presumably positive social effects, as the most important kind of artwork.

The evidence of centuries does not suggest that wisdom can be easily taught, if it can be taught at all, so invoking wisdom is unrealistic. Perhaps more achievable would be to seek a modest advance in social consciousness that can help relieve oppression, a leading idea of which is the development of *trust*, a second of which is *interdependency*, that can issue from trust, and a third of which is a *stronger disposition to share*, given the howling magnitude of greed that presently exists in certain powerful quarters. From the standpoint of moral philosophy, trust is a reasonable quality upon which to focus, since philosophers in both Western and Asian traditions have argued that it is close to the center of our moral thinking.[106] From the standpoint of politics, trust is also crucial, as is evident from the words of Javier Solana, the European Union's High Representative for the Common Foreign and Security Policy, speaking in 2007:

> This brings me to the matter of trust. What the current system often lacks is trust among the relevant players. And it is the task of politics to create trust where it does not exist.
>
> We all know that without trust – and the law – there is no security. Trust is the basis of everything. It is trust which provides security. . .
>
> Above all, we need to revive the view of politics as the art of building trust where it does not exist. In international life, determination and good will are important. But they are not enough.[107]

---

[106] Annette Baier is a leading Western thinker in this regard. Among her publications that address the concept of trust, we can mention here the essay, "What Do Women Want in a Moral Theory?" In the Asian tradition, Yutaka Yamamoto, inspired by the neo-Confucianist, Nishimura Shigeki (1828–1902), also argues that trust is at the center of Confucian values. See his "A Morality Based on Trust."
[107] Speech by EUHR Javier Solana at the Arthur Burns Dinner, New York, February 14, 2007.

Trust is crucially lacking in situations of social oppression, for social oppressors typically believe that the people whom they oppress are less than fully human, and hence need to be kept degradingly under surveillance, control, and castigation, much as Freud maintained that the superego needs to control the ego and Id by oppressing instinctual drives with a persecuting eye and a corresponding sense of self-inflicted guilt. Oppressive leaders rarely trust their people to exercise their freedom well, and oppressed people rarely trust their leaders to look after the general population's interests, as the oppressors impose their strict legal and military control, whether it be in the form of a Roman spear or a surveillance satellite.

Foucault advocated an individualistically centered "aesthetics of existence" as a mode of liberation, where one reforms oneself according to one's own personal lights in a rule-governed, self-controlled way. As a socially revisionary alternative, one can imagine an "art of trust," where art and artistically cultivated modes of behavior derive their primary social value by helping to build trust, as they aim to soften feelings of fear and hostility. Differences of opinion can resolve more peacefully with a background of increased trust, and avoiding war is among the most serious issues today. Such exemplary works of art would present trusting human relationships as models, illustrate dimensions of our human commonality that can foster trust, and exhibit values and shared interests as a species, on either a small scale or a large scale, that are trust-enhancing.

John F. Kennedy's commencement address at American University on June 10, 1963 offers an appropriate baseline picture:

> So, let us not be blind to our differences – but let us also direct attention to our common interests and to the means by which those differences can be resolved. And if we cannot end now our differences, at least we can help make the world safe for diversity. For, in the final analysis, our most basic common link is that we all inhabit this small planet. We all breathe the same air. We all cherish our children's future. And we are all mortal.

Extrapolating from the thought that we all cherish our children's future, Kennedy might have added that we are all human, and that since our common interests issue from the same human character, they transcend national, religious, and racial differences. Self-consciousness has no color, and when a person says "I" to him or herself, it is exactly the same feeling of self-consciousness that is instantiated in me, in you, or in anyone else, whether it happens to be a past, present, or future person.

The idea of an art that emphasizes trust brings us full circle, in a self-conscious return to the disappointing French Revolution, to the abuse of Kant's ethics of duty by the German army during World War II (viz., "*Befehl ist Befehl*" ["an order is an order"]), to the oppressive rationality of the ancient Greeks about which Nietzsche complained, and to those respectively supportive theories of human nature that emphasize human commonality rather than human difference in a vision of freedom, justice, and social balance. Judging from the aesthetic theories that have tried to embody this ideal, especially in light of their failures in social implementation, one can conclude that the rational truth that we are all essentially one is a delicate and volatile idea.

The undermining of reason occurs when those who supposedly advocate reason fail to realize that reason itself requires a balance of respect across humanity. We see this failure described by Foucault in reference to the Classical Age's – that is, the so-called Age of Reason's – mental institutions that incarcerated the sick, mentally deficient, and elderly. It resides also in the French Revolutionaries who indiscriminately employed the guillotine, and in the Nazis who instituted the murder of innocent civilians on an industrial scale. To develop human sensibilities in the opposite direction, an art that emphasizes trust would aspire to promote and cultivate trust with an aim towards more effectively instantiating the idea of balanced respect, in accord with the aspirations the theorists we have been considering between 1790 and 1990 had for art in its relation to society.

The idea of an art of trust is consistent with one that aims generally to repair weaknesses in social bonds through the creation of festive atmospheres in museum exhibitions, as expressed in relational aesthetics.[108] In our present context, we are considering the situation from a different angle, namely, in view of the history of aesthetics we have surveyed, insofar as one can project

---

[108] See Bourriaud, *Relational Aesthetics*.

the contours of a contemporary art that retains the social spirit of their projects. Coming to the fore is a central characteristic of moral awareness, namely, trust, that is independent of rationality and non-rationality, consistent with them both, and acknowledged by moral and political theorists as essential to a flourishing and fair society. Somewhat utopian, the hope inherent in this kind of art is that a greater infusion of trust into the world at large could positively stimulate a social domino effect.

A difficulty regarding the feasibility of an art that emphasizes trust – and this would apply with parallel reasoning to most aesthetic theories that emphasize moral values – concerns the disruption generated by the widespread illusions of trust. Potential artistic subjects such as smiling and inviting faces, handshakes, acts of promising, expressions of camaraderie, loving looks, friendly slaps on the back, warm congratulations, and forgiving and consoling speech can be unscrupulously employed. An art that promotes such subject matters may be largely ineffective within a social atmosphere where expressions and representations of trust are *a priori* assumed to be false and deceptive. When a fundamental distrust pervades either the social consciousness or an individual's attitude, the reactions to such artistic expressions of trust promise to be cynical or scornful.

Such a distrusting attitude is a widespread feature of the present world, given how television's friendly faces mask corporate interests, how newspapers often lack the courage to explore the truth of politically explosive happenings, and how reporters and photographers are muzzled for attempting to document contemporary history. The 1988 popular song, "Everybody Knows," by Leonard Cohen and Sharon Robinson, expresses well the sense of cynicism that arises when a social system is permeated with dishonesty and distrust. Everybody knows that the system is corrupt; everybody knows that the newspapers lie; everybody knows that the world is a cheat. Everybody knows that the war is over and that the bad guys won.

As we know, a prevailing attitude of distrust is nonetheless not the natural human condition, for if we consider how infants and young children naturally trust their caretakers – and this kind of trust is sometimes also observed in tribal cultures that have been far removed from contemporary civilization – then tapping into this dimension of what is most basic in our social relationships with others might help foster a culture of increased trust. Nurturing that trust in the next generation of young people, when the individuals are still young – and this would not be through art alone, but through a variety of means – may be the key to instantiating the social dreams of the writers we have considered who believed that art could assist in the great task of improving society, for the problem of social improvement goes beyond the sphere of art and beauty. Since the future significantly resides in the hands of those who instill values in our children, Schiller's observation that the pleasure taken in natural beauty is a moral pleasure related to feelings of love, much like our affection for children and their innocence, remains significant and instructive.

From the standpoint of aesthetic theory, though, an art that emphasizes trust is imperfect, since it does not immediately discriminate well between great art and poorly crafted art. High artistic quality is not essential for invoking a socially beneficial content. Tolstoy, who was interested in promoting feelings of universal kinship, preferred happy, community-solidifying folk songs over Beethoven's symphonies and ballets precisely for their simplicity and easy communicability, and his theory is criticized often for having ignored the importance of artistic excellence. On the other hand, the inspirational value of artistic masterpieces as such, centers around morally neutral excellences such as ingenuity, creativity, complexity, dedication, courage, intelligence, and intuition, none of which needs to work in favor of instantiating the visions of social liberation and improvement that have inspired the aesthetic theories we have been considering from 1790 to 1990.

Considered in isolation, artistic excellence and the enhancement of trust are independent; neither implies the other. Neither, however, are they inconsistent. A work that is both artistically excellent and whose subject fosters trust would be good on two counts, since the artistic excellence can reinforce the subject matter's expression, along with helping to develop taste, which in turn can be applied to develop wisdom.

Another precaution to be taken with an art that emphasizes trust resides in the possible domination of the general quest for social improvement and the accompanying assumption and expectation that art can assist significantly in this effort. The more that fine art is believed to be effective in the project of building trust, the greater likelihood that works that fit these aims will be socially preferred over others, precipitating the kind of moralistic narrowness that attends Marxist, Tolstoyan or, worse, Nazi aesthetics. This narrowness arises from the content-oriented nature of an art that emphasizes trust, or, for that matter, any moralistic aesthetics where the artwork's message is deemed more important than its design or level of artistic excellence.

Given these pitfalls, it is more prudent to rest with a more ground-clearing approach, as opposed to attempting to institute some particular moralistic vision through fine art, as do most of the theorists we have examined. Some, however, more modestly remain content to indicate simply how art can awaken people to the presence of social problems. Barthes' theory of photography that contrasts a status quo *studium* with an interrupting *punctum* operates at this level. Marxist aesthetics also instructs artists to present works that display the injustices of capitalism, quite aside from the socialist vision. Nietzsche admittedly advocates an aesthetics of health, but his more general philosophy urges that we create new perspectives of all kinds. Sartre is adamant about the need to question authority, as is Derrida. Heidegger notes, as well, how the human being is a fundamentally questioning being.

Emerging from these reflections is the familiar message that one of art's central functions is to be socially critical. Recalling the more positively and substantially advanced visions of society, and recognizing Schiller's fundamental insight that no revolutions can be successful if the revolutionaries themselves are morally undeveloped, one can add the analogous assertion that, in the spirit of the artists in our survey, the first responsibility of artists is not to be "artists," but to express visions that are at least decently human. Social transformation depends upon change from within the person, and upon the quality of the characters who either clear the way with morally guided social criticism, or, more ambitiously, enact humane ideals.

Artistic excellence re-enters the equation on this conceptualization, since even when one is concerned mainly with social criticism, a talent for portraying depth of feeling and sensitivity can be of great value. As a final example, witness a revealing painting by Honoré Daumier (1808–79), *Third-Class Carriage* (1862) (Plate 10), which presents a picture of underprivileged humanity within industrialized culture, silently cramped into a traincar, riding to an undefined destination. One cannot help but reflect analogously and existentially upon the movement of our planet earth through the cosmos, and, more objectively, upon our human situation at large.

FURTHER READING

CHAPTER 1

Allison, Henry. *Kant's Theory of Taste – A Reading of the* Critique of Aesthetic Judgment. Cambridge: Cambridge University Press, 2001.

Burnham, Douglas. *An Introduction to Kant's* Critique of Judgment. Edinburgh: Edinburgh University Press, 2001.

Cohen, Ted, and Guyer, Paul (eds). *Essays in Kant's Aesthetics.* Chicago and London: University of Chicago Press, 1982.

Crawford, Donald W. *Kant's Aesthetic Theory.* Madison: University of Wisconsin Press, 1974.

Guyer, Paul. *Kant and the Claims of Taste.* Cambridge and London: Harvard University Press, 1979.

Kemal, Salim. *Kant's Aesthetic Theory: An Introduction.* New York: St. Martin's Press, 1992.

Pillow, Kirk. *Sublime Understanding: Aesthetic Reflection in Kant and Hegel.* Cambridge: MIT Press, 2000.

Wenzel, Christian. *An Introduction to Kant's Aesthetics: Core Concepts and Problems.* Oxford: Blackwell, 2006.

Wicks, Robert. *Routledge Philosophy Guidebook to Kant on Judgment.* London: Routledge, 2007.

Zuckert, Rachel. *Kant on Beauty and Biology : An Interpretation of The Critique of Judgment.* Cambridge: Cambridge University Press, 2007.

CHAPTER 2

Beiser, Frederick. *Schiller as Philosopher: A Re-Examination.* Oxford: Oxford University Press, 2005.

Miller, R. D. *Schiller and the Ideal of Freedom.* Oxford: Clarendon Press, 1970.

Norton, Robert. *The Beautiful Soul – Aesthetic Morality in the Eighteenth Century.* Ithaca: Cornell University Press, 1995.

Regin, Deric. *Freedom and Dignity: The Historical and Philosophical Thought of Schiller.* The Hague: Nijhoff, 1965.

Sharpe, Lesley. *Friedrich Schiller: Drama, Thought and Politics.* Cambridge: Cambridge University Press, 1991.

CHAPTER 3

Bungay, Stephen. *Beauty and Truth*. Oxford: Oxford University Press, 1984.

Desmond, William. *Art and the Absolute – A Study of Hegel's Aesthetics*. Albany: SUNY Press, 1986.

Houlgate, Stephen (ed.). *Hegel and the Arts*. Evanston, Ill.: Northwestern University Press, 2007.

Knox, Israel. *The Aesthetic Theories of Kant, Hegel and Schopenhauer*. New York: Colombia University Press, 1936.

Maker, William (ed.). *Hegel and Aesthetics*. Albany: SUNY Press, 2000.

Rutter, Benjamin. *Hegel on the Modern Arts*. Cambridge: Cambridge University Press, 2010.

CHAPTER 4

Berger, John. *Ways of Seeing*. New York: Penguin, 1972.

Daly, Macdonald. *A Primer in Marxist Aesthetics*. York: Zoilus Press, 1999.

Eagleton, Terry. *The Ideology of the Aesthetic*. Oxford and Malden, MA: Blackwell, 1990.

Johnson, Pauline. *Marxist Aesthetics: The Foundations Within Everyday Life for an Emancipated Consciousness*. London, Boston, Melbourne, and Henley: Routledge & Kegan Paul, 1984.

Laing, Dave. *The Marxist Theory of Art*. Sussex: The Harvester Press; Atlantic Highlands, NJ: Humanities Press, Inc., 1978.

Marcuse, Herbert. *The Aesthetic Dimension: Toward a Critique of Marxist Aesthetics*. Boston: Beacon Press, 1978.

Rose, Margaret A. *Marx's Lost Aesthetic: Karl Marx and the Visual Arts*. Cambridge: Cambridge University Press, 1984.

CHAPTER 5

Jacquette, Dale (ed.). *Schopenhauer, Philosophy and the Arts*. Cambridge: Cambridge University Press, 1996.

Magee, B. *The Philosophy of Schopenhauer*. Oxford: Clarendon Press, 1983.

Neill, Alex, and Janaway, Christopher (eds). *Better Consciousness: Schopenhauer's Philosophy of Value*. West Sussex, UK: Wiley-Blackwell, 2009.

Wicks, Robert. *Schopenhauer*. West Sussex, UK: Wiley-Blackwell, 2008.

Young, Julian. *Schopenhauer*. London and New York: Routledge, 2005.

CHAPTER 6

Kemal, Salim, Gaskell, Ivan, and Conway, Daniel W. (eds). *Nietzsche, Philosophy and the Arts*. Cambridge: Cambridge University Press, 1998.

Liebert, Georges. *Nietzsche and Music*, trans. by David Pellauer and Graham Parkes. Chicago: University of Chicago Press, 2004.

Nabais, Nuno. *Nietzsche and the Metaphysics of the Tragic*, trans. Martin Earl. London and New York: Continuum, 2006.

Nehamas, Alexander. *Nietzsche: Life as Literature*. Cambridge, Mass.: Harvard University Press, 1985.

Ridley, Aaron. *Nietzsche on Art*. London: Routledge, 2007.

Witt, Mary Ann Frese (ed.). *Nietzsche and the Rebirth of the Tragic*. Madison, NJ: Fairleigh Dickenson University Press, 2007.

Young, Julian. *Nietzsche's Philosophy of Art*. Cambridge: Cambridge University Press, 1992.

CHAPTER 7

Adorno, Theodor W. *Kierkegaard: Construction of the Aesthetic*, trans. Robert Hullot-Kentor. Minneapolis: University of Minnesota Press, 1989.

Mackey, Louis. *Kierkegaard: A Kind of Poet*. Philadelphia: University of Pennsylvania Press, 1971.

Pattison, George. *Kierkegaard: The Aesthetic and the Religious*. London: Macmillan, 1992.

Schleifer, Ronald, and Markley, Robert (eds). *Kierkegaard and Literature: Irony, Repetition, and Criticism*. Norman: University of Oklahoma Press, 1984.

Walsh, Sylvia. *Living Poetically: Kierkegaard's Existential Aesthetics*. University Park, Pennsylvania: Pennsylvania State University Press, 1994.

CHAPTER 8

Bersani, Leo. *The Freudian Body: Psychoanalysis and Art*. New York: Columbia University Press, 1986.

Glover, Nicky. *Psychoanalytic Aesthetics: An Introduction to the British School* [1998]. London: Karnac Books, 2009.

Kofman, Sarah. *The Childhood of Art: An Interpretation of Freud's Aesthetics*, trans. Winifred Woodhull. New York: Colombia University Press, 1988.

Ranciere, Jacques. *The Aesthetic Unconscious*. Oxford: Polity Press, Blackwell, 2009.

Sayers, Janet. *Freud's Art: Psychoanalysis Retold*. London: Routledge, 2007.

Spector, Jack J. *The Aesthetics of Freud: A Study in Psychoanalysis and Art*. New York: Praeger, 1973.

CHAPTER 9

Benjamin, Andrew (ed.). *Walter Benjamin and the Architecture of Modernity*. Melbourne: re.press, 2009.

Eagleton, Terry. *Walter Benjamin: Or Towards a Revolutionary Criticism*. London: Verso/New Left, 1985.

Koepnick, Lutz. *Walter Benjamin and the Aesthetics of Power: Politics in the Age of Industrial Mass Culture*. Lincoln, NE: University of Nebraska Press, 1999.

Rochlitz, Rainer. *The Disenchantment of Art: The Philosophy of Walter Benjamin*, trans. Jane Marie Todd. New York and London: Guilford Press, 1996.

Smith, Gary (ed.). *Benjamin: Philosophy, Aesthetics, History*. Chicago and London: University of Chicago Press, 1989.

Spotts, Frederic. *Hitler and the Power of Aesthetics*. Woodstock and New York: Overlook Press, 2002.

Wolin, Richard. *Walter Benjamin: An Aesthetic of Redemption*. Berkeley, CA: University of California Press, 1994.

CHAPTER 10

Coulson, Shea. *Adorno's Aesthetics of Critique*. Newcastle, UK: Cambridge Scholars Publishing, 2007.

Huhn, T., and Zuidervaart, L. (eds). *The Semblance of Subjectivity: Essays in Adorno's Aesthetic Theory*. Cambridge, MA: MIT Press, 1997.

Menke, C. *The Sovereignty of Art: Aesthetic Negativity in Adorno and Derrida*, trans. N. Solomon. Cambridge, MA: MIT Press, 1998.

Paddison, M. *Adorno's Aesthetics of Music*. New York: Cambridge University Press, 1993.

Roberts, David. *Art and Enlightenment: Aesthetic Theory After Adorno*. Lincoln, NE: University of Nebraska Press, 1991.

Wellmer, A. *The Persistence of Modernity: Essays on Aesthetics, Ethics, and Postmodernism*, trans. D. Midgley. Cambridge, MA: MIT Press, 1991.

Zuidervaart, L., *Adorno's Aesthetic Theory: The Redemption of Illusion*. Cambridge, MA: MIT Press, 1991.

CHAPTER 11

Dreyfus, H. L., and Wrathall, M. A. (eds). *A Companion to Heidegger*. Oxford: Blackwell, 2005.

Edwards, C. *The Shoes of Van Gogh: A Spiritual and Artistic Journey to the Ordinary*. New York: Crossroad Publishing Company, 2004.

Kockelmans, J. *Heidegger on Art and Art Works*, Dordrecht: Nijhoff, 1985.

Risser, J. (ed.). *Heidegger Toward the Turn: Essays on the Work of the 1930s*. Albany: SUNY Press, 1999.

Sallis, J. (ed.). *Reading Heidegger: Commemorations*. Bloomington: Indiana University Press, 1993.

Sheehan, T. (ed.). *Heidegger: The Man and the Thinker*. Chicago: Precedent Publishing, 1981.

Young, Julian. *Heidegger's Philosophy of Art*. Cambridge: Cambridge University Press, 2001.

CHAPTER 12

Hahn, Lewis Edwin (ed.). *The Philosophy of Hans-Georg Gadamer*, Library of Living Philosophers XXIV. Chicago: Open Court, 1997.

Hirsch, E. D. *Validity in Interpretation*. New Haven and London: Yale University Press, 1967.

Hoy, David Couzens. *The Critical Circle: Literature, History, and Philosophical Hermeneutics*. Berkeley, Los Angeles, London: University of California Press, 1982.

Palmer, Richard E. *Hermeneutics: Interpretation Theory in Schleiermacher, Dilthey, Heidegger and Gadamer*. Evanston: Northwestern University Press, 1969.

Warnke, Georgia. *Gadamer: Hermeneutics, Tradition and Reason*. Stanford: Stanford University Press, 1987.

Weinsheimer, Joel. *Gadamer's Hermeneutics: A Reading of "Truth and Method."* New Haven: Yale University Press, 1985.

CHAPTER 13

Batchen, Geoffrey (ed.). *Photography Degree Zero: Reflections on Roland Barthes's* Camera Lucida. Cambridge, MA: MIT Press, 2009.

Bensmaïa, Réda. *The Barthes Effect: The Essay as Reflective Text*. Minneapolis: University of Minnesota Press, 1987.

Jay, Paul. *Being in the Text: Self-Representation from Wordsworth to Roland Barthes*. Ithaca and London: Cornell University Press, 1984.

Knight, Diana (ed.). *Critical Essays on Roland Barthes*. New York: G. K. Hall, 2000.
Moriarty, Michael. *Roland Barthes*. Stanford: Stanford University Press, 1991.
Thody, Philip. *Roland Barthes: A Conservative Estimate*. London and Basingstoke: Macmillan, 1977.
Wiseman, Mary Bittner. *The Ecstasies of Roland Barthes*. London and New York: Routledge, 1989.

CHAPTER 14

Bernauer, James, and Rasmussen, David (eds). *The Final Foucault*. Cambridge, MA: MIT Press, 1994.
Nehamas, Alexander. *The Art of Living, Socratic Reflections from Plato to Foucault*. Berkeley: University of California Press, 1998.
Rajhman, John. *Michel Foucault – The Freedom of Philosophy*. New York: Columbia University Press, 1985.
Shapiro, Gary. *Archaeologies of Vision: Foucault and Nietzsche on Seeing and Saying*. Chicago: Chicago University Press, 2003.
Tanke, Joseph J. *Foucault's Philosophy of Art: A Genealogy of Modernity*. London and New York: Continuum, 2009.

CHAPTER 15

Cohen, Tom. *Jacques Derrida and the Humanities: A Critical Reader*. Cambridge: Cambridge University Press, 2001.
Hobson, Marian. *Jacques Derrida: Opening Lines*. London and New York: Routledge, 1998.
Jameson, Frederic. *Postmodernism, or the Cultural Logic of Late Capitalism*. London: Verso, 1990.
McCance, Dawne. *Medusa's Ear: University Foundings from Kant to Chora L*. Albany: State University of New York Press, 2004.
Rapaport, Herman. *Heidegger and Derrida: Reflections on Time and Language*. Lincoln: University of Nebraska Press, 1989.

CHAPTER 16

Bogue, Ronald. *Deleuze on Cinema*. London and New York: Routledge, 2003.
Bogue, Ronald. *Deleuze on Literature*. London and New York: Routledge, 2003.

Bogue, Ronald. *Deleuze on Music, Painting and the Arts*. London and New York: Routledge, 2003.

Buchanan, Ian, and MacCormack, Patricia (eds). *Deleuze and the Schizoanalysis of Cinema*. London and New York: Continuum, 2008.

Flaxman, Gregory (ed.). *The Brain is the Screen – Deleuze and the Philosophy of Cinema*. Minneapolis and London: University of Minnesota Press, 2000.

Holland, Eugene, Stivale, Charles J., and Smith, Daniel W. (eds). *Gilles Deleuze: Image and Text*. London and New York: Continuum, 2009.

Marrati, Paola. *Deleuze: Cinema and Philosophy*, trans. Alisa Hartz. Baltimore: Johns Hopkins University Press, 2008.

Martin-Jones, David. *Deleuze, Cinema and National Identity: Narrative Time in National Contexts*. Edinburgh: Edinburgh University Press, 2007.

Rodowick, D. N. (ed.). *Afterimages of Gilles Deleuze's Film Philosophy*. Minneapolis: University of Minnesota Press, 2009.

Rodowick, D. N. *Gilles Deleuze's Time Machine*. Durham and London: Duke University Press, 1997.

BIBLIOGRAPHY

Adorno, Theodor. *Aesthetic Theory*, trans. C. Lenhardt. London and New York: Routledge & Kegan Paul, 1984.

Adorno, Theodor. *Essays on Music: Theodor W. Adorno*, ed. R. D. Leppert, trans. S. H. Gillespie et al. Berkeley: University of California Press, 2002.

Adorno, Theodor. *Negative Dialectics*, trans. E. B. Ashton [1966]. New York: Seabury Press, 1973.

Adorno, Theodor. *Philosophy of New Music*, trans. R. Hullot-Kentor [1949]. Minneapolis: University of Minnesota Press, 2006.

Adorno, Theodor, and Horkheimer, Max. *The Dialectic of Enlightenment: Philosophical Fragments*, ed. G. S. Noerr, trans. E. Jephcott [1947]. Stanford: Stanford University Press, 2002.

Baier, Annette. "What Do Women Want in a Moral Theory?" *Noûs*, 19, 1 (1985), pp. 53–63.

Barthes, Roland. *Camera Lucida – Reflections on Photography* [1980], trans. Richard Howard. London: Vintage, 2000.

Barthes, Roland. *Image, Music, Text*, trans. S. Heath. London: Fontana, 1977.

Barthes, Roland. *Mythologies*, trans. Annette Lavers. New York: Hill and Wang, 1972.

Baudrillard, Jean. *Jean Baudrillard: Selected Writings*, ed. M. Poster. Stanford, California: Stanford University Press, 1988.

Benjamin, Walter. *Illuminations*, trans. Harry Zohn. New York: Schocken Books, 1968.

Benjamin, Walter. *The Origin of German Tragic Drama*. London: Verso, 1990.

Bloch, Ernst. *The Utopian Function of Art and Literature*, trans. Jack Zipes and Frank Mecklenburg. Cambridge, MA and London, MIT Press: 1988.

Bourriaud, Nicholas. *Relational Aesthetics*. Dijon: Les presses du réel, 1998.

Brown, Jonathan. *Images and Ideas in Seventeenth-Century Spanish Painting*. Princeton: Princeton University Press, 1978.

Bungay, Stephen. *Beauty and Truth – A Study of Hegel's Aesthetics*. Oxford: Oxford University Press, 1994.

Chytry, Josef. *The Aesthetic State: A Quest in Modern German Thought.* Berkeley and Los Angeles: University of California Press, 1989.

Croce, Benedetto. *Aesthetic*, trans. Douglas Ainslie. New York: Noonday Press, 1909.

Deleuze, Gilles. *Cinema 1: The Movement Image*, trans. Hugh Tomlinson and Barbara Habberjam [1983]. London and New York: Continuum, 1986.

Deleuze, Gilles. *Cinema 2: The Time Image*, trans. Hugh Tomlinson and Robert Galeta [1985]. London: Athlone Press, 1989.

Deleuze, Gilles. *Francis Bacon: The Logic of Sensation* [1981], trans. Daniel W. Smith. London and New York: Continuum, 2003.

Deleuze, Gilles. *Negotiations – 1972–1990*, trans. Martin Joughin [1990]. New York: Colombia University Press, 1995.

Derrida, Jacques. *Memoirs of the Blind – The Self-Portrait and Other Ruins* [1990], trans. Pascale-Anne Brault and Michael Naas. Chicago and London: University of Chicago Press, 1993.

Derrida, Jacques. *The Truth in Painting*, trans. G. Bennington and I. McLeod [1978]. Chicago: University of Chicago Press, 1987.

Eagleton, Terry. *The Ideology of the Aesthetic.* Oxford: Basil Blackwell, 1990.

Ferry, Luc. *Homo Aestheticus: The Invention of Taste in the Democratic Age* [1990], trans. R. de Loaiza. Chicago and London: University of Chicago Press, 1993.

Foster, Nelson, and Shoemaker, Jack (eds). *The Roaring Stream – A New Zen Reader.* Hopewell, NJ: Ecco Press, 1996.

Foucault, Michel. *Aesthetics, Method and Epistemology*, ed. J. D. Faubion, trans. R. Hurley *et al.* New York: New Press, 1998.

Foucault, Michel. *Death and the Labyrinth: The World of Raymond Roussel*, trans. Charles Ruas. Garden City, NY: Doubleday & Company, Inc., 1986.

Foucault, Michel. *Discipline and Punish: The Birth of the Prison* [1975], trans. Alan Sheridan. London: Penguin Books, 1977.

Foucault, Michel. *Madness and Civilization*, trans. Richard Howard. New York: Pantheon, 1965.

Foucault, Michel. *Manet and the Object of Painting*, trans. Matthew Barr. London: Tate Publishing, 2009.

Foucault, Michel. *Maurice Blanchot: The Thought from Outside.* New York: Zone Books, 1966.

Foucault, Michel. *The Order of Things.* New York: Vintage, 1973.

Foucault, Michel. *Politics, Philosophy, Culture: Interviews and Other Writings*, trans. A. Sheridan *et al.* London: Routledge, 1988.

Foucault, Michel. *Power/Knowledge: Selected Interviews and Other Writings 1972–7*, ed. Colin Gordon, trans. Colin Gordon, Leo Marshall, John Mepham, and Kate Soper. New York: Pantheon Books, 1980.

Foucault, Michel. *This Is Not a Pipe*, trans. James Harkness. Berkeley: University of California Press, 1983.

Freud, Sigmund. *Civilization and Its Discontents*, trans. James Strachey. New York: W. W. Norton & Company, Inc., 1961.

Freud, Sigmund. *Five Lectures on Psychoanalysis*, trans. James Strachey. New York: W. W. Norton & Company, Inc., 1977.

Freud, Sigmund. *The Interpretation of Dreams*, trans. James Strachey. New York: Avon Books, 1965.

Freud, Sigmund. *Introductory Lectures on Psychoanalysis*, trans. James Strachey. New York: W.W. Norton & Company, Inc., 1966.

Freud, Sigmund. *Leonardo da Vinci – A Study in Psychosexuality*, trans. A. A. Brill. New York: Vintage Books, 1947.

Freud, Sigmund. *New Introductory Lectures on Psychoanalysis*, trans. James Strachey. New York: W.W. Norton & Company, Inc., 1965.

Fry, Roger. "Vincent Van Gogh," in *Transformations – Critical and Speculative Essays on Art* [1926]. New York: Anchor Books, 1956.

Gadamer, Hans-Georg. *Philosophical Hermeneutics*, trans. David E. Linge. Berkeley, Los Angeles and London: University of California Press, 1976.

Gadamer, Hans-Georg. *The Relevance of the Beautiful*, trans. Nicholas Walker. Cambridge: Cambridge University Press, 1986.

Gadamer, Hans-Georg. *Truth and Method*. New York: Crossroad, 1982.

Gauzi, F. "Vincent van Gogh (1886–87)," in *Van Gogh in Perspective*, ed. B. Welsh-Ovcharo. Englewood Cliffs, NJ: Prentice-Hall, 1974.

Goodman, Nelson. *Languages of Art*. Indianapolis: Hackett Publishing Company, Inc., 1976.

Hamann, Johann Georg. "Aesthetica in nuce," in *German Aesthetic and Literary Criticism: Winckelmann, Lessing, Hamann, Herder, Schiller and Goethe*, ed. H. B. Nisbet. Cambridge: Cambridge University Press, 1985.

Hammermeister, Kai. *The German Aesthetic Tradition*. Cambridge: Cambridge University Press, 2002.

Hegel, G. W. F. *Early Theological Writings*, trans. T. M. Knox. Philadelphia: University of Pennsylvania Press, 1948.

Hegel, G. W. F. *Hegel's Aesthetics – Lectures on Fine Art, Volumes I and II*, trans. T. M. Knox. Oxford: Oxford University Press, 1975.

Hegel, G. W. F. *Phenomenology of Spirit*, trans. A. V. Miller. Oxford: Oxford University Press, 1977.

Hegel, G. W. F. *Science of Logic*, trans. A. V. Miller. Amherst, NY: Humanity Books, 1999.

Heidegger, Martin. *Being and Time* [*Sein und Zeit*, 1927], trans. John Macquarrie and Edward Robinson. New York: Harper & Row, 1962.

Heidegger, Martin. *Off the Beaten Track* [*Holzwege*, 1950], ed. and trans. Julian Young and K. Haynes. Cambridge: Cambridge University Press, 2002.

Heidegger, Martin. "What Are Poets For?," in *Poetry Language, Thought*, trans. Albert Hofstadter. New York: Harper & Row, 1971.

Hirsch, E. D. *Validity in Interpretation*. New Haven and London: Yale University Press, 1967.

Holmes, Lewis M. *Kosegarten's Cultural Legacy*. New York, Bern, Berlin, Brussels, Frankfurt am Main, Oxford and Vienna: Peter Lang, 2005.

Kant, Immanuel. *Correspondence*, trans. Arnulf Zweig (Cambridge Edition of the Works of Immanuel Kant). Cambridge: Cambridge University Press, 1999.

Kant, Immanuel. *Critique of The Power of Judgment*, trans. J. H. Bernard. New York: Hafner Press, 1951.

Kant, Immanuel. *Critique of Practical Reason*, trans. Lewis White Beck. Indianapolis: Bobbs-Merrill Co., Inc., 1956.

Kant, Immanuel. *Critique of Pure Reason*, trans. Norman Kemp Smith. New York: St Martin's Press, 1965.

Kater, Michael H. *Different Drummers – Jazz in the Culture of Nazi Germany*. Oxford: Oxford University Press, 1992.

Kierkegaard, Søren. *Concluding Unscientific Postscript*, trans. David Swenson and Walter Lowrie. Princeton: Princeton University Press, 1968.

Kierkegaard, Søren. *Either/Or, Volumes I and II*, trans. Howard and Edna Hong. Princeton: Princeton University Press, 1988.

Kierkegaard, Søren. *The Last Years – Journals 1853–5*, ed. Ronald Gregor Smith. London: Fontana Library, 1965.

Krukowski, Lucian. *Aesthetic Legacies*. Philadelphia: Temple University Press, 1992.

Littlefield, Henry N. "The Wizard of Oz: Parable on Populism." *American Quarterly*, 16, 3 (1964), pp. 47–58.

Lukács, György. *The Destruction of Reason*, trans. Peter Palmer. London: Merlin, 1980.

Lyotard, Jean-François. *The Postmodern Condition*, trans. Geoff Bennington and Brian Massumi. Minneapolis: University of Minnesota Press, 1984.

Maher, Winifred Barbara, and Maher, Brendan. "The Ship of Fools: *stultifera navis* or *ignis fatuus*?" *American Psychologist*, 37, 7 (1982), pp. 756–761.

Marx, Karl. *Capital, Volume I*. Moscow: Progress Publishers, 1887.

Marx, Karl. "Manifesto of the Communist Party" in *The Marx-Engels Reader* (2nd edition), ed. Robert C. Tucker. New York: W. W. Norton & Company, 1978.

Marx, Karl and Engels, Friedrich. *Marx and Engels on Literature and Art*. Moscow: Progress Publishers, 1976.

The Marx-Engels Reader (2nd edition), ed. Robert C. Tucker. New York and London: W.W. Norton & Company, 1978.

Merleau-Ponty, Maurice. *Sense and Non-Sense*, trans. H. Dreyfus and A. Dreyfus. Evanston, IL: Northwestern University Press, 1964.

Michelfelder, Diane P., and Palmer, Richard E. (eds). *Dialogue and Deconstruction: The Gadamer-Derrida Encounter*. Albany: State University of New York Press, 1989.

Moffitt, John F. "Velázquez in the Alcázar Palace in 1656: The Meaning of the Mise-en-scéne of *Las Meninas*." *Art History*, 6, 3 (1983), pp. 271–300.

Moon in a Dewdrop: Writings of Zen Master Dōgen, ed. Kazuaki Tanahashi. New York: North Point Press, 1985.

Nietzsche, Friedrich. *The Birth of Tragedy*, trans. Walter Kaufmann. New York: Vintage Books, 1967.

Nietzsche, Friedrich. *The Will to Power*, trans. Walter Kaufmann and R. J. Hollingdale. New York: Vintage Books, 1968.

Pippin, Robert. *Modernism as a Philosophical Problem: On the Dissatisfactions of European High Culture*. London: Basil Blackwell, 1991.

Plekhanov, G. V. *Unaddressed Letters. Art and Social Life*. Moscow: Foreign Languages Publishing House, 1957.

Plutarch. *Moralia II*, trans. Frank Cole Babbit. Cambridge, MA: Loeb Classical Library, Harvard University Press, 1928.

Rohter, Larry. "New Doubts Raised over Famous War Photo." *New York Times*, August 17, 2009.

Roosevelt, Theodore. "A Layman's Views of an Art Exhibition." *Outlook*, 103 (29 March 1913), pp. 718–20.

Schaeffer, Jean-Marie. *Art of the Modern Age: Philosophy of Art from Kant to Heidegger*, trans. Steven Rendall. Princeton: Princeton University Press, 2009.

Schapiro, Meyer. "The Still Life as a Personal Object – A Note on Heidegger and van Gogh," in Marianne L. Simmel, ed., *The Reach of the Mind: Essays in Memory of Kurt Goldstein, 1878–1965*. Springer: New York, 1968.

Schelling, Friedrich Wilhelm Joseph. *System of Transcendental Idealism*, trans. Peter Heath. Charlottesville: University Press of Virginia, 1981.

Schiller, Friedrich Wilhelm Joseph. *On the Aesthetic Education of Man*, trans. Reginald Snell. New York: Frederick Ungar Publishing Co., 1965.

Schopenhauer, Arthur. *The World as Will and Representation*, Volume I and Volume II, trans. E. F. J. Payne. New York: Dover Publications, Inc., 1966.

Snyder, Joel, and Cohen, Ted. "Reflections on '*Las Meninas*': Paradox Lost." *Critical Inquiry*, 7, 2 (1980), pp. 429–47.

Sophocles. "Oedipus at Colonus," in *The Complete Greek Tragedies, Sophocles I*, trans. Robert Fitzgerald. New York: Washington Square Press, 1967.

Theognis. *The Elegies of Theognis and Other Elegies Included in the Theognidean Sylloge: A Revised Text Based on a New Collation of the Mutininensis MS*, trans. T. Hudson-Williams. New York: Arno Press, 1979.

Thompson, Ian. "Heidegger's Aesthetics," in *The Stanford Encyclopedia of Philosophy* (online) [http://plato.stanford.edu/entries/heidegger-aesthetics], 2010.

Vattimo, Gianni. *Art's Claim to Truth* [1985], trans. Luca D'Isanto. New York: Colombia University Press, 2008.

Weill, M. A. "Schopenhauer Only an Actor." *New York Times*, May 16, 1886.

Wicks, R. "Kant on Beautifying the Human Body." *British Journal of Aesthetics*, 39, 2 (1999), pp. 163–178.

Wicks, Robert. "Using Artistic Masterpieces as Historical Examples: The Case of *Las Meninas*." *Journal of Aesthetics and Art Criticism*, 68, 3 (2010), pp. 259–72.

Yamamoto, Yutaka. "A Morality Based on Trust: Some Reflections on Japanese Morality." *Philosophy East & West*, 40, 4 (1990), pp. 451–69.

INDEX OF NAMES

Dante Alighieri, 128
Daumier, Honoré, 169n, 323
Davies, Arthur B., 169n
Davis, Miles, 193
Davis, Stuart, 169n
Degas, Edgar, 169n, 248
Delacroix, Eugène, 169n
Deleuze, Gilles, 185, 239n, 289–308, 311, 317
Derrida, Jacques, 7, 129, 223, 230, 260, 271–288, 311, 323
Descartes, René, 14, 15, 59, 283, 284, 299
Dickens, Charles, 300
Dionysus, 118, 120
Dix, Otto, 168n
Dōgen, 304
Dostoevsky, Fyodor, 179
Duchamp, Marcel, 169n, 248, 314
Dufrenne, Mikel, 6

Einstein, Albert, 198
Ellington, Duke, 192
Ernst, Max, 168n

Feininger, Lyonel, 168n
Fichte, Johann Gottlieb, 58, 59
Fish, Stanley, 268
Foucault, Michel, 3, 178, 249–270, 277, 295n, 297n, 299, 311, 319, 320
Frege, Gottlob, 198
Freud, Sigmund, 7, 95, 114, 129, 130, 147–161, 168, 194, 200, 209, 274, 285, 286, 288, 311, 319
Friedrich, Caspar David, 5n
Fry, Roger, 97

Gadamer, Hans-Georg, 25, 129, 218–233, 252, 288, 310–312
Galilei, Galileo, 290
Galton, Francis, 246
Gardner, Alexander, 240
Gauguin, Paul, 169n
Gauzi, François, 275
Genet, Jean, 249
Gerard, Alexander 16

Goethe, Johann Wolfgang von, 49, 126, 165
Goldstein, Kurt, 283
Goodman, Benny, 192
Goodman, Nelson, 175
Goya, Francisco, 169n, 261
Grosz, George, 168n

Hamann, Johann Georg, 210
Hamlet, 153–154
Hartmann, Eduard von, 147
Hassam, Childe, 169n
Heckel, Erich, 168n
Hegel, G. W. F., 2, 4, 7, 44, 45n, 53, 55–78–82, 85, 88, 90, 91, 95, 96, 98, 106, 112, 114, 117, 122, 128, 133, 139, 141, 143, 145, 160, 161, 174, 189, 194, 195, 200, 217, 244, 287, 301, 310, 311
Heidegger, Martin, 3, 202–217, 226, 233, 253, 264, 266, 272–286, 295n, 306, 310, 311, 315, 323
Henri, Robert, 169n
Hirsch, E. D., 228
Hitchcock, Alfred, 299
Hitler, Adolf, 166–168, 171–173, 178, 179, 208, 241, 250, 296, 297, 307
Hodler, Ferdinand, 169n
Hölderlin, Friedrich, 211, 212, 215
Hopper, Edward, 169n
Horkheimer, Max, 186–191, 210, 212, 297
Hübner, Carl Wilhelm, 90
Hugo, Victor, 128
Hume, David, 16
Husserl, Edmund, 306
Hutcheson, Francis, 16

Iser, Wolfgang, 268
Ixion, 114

Jauss, Hans Robert, 268
Jawlensky, Alexej von, 168n
Jean Paul, 147
Jesus, 71, 126, 132, 134, 143, 146

INDEX OF SUBJECTS